LET'S STUDY LUKE

In the same series:

LET'S STUDY MARK by Sinclair B. Ferguson
LET'S STUDY JOHN by Mark Johnston
LET'S STUDY ACTS by Dennis E. Johnson
LET'S STUDY 1 CORINTHIANS by David Jackman
LET'S STUDY 2 CORINTHIANS by Derek Prime
LET'S STUDY GALATIANS by Derek Thomas
LET'S STUDY PHILIPPIANS by Sinclair B. Ferguson
LET'S STUDY 1 & 2 THESSALONIANS by Andrew W. Young
LET'S STUDY HEBREWS by Hywel R. Jones
LET'S STUDY 1 PETER by William W. Harrell
LET'S STUDY REVELATION by Derek Thomas

Series Editor: SINCLAIR B. FERGUSON

Let's Study
LUKE

Douglas J. W. Milne

THE BANNER OF TRUTH TRUST

THE BANNER OF TRUTH TRUST
3 Murrayfield Road, Edinburgh EH12 6EL, UK
P.O. Box 621, Carlisle, PA 17013, USA

*

First Published 2005
ISBN 0 85151 896 6

*

*

Typeset in 11/12.5 pt Ehrhardt MT by
Initial Typesetting Services,
Edinburgh

Printed in the U.S.A. by
Versa Press, Inc.,
Peoria, IL

For my son
Mark

Contents

Publisher's Preface

Let's Study Luke is part of a series of books which seek to explain and apply the message of Scripture. The series is designed to meet a specific and important need in the church. While not technical commentaries, the volumes comment on the text of a biblical book; and, without being merely lists of practical applications, they are concerned with the ways in which the teaching of Scripture can affect and transform our lives today. Understanding the Bible's message and applying its teaching are the aims.

Like other volumes in the series, *Let's Study Luke* seeks to combine explanation and application. Its concern is to be helpful to ordinary Christian people by encouraging them to understand the message of the Bible and apply it to their own lives. The reader in view is not the person who is interested in all the detailed questions which fascinate the scholar, although behind the writing of each study lies an appreciation for careful and detailed scholarship. The aim is exposition of Scripture written in the language of a friend, seated alongside you with an open Bible.

Let's Study Luke is designed to be used in various contexts. It can be used simply as an aid for individual Bible study. Some may find it helpful to use in their devotions with husband or wife, or to read in the context of the whole family.

In order to make these studies more useful, not only for individual use but also for group study in Sunday School classes and home, church or college, study guide material will be found on pp. 287–306. Sometimes we come away frustrated rather than helped by group discussions. Frequently that is because we have been encouraged to discuss a passage of Scripture which we do not understand very well in the first place. Understanding must always be the foundation for enriching discussion and for thoughtful, practical application. Thus, in addition to the exposition of Luke, the additional material provides questions to encourage personal thought and study, or to be used as discussion starters. The Group Study Guide divides the material into thirteen sections and provides direction for leading and participating in group study and discussion.

Introduction

WHO WAS LUKE?

Judging from the quality of his writing Luke was a well-educated Greek-speaker, perhaps from the cultured centre of Antioch (that is the tradition about him) or from Philippi which he seems to have known well (*Acts* 16).

Luke accompanied Paul on some of his journeys around the Mediterranean, if the 'we' passages (*Acts* 16:10–17; 20:5–16; 21:1–18; 27:1–28:16) are taken seriously as including the author of Acts. He is called a physician (*Col.* 4:14), which would explain his intense and sympathetic interest and treatment of people throughout his Gospel (and Acts).

He introduces himself in his preface to the Gospel (*Luke* 1:1–4), unlike the other Gospel writers who remain anonymous. Judged from his writing as a whole Luke was a caring, learned and artistically gifted individual who was committed, like Jesus, to the welfare of the men and women of his world. His outstanding quality was his feeling for people.

WHEN AND WHY DID HE WRITE HIS GOSPEL?

An earlier rather than later date for the writing of Luke's Gospel seems preferable. This means a date around the 60s AD since no event later that that is mentioned by Luke in his second writing in Acts (such as the death of Paul or the destruction of Jerusalem).

Luke wrote for Theophilus as one educated Greek-speaker to another (*Luke* 1:1–4). Following the practice in Hellenistic writings of that time Luke dedicates his Gospel to Theophilus as his patron and publisher. Theophilus may have been either a new convert to Christianity or a serious enquirer about it. Either way Luke has composed his Gospel for him and all like him, who want to learn about the reliable facts of the beginnings of Christianity so as to have a well-grounded faith of their own.

WHAT ARE THE SPECIAL THEMES OF LUKE'S GOSPEL?

As a narrative theologian Luke has special interest themes that run through his Gospel. He has picked these up from the life and teaching of Jesus and woven them artistically into the fabric of his writing. They give the reader a clear indication of what salvation means and how it ought to impact human lives. Some of the major themes are:

SALVATION (1:76–79; 2:10–11, 30–32; 19:10)

UNDER-CLASSES (2:8–20; 7:11–12, 36–50; 8:1–3; 10:38–42; 14:12–14; 15:1–2; 19:1–6; 21:1–4)

WEALTH (1:53; 6:24; 12:16–21; 16:1–12, 19–35; 19:1–10; 18:18–27)

PRAYER (2:28–32; 5:16; 11:1–13; 18:9–14; 23:34, 46)

JOYFUL PRAISE (1:46–55, 67–79; 2:13–14; 10:21–22; 19:37–40; 24:52–53)

THE HOLY SPIRIT (1:35, 41–42, 67; 2:26–27, 3:16, 21–22; 4:1, 14, 18; 10:21; 11:13; 24:49)

HOSPITALITY (1:39; 2:6; 4:16–30; 7:36–48; 10:30–37, 38–41; 14:15–24; 15:11–32; 19:1–10; 22:14–20; 23:42–43; 24:28–31)

FAITH, REPENTANCE AND FORGIVENESS (1:26–38, 45; 5:17–25, 32; 7:1–10, 48–50; 8:41–50; 13:1–5; 15:11–24; 17:5–6; 18:8; 24:46–47)

DISCIPLESHIP (5:8–11; 9:23–26, 57–62; 14:25–34).

HOW SHOULD WE READ HIS GOSPEL?

Luke's Gospel is well suited to 21st-century readers because he has written in a narrative style that appeals to the imagination, deals with people's lives, is easy to read and wholly enjoyable. Through his narratives/stories Luke has made Jesus alive and accessible for anyone who seriously reads him. This is narrative theology at its best.

Modern writers who have studied the place and power of narratives in human life and culture have come up with the opinion that human beings need authoritative narratives to identify themselves by and to bring organization and meaning into their existence. A post-modern and relativistic age delights in stories but disowns meta-narratives, the big stories that provide a total framework for giving meaning to existence and the future by speaking with final authority. But in the absence of such narratives men and women suffer irreparably by losing hope and something to believe in that transcends themselves. The story of Jesus is the best and brightest of all the meta-narratives, one that more than any other has the power to shape our destinies and remake us in his own moral and spiritual likeness.

Luke's Gospel is like an extended story made up of a patchwork of many shorter stories taken from the life of Jesus, who is the central figure through every narrative. Luke retells in his own selective way the leading incidents from the lifetime of Jesus beginning with his birth and going right through to his death. But the storyline does not stop there because Jesus is no ordinary human being; he is the pre-existent Son of God who came into this world to claim his father David's throne over the whole of time and space. As a result his story does not stop at his death but takes on a new beginning with his resurrection and ascension into God's heavenly presence where the crucified one now rules as Lord and Christ (*Acts* 2:36).

Luke wants his readers to enter sympathetically into his narratives and through this contact with Jesus to know, love and trust him as Lord and Saviour. Through experiencing the grace and forgiveness of Jesus, readers of the Gospel, like the individuals who met Jesus in the Gospel narratives, will find the other relationships of their lives restored as well. In fact, their whole humanity will come alive as they experience the joy and freedom of God's salvation.

The narratives of Luke's Gospel are not only the stories about Jesus but Jesus' own stories told in his parables. This means that the reader must be able to read narrative in a way that is true to the style and purpose of narrative writing. This means reading each section of the Gospel by itself as a single unit and at a single sitting.

The parts of the story or the teaching must be viewed in the light of the whole unit and interpreted in a way that is consistent with the whole.

Every narrative contains its own clues to the main meaning and message. This may take the form of editorial comment from Luke (19:11), a single theme (23:50–56), a preliminary request or question (17:5), Jesus' own explanation (8:11–15), Old Testament background (11:29–32), the focus of the narrative (18:18), a particular context (4:14–15) and so on. The reader should look out for these and draw the lessons of each narrative from there. Even with these keys some narratives and sayings of Jesus remain a challenge to interpretation and application (11:33–36). Above all, the narratives appeal to a human-interest factor that we all share.

These narratives about and by Jesus form part of the total biblical narrative that is the story of God's saving acts in the world. The story of Jesus is the high-point of that story that reaches back to the beginning of creation (3:23–38), moves through the history of Israel (1:67–79), interacts with Roman and Jewish first century history (2:1–2; 3:1), and reaches forward to the end of the age and the new creation (20:34–38). Within this total framework the stories about Jesus are the middle of God's saving plan for the world. Above all Jesus' death, resurrection and ascension lay the foundation of the kingdom of God (24:44–49). Believing the gospel means identifying with the biblical accounts about Jesus so as to make them our own, the foundation of our existence and our view of the world.

The narrative of Jesus begins with a virgin's miraculous conception of a holy child and climaxes some thirty-three years later on a gallows, a rough cross of wood erected outside the holy city of Jerusalem under the imperial rule of Tiberius Caesar. Nor did his life story stop there for Luke discerns that there is a mid-point of the story of Jesus in his ascension from earth to heaven, when he finally exchanged the humble forms of earth for the regal powers of heaven. Through his faithful witness Luke, and his orderly account, the risen and coronated Jesus calls modern readers to take up their cross and follow him into servanthood, suffering and obedience, then to receive the servant's crown and a gracious share in the eternal glories of his Father's kingdom.

Outline of Luke's Gospel

Luke's Gospel records the beginnings of Christianity in the events of Jesus' birth, public ministry, death, resurrection and ascension. His narrative moves through a number of natural stages.

PROLOGUE (1:1–4)

Luke states his reasons for writing his Gospel and also explains his methods in doing so.

INTRODUCTORY EVENTS (1:5–2:52)

Luke records events leading up to and surrounding the births of John the Baptist and Jesus. John and Jesus are God's principal agents in the coming of his Kingdom into the world. There is also a story from Jesus' later childhood.

PREPARATION FOR MINISTRY (3:1–4:13)

This included three items – Jesus listening to the preaching of John the Baptist, his baptism at John's hands, his private temptation in the desert. Only then was Jesus ready to take up his work as the Lord's Christ to Israel and the Gentiles.

MINISTRY IN GALILEE (4:14–9:50)

Jesus' public ministry began with his preaching at Nazareth, but it led into an itinerant-style ministry that involved preaching, teaching and healing throughout most of the northern parts of Palestine.

JOURNEY TOWARDS JERUSALEM (9:51–19:27)

Throughout this section Jesus is slowly making his way to Jerusalem for the last time. Luke includes several notable examples of Jesus' parables and miracles.

THE JERUSALEM MINISTRY (19:28–21:38)

Jesus enters Jerusalem triumphantly, debates repeatedly with the religious authorities, and finally predicts the future events of this age.

THE PASSION (22:1–23:56)

Jesus shares his last meal with his disciples, before visiting the garden of Gethsemane. There he is betrayed by one of his disciples who hands him over to the Romans. Pilate the governor gives in to the Jewish authorities and agrees to condemn Jesus to death by crucifixion. After his execution Jesus is buried in a privately-owned tomb.

THE RESURRECTION AND ASCENSION (24:1–53)

Jesus appears to many of his disciples and teaches them further from the Scriptures. His final act is to ascend into heaven as Lord of all.

The Larger Setting

Luke's Gospel is the first of two narratives that he wrote, the other being the Acts of the Apostles. Ideally, the Gospel should be read along with the Acts as a continuous story. Then readers gain a panoramic view of God's saving plan of history in three parts:

Luke 1–2 : the transitional age of the Old Testament
Luke 3–Acts 1: the foundational time of Jesus' ministry
Acts 2–28: the era of Christianity and the Church

This is a theological-historical way of seeing the ministry of Jesus as Luke himself represents it.

I

What Is a Gospel?

Inasmuch as many have undertaken to compile a narrative of the things that have been accomplished among us, [2] just as those who from the beginning were eyewitnesses and ministers of the word have delivered them to us, [3] it seemed good to me also, having followed all things closely for some time past, to write an orderly account for you, most excellent Theophilus, [4] that you may have certainty concerning the things you have been taught (Luke 1:1–4).

Luke addressed his Gospel to Theophilus who was a Roman patrician wanting to learn more about the Christian faith. In the first four verses Luke explains how he went about writing his Gospel. These first verses stand as an introduction to the whole Gospel and give us some idea of what to expect in what follows. Luke indicates that a Gospel is a special kind of writing for a number of reasons.

- a Gospel is a certain type of writing (verse 1). Many others had already attempted to write one. It is possible Luke was able to make some use of other Gospel accounts like Mark's Gospel to help him write his. There are no less than four Gospels in the New Testament to nurture our faith. How thankful we should be for these parallel sources for knowing about our blessed Lord and Saviour and how regularly we should be found reading them!
- a Gospel is a narrative or account of something (verse 1). So Luke's Gospel is made up of true stories about Jesus that come together to form a connected and single narrative about him, his person, life, and times. We should read the Gospel through from

beginning to end because it forms one connected account of his human life. It begins in Jerusalem and ends in Jerusalem as the centre of all God's great purposes and works.

- a Gospel is about things that have been fulfilled (verse 1). This suggests a purpose or plan that has been formed and carried out in the fullness of time. The plan in this case is God's plan, outlined and promised in the Scriptures of the Old Testament and centred in the person of Jesus Christ. The first two chapters will illustrate this Old Testament background and underpinning of the whole life and work of Jesus as he fulfils the true meaning of the history of the people of Israel.
- a Gospel is based on the first-hand reports of people who knew Jesus from the beginning because they listened to him and observed him carefully (verse 2). They were then able to pass on to other people the evidence for Jesus' claims and achievements. This means that as we read through Luke's Gospel we are listening to the reports of people who lived through these events and are its primary witnesses. Nothing could be further from legend or make-belief than Luke's Gospel.
- a Gospel involves the pain-staking efforts and researches of its author (verse 3). Luke is a true historian who has investigated his sources carefully and written up his material methodically. Luke compares well with the most reliable historians of the ancient world and has proved reliable again and again in his geographical and historical references to people and events. He knew his times and his world.
- a Gospel is written so that people can gain a well-grounded faith in God on the basis of the real-life facts about Jesus' life, death, resurrection, and ascension (verse 4). The stories that make up the story of Jesus are here in Luke's Gospel for a definite reason – to awaken our interest, answer our doubts and questions, lead us to faith in Jesus as Christ, and nurture our knowledge in following him. Luke would wish us to make this journey with him as we travel through his Gospel in the footsteps of Jesus of Nazareth in first-century Palestine. Then, like the two walking together on the way (*Luke* 24:13–35), we may be surprised by the presence of Jesus as he opens our minds to understand the Scriptures and causes our hearts to burn within us.

Oct 12

2

A Promised Child

5 In the days of Herod, king of Judea, there was a priest named
Zechariah, of the division of Abijah. And he had a wife from
the daughters of Aaron, and her name was Elizabeth. 6 And they
were both righteous before God, walking blamelessly in all the
commandments and statutes of the Lord. 7 But they had no child,
because Elizabeth was barren, and both were advanced in years.
8 Now while he was serving as priest before God when his division
was on duty, 9 according to the custom of the priesthood, he was
chosen by lot to enter the temple of the Lord and burn incense.
10 And the whole multitude of the people were praying outside at
the hour of incense. 11 And there appeared to him an angel of the
Lord standing on the right side of the altar of incense. 12 And
Zechariah was troubled when he saw him, and fear fell upon him.
13 But the angel said to him, 'Do not be afraid, Zechariah, for
your prayer has been heard, and your wife Elizabeth will bear
you a son, and you shall call his name John. 14 And you will have
joy and gladness, and many will rejoice at his birth, 15 for he will
be great before the Lord. And he must not drink wine or strong
drink, and he will be filled with the Holy Spirit, even from his
mother's womb. 16 And he will turn many of the children of Israel
to the Lord their God, 17 and he will go before him in the spirit
and power of Elijah, to turn the hearts of the fathers to the
children, and the disobedient to the wisdom of the just, to make
ready for the Lord a people prepared.'
18 And Zechariah said to the angel, 'How shall I know this? For
I am an old man, and my wife is advanced in years.' 19 And the
angel answered him, 'I am Gabriel, who stands in the presence
of God, and I was sent to speak to you and to bring you this good

news. [20] *And behold, you will be silent and unable to speak until the day that these things take place, because you did not believe my words, which will be fulfilled in their time.'* [21] *And the people were waiting for Zechariah, and they were wondering at his delay in the temple.* [22] *And when he came out, he was unable to speak to them, and they realized that he had seen a vision in the temple. And he kept making signs to them and remained mute.* [23] *And when his time of service was ended, he went to his home.*

[24] *After these days his wife Elizabeth conceived, and for five months she kept herself hidden, saying,* [25] *'Thus the Lord has done for me in the days when he looked on me, to take away my reproach among people'* (Luke 1:5–25).

Luke is now ready to begin his narrative about the beginnings of Christianity. But he does this by going back before the birth of Jesus to the birth-story of John, the cousin of Jesus.

A CHILDLESS COUPLE (verses 5–7)

The time is the last days of 'Herod the Great' who was king under the Romans of a part of their empire called Judea, in Palestine, for about thirty-three years. This was the Herod who ordered the slaughter of the Jewish male children after Jesus was born (*Matt.* 2:1–18). Luke refers to Herod because he wants to place the life of Jesus in an historical frame.

The place is the house of an elderly Jewish couple called Zechariah and Elizabeth. They belonged to prestigious priestly families in Israel. They were God-fearing folk who honoured God by adhering strictly to his commandments for living (verse 6). They represented the true Israel within Israel who, like Mary, Simeon, Annas, Cleopas, and many others, feared God and were looking out for the redemption of God's people through the coming of his Messiah (*Luke* 2:25, 38; 24:21a). Although they did not yet know it, Zechariah and Elizabeth belonged to the generation that would see God's salvation in the person of his Son (*Luke* 2:26–32).

The most significant fact about them for the story is that they were childless. This was a source of shame particularly for married Jewish women since God had promised to make his people fruitful as a sign of his blessing (*Deut.* 28:1, 11, *Gen.* 30:22–23, *1 Sam.* 1:5–8). In this chronic testing of their faith they had prayed fervently for a child and God was about to give them their heart's desire (verse 13).

By choosing and using people like Zechariah and Elizabeth God teaches us that humble, believing people can be the channels of his blessing to the world.

AN ANGEL VISITOR (verses 8–12)

The priesthood in those days was organised around divisions of the families of Israel (*1 Chron.* 24, *2 Chron.* 35:5). Priests from town and country (Zechariah was from the hill-country, verse 39) were rostered for service in the temple in Jerusalem, so that all of them could have the honour of leading temple worship on behalf of their nation. It was Zechariah's turn to perform the ceremonies by offering incense inside the sanctuary (*Exod.* 30:1–8), while the people prayed outside.

Alone inside the sacred area, Zechariah was suddenly accompanied by an angel of the Lord. Angels are spirit-beings who actively serve God and his people (*Heb.* 1:14).

The site of this visitation in the heart of the temple should not be missed. Since the days of David and Solomon (*1 Kings* 8), the temple had been a visible sign of the Lord's real presence with his people Israel. Because of the idolatry of his people the Lord had sent them into exile for seventy years. During this time the temple had lain in ruins until the exiles returned to rebuild it. Malachi, the last of the prophets, predicted that in a future time of salvation the Messiah would appear in the temple to cleanse and reclaim it (*Mal.* 3:1–4). In the angel's announcement to the elderly Zechariah we should hear the in-breaking of that promised day when God would act decisively for the world's salvation (*Luke* 1: 67–79). In verse 19 the angel declares that he has brought to Zechariah the good news of these events, intimating the arrival of the Gospel era.

A PROMISED SON (verses 13–17)

Zechariah was naturally alarmed by the sudden appearance of an angel. But the angel informed him that the Lord had heard his prayer for a child, even in old age. Elizabeth was going to conceive and have a boy, to be called John, meaning 'the Lord is gracious'. This was a promise that a new age of God's favour was dawning and would be heralded by John as the Lord's prophet to the nation. Everyone was going to rejoice at John's birth because he would speak God's word to Israel after four hundred years of silence. His message would be one of mercy and hope.

John must refrain from intoxicating liquor all his life, in the tradition of the Nazirites (*Num.* 6:1–4, *Judg.* 13:2–5) and Rechabites (*Jer.* 35). He would be filled with the Holy Spirit from the womb, a sign of his pre-eminence as a special prophet of the Lord. The Spirit is the source of prophetic utterance in both of Luke's writings (*Acts* 2:4, 16–18). He would bring many of the people of Israel back to the Lord their God through personal repentance and faith. He would resemble his great predecessor Elijah, both in message and in lifestyle (*1 Kings* 18, *Mal.* 4:5–6).

But John's greatest claim to fame would lie in the fact that he was the one appointed by God to introduce Israel to her Messiah (*John* 1:31–33). Through preaching about the Messiah and God's grace to the nation, John was going to reconcile people to their God and people to one another, across the generations.

John was helped in all this by a public rite of water-baptism that symbolised a radical change of heart and a cleansing of the whole of life both past and present (*Luke* 3:15–17, *John* 1:6–8, 29–34). No wonder Jesus declared that of those born of woman none was greater than John (*Luke* 7:24–28). Yet John still lacked something because he belonged to the provisional dispensation of the law and the prophets (*Luke* 16:16). Jesus the Messiah has brought the final age of redemption in which God's glory is more amply revealed and his power more richly given (*2 Cor.* 3).

UNBELIEVING ZECHARIAH AND HIS CHASTENING (verses 18–25)

Unfortunately Zechariah foolishly questioned the truth of the angel's promise thereby exposing himself to the Lord's chastening. Really, there was no excuse for Zechariah's response since the Scriptures contained stories of childless women who conceived, even when old

(*Gen.* 17:15–22, *Judg.* 13:2–3, *1 Sam.* 1:1–2:11). Further, the angel who called was none other than Gabriel, an archangel who waited and worshipped in the Lord's very presence.

By doubting the angel's words Zechariah cast doubt on the Lord through his messenger. As a result the Lord disabled him from speaking, so he could not share the good news with the people. Instead they could see that Zechariah was deeply affected by something that had happened to him inside the temple. Using sign language he explained that he had seen a vision that had taken away his power of speech.

Predictably Elizabeth did become pregnant but she secluded herself for the first five months until her pregnancy could no longer be hidden. Privately Zechariah must have regretted his rashness while Elizabeth rejoiced in the goodness of the Lord.

How often do we forfeit the intended blessings of the Lord for similar reasons? We do not believe or act on his word because we justify our fears and discredit God's promises. Like Zechariah we come under God's fatherly displeasure, thus setting limits to our usefulness to God. But the Lord is gracious and when we have learned from his chastening, he restores us to his service (*Luke* 1:59–79; 22:31–34, *Heb.* 12:5–11).

3

The Incarnation

[26] In the sixth month the angel Gabriel was sent from God to a
city of Galilee named Nazareth, [27] to a virgin betrothed to a man
whose name was Joseph, of the house of David. And the virgin's
name was Mary. [28] And he came to her and said, 'Greetings, O
favored one, the Lord is with you!' [29] But she was greatly troubled
at the saying, and tried to discern what sort of greeting this might
be. [30] And the angel said to her, 'Do not be afraid, Mary, for
you have found favor with God. [31] And behold, you will conceive
in your womb and bear a son, and you shall call his name Jesus.
[32] He will be great and will be called the Son of the Most High.
And the Lord God will give to him the throne of his father David,
[33] and he will reign over the house of Jacob forever, and of his
kingdom there will be no end.'
[34] And Mary said to the angel, 'How will this be, since I am a
virgin?'
[35] And the angel answered her, 'The Holy Spirit will come upon
you, and the power of the Most High will overshadow you;
therefore the child to be born will be called holy – the Son of God.
[36] And behold, your relative Elizabeth in her old age has also
conceived a son, and this is the sixth month with her who was
called barren. [37] For nothing will be impossible with God.' [38] And
Mary said, 'Behold, I am the servant of the Lord; let it be to
me according to your word.' And the angel departed from her
(Luke 1:26–38).

After the announcement of John's forthcoming birth to Zechariah and Elizabeth, Luke records another angelic visit to the future mother of Jesus. The Annunciation or announcement of the angel to Mary of her impending pregnancy is a favourite scene in Christian art. This is because of the sheer importance of the moment in the history of salvation, the arrival in time of the eternal Son of God our Saviour.

THE VIRGIN MARY (verses 26–30, 36–38)

Six months after Elizabeth became pregnant (verse 36) the angel Gabriel carries out the second part of God's plan of salvation. Mary was already betrothed to a man called Joseph who belonged to the ancient royal family line of David, Israel's greatest king. Betrothal meant that a marriage covenant had been entered into by both parties but without the relationship being consummated sexually. This is important for understanding Mary's question in verse 34. It also protects her personal reputation in her relationship to Joseph. It is also unthinkable that the holy God would use a promiscuous woman to be the mother of his sinless Son.

The Lord makes it clear that he has chosen Mary in grace (verses 28, 30) to be his special instrument of blessing to the world. The coming of Jesus was a matter of grace – of unspeakable favour, exceptional love, and overwhelming kindness – from beginning to end (*Titus* 3:4–5). No suggestion is made that Mary possesses special merit or sinlessness in becoming the mother of Jesus the Christ.

There is a special grace extended to women here since another woman, Eve, had opened the door for sin to come into the world (*1 Tim*. 2:14), bringing down the curse of God on womankind (*Gen*. 3:16). Now the Lord is opening the history of salvation through a different woman, the God-fearing and submissive Mary. Through her and her maternal role the Lord has restored the honour of women, replacing the curse with a blessing, because of her Son (*1 Tim*. 2:15).

Mary is a leading example in the Bible of what it means to receive the word of God and to do his will. Unlike Zechariah Mary asks about the angel's announcement in a spirit of faith and respect (verse 34). We may never make Mary into a source of salvation but we may genuinely learn from her faith and obedience. She personifies what is most attractive in female piety in particular (*1 Pet*. 3:3–5) and in Christian character generally.

THE VIRGIN'S CHILD (verseS 31–33)

The angel informs Mary about the child she was going to have. Four things are predicted. Firstly, he will be called Jesus because 'the Lord will save' his people through him (*Matt.* 1:21). Secondly, he will be great – the key-player in the plan of God (*Isa.* 52:13; 53:12). Thirdly, he will be the Son of the Most High God, a title that points to Jesus' eternal Sonship (*John* 1:18). Fourthly, he will rule as king just like David his forefather, but his kingdom will endure forever (*Acts* 2:29–36).

This announcement pinpoints some of the themes that Luke will develop in the rest of his Gospel. Jesus appears throughout as a transcendent Person who is also fully human; he presents himself as the Saviour of all kinds of people by mixing with them freely; he travels to Jerusalem in order to die for others; he comes to kingly rule through resurrection and ascension; he administers a kingdom of justice and joy for men and women everywhere and across the ages since. This variegated role begins with his miraculous conception in the womb of his earthly mother and will not end until he returns in heavenly glory as creation's King.

THE VIRGIN CONCEPTION (verses 34–35)

Jesus' conception was miraculous, which means that God by-passed in part the normal process of reproduction to create a new life. Firstly, Mary was a virgin and had never engaged in sexual relations with anyone (verse 34). Secondly, the Holy Spirit created Jesus as a child in Mary's womb by a special act of power (verse 35). Thirdly, the other case of Elizabeth's pregnancy in old age gives credence to Mary's conception (verse 36). Fourthly, the virgin conception illustrates that there are no limits to what God can do (verse 37).

Today we know that genetic mixing takes place at conception resulting in the creation of a new human being, when male sperm penetrates and fertilises a female egg. Since Mary did not conceive in the normal way with Joseph or anyone else and Jesus was male, we are led to believe that the Holy Spirit supernaturally created the embryo Jesus by mixing male genes with those taken from Mary on the female side. This miraculous method of working meant that the eternal God has become truly, permanently and sinlessly human in Jesus.

The incarnation (becoming flesh) of God in the man Jesus (*John* 1:14) is the most astonishing act of self-giving love on the part of God. Without necessity the Creator chose in amazing grace to become one of his own creatures, for the creature's sake. The incarnation means that our humanity is forever joined to God and hidden in God (*Col.* 3:3).

The incarnation further means that our human dignity is now rooted in the love of God, personified in the man Jesus. He is the measure of our worth to God as men and women. We can truly behold in Jesus the dignity the Father has bestowed on us to call us his children and to appoint us a new headship over the whole creation (*Heb.* 2:5–9).

4

The Grandeur of God

[39] *In those days Mary arose and went with haste into the hill*
country, to a town in Judah, [40] *and she entered the house of*
Zechariah and greeted Elizabeth. [41] *And when Elizabeth heard*
the greeting of Mary, the baby leaped in her womb. And
Elizabeth was filled with the Holy Spirit, [42] *and she exclaimed*
with a loud cry, 'Blessed are you among women, and blessed is
the fruit of your womb! [43] *And why is this granted to me that*
the mother of my Lord should come to me? [44] *For behold, when*
the sound of your greeting came to my ears, the baby in my womb
leaped for joy. [45] *And blessed is she who believed that there would*
be a fulfillment of what was spoken to her from the Lord.'
[46] *And Mary said,*
'My soul magnifies the Lord,
[47] *and my spirit rejoices in God my Saviour,*
[48] *for he has looked on the humble estate of his servant.*
For behold, from now on all generations will call me blessed;
[49] *for he who is mighty has done great things for me,*
and holy is his name.
[50] *And his mercy is for those who fear him*
from generation to generation.
[51] *He has shown strength with his arm;*
he has scattered the proud in the thoughts of their hearts;
[52] *he has brought down the mighty from their thrones*
and exalted those of humble estate;
[53] *he has filled the hungry with good things,*
and the rich he has sent empty away.
[54] *He has helped his servant Israel,*

in remembrance of his mercy,
[55] *as he spoke to our fathers,*
to Abraham and to his offspring forever.'
[56] *And Mary remained with her about three months and returned*
to her home (Luke 1:39–56).

Events now bring together, in a preliminary way, the two children of promise, through the meeting of their mothers, just as their lives and ministries were to cross in adult years. Mary immediately set off to visit her cousin, having heard the exciting news of her pregnancy (verse 36). No doubt she could hardly wait to tell Elizabeth in person of the angel's visit and announcement and to hear Elizabeth's story in turn.

MARY'S VISIT (verses 39–45)

The scene moves to a quiet town in the hill country (verse 39). Mary greeted Elizabeth in normal Jewish fashion, on entering her home. At Mary's voice the foetus John leaps in Elizabeth's womb, as though in recognition of Mary and her unborn child. At the same moment Elizabeth is inspired by the Holy Spirit to put into words this blessing on Mary and her holy child.

Twice she pronounces a blessing, the first time because of Mary's privileged role as the human mother of the Messiah (verse 42); the second time because Mary had believed (unlike Zechariah) that the Lord would fulfil the thing that he had spoken (verse 45). Elizabeth further declares herself honoured and humbled that the mother of her Lord should visit her (verse 43). She also relates how she had felt her child leap for joy at the sound of Mary's voice (verse 44). These physical movements of the unborn John already point to the public ministry he is going to have of announcing the good news of Jesus' arrival as the servant-king of Israel (*Luke* 3:1–18).

Mary we understand had been pregnant with Jesus since the visit of the angel. Elizabeth by now was about six months pregnant with John (verse 36). Mary was going to stay with her cousin for the remainder of her pregnancy when she herself would be near the end of the first three months of her pregnancy (verse 56).

Being Filled with the Holy Spirit

Throughout the writings of Luke being filled with the Holy Spirit (as Elizabeth was here, verse 41) means being powerfully moved by the Spirit of God to utter something of praise to God, or witness about him, or both (*Luke* 10:21; 24:48–49, *Acts* 1:8; 2:4; 4:8–12, 31; 7:55–56; 10:44–46; 13:9–11; 13:48–52). So at Pentecost all the disciples, filled with the Holy Spirit, began to prophesy or witness, to the mighty deeds of God in Jesus, through his life, death, resurrection and ascension (*Acts* 2:1, 4, 11). Joel had predicted that in the last days, following the outpouring of God's Spirit on all flesh, all God's people would be able to engage in this kind of 'prophesying' – by praising God joyfully and boldly telling other people about him (*Joel* 2:28–29).

Already at the time of the Saviour's coming into the world by incarnation these wonderful powers were being given to ordinary believers like Elizabeth, Mary and Zechariah (verses 41, 46, 67). This was happening in anticipation of Jesus' heavenly enthronement when, having accomplished the work that his Father had given him to do in the world, he would richly receive and generously give the gift of the Holy Spirit to his people (*Acts* 2:33–36). The very conception of the Son of God was enough to trigger the beginning of the age of salvation in songs of praise to God's saving power in Jesus (*Luke* 2:11, 30; 4:21).

MARY'S SONG (verseS 46–56)

Like Elizabeth Mary is filled with the Holy Spirit and gives utterance to an inspired song of confessional praise. It has become known as the 'Magnificat' from the first word of the Latin translation of verse 47 ('magnifies' or makes great).

In the background of Mary's song is that of another Israelite woman, Hannah. Her song is found in 1 Samuel 2:1–10. She too became pregnant and a joyful mother through the goodness of God. Mary would have known Hannah's song and the occasion of it. The Holy Spirit made use of this biblical knowledge when inspiring Mary's song with similar themes and language.

Mary's song is in three parts.

- Firstly (verses 47–50), Mary tells of her own experience of the mighty God who has shown himself to be her Saviour God. Mary was a simple Jewish girl whom the Lord chose for a remarkable service. He has used his boundless strength to do great things for her. All future generations – as has happened – will say that she was specially blessed by the Lord (following the lead of Elizabeth, verse 45).

- Secondly (verses 51–53), the heart of Mary's song draws lessons from her experience for all mankind. The Lord topples the proud, the powerful and the wealthy who trust in their attainments; he lifts up those who put their trust in him, the hungry and the lowly in spirit and circumstance. The values and goals of this world are not those of God's kingdom (*Isa.* 55:8–9). The story of Jesus will provide many illustrations of this principle of reversal of fortunes (*Luke* 7:36–50; 8:26–39; 10:25–37; 13:10–17; 15:1–7; 17:11–19; 18:9–14; 19:1–10).
- Thirdly (verses 54–55), Mary proclaims the meaning of her experience for Israel. Mary is enlightened to see that the events of her life herald the arrival of the promised age of salvation. The Lord had spoken in these terms long ago, especially to Abraham (*Gen.* 12:3, *Gal.* 3:16), by looking forward to someone who would be the glory of Israel and the light of the world (*Isa.* 49:5–6; *Luke* 2:28–32).

Mary's song is inspired Scripture and ranks as one of the finest examples of sacred song. Its joyful themes and liturgical expressions blend beautifully into the cycle of events it celebrates. Although not mentioned by name Jesus Christ is hidden in every canto. He inspires its message of human hope and liberation. Mary invites us to join with her in discovering God's greatness and goodness by making his gracious acts our own. Jesus is the key to personal existence, the life of believers and the history of the world.

Tell out, my soul, the greatness of the Lord!
    Unnumbered blessings, give my spirit voice;
Tender to me the promise of His Word;
    In God my Saviour shall my heart rejoice.

Tell out, my soul, the greatness of His Name!
    Make known His might, the deeds His arm has done;

His mercy sure, from age to age the same;
His holy Name – the Lord, the Mighty One.

Tell out, my soul, the greatness of His Name!
Powers and dominions lay their glory by;
Proud hearts and stubborn wills are put to flight,
The hungry fed, the humble lifted up.

Tell out, my soul, the glories of His Word!
Firm is his promise and his mercy sure.
Tell out, my soul, the greatness of the Lord
To children's children and for evermore!

Timothy Dudley-Smith

5

Zechariah's Song

*[57] Now the time came for Elizabeth to give birth, and she bore a
son. [58] And her neighbours and relatives heard that the Lord had
shown great mercy to her, and they rejoiced with her. [59] And on
the eighth day they came to circumcise the child. And they would
have called him Zechariah after his father, [60] but his mother
answered, 'No; he shall be called John.' [61] And they said to her,
'None of your relatives is called by this name.' [62] And they made
signs to his father, inquiring what he wanted him to be called. [63]
And he asked for a writing tablet and wrote, 'His name is John.'
And they all wondered. [64] And immediately his mouth was opened
and his tongue loosed, and he spoke, blessing God.*

*[65] And fear came on all their neighbours. And all these things
were talked about through all the hill country of Judea, [66] and
all who heard them laid them up in their hearts, saying, 'What
then will this child be?' For the hand of the Lord was with him.*

*[67] And his father Zechariah was filled with the Holy Spirit and
prophesied, saying,*

[68] 'Blessed be the Lord God of Israel,
for he has visited and redeemed his people
[69] and has raised up a horn of salvation for us
in the house of his servant David,
[70] as he spoke by the mouth of his holy prophets from of old,
[71] that we should be saved from our enemies
and from the hand of all who hate us;
[72] to show the mercy promised to our fathers
and to remember his holy covenant,
[73] the oath that he swore to our father Abraham, to grant us

74 *that we, being delivered from the hand of our enemies,*
might serve him without fear,
75 *in holiness and righteousness before him all our days.*
76 *And you, child, will be called the prophet of the Most High;*
for you will go before the Lord to prepare his ways,
77 *to give knowledge of salvation to his people*
in the forgiveness of their sins,
78 *because of the tender mercy of our God,*
whereby the sunrise shall visit us from on high
79 *to give light to those who sit in darkness and in the shadow of death,*
to guide our feet into the way of peace.'
80 *And the child grew and became strong in spirit, and he was in*
the wilderness until the day of his public appearance to Israel
(Luke 1:57–80).

Luke picks up again his original story about Zechariah, Elizabeth and John, having diverted in the meantime to the story of Jesus and his beginnings. The story of Zechariah resumes by informing us of his recovery and climaxes with another canticle of praise like Mary's song, inspired by the Spirit of Christ (*1 Pet*. 1:10–12).

ZECHARIAH'S RELEASE (verses 57–66)

Elizabeth gives birth to a boy, a cause of gratitude to God for his great mercy (verse 57).

The truth about John came out on the day of the child's circumcision, eight days after his birth. Normally parents chose the name of one of the parents or grandparents as a sign of a continuing lineage. Zechariah was the obvious choice but Elizabeth insisted that the boy's name should be John, meaning 'the Lord is gracious'. In their astonishment the relations turned to Zechariah expecting him to correct Elizabeth's supposed mistake. Imagine their consternation when the father confirmed what his wife had told them! The child's name must be John!

At this moment of restored obedience to the Lord Zechariah regained his powers of speech and praised God (verse 64). But the whole incident had left a deep impression so that this newborn child of Zechariah and Elizabeth became a talking point throughout the hill-county of Judea (verse 65). The question on everybody's lips was, 'What will this child become?', a question that we share as the readers of Luke's Gospel. Clearly John has been marked out for great things under the hand of God (for the same expression see Acts 11:21).

ZECHARIAH'S SONG (verses 67–80)

Like Elizabeth (*Luke* 1:41–42) and Mary (*Luke* 1:46–55), Zechariah is filled with the Holy Spirit and gives utterance to a great announcement of the coming of the Lord's salvation, as foreshadowed in the birth of John. The opening word of the Latin version has given its name to the whole song – the Benedictus ('blessed').

Zechariah's song is in two parts. The belief that is common to them both is that God is again visiting his people after years of silence and neglect (verses 68, 78). The visitation of God is cause for rejoicing and hope, as elsewhere in Scripture (*Acts* 15:14, *1 Pet*. 2:12).

- First (verses 67–75), Zechariah celebrates the acts of God on behalf of his suffering people Israel in fulfilment of his ancient promises. In particular Zechariah recalls God's words to David that he would eventually raise up a successor who would bring salvation to his people by delivering them from their enemies (verses 69–71). This was in accordance with God's earlier covenant oath to Abraham the father of Israel (verse 72–73). The goal of God's dealings with Israel was the positive one that they should serve him without fear in holiness and justice all their lives (verses 74–75).
- Secondly (verses 76–79), Zechariah addresses his own son in a predictive way. He will be called prophet of God Most High and fulfil the role of Elijah in preparing the way for the Lord's coming to his people (verse 76). His message will be salvation, consisting in the forgiveness of people's sins in a rich display of the mercies of Israel's God (verses 77–78). A new day is dawning for Israel, its light falling on those in darkness to lighten their way to the Lord's peace (verses 78–79).

A number of valuable lessons of a general kind come out of Zechariah's song.

- First, we cannot understand the events of the New Covenant, starting with John and Jesus, apart from the prior history of Israel. Zechariah speaks of the new day of the gospel but he explains it with the help of many Old Testament references.
- Secondly, the story of Israel is largely set up by a series of divine covenants through which the Lord promised to be gracious to people like Abraham (*Gen.* 12:1–3), the Israelites (*Exod.* 19–20) and David (*2 Sam.* 7:12–16). Jesus is the embodiment of those covenants of promise (*Rom.* 9:4–5).
- Thirdly, John's role is the special one of preparing the way of the Messiah by announcing God's amazing grace in a message of forgiveness. While John remains a prophet, the Messiah is the Son of the Most High God (*Luke* 1:32).

Before closing his narrative Luke informs us of John's steady growth to manhood in body and spirit (verse 80). More significantly, he was taken into the wilderness in readiness for the time when he would burst upon the scene by calling the nation to repentance before their Messiah-King.

6

Jesus the Saviour Is Born

In those days a decree went out from Caesar Augustus that all
the world should be registered. 2 This was the first registration
when Quirinius was governor of Syria. 3 And all went to be
registered, each to his own town. 4 And Joseph also went up from
Galilee, from the town of Nazareth, to Judea, to the city of
David, which is called Bethlehem, because he was of the house
and lineage of David, 5 to be registered with Mary, his betrothed,
who was with child. 6 And while they were there, the time came
for her to give birth. 7 And she gave birth to her firstborn son
and wrapped him in swaddling cloths and laid him in a manger,
because there was no place for them in the inn.
8 And in the same region there were shepherds out in the field,
keeping watch over their flock by night. 9 And an angel of the Lord
appeared to them, and the glory of the Lord shone around them,
and they were filled with fear. 10 And the angel said to them, 'Fear
not, for behold, I bring you good news of a great joy that will be
for all the people. 11 For unto you is born this day in the city of
David a Saviour, who is Christ the Lord. 12 And this will be a sign
for you: you will find a baby wrapped in swaddling cloths and lying
in a manger.' 13 And suddenly there was with the angel a multitude
of the heavenly host praising God and saying,

14 'Glory to God in the highest,
and on earth peace among those with whom he is pleased!'

15 When the angels went away from them into heaven, the
shepherds said to one another, 'Let us go over to Bethlehem and
see this thing that has happened, which the Lord has made known
to us.' 16 And they went with haste and found Mary and Joseph,
and the baby lying in a manger. 17 And when they saw it, they

made known the saying that had been told them concerning this child. [18] *And all who heard it wondered at what the shepherds told them.* [19] *But Mary treasured up all these things, pondering them in her heart.* [20] *And the shepherds returned, glorifying and praising God for all they had heard and seen, as it had been told them* (Luke 2:1–20).

This whole chapter is about the first years of Jesus' life. Luke has chosen three cameos that illustrate Jesus' personal development (verse 40). First he arrives as a newborn (verses 1–21), then he appears as a baby in arms (verses 22–40), finally he makes his way as an adolescent boy of twelve (verses 41–52).

JESUS APPEARS (verses 1–7)

The story of Jesus' birth is told in the simplest way. In the western world of that time the sole superpower was imperial Rome. Caesars ruled the empire together with the senators of Rome, through a system of regional provinces. Augustus was the Caesar when Jesus was born and it was due to him that Jesus was born just where God's prophet Micah had said (*Mic.* 5:2). As part of his administrative reforms Augustus decreed a census throughout the empire, as a basis for raising revenue through taxes.

Luke tells us that this census took place while Quirinius was governor of the province of Syria. Since we understand that Quirinius only became governor in A.D. 6 there are historical difficulties here, though not insuperable ones. For example, Quirinius was active in the eastern provinces before he became governor there and may have been given special powers to conduct a census at that time. Or possibly the census was begun earlier but only completed after Quirinius had become governor.

The taking of a census meant a great upheaval for people in the provinces since every person had to return to the place of their birth to register (verse 3). This is why we read of Jesus' father Joseph, together with his engaged wife Mary, now pregnant with Jesus and ready to give birth, travelling to the little town of Bethlehem. Joseph belonged to the royal family of David whose father came from there

(*1 Sam.* 16:1). Bethlehem was known as David's city (verse 11) because David grew up there as a boy and often visited there as an adult (*1 Chron.* 11:17). Perhaps because of Mary's condition and the need to travel more slowly they were some of the last to seek lodgings on arrival at Bethlehem. As a result Jesus was born in a cattle shed and laid in a manger for a cot (verse 7).

What an astounding beginning for the Lord of glory on entering our world! Already he embraces the life of poverty, rejection and weakness that must be his in order to be our Saviour.

Child in a manger,
  Infant of Mary;
Outcast and stranger,
  Lord of all!
Child who inherits
  All our transgressions,
All our demerits
  On Him fall.
    Mary MacDonald

Here is the beginning of the world's salvation, when God became man and dwelt among us, making our world his home (*John* 1:14). The stooping-down of God in this event is truly staggering in its proportions and in its implications for the world and for you and me. Consider 'this humble God, lying in a manger' (Bonaventure, the mediaeval theologian).

ANGELS SING (verses 8–14)

As soon as Jesus' birth takes place a host of angels arrives to bring the glad news to a band of shepherds watching over their flocks that night. Like Zechariah the shepherds were terrified by the sudden arrival of the Lord's angel, largely because he appeared in the other-worldly light of God's glory. But the angel reassured them by telling them a Saviour had been born for them, who is Christ the Lord (verse 11). This announcement was cause for great joy (verse 10), a sentiment that Mary had already shared in (*Luke* 1:47) and that Luke will mention throughout his Gospel.

The angel bestows three names on this child of wonder.

- The child is Saviour or Deliverer, the one who raises up the 'horn of salvation' in David's house (*Luke* 1:69), who will personally 'save' Israel from her enemies (*Luke* 1:71) and who will spread the 'knowledge of salvation', that is, the forgiveness of sins (*Luke* 1:77).
- The child is Christ or Messiah, the one anointed with God's Spirit to proclaim the era of the Lord's grace, to set the prisoners free, and to give sight to the blind (*Luke* 4:18–19).
- The child is the Lord, the God of Israel incarnated, who has come in personal human form to rescue his people and to restore the whole creation. Jesus is Immanuel, God with us (*Matt.* 1:23); the One who was eternally in the form of God but chose to empty himself by taking to himself the form of a servant in becoming man and, as a man, he became obedient even to the point of dying on a cross for others (*Phil.* 2:5–8).

This was the first gospel preaching, by angels to shepherds, the night that Jesus was born. The angel's final assurance was the giving of a sign – the shepherds would recognise the baby by finding him wrapped in cloths and lying in a feeding-trough in Bethlehem town.

Suddenly there appeared a host of other angels praising God in heavenly music (verse 13). In their song they ascribe glory to God in heaven high because he has given peace on the earth below. This spatial language (above, below) is unavoidable in trying to explain something about the heavenly world. We should not take this kind of language literally. But the main point of the angels' song is clear, that God has begun to reconcile heaven and earth through the birth of the male child Jesus.

Jesus was born into a world that had won a political peace after decades of civil war. Augustus was acclaimed as the architect of this *pax Romana* that stretched around the Mediterranean world. But the peace that Jesus came to bring to the world was of a higher order. It was the peace of God that means the restoration of peaceful relations between God and man through the reconciling death of the cross (*Col.* 1:19–20).

This peace is his gift, the result of his goodwill and a favour that the world can never earn. The God of Jesus is a peace-loving and peace-making God who has taken the initiative in coming to earth from heaven. The story of Jesus' birth is the greatest good news that has ever been told and its relevance never fades for a world that is still searching for lasting peace.

SHEPHERDS VISIT (verses 15–20)

Welcoming the message of a Saviour, the shepherds immediately agreed to set off for Bethlehem to see for themselves the peace-child of the angels' song. Following the clues the angels had given, the shepherds discovered the family of Joseph, Mary, and Jesus. The newborn infant was indeed lying, wrapped, in the manger. They explained their presence by recounting all that happened that night. Everyone to whom their story was told was amazed, but most of all Mary who stored up these events and words in her heart (verse 19). She already had a store of memories of God's wonderful acts and would have many more before her Son had completed his earthly course (*Luke* 2:33–35).

In 'glorifying and praising God' (verse 20), the shepherds, like many others in the Gospel (*Luke* 5:25–26), showed that they were truly receptive of God's grandeur and grace. They returned home rejoicing in the fact that a Child had been given them and a Son had been born for them (*Isa.* 9:6). There is a message here for each one of us.

> The shepherds sing; and shall I silent be?
> My God, no hymn for thee?
> My soul's a shepherd too; a flock it feeds
> Of thoughts and words and deeds.
> The pasture is thy word: the streams thy grace
> Enriching all the place.
> Shepherd and flock shall sing and all my powers
> Out-sing the day-light hours.
>
> *George Herbert*

7

Simeon's Song and Anna's Witness

21 And at the end of eight days, when he was circumcised, he was
called Jesus, the name given by the angel before he was conceived
in the womb.
22 And when the time came for their purification according to
the Law of Moses, they brought him up to Jerusalem to present
him to the Lord 23 (as it is written in the Law of the Lord, 'Every
male who first opens the womb shall be called holy to the Lord')
24 and to offer a sacrifice according to what is said in the Law of
the Lord, 'a pair of turtledoves, or two young pigeons.' 25 Now
there was a man in Jerusalem, whose name was Simeon, and this
man was righteous and devout, waiting for the consolation of
Israel, and the Holy Spirit was upon him. 26 And it had been
revealed to him by the Holy Spirit that he would not see death
before he had seen the Lord's Christ. 27 And he came in the Spirit
into the temple, and when the parents brought in the child Jesus,
to do for him according to the custom of the Law, 28 he took him
up in his arms and blessed God and said,

29 'Lord, now you are letting your servant depart in peace,
according to your word;
30 for my eyes have seen your salvation
31 that you have prepared in the presence of all peoples,
32 a light for revelation to the Gentiles,
and for glory to your people Israel.'

33 And his father and his mother marvelled at what was said
about him. 34 And Simeon blessed them and said to Mary his
mother, 'Behold, this child is appointed for the fall and rising of
many in Israel, and for a sign that is opposed 35 (and a sword

will pierce through your own soul also), so that thoughts from
many hearts may be revealed.'
36 *And there was a prophetess, Anna, the daughter of Phanuel,*
of the tribe of Asher. She was advanced in years, having lived
with her husband seven years from when she was a virgin, 37 *and*
then as a widow until she was eighty-four. She did not depart
from the temple, worshiping with fasting and prayer night and
day. 38 *And coming up at that very hour she began to give thanks*
to God and to speak of him to all who were waiting for the
redemption of Jerusalem.
39 *And when they had performed everything according to the Law*
of the Lord, they returned into Galilee, to their own town of
Nazareth. 40 *And the child grew and became strong, filled with*
wisdom. And the favour of God was upon him (Luke 2:21–40).

The main incident in this section is the inspired prophecy of the old man Simeon and the public witness of the widowed Anna. But in order to set up these meetings Luke explains how it was that Jesus' family came to be in Jerusalem at that time.

FULFILLING THE LAW (verses 21–24)

Every Jewish child was required to be circumcised on the eighth day after birth (*Lev.* 12:2–3). This was also the time when the child received a name. Jesus' name, like that of John, had been decided by the angel (*Luke* 1:31). Jesus means 'the Lord saves' because Jesus was God's agent in saving his people from their sin (*Matt.* 1:21). The names of both the boys pointed to the new age of grace that was dawning.

Circumcision was a surgical operation performed on male children at eight days (*Lev.* 12:2–3). It signified the separation of the child from a life of sin and death to a life lived for the Lord. Through circumcision a person was obliged to keep the whole of God's law, something that Jesus did perfectly for everyone (*Gal.* 5:3–4). By putting final confidence in Jesus' obedience in our place we will inherit a share in his righteousness and Spirit (*Gal.* 3:10–14; 4:4–6).

About three weeks later Mary and Joseph brought the infant Jesus up to the temple to perform the customary rites for Mary's purification. That they offered two birds shows that they were too poor to afford a lamb. This gives us a little insight into the socio-economic circumstances in which Jesus grew up (*Lev.* 12:6–8).

Moses' law also required that a newborn male child should be redeemed by paying five shekels (*Num.* 18:15–16). This practice recalled the time when the Lord saved the first-born children of Israel from the fate inflicted on the first-born Egyptians at the Exodus (*Exod.* 12:21–32). Instead of dying they lived, through the lambs offered in their place. In the same way Jesus was going to be our sacrificial lamb by shedding his life-blood on the cross (*1 Cor.* 5:7, *Heb.* 9:11–14).

Rather than telling us how Mary and Joseph paid the redemption money, Luke draws attention to their desire to present Jesus to the Lord for his service as long as he might live (verse 22, see 1 Sam. 1:1–28). In doing so Luke shows how Jesus' parents were bound by the ties of faith and love that inspired them to go beyond the minimal demands of the law.

SIMEON'S SONG (verses 25–35)

Now comes one of the great moments in the Gospel history. We are introduced to an old man called Simeon, who was a true and devout believer, watching for Israel's promised deliverance. The Holy Spirit was upon him and had revealed to him that he would not die until he had seen with his own eyes the deliverer of Israel. As the Spirit would have it, Simeon came into the temple just as Jesus' family came there too. Immediately Simeon recognised the infant Jesus, took him in his arms and prophesied about him.

Like the songs of Mary and Zechariah Simeon's borrows heavily from the Old Testament. Simeon can now die in peace because he has seen the Lord's Saviour who will bring light to the Gentile world as well as glory to his people Israel (notice the surprising order, another example of God's unexpected reversal, verses 29–32). In saying so Simeon links Jesus with the Lord's Servant who was going to bring God's salvation to the whole world (*Isa.* 42:6; 49:6; 52:9–10). Simeon's announcement sums up Luke's double theological perspective on Jesus – in him God's salvation is present for us and offered to us and he is the Saviour of no one group, but of the whole world of humankind. He is the people's Saviour.

Simeon then blessed Jesus' father and mother, before addressing his final words to Mary (verse 34). Unlike the triumphant words of the first part of his song these appended words are heavy with the themes of judgement and pain. Jesus in his lifetime will divide people, be spoken against and be the cause of anguish to Mary (verses 34–35). The sword that will pierce Mary (verse 35) may not be the trauma of the cross (*John* 19:25–27) but more generally the anguish of surrendering her Son to a life of suffering and rejection (*Luke* 2:48–49). With unerring foresight Simeon foreshadows the path that Jesus must travel in order to be the world's salvation. The Gospel of Luke will bear this out.

ANNA'S WITNESS (verses 36–38)

Simeon is not alone in his witness to what Jesus will do. A prophetess called Anna, a member of one of Israel's ancient tribes, and of a great age (she had lived ninety-one years since being married), was moved to speak of Jesus to the crowds. That a woman was so inspired heralds the new day when the Lord will pour out his Spirit on his sons and daughters to bear witness together (*Acts* 2:16–17). Those who were looking for Israel's redemption could resonate with Anna's message.

In the meantime Joseph and Mary returned to Nazareth where Jesus grew up, having fulfilled all the requirements of the law (verse 39). Jesus himself grew like any other child but was filled with God's wisdom, as the next incident will illustrate (*Luke* 2:41–52). While being always the eternal God, incapable of changing, as the man Christ Jesus the Son of God continued to develop mentally, physically and spiritually, following the lines of natural human growth. Being 'filled with wisdom' is the same as being filled with the Holy Spirit. This was for his private development; later (*Luke* 3:21–22) Jesus would receive the gifts of the same Spirit for public ministry. Strength and grace marked his development as a boy.

Simeon and Anna are continuous with Israel's past. They speak for all those who by faith held on to God's promises through the long watches of Israel's troubled history (*Heb*. 11:39–40). They show us that even in the darkest and leanest times of the history of the covenant people there is a believing remnant of God's gracious choosing. Historically salvation is from the Jews but it is for the whole world (*John* 4:21–24, *Rom.* 9:4–5).

8

The Adolescent Jesus

41 *Now his parents went to Jerusalem every year at the Feast of*
the Passover. 42 *And when he was twelve years old, they went up*
according to custom. 43 *And when the feast was ended, as they*
were returning, the boy Jesus stayed behind in Jerusalem. His
parents did not know it, 44 *but supposing him to be in the group*
they went a day's journey, but then they began to search for him
among their relatives and acquaintances, 45 *and when they did*
not find him, they returned to Jerusalem, searching for him.
46 *After three days they found him in the temple, sitting among*
the teachers, listening to them and asking them questions. 47 *And*
all who heard him were amazed at his understanding and his
answers. 48 *And when his parents saw him, they were astonished.*
And his mother said to him, 'Son, why have you treated us so?
Behold, your father and I have been searching for you in great
distress.' 49 *And he said to them, 'Why were you looking for me?*
Did you not know that I must be in my Father's house?'
50 *And they did not understand the saying that he spoke to them.*
51 *And he went down with them and came to Nazareth and was*
submissive to them. And his mother treasured up all these things
in her heart.
52 *And Jesus increased in wisdom and in stature and in favour*
with God and man (Luke 2:41–52).

This is the only story that breaks the silent years between Jesus' birth and his public mission thirty years later (*Luke* 3:23). Following Jewish custom (*Exod.* 23:17, *Deut.* 16:16) Jesus' parents went up to Jerusalem for the Passover. On this occasion Jesus had turned twelve, the age when Jewish boys were said to reach adulthood and were expected to take responsibility for their own decisions. This is the key to the story.

JESUS IS LOST (verses 43–45)

At the end of the festival Jesus chose to stay in Jerusalem for reasons that he will later explain to his parents. They were unaware of this decision and so set out for home in the confidence that Jesus was somewhere in the family travelling group. Imagine their shock, after a whole day's travel, to discover that Jesus was still somewhere in Jerusalem! After three days they found him in the temple oblivious to their anxiety.

JESUS IS FOUND (verses 46–51)

Jesus was in his element among the rabbinical teachers, listening to their answers and asking them questions. His precociousness was apparent to everyone who heard him in debate with the teachers of the law. But his parents did not share the general enthusiasm for their son. Immediately Mary remonstrated with him for his thoughtlessness in treating his parents like this and explaining their anxiety (verse 48).

But Jesus is equally astonished at their failure to understand him. He is taking responsibility for his own life in accordance with God's law. At this point Jesus utters his first recorded words in this Gospel and they are truly prophetic, 'Did you not know that I must be in my Father's house [or 'about my Father's business']?' (verse 49). In speaking like this Jesus opens a window on himself. Firstly, Jesus was conscious of a divine constraint throughout his life; he must be active in the service of his Father. He will refer again to this heavenly 'must' (*Luke* 9:22; 13:33; 19:5; 22:37). Secondly, he has a heavenly Father as well as an earthly one. In fact, his heavenly Father is closer to him since Joseph is his father by law but God is his Father by eternal generation (*John* 5:17–18). Thirdly, within this set of relationships he owes obedience to his heavenly Father over his earthly father and mother (*John* 8:29). Hence his incomprehension over their anxiety about him and displeasure with him.

His parents are unable to assimilate this fresh information about their Son (verse 50). Even with the hindsight of the birth prophecies they could not grasp the truth about him. One thing they did know – that their son was different in some way and did the unexpected. Yet Jesus did not fail to honour his father and mother, because he returned with them to Nazareth and was obedient to them. After twelve years Mary again had cause to keep in her heart strange events in the life of her son (verse 51, *Luke* 2:19).

By his example here Jesus teaches us that where two loyalties clash there is the need to put God first. Later Peter enunciated this principle as a guide to public action (*Acts* 5:29). At the same time Jesus shows us that in putting God first we do not have to be disrespectful to those human authority figures who are legally over us (for example, parents, teachers, pastors, civil leaders).

Finally, Luke tells us about Jesus' natural growth as a young man (verse 52). He developed inwardly in wisdom and outwardly in physique; he nurtured his relationships with God and people, so becoming a well-rounded and perfectly balanced individual. Luke's description of the maturing Jesus assures us that the eternal Son of God became a true man and has shared in every stage of our human journey from conception to death. This was necessary if he was truly to act and speak for us to God. It further assures us that the One who acts for us understands us inside and outside (*Heb*. 2:10–18).

The Infancy Stories

At the end of this cycle of stories connected with the births of Jesus and John we can observe a pattern in which God's kingly powers work through the everyday lives of ordinary people. We can think here of Zechariah and Elizabeth, an elderly couple doomed, it would seem, to childlessness; Mary a poor and obscure young Galilean girl; Simeon and Anna, a couple of old believers living out their days in the strong hope of Israel's deliverance. The sites of God's intervention are equally insignificant – the little town of Bethlehem, the open fields of Judea, the backwoods settlement of Nazareth.

All this tells us that God has chosen to work out his purposes for the world through ordinary men and women by matching his power with their weaknesses. Thus Zechariah fails to believe the angel but gets a second chance to proclaim the Lord's greatness; Mary believes the angel but has to have her baby in an animal shed; Zechariah's family interfere in the naming of John but submit in astonishment to the father's revelation; Mary rejoices in the glory surrounding the birth of her son but must live with the heart-break of his sufferings and rejection; Joseph and Mary have the privilege of bringing up God's Son but must let him do his Father's work.

We too may look for God to intervene in our daily routines and struggles. We may not look for this in precisely the same terms since the times have changed and the first two chapters of Luke record the unique events of salvation history. Yet we may experience the triumphs of God's grace and live on the strength of his promises, just as Zechariah, Elizabeth, Mary, Simeon and Anna did. Their stories are cameos of our time.

9

The Prophet John

In the fifteenth year of the reign of Tiberius Caesar, Pontius
Pilate being governor of Judea, and Herod being tetrarch of
Galilee, and his brother Philip tetrarch of the region of Ituraea
and Trachonitis, and Lysanias tetrarch of Abilene, [2] during the
high priesthood of Annas and Caiaphas, the word of God came
to John the son of Zechariah in the wilderness. [3] And he went
into all the region around the Jordan, proclaiming a baptism of
repentance for the forgiveness of sins. [4] As it is written in the book
of the words of Isaiah the prophet,

'The voice of one crying in the wilderness:
Prepare the way of the Lord,
make his paths straight.
[5] Every valley shall be filled,
and every mountain and hill shall be made low,
and the crooked shall become straight,
and the rough places shall become level ways,
[6] and all flesh shall see the salvation of God.'

[7] He said therefore to the crowds that came out to be baptized by
him, 'You brood of vipers! Who warned you to flee from the
wrath to come? [8] Bear fruits in keeping with repentance. And do
not begin to say to yourselves, 'We have Abraham as our father.'
For I tell you, God is able from these stones to raise up children
for Abraham. [9] Even now the axe is laid to the root of the trees.
Every tree therefore that does not bear good fruit is cut down
and thrown into the fire.'

[10] And the crowds asked him, 'What then shall we do?' [11] And he
answered them, 'Whoever has two tunics is to share with him who
has none, and whoever has food is to do likewise.' [12] Tax collectors

also came to be baptized and said to him, 'Teacher, what shall we do?' [13] *And he said to them, 'Collect no more than you are authorized to do.'* [14] *Soldiers also asked him, 'And we, what shall we do?' And he said to them, 'Do not extort money from anyone by threats or by false accusation, and be content with your wages.'*
[15] *As the people were in expectation, and all were questioning in their hearts concerning John, whether he might be the Christ,* [16]
John answered them all, saying, 'I baptize you with water, but he who is mightier than I is coming, the strap of whose sandals I am not worthy to untie. He will baptize you with the Holy Spirit and with fire. [17] *His winnowing fork is in his hand, to clear his threshing floor and to gather the wheat into his barn, but the chaff he will burn with unquenchable fire.'*
[18] *So with many other exhortations he preached good news to the people.* [19] *But Herod the tetrarch, who had been reproved by him for Herodias, his brother's wife, and for all the evil things that Herod had done,* [20] *added this to them all, that he locked up John in prison* (Luke 3:1–20).

The last time John appeared he was in the deserts of Judea, waiting for God's call (*Luke* 1: 80). Now the time has come. John will be revealed to Israel and introduce the Messiah.

JOHN'S TIMES (verses 1–2)

Luke carefully notes time on the world clock. Tiberius was emperor in Rome, Pontius Pilate the provincial governor of Judea, Herod's house ruled over Palestine and its neighbouring territories and the household of Annas controlled the high-priestly office in Jerusalem. In this way Luke registers the fact that what was taking place in the lonely deserts of Palestine was beginning a chain of events that would change the course of world history. He also wants his readers to know that what he is recording in his Gospel belongs to the actual history of the world and is other than religious symbol or spiritual fantasy. The Roman Empire has crumbled and Herod's house has long since gone but the kingdom of Jesus Christ continues. Annas and Pilate passed judgement on Jesus but one day Jesus will judge all the world's rulers. After four hundred years of silence (since the days of

Malachi), the word of God was again being heard in Palestine, through John the son of Zechariah and Elizabeth, just as the angel predicted (*Luke* 1:13–17). As in the days of Samuel (*1 Sam* 3:1) and those that Amos forecast (*Amos* 8:11–12) there was a great famine of God's prophetic word; now 'the word of God came to John' in a grand, new revelation of God's grace and truth for the whole of humankind.

JOHN'S MINISTRY (verses 3–6)

Having placed John historically and geographically Luke now fits him into a biblical context. He sums up John's message in two main themes – repentance and forgiveness. This places John within the long tradition of messengers of the Lord. True prophets of the Lord authenticate themselves by calling for radical repentance; at the same time they wooed the people back to God by renewing his promise of unqualified forgiveness. In the writings of Luke these twin themes often go together (*Luke* 4:16–21; 13:1–5; 24:47). An adjunct to John's message of repentance and forgiveness is a rite of water baptism symbolizing both (verse 3).A passage from Isaiah (*Isa.* 40:3–5) helps locate John in God's scheme of things. From this readers learn that

- John is only a voice crying out for God in a spiritual wasteland (verse 4). Great as he is, John is overshadowed by the One whose way he is preparing. This was his own preference (*John* 3:26–30).
- repentance means the straightening out of lives as a place for the Lord to walk (verse 4). The rubble and overgrown pathways of life must be cleared and made ready for his arrival.
- the One whose way is being prepared is none other than the Lord himself (verse 4). Already at the time of his conception and again at his birth, angels announced Messiah's heavenly beginnings (*Luke* 1:30–35, 2:11). This is the paradox of Jesus' person that he is God's servant and yet the Lord, David's Lord but also his Son (*Matt.* 1:23, *Luke* 20:41–44).
- God is about to transform through Jesus the spiritual and human landscape by turning people's lives and times upside down – the valleys will be filled in, the hilltops will be levelled, what is twisted

will be straightened and the rough ground will become smooth for walking (verse 5).
- 'all flesh will see the salvation of God' (verse 6). Though Jesus confined his ministry to the Jewish people *(Matt* 15:24), yet the world at large has 'seen' his salvation through the Bible and the witness of his missionary people. He has been preached among the nations and believed on in the world (*1 Tim.* 3:16).

The priority of repentance towards God and receiving his forgiveness through Christ is more pressing now than at any time in the history of this planet as world population outstrips conversions to Jesus. The offer of forgiveness inspires repentance and repentance is always the pledge of forgiveness. God requires repentance because he is holy; he offers forgiveness because he is gracious.

JOHN'S MESSAGE (verses 7–9)

John's preaching is strongly eschatological, which means that he sets his demand for repentance within the endpoint of God's judgement and salvation (verse 7). Jesus the Messiah will be a sign in the present of both judgement and grace. John speaks of 'the wrath to come' as an axe already laid to the roots of the trees. Messiah will cut down unfruitful trees and throw them into the eternal fire (verse 9). Repentance is made visible through moral changes and stands opposed to all presumptions based on religious heritage, such as Abraham. Biological ties mean nothing in the era of salvation, because God can make disciples from stones.

As fallen human beings people instinctively take refuge in the externals of religion. The evangelical preaching of John and Jesus calls for a change of heart so deep that the whole of life is directed henceforth to God. What the appropriate signs of repentance might be John is about to make known.

JOHN'S PRACTICAL COUNSELS (verses 10–14)

It is always easier to speak about repentance in general terms than to give specific examples, but John does not fail at this point. Different groups in society approached him with the same question

– 'What shall we do?' (verses 10, 12, 14). For the ordinary people John advises practical generosity and hospitality (verse 11); for tax collectors he advises strict honesty (verse 13); for soldiers he advises non-violence and contentment (verse 14).

Running through all these counsels is a theme of Luke's Gospel – the dangerous attraction of wealth and possessions. By the parables of Jesus, the real-life stories of individuals (like Zacchaeus), and the warnings of Jesus' wisdom sayings, Luke exposes the seduction of riches for the unwary. Repentance always effects a changed attitude to wealth and its uses *(Matt.* 6:19–21).

JOHN'S GOSPEL (verses 15–17)

John is an evangelist who proclaims Christ to the people. John awakened all sorts of expectations among the people by his fiery manner and radical demands. As a result there were murmurings among the crowds that John might be the Messiah (verse 15). In reply John contrasted what he was doing with what Jesus would do: John baptised the body with water but the Christ would baptise the whole person with the Holy Spirit and fire. John is like a simple servant while Jesus is the master of the house (verse 16). John's whole reason for being is to deflect attention away from himself to Jesus, as God's sacrificial lamb slain for the sins of the world (*John* 1:29). In this John represents every faithful preacher of the word of God.

But John's preaching is a mixture of judgement and mercy. In this also he speaks for all true preachers of the word. Jesus will cause the fall as well as the rise of many in Israel *(Luke* 2:34). This may not be his primary purpose but it is the inevitable result of his being who he is (*John* 3:17–21). Jesus is like a farmer who separates the chaff from the grain of his harvest, tossing away the chaff and storing the grain. At the close of this age Jesus will come again as Judge of all humankind, to separate forever the penitent from the impenitent. Present repentance is the moral foundation of his future rule.

JOHN'S IMPRISONMENT (verses 18–20)

John paid with his life for his attachment to Christ and his word. Herod Antipas, the Jewish ruler *(Luke* 3:1) talked his half brother into divorcing his wife Herodias, so that he could enjoy her. (He was later to divorce his own wife, the daughter of a Nabatean king, who would seek revenge by engaging Herod in a costly war.) John openly rebuked Herod for his marital infidelities and was cast into prison at Machaerus, east of the Dead Sea for doing so. In this way Herod added to the stockpile of his indiscretions.

John epitomizes what is best in preaching that honours God and helps humankind. Motivated by the fear of God and desiring the good of people John preached both the law of repentance and the gospel of forgiveness; the framework of his preaching was the endtime plan of God, illumined and centred in Jesus Christ, the present time of grace and the future time of wrath; his preaching laid bare the secrets of the human heart and the moral dilemmas of daily living; he preached for the common people and the ruling classes; he was faithful to the past and relevant to the present.

10

Jesus Is Baptized

[21] Now when all the people were baptized, and when Jesus also had been baptized and was praying, the heavens were opened, [22] and the Holy Spirit descended on him in bodily form, like a dove; and a voice came from heaven, 'You are my beloved Son; with you I am well pleased' (Luke 3:21–22).

Once again Luke picks up the story of Jesus after dealing with John's career. Just as their birth-stories were intertwined so were their adult lives. Crowds of people came to John and willingly submitted to his baptism, confessing their sins in a show of national reconciliation. Out of the crowd stepped Jesus to submit with the others to John's religious rite. Luke tells the story of Jesus' baptism with an economy of words but it comes in line with all that we have learned about Jesus so far. As the eternal Son of God (*Luke* 1:32) he chose to save us through becoming man himself. In his baptism he shows the extent of this by standing with us in our sinfulness, though he himself never sinned nor had any need to repent (*Heb*. 4:15).

Jesus was praying at the time of his baptism when the heavens opened (verse 21). Jesus was in the habit of praying, especially at defining moments in his life – choosing the disciples (*Luke* 6:12), leading them to faith in him (*Luke* 9:18), at the transfiguration (*Luke* 9:28–29), at the commissioning of the disciples (*Luke* 10:21–22), before teaching the disciples to pray (*Luke* 11:1), in the garden (*Luke* 22:41–46), on the cross (*Luke* 23:34, 46). Since Jesus is our perfect human example we learn from him how natural and right it is for men and women to pray. By praying Jesus was putting his personal faith in God his Father and entrusting every responsibility to him.

How much more do we need to commit our ways to God as a natural way to live?

At the time of his baptism Jesus visibly received the Holy Spirit and was audibly attested by God the Father (verse 22). The Spirit anointed Jesus with heavenly power for his human work of saving the world from sin and death (*Acts* 10:37–38). When Jesus preaches the word of the kingdom at Nazareth he shows publicly the truth of this anointing (*Luke* 4:18–19). In the same way Jesus commanded his disciples to wait for the anointing of the Spirit for their life's work of world mission (*Luke* 24:46–49). Jesus' Spirit-baptism was his personal Pentecost when he received the Spirit's charisms for the work he came to do.

The Father addressed Jesus in the second person as his very own Son, beloved and well-pleasing (verse 22), making use of prophetic scriptures which united the rich themes of the Messiah-King and the suffering Servant of the Lord (*Psa*. 2:7, *Isa*. 42:1). The baptism of Jesus illustrates the doctrine of the Trinity. The Father spoke, the Spirit came down, and the Son incarnate was the subject of the drama. Though separate in their persons they are one in willing and acting for the world's salvation.

By joining in John's baptism for sinners Jesus showed his willingness to be obedient in everything to do the Father's will. He did not draw back from associating openly with sinful men and women who need to repent of their sinful lives. No wonder the Father was pleased with him! Here was the first instalment of that obedience that would lead him all the way to the cross (*Phil*. 2:5–8). The one who knew no sin of his own was made sin for us in his lifetime so that we might become God's righteousness in him forever (*2 Cor*. 5:21).

11

Jesus' Family Tree

23 Jesus, when he began his ministry, was about thirty years of
age, being the son (as was supposed) of Joseph, the son of Heli,
24 the son of Matthat, the son of Levi, the son of Melchi, the son
of Jannai, the son of Joseph, 25 the son of Mattathias, the son of
Amos, the son of Nahum, the son of Esli, the son of Naggai,
26 the son of Maath, the son of Mattathias, the son of Semein,
the son of Josech, the son of Joda, 27 the son of Joanan, the son of
Rhesa, the son of Zerubbabel, the son of Shealtiel, the son of Neri,
28 the son of Melchi, the son of Addi, the son of Cosam, the son
of Elmadam, the son of Er, 29 the son of Joshua, the son of Eliezer,
the son of Jorim, the son of Matthat, the son of Levi, 30 the son
of Simeon, the son of Judah, the son of Joseph, the son of Jonam,
the son of Eliakim, 31 the son of Melea, the son of Menna, the
son of Mattatha, the son of Nathan, the son of David, 32 the son
of Jesse, the son of Obed, the son of Boaz, the son of Sala, the
son of Nahshon, 33 the son of Amminadab, the son of Admin, the
son of Arni, the son of Hezron, the son of Perez, the son of Judah,
34 the son of Jacob, the son of Isaac, the son of Abraham, the son
of Terah, the son of Nahor, 35 the son of Serug, the son of Reu,
the son of Peleg, the son of Eber, the son of Shelah, 36 the son of
Cainan, the son of Arphaxad, the son of Shem, the son of Noah,
the son of Lamech, 37 the son of Methuselah, the son of Enoch,
the son of Jared, the son of Mahalaleel, the son of Cainan,
38 the son of Enos, the son of Seth, the son of Adam, the son of
God (Luke 3:23–38).

People like to trace their family tree to learn who their forebears were. They get excited if they can find an important historical person in their family line. The Jews were also interested in genealogies because it was by this means that a man could prove his right to be a priest in Israel. So the genealogy of Jesus is of more than historical interest; it serves a theological purpose by linking Jesus with Israel and pointing to his suitability as the Saviour of the world.

But first we are told that Jesus was about thirty years old when he began travelling, teaching, healing and suffering (verse 23).

By a careful use of words ('as was supposed', verse 23) Luke attests in passing to Jesus' miraculous conception by the Holy Spirit (*Luke* 1:35). Joseph was the legal though not the biological father of Jesus. Most people knew nothing of the inside story of Jesus' beginnings; they assumed that he was a normal child from the union of Joseph and Mary. Matthew achieves the same effect in his genealogy by linking Jesus with Mary but not with Joseph (*Matt.* 1:16).

Factual differences exist between Luke's genealogy and that of Matthew. The best solution may be to understand Luke as giving the actual line of Joseph's family while Matthew gives the royal line of David's descendants who were related to Mary.

So who were Jesus' ancestors and what can we learn from this information?

First, there was King David (verse 31). To him the Lord had promised a successor who was going to rule over Israel and the nations (*Isa.* 7:14; 9:6–7). Even before he was born Jesus was already named as this wonder-child whose kingdom would never end (*Luke* 1:31–33). By his ascension Jesus entered into his royal position before God as Lord and Christ (*Acts* 2:33–36).

Secondly, there was Abraham (verse 34), the father of the Jewish people and the man to whom God gave special promises. These promises pointed to the coming of an individual who would channel the spiritual blessings of Abraham's covenant – the free gift of righteousness and the Holy Spirit – to the whole of humankind (*Gen.* 12:3, *Gal.* 3:16). Jesus fulfilled this by extending a welcome to outsiders and strangers so that they also can share in the glory of his kingdom.

Finally, there is Adam (verse 38) the first man, created in God's image and called God's son (*Gen.* 1:26). By his human birth from Mary, Jesus became the son of Adam at the same time being the Son of God, so that we might become the children of God. This is the logic of the incarnation (*Heb*. 2:10–18). Jesus is the man for others, the proper man, the man of love, the crucified.

So Jesus' family tree has shown us some interesting and important connections – David the king, Abraham the man who received God's promises, and Adam the first human! Having David for an ancestor links Jesus to God's royal house; having Abraham for an ancestor links him to God's covenant people, east, west, north, and south; having Adam for his ancestor links him to the whole human family. By being David's son Jesus rules the world; by being the son of Abraham he fulfils the promises (*2 Cor*. 1:20); by being Adam's son he acts for human beings.

12

The Temptation of Jesus

And Jesus, full of the Holy Spirit, returned from the Jordan and
was led by the Spirit in the wilderness 2 *for forty days, being*
tempted by the devil. And he ate nothing during those days.
And when they were ended, he was hungry. 3 *The devil said*
to him, 'If you are the Son of God, command this stone to
become bread.' 4 *And Jesus answered him, 'It is written, "Man*
shall not live by bread alone."' 5 *And the devil took him up and*
showed him all the kingdoms of the world in a moment of time,
6 *and said to him, 'To you I will give all this authority and*
their glory, for it has been delivered to me, and I give it to
whom I will. 7 *If you, then, will worship me, it will all be*
yours.' 8 *And Jesus answered him, 'It is written,*

> *"You shall worship the Lord your God,*
> *and him only shall you serve."*

9 *And he took him to Jerusalem and set him on the pinnacle of*
the temple and said to him, 'If you are the Son of God, throw
yourself down from here, 10 *for it is written,*

> *"He will command his angels concerning you,*
> *to guard you,"*

11 *and*

> *"On their hands they will bear you up,*
> *lest you strike your foot against a stone.'*

12 *And Jesus answered him, 'It is said, "You shall not put the*
Lord your God to the test." 13 *And when the devil had ended*
every temptation, he departed from him until an opportune time
(Luke 4:1–13).

Jesus had now received the Holy Spirit to carry him through his life of suffering and service (*Luke* 3:21–22). Next his willingness for that way of life must be tested to the limit. The Holy Spirit is the one, therefore, who leads him out into the desert. God makes use of the great enemy of humankind, the devil, who caused humankind at the beginning of human history to fall away from God (verse 1).

There are two representatives in the Bible history who help us to understand this experience of Jesus in the course of salvation-history. These are Adam and Israel. Adam was tempted by the devil in God's garden paradise (*Gen*. 3:1–6); Israel was tempted during her desert journeys (*Deut*. 8:2). Jesus was therefore being put to the test as the true Man and the true Israel. Both were meant to do God's will but failed; Jesus came to do God's will and succeeded. By succeeding against the devil Jesus laid the foundation of his messianic work that would lead him to the cross where he finally broke the devil's power (*John* 14:30). He has effectively bound the strong man and now can spoil his goods (*Luke* 11:20–22).

Having won the initial victory in the history of salvation Jesus has put those who belong to him in the position of being able to resist the devil in their lifetime. For this reason Paul can exhort believers to be strong in the Lord and in the power of his might and so stand against all the wiles of the devil (*Eph*. 6:10–13). Christians do not need to defeat Satan for themselves; rather they build on the victory of Christ. They fight the good fight in Christ.

In one way Jesus' temptations are uniquely his own, in another way they are typical of the temptations that assail us all. Like our temptations his made a strong appeal to his immediate self-interest by urging him to compromise by choosing the easier way. Jesus' experience should warn us that Satanic temptations are both deceptive and persuasive, suited to our situation and temperament.

Like our temptations Satan insinuated his temptations as suggestions into Jesus' mind so that they seemed to be his own thoughts. Unlike us Jesus rejected these suggestions by not allowing them to take hold in his thoughts or desires so as to influence him to act. The account of the temptations discloses how he did this by recording the spiritual reasonings that he used from Scripture to bring about his victory. Temptation is a common human experience; overcoming it is not. But in Christ we have new resources (*1 Cor.* 10:13).

There were three temptations, representing the triad of evil through which Satan still corrupts the world. There was an appeal to Jesus' senses (satisfy your hunger), a temptation from the world to his consciousness of being a king (enjoy worldly power and glory), and a temptation to false worship (surrender to evil). These temptations were physical, social and religious in nature. They covered the whole spectrum of human nature and experience.

The order of the second and third temptations differs in Luke and Matthew, perhaps for theological reasons in each case. Matthew has the temptations climaxing on a mountain (following his mountain motif in chapters 5, 17, and 28). Luke has the temptations climaxing in Jerusalem where Jesus' life would finish and Israel's destiny was going to be decided. These editorial decisions do not change the event itself.

THE FIRST TEMPTATION (verses 2–5)

Satan comes to Jesus after he has fasted for forty days, when he is hungry, tired and vulnerable. The devil matches the first temptation to Jesus' physical condition. He encourages Jesus to draw on his divine powers as the Son of God instead of waiting on God to supply his needs. Jesus quotes Deuteronomy 8:3 ('man will not live by bread alone'). By this Jesus shows his primary concern is doing God's will even when it means suffering hunger. Eve was drawn to the food of the tree just as Israel craved food in the desert; both took their needs into their own hands instead of trusting God to provide them. They put the physical ahead of the spiritual (*Psa.* 106:13–15). So may we under the pressure of materialistic advertising that appeals to our senses and diverts us from the spiritual disciplines of true obedience.

THE SECOND TEMPTATION (verses 5–8)

By some demonic power Satan flashes before Jesus a scintillating picture of all the civilisations of history with their entrancing political power, wealth and glory. The beauty of the tree had mesmerised Eve (*Gen.* 3:6). The devil deals in half-truth when he claims the ownership of these (*1 Tim.* 6:15–16). The temptation requires Jesus to choose how he will become a king – immediately, by surrendering to the devil or as a future reward for being faithful to God; the crown without a cross or the crown because of a cross (*Luke* 1:32–33).

Jesus appeals to Deuteronomy 6:13 ('You shall worship the Lord your God and him only shall you serve'). The 'only', missing in the original text but implied from the context (verse 14), exposes the falsehood at the heart of the temptation. Israel had embraced other gods in place of her true spouse but Jesus will be only, always, all for God (*Acts* 2:22–36).

This is the requirement of the first commandment to have no other gods before the Lord and to love the Lord with all our heart, soul, mind and strength. This is still the starting-point of godliness.

THE THIRD TEMPTATION (verses 9–12)

Finally, Satan conducts Jesus to the temple where he summons all his subtlety by telling Jesus to throw himself out into space to force the hand of God in saving him. Here the devil tries to play Jesus at his own game by quoting Scripture for his own ends: Psalm 91:11–12, 'He will give his angels charge of you, to guard you' and 'On their hands they will bear you up, lest you strike your foot against a stone.' The devil wants to destroy Jesus, but he knows that he must first get Jesus to agree. He can only achieve this end by deceiving Jesus (*Luke* 22:3).

But Jesus sees through the devil's tactics. In the same way Israel put the Lord to the test by acts of self-will and bravado that had nothing to do with trust and obedience (*Psa.* 95:6–11). Again Jesus deflects Satan's lie by quoting Deuteronomy 6:16 ('You shall not tempt the Lord your God'). Jesus refused to be an entertainer who gained the applause of the crowds at the expense of his worth to God. Neither should those who are responsible for teaching and shepherding other human beings. Jesus shows us the proper style of leadership is in self-giving surrender to God through personal integrity.

After the third temptation the devil left Jesus, to try again another time (verse 13). In the garden of Gethsemane Satan would unleash his arts and darts against Jesus again (*Luke* 22:39–46). The temptations of Jesus were real tests of his obedience, made all the more so by his sinless nature.

The devil targeted Jesus and he will do the same with everyone who sides with Jesus. Being periodically harassed by the powers of darkness is a hallmark of all Christian leaders, churches, and causes. Jesus shows us the need to know the Scriptures in context if we are to survive the onslaught of the devil's attacks (*Eph.* 6:16–17). Temptations appeal to something in us; the Lord calls us to something outside us. His word gives us a place to stand in the midst of the storm (*1 Cor.* 10:13).

13

Popularity and Rejection

14 And Jesus returned in the power of the Spirit to Galilee, and
a report about him went out through all the surrounding country.
15 And he taught in their synagogues, being glorified by all.
16 And he came to Nazareth, where he had been brought up. And
as was his custom, he went to the synagogue on the Sabbath day,
and he stood up to read. 17 And the scroll of the prophet Isaiah
was given to him. He unrolled the scroll and found the place
where it was written,
18 'The Spirit of the Lord is upon me,
because he has anointed me
to proclaim good news to the poor.
He has sent me to proclaim liberty to the captives
and recovering of sight to the blind,
to set at liberty those who are oppressed,
19 to proclaim the year of the Lord's favour.'
20 And he rolled up the scroll and gave it back to the attendant and
sat down. And the eyes of all in the synagogue were fixed on him.
21 And he began to say to them, 'Today this Scripture has been
fulfilled in your hearing.' 22 And all spoke well of him and marvelled
at the gracious words that were coming from his mouth. And they
said, 'Is not this Joseph's son?' 23 And he said to them, 'Doubtless
you will quote to me this proverb, "Physician, heal yourself." What
we have heard you did at Capernaum, do here in your hometown
as well.' 24 And he said, 'Truly, I say to you, no prophet is acceptable
in his hometown. 25 But in truth, I tell you, there were many widows
in Israel in the days of Elijah, when the heavens were shut up three
years and six months, and a great famine came over all the land, 26
and Elijah was sent to none of them but only to Zarephath, in the

land of Sidon, to a woman who was a widow. [27] *And there were many lepers in Israel in the time of the prophet Elisha, and none of them was cleansed, but only Naaman the Syrian.'* [28] *When they heard these things, all in the synagogue were filled with wrath.* [29] *And they rose up and drove him out of the town and brought him to the brow of the hill on which their town was built, so that they could throw him down the cliff.* [30] *But passing through their midst, he went away* (Luke 4:14–30).

Having passed the temptation to surrender to the world, the flesh and the devil, Jesus is now set to begin his lifework. His first port of call will be his hometown Nazareth where he will declare his manifesto of God-appointed servanthood at a Sabbath day service. In the meantime Luke tells how Jesus travelled north into Galilee where he conducted the first part of his public mission. He was flushed with God's power after the triumph of the temptation in the desert. Initially he rode the crest of a wave of popularity (verses 14–15).

WELCOME (verses 16–21)

The highlight of any synagogue service was the reading of the Law, possibly though not always, followed by a passage from the Prophets. As a visitor Jesus had the opportunity to speak from the biblical passage for the day (*Acts* 13:14–16). That day it was from Isaiah chapter 61 describing the ministry of the Lord's Servant. Already we can see the overriding plan of God in this coincidence. Having stood up to read Jesus sat down to speak, the normal Jewish practice.

In Isaiah the Lord's Servant speaks in the first person, declaring how the Lord has anointed him with the Holy Spirit to proclaim the joyful message of the Lord's salvation. This message is about release from the burden and bondage of sin which is like a prison. The Servant will throw open the prison doors of the human spirit and lead into the light of day. Malachi had predicted that the Messiah's arrival would be like the warm sun rising with healing in his wings (*Mal.* 4:2). This is reflected in Charles Wesley's description of personal conversion:

Long my imprisoned spirit lay
  Fast bound in sin and nature's night;
Thine eye diffused a quickening ray,
  I woke, the dungeon flamed with light;
My chains fell off, my heart was free,
  I rose, went forth and followed Thee.

Jesus made the startling announcement that Isaiah's words had been fulfilled that day (verse 21)! 'Today' is more than a simple statement of time; it is part of Luke's theology of salvation (*Luke* 13:33; 19:10; 23:43). On each of these occasions Jesus is claiming and promising that salvation has already arrived in him, through his personal presence, his miracles, and his teachings.

Into the quotation from Isaiah 61 Jesus inserted a line from Isaiah 58:6 where the prophet calls the nation to practise social justice and kindness to their neighbours. Through individual, inner renewal a new kind of society will emerge where everyone is cared for and justice, truth, and goodness prevail universally (*Luke* 1:46–55). But the only way to such a future of brotherhood, justice, and peace is through personal acceptance of Jesus and his programme of righteousness and repentance. Because they ignore the gospel of Jesus all human utopias have always and will always fail. His kingdom alone can bring human justice and joy.

As well as adding, Jesus also omits from the Isaiah passage the line about God's forthcoming judgement and vengeance (*Isa*. 61:2). Judgement will come, but for now Jesus has come to announce God's end-time amnesty, a day of salvation. That day of opportunity and grace still beckons the world in Jesus (*2 Cor*. 6:2).

There was something about Jesus and the way he explained the Scriptures that held the people's attention. The whole congregation recognised him as a local boy and took pride in him. At least to start with. Shortly their mood was going to change dramatically.

REJECTION (verses 22–30)

True to his calling as outlined by Isaiah Jesus preferred the approval of God to the approbation of men and women. Aware of their pride and apathy, Jesus deliberately challenged them by quoting the proverb, 'Physician, heal yourself!' In terms of Jesus' ministry this means, 'What we, your own townspeople, have heard you did in other centres, perform for us here in Nazareth!' In so saying Jesus read their thoughts and they were not pleased. To reinforce the point, he quotes another proverb, 'A prophet is accepted everywhere except in his hometown'.

He shocked their sensibilities further by announcing that his ministry will be like the reforming prophets Elijah and Elisha who reached out to non-Jewish people. Elijah went to the poor widow of Sidon (*1 Kings* 17:8–16), Elisha served Naaman from Syria (*2 Kings* 5:1–14). Although there were many widows and many lepers in Israel at that time God directed his servants elsewhere. Jesus refused to conform to local expectations or popular stereotypes of the Messiah. He was going to be God's universal Saviour.

The initial response to Jesus in the synagogue at Nazareth had been warm and approving, now the atmosphere became icy cold and hostile. Jesus had exposed the underlying pride and prejudices of his fellow citizens. They were openly offended by the implications of his teaching. In their aggression they moved against him to throw him down the cliff on which Nazareth was partly built.

Although Jesus is immune to their violent action and goes his way, their intended deed foreshadows the final drama of Jesus' sufferings and rejection (*Luke* 13:31–33). For this reason the incident at Nazareth is 'programmatic' in laying before us the plan of Jesus' campaign and the end that awaits him. The one who came to serve will give his life as a ransom for many.

Jesus' message and mission of human freedom are as relevant today as they were in Nazareth. The eighteenth-century French philosopher Jean-Jacques Rousseau said that man was born to freedom but was everywhere in chains. Jesus would have agreed with the diagnosis though not with the cure. The Lord offers human freedom but through the liberation of the human person from within. If Jesus makes people free then they will be free indeed (*John* 8:36).

14

Jesus' Authority

> [31] *And he went down to Capernaum, a city of Galilee. And he was*
> *teaching them on the Sabbath,* [32] *and they were astonished at his*
> *teaching, for his word possessed authority.* [33] *And in the synagogue*
> *there was a man who had the spirit of an unclean demon, and he*
> *cried out with a loud voice,* [34] *'Ha! What have you to do with us,*
> *Jesus of Nazareth? Have you come to destroy us? I know who you*
> *are – the Holy One of God.'* [35] *But Jesus rebuked him, saying,*
> *'Be silent and come out of him!' And when the demon had thrown*
> *him down in their midst, he came out of him, having done him no*
> *harm.* [36] *And they were all amazed and said to one another, 'What*
> *is this word? For with authority and power he commands the*
> *unclean spirits, and they come out!'* [37] *And reports about him went*
> *out into every place in the surrounding region* (Luke 4:31–37).

Luke describes the kind of ministry acts Jesus performed in his early time in Galilee. There are three examples each of which involves Jesus with evil powers. He casts out one demon, 'rebukes' a fever and drives out many evil spirits. In all this Jesus displays a new kind of authority that proves he is able to control natural and spiritual forces.

The three episodes take place in a 24 hour period in Capernaum, on the north-west shoreline of the Sea of Galilee, where Jesus had made his new home (*Matt.* 4:13).

JESUS' AUTHORITY IN TEACHING (verses 31–32)

Just as Jesus was teaching in the local synagogue one Sabbath day a member of the audience cried out to Jesus. He did not speak for himself but an evil spirit was speaking through him like a medium. The demon cried out in recognition of who Jesus was (Jesus of Nazareth and the Holy One of God). It also cried out in dread because Jesus' arrival could mean only one thing – the day of their doom had come (verse 34).

That the demon confessed the truth about Jesus reminds us of James' saying about religious faith that consists only in doctrinal knowledge. It is dead and will not save anyone until it is translated into works of love (*James* 2:18–19, *Gal.* 5:6).

We may also notice how the demon is addressed in the singular but answers in the plural. Apparently demons move in packs (*Luke* 8:30), not choosing to act or be alone (*Luke* 11:24–26).

JESUS' AUTHORITY OVER THE SPIRIT WORLD (verses 33–37)

Jesus' response was immediate. He silenced the demon, a practice of Jesus that Luke will comment on later (verse 41). Then he commanded the demon to leave the man. The demon departed but not before throwing the man down without injury.

The action was over in moments but the discussion went on for longer. The bystanders were astonished that Jesus with a word could command the evil powers. They knew they had witnessed something from another world. Jesus became the talking point of the whole region of Galilee.

How should we interpret and use stories of Jesus that involve supernatural evil? Christians in the West have been conditioned by a technological and scientific culture to explain everything naturalistically. With this method they would explain this man by means of psychological and social causes. He was mentally and emotionally sick and stood in need of counselling and rest. But the story itself invites a realistic reading in which the demons exist and the man was controlled by them. There is more here than psychological and social causes, the dominant causes are spiritual which science cannot explain because they fall outside its ambit. The story now becomes an illustration of how evil powers can inhabit and destroy human personality and behaviour.

Western Christians tend to associate such powers with developing countries where spiritual darkness in the forms of idolatry, witchcraft, and superstition, has prevailed for centuries. But demonic powers will return to fill a spiritual vacuum (*Luke* 11:24–26). Do we not observe a return of evil powers in Western countries once blessed with Gospel liberty, through addictive and destructive practices like abortion, gambling, drugs, pornography, cults, mysticism, and the occult? As in Jesus' day these evil powers can allure, penetrate, and corrupt human lives, families, communities, and institutions.

Jesus had bound the strong man Satan in the desert encounter on the eve of his ministry (*Luke* 4:1–13); now Jesus is destroying his minions. These encounters with the demons are like skirmishes on the way to the last battle of Gethsemane and the cross when Jesus will finally cast out the prince of darkness (*Luke* 22:53).

15

Jesus' Varied Ministry

38 And he arose and left the synagogue and entered Simon's house. Now Simon's mother-in-law was ill with a high fever, and they appealed to him on her behalf. 39 And he stood over her and rebuked the fever, and it left her, and immediately she rose and began to serve them.
40 Now when the sun was setting, all those who had any who were sick with various diseases brought them to him, and he laid his hands on every one of them and healed them. 41 And demons also came out of many, crying, 'You are the Son of God!' But he rebuked them and would not allow them to speak, because they knew that he was the Christ.
42 And when it was day, he departed and went into a desolate place. And the people sought him and came to him, and would have kept him from leaving them, 43 but he said to them, 'I must preach the good news of the kingdom of God to the other towns as well; for I was sent for this purpose.' 44 And he was preaching in the synagogues of Judea (Luke 4:38–44).

Luke continues his 'day in the life of Jesus' by recording a variety of situations in which Jesus proved his independence and sufficiency. His three typical activities are healing the sick, exorcising evil spirits, and proclaiming God's word. As Jesus' ministry lengthens and intensifies his preaching and teaching become more urgent and insistent. But in this earlier phase of his ministry the three activities overlap. Here Jesus appears as the Healer, the Liberator, and the Teacher.

HEALING (verses 38–40)

Immediately Jesus left the synagogue he went to the house of Peter where Peter's mother-in-law (*1 Cor.* 9:5) was ill with a burning fever. Requested to help, Jesus readily responded. He stood over the patient as a sign of his authority over sickness and with a word he healed her. So complete and sudden was the woman's cure that she immediately got up and thanked Jesus by serving them all.

The other notable part of the story is the 'rebuke' that Jesus gave to the fever, just as he had done to the evil spirit in the man (Luke uses the same word in verse 35). Jesus could discern that this was no normal sickness but one induced by the same evil powers. His word was addressed to those powers manipulating the sickness in the body of Peter's wife's mother.

Jesus repeated this healing help many times over that evening when the local people brought their sick to him as the sun was setting. This was either because it was the end of the Sabbath day and they could do their normal activities again, or because the blistering heat of the day was passing into the cool of the evening, when people in middle-eastern countries still congregate outdoors for neighbourly chatter. Whatever kind of sickness people had, Jesus was equal to the task.

He laid his hands on all of them, perhaps a sign of his patience and compassion for every human being. He may also have wanted to awaken or strengthen their faith in him. Jesus used the gift of healing he possessed for the relief of others and the glory of the God of Israel. This was a visible proof that he was the Lord's Christ and the bearer of the age of salvation (*Luke* 7:19–22).

Does Jesus heal today? Although the special gift of healing may no longer be present among Christ's followers, he may still answer prayers for such an outcome (*James* 5:14–16; *Phil.* 2:23; *2 Tim.* 4:20).

EXORCISING (verse 41)

Many of those who came to Jesus were not medical cases but spiritual ones, people living with the devastating effects of demon-possession. The fact that Luke clearly differentiates the two types of human trauma is enough to refute the idea that what Luke calls demon-possession we today would call a pathological illness.

The demons show their spiritual origins by shouting out the truth about Jesus, that he is the eternal Son of God and the Messiah. This confession is wrung from them by the force of Jesus' personal presence among them, not from any desire to make him known. In the same way he will elicit the worship of all created things, willingly or otherwise, in the day of his coming (*Phil.* 2:9–11).

But why did Jesus silence the demons when they exclaimed about him? Different reasons have been given. This type of publicity ran counter to his mission as the self-effacing Servant of the Lord who would not draw special attention to himself (*Isa.* 42:2–3). Again, since Jesus had come as a man and for men and women, it was their witness he desired, born out of love, not the bloodcurdling yells of demons (*Heb.* 2:14–18).

PREACHING (verses 42–44)

The twenty-four hour cycle is completed next morning when Jesus rises very early to find privacy and time to pray. But the crowds are determined to be with him. Like the folks at Nazareth they make the mistake of attaching to his physical presence and so controlling him, instead of believing in his message and so being one with him forever. Just as at Nazareth, Jesus declares his determination to complete his commission to the whole nation and beyond.

Jesus states this as an obligation from God to proclaim the kingdom. Already at adolescence Jesus had sensed and privately declared this same divine claim upon his life (*Luke* 2:49). He will continue under it until the end (*Luke* 9:22; 13:32–33; 22:37). This was his God-given destiny.

Jesus was busy from sun-up to sunset, following a punishing programme in the service of humanity. How could he keep this up and what motivated him in doing so? Verse 43 tells us that:

- he replenished himself by regular times of communion with God
- he did not allow himself to be controlled by the whims of the people
- Jesus' message was always centred on God and his kingdom
- he enjoyed a divine constraint in preaching to the people

- preaching the word of the kingdom was the main reason for his mission to the world
- he was committed to evangelising people everywhere (verse 44 reads 'Judea' although Jesus was presumably in Galilee).

From this verse we can glean a rich theology of mission according to Jesus.

16

A Sinful Man

On one occasion, while the crowd was pressing in on him to hear the word of God, he was standing by the lake of Gennesaret, [2] and he saw two boats by the lake, but the fishermen had gone out of them and were washing their nets. [3] Getting into one of the boats, which was Simon's, he asked him to put out a little from the land. And he sat down and taught the people from the boat. [4] And when he had finished speaking, he said to Simon, 'Put out into the deep and let down your nets for a catch.' [5] And Simon answered, 'Master, we toiled all night and took nothing! But at your word I will let down the nets.' [6] And when they had done this, they enclosed a large number of fish, and their nets were breaking. [7] They signalled to their partners in the other boat to come and help them. And they came and filled both the boats, so that they began to sink. [8] But when Simon Peter saw it, he fell down at Jesus' knees, saying, 'Depart from me, for I am a sinful man, O Lord.' [9] For he and all who were with him were astonished at the catch of fish that they had taken, [10] and so also were James and John, sons of Zebedee, who were partners with Simon. And Jesus said to Simon, 'Do not be afraid; from now on you will be catching men.' [11] And when they had brought their boats to land, they left everything and followed him (Luke 5:1–11).

Up to this point Jesus has acted alone, now he begins to gather a circle of disciples who will learn from him by being near him. They will become the future leaders of his church.

The story centres around Peter whom Jesus had met previously (*John* 1:40–42). Before his training finished, Peter was to have several more encounters with Jesus (*Luke* 9:33; 22:31–34).

The place is the open-air on the shore of Lake Galilee, or Gennesaret as Gentiles called it. The crowd was large enough to force Jesus down to the water's edge where he caught sight of two empty fishing-boats. The owners were washing their nets after a fruitless night's work. Jesus asked Peter for the use of his boat as a pulpit. He pushed out a little from the shore and sat down (*Mark* 4:1–9).

In all this we have a remarkable example of the providence of God in bringing Jesus and Peter together in circumstances that would bring glory to Jesus and grace to Peter. God works everything together for good for those who are called according to his purpose (*Rom*. 8:28).

PETER WITNESSES JESUS' GLORY (verses 4–7)

After preaching to the people Jesus turned to Peter telling him to repeat the fishing of the night before. He was to row out to the deepest part of the lake and let his nets down for a catch of fish. Peter was sceptical but there was a note of authority in Jesus' words that compelled him to obey. The result was a bumper catch so that the nets were going to break under the pressure of so many fish. Peter summoned his partners to help with the load. They emptied the fish into the boats but then the boats were going to sink. Truly something miraculous had happened here and Peter was touched by it. He turned to Jesus who had managed the miracle and made his confession.

PETER CONFESSES HIS SINFULNESS (verses 8–10)

For Peter this was a moment of personal epiphany when God drew near and Peter was filled with awe. In the presence of Jesus Peter could see two things most clearly. First, he saw Christ's glory as Lord and God. The miracle was a sign pointing to Jesus and the truth about him. Secondly, Peter saw himself in the light of Jesus and what he saw horrified him. He could not exist in the same company, so he asked Jesus to depart from him, a sinful or sin-filled man.

Peter's encounter and response is a paradigm for others. Isaiah experienced the same trauma from being in the Lord's presence in the temple (*Isa*. 6:1–7). His reaction was the same as Peter's. Isaiah saw himself (as Peter did) as unclean in God's sight and in need of cleansing. John tells us it was Christ's glory that Isaiah saw in the temple that day (*John* 12:39–41). No wonder there are similarities between the two accounts so separated in time! In the same way the tax-collector lamented his moral failures and pled with God for mercy (*Luke* 18:13). Before anyone can serve or speak in God's name they must first be broken in the presence of the Lord and lifted up by him. Here is a prerequisite for fruitful labour.

Peter's confession deserves closer study. Not content to confess a single wrongdoing, he recognizes himself as a sinful person. The inner channels of his moral nature are polluted with sin and self. Paul expressed this consciousness in one of his letters in a psychological analysis of sin (*Rom*. 7:18). Not what he has done so much as what he is, is what disturbs the future apostle of Jesus. Peter was changed by Jesus that day; his training for kingdom service had begun.

PETER RECEIVES A COMMISSION (verses 10–11)

Now Peter is ready to receive Christ's commission. Instead of catching fish, under Christ's authority he will catch men. The work will be the same but the subjects will differ. Jesus calls on Peter's skills as a fisherman to help him catch human beings. No training, knowledge or skills are wasted in the service of Christ. Yet only Christ's call should make us leave the trade, profession or job we have trained for (*1 Cor*. 7:17–24). Jesus wants Christian fishermen as well as servant leaders for his kingdom.

Once again Jesus implies the greater value of human beings to the rest of his creation. How well Peter was going to succeed in his new work of man-fishing was put to the test on the day of Pentecost when he preached Jesus his Lord to a crowd of thousands. Three thousand people were 'caught' in his net that day, no mean harvest for a single sermon (*Acts* 2:14–42)!

But in order to achieve this goal Peter and his friends leave their business to be with Jesus. Peter would only momentarily return (*John* 21:1–14).

> A Man once came from Galilee.
>   No man so great as He.
> We left our work and went with him,
>   His followers to be.

A Sinful Man

Lord Jesus be our Teacher now,
And may we learn from You
To love and serve the living God
And other people too.
Margaret Old

Jesus is still in the business of 'catching' people and he still chooses others to do it for him. There are three lessons in his training: first, to know him in his glory and grace; then to know ourselves in our sinfulness and need; then to know others in their human worth before him.

17

A Leper Cleansed

> [12] *While he was in one of the cities, there came a man full of*
> *leprosy. And when he saw Jesus, he fell on his face and begged*
> *him, 'Lord, if you will, you can make me clean.'* [13] *And Jesus*
> *stretched out his hand and touched him, saying, 'I will; be clean.'*
> *And immediately the leprosy left him.* [14] *And he charged him to*
> *tell no one, but 'go and show yourself to the priest, and make an*
> *offering for your cleansing, as Moses commanded, for a proof to*
> *them.'* [15] *But now even more the report about him went abroad,*
> *and great crowds gathered to hear him and to be healed of their*
> *infirmities.* [16] *But he would withdraw to desolate places and pray*
> (Luke 5:12–16).

The next three episodes form a series. Jesus deals with people from the lower classes of society – a leper, a paralytic and a tax-collector. By responding to their needs as real individuals in the way he does Jesus makes known the breadth of God's mercies. Jesus has not come to approve the self-righteous but to call moral failures to his side.

THE CLEANSING (verses 12–13)

Of all ancient diseases leprosy was the most loathsome and painful. Because of the danger of contagion the leper was driven out from his local community to a life of isolation and poverty. In Jewish law a person with leprosy had to cry out as he went along, 'Unclean! Unclean!' and to live away from the camp of Israel (*Lev.* 13:45–46).

Such an individual (this was a bad case, Luke says he was 'full of leprosy') one day confronted Jesus. He announced his confidence in Jesus' ability to heal him, if only he was willing. As always Jesus responded immediately to human need by assuring the man of his willingness to heal him. To prove his point Jesus did the unthinkable – he reached out to him and touched him. What clearer evidence could there be of Jesus' compassion and power? Jesus' word of willingness brought the change and a remarkable miracle of healing took place.

The physical healings of Jesus are allegories of the spiritual recovery he gives to polluted men and women. As with this leper, sin has penetrated deep within us all and driven us away from the presence of God and the fellowship of humankind. Sin isolates and stigmatises us all. Only Jesus can restore us to ourselves, to God, and humankind. 'To him our sinning conscience cries out like the faithful leper, "Lord, if you wish you can make me clean"' (Bonaventure). Let no one doubt that Jesus is willing to restore them from the sickness of sin that leads to death.

THE COMMAND (verses 14–16)

Jesus did not patronise this man whom he had helped. He commanded him to take responsibility for his new life by reporting to the local priest. In Israelite life the priest was a kind of local health officer who diagnosed and prescribed cases of disease. This was because disease and ritual uncleanness were connected in Jewish law. Once declared clean by the priest, the leper was required to make atonement before the Lord (*Lev.*14:2–32). By telling this man to comply with the Mosaic requirements Jesus was showing his own adherence to the law (*Gal.* 4:4–5). By his obedience and sacrifice Jesus has abolished the ritual laws of Israel (*Gal.* 3:23–25).

Despite Jesus' plea for secrecy the news of this remarkable healing spread far and wide, due to the leper himself (*Mark* 1:45). The result was larger crowds and more demands on Jesus. But Jesus was unflinching in his devotion to God and the work he was given to do. Instead of being diverted by popularity, Jesus kept up his practice of early morning prayer with God. Throughout this Gospel Jesus appears as a man of prayer. No effective ministry can be maintained without regular, personal prayer with God. If that was true for Jesus, how much more for those who serve in his Name.

18

A Paralytic Healed

17 On one of those days, as he was teaching, Pharisees and
teachers of the law were sitting there, who had come from every
village of Galilee and Judea and from Jerusalem. And the power
of the Lord was with him to heal. 18 And behold, some men were
bringing on a bed a man who was paralysed, and they were
seeking to bring him in and lay him before Jesus, 19 but finding
no way to bring him in, because of the crowd, they went up on
the roof and let him down with his bed through the tiles into the
midst before Jesus. 20 And when he saw their faith, he said, 'Man,
your sins are forgiven you.' 21 And the scribes and the Pharisees
began to question, saying, 'Who is this who speaks blasphemies?
Who can forgive sins but God alone?' 22 When Jesus perceived
their thoughts, he answered them, 'Why do you question in your
hearts? 23 Which is easier, to say, "Your sins are forgiven you,"
or to say, "Rise and walk"? 24 But that you may know that the
Son of Man has authority on earth to forgive sins' – he said to
the man who was paralysed – 'I say to you, rise, pick up your
bed and go home.' 25 And immediately he rose up before them and
picked up what he had been lying on and went home, glorifying
God. 26 And amazement seized them all, and they glorified God
and were filled with awe, saying, 'We have seen extraordinary
things today.' (Luke 5:17–26).

The second episode concerns a paralysed individual. As it turns out this man required the deeper healing of heart and conscience. Jesus administers both and in such a way that his enemies are put to shame.

THE SCENE (verse 17)

The scene is set inside a house. Jesus is teaching the people who are so numerous and eager that there is no way in or out. A delegation of teachers of the law and their Pharisees had come together from as far away as Jerusalem. Their presence testifies to the impact Jesus was making and their concern to find grounds against him. They were not impartial seekers after truth.

The atmosphere is charged. The judgemental attitude of the religious leaders is almost tangible. But the power of the Lord is present to heal many people. These were counter forces about to clash head-on.

AN UNEXPECTED DISTURBANCE (verses 18–19)

While Jesus was speaking inside the house another action was taking place outside. Four men had brought a paralysed friend for Jesus to heal. The man was lying on a stretcher that the four were carrying. Because of the crowd they could not possibly reach Jesus inside. Not to be outdone, they formed a plan to get onto the roof through which they could let their friend down to Jesus. The flat roofs of Palestinian homes were an asset at a time like this because they were easily broken through. An outside stairway gave easy access to the roof.

The friends did what they planned and let the paralysed man down into the crowded room below. What a sensational entrance for the poor man lying helpless on his hammock bed and what a challenge to Jesus in the middle of his teaching! Responding to the clear faith of the four friends and given the parties present in the room Jesus chose to heal the man in two stages: first, he would perform the more difficult task of pardoning his sins; then would follow the lesser miracle of restoring his body.

Incidentally, this shows what other people's faith can do for another person who may lack faith. No one can believe for another person since each person must come to their own faith. Yet people can believe for others when their faith works for that other person or group through prayer and acts of love. The result may well be the full recovery of that person to God.

JESUS FORGIVES SINS AND HEALS THE BODY (verses 20–24)

Jesus could see the faith of the paralytic's friends by their action in breaking through to Jesus. They had persisted in the face of difficulties until they achieved what they wanted for their friend. In the presence of such faith Jesus was more than willing to respond.

But Jesus first addressed the man's deeper need, the inner need of cleansing before God in his conscience. There is a greater evil than physical ill-health. True quality of life begins from the time we receive God's forgiveness. Jesus himself wants his hearers to understand the two levels at which he operates for the salvation of men and women.

Jesus' pronouncement of absolution sounds like blasphemy in the ears of his judges. They lack the courage to say what they think but Jesus does it for them anyway. They were correct in their theology that only God can forgive sins. This is because all human sin is a breach of God's laws and only he can pardon the offender. They were wrong in their assessment of Jesus. Instead of allowing for God's authority invested in him, they excluded the possibility and so squandered another opportunity to learn the truth. How many people make the same mistake of pre-judging Jesus and in this way have blinded their own eyes.

Gifted with prophetic insight Jesus could discern the real thoughts of people (*Luke* 6:8; 7:39). As a result, he confidently challenged the religious teachers with a searching question that put them on the spot. Which was easier, to forgive someone their sins or to make them walk? If Jesus could do the former how could he not perform the latter? Leaving his judges to ponder his saying Jesus effected the man's healing, telling him to get up, pick up his bed and go home.

THE OUTCOME (verses 25–26)

The working relation of the inner and outer life of the human person is complex and mysterious. There is no hint that this man was paralysed because of personal sin. But Jesus takes the opportunity to separate the two spheres of human life and ranks them in order of importance. Human health is more than physical fitness; spiritual health can exist in a paralysed frame. Jesus is ultimately the Giver of both.

Jesus' main aim was to show people God's glory as a God of grace and a God of power. At the same time the people experienced both awe and wonder in the presence of God's servant. They rejoiced in God's goodness but trembled for his glory. This mixture of emotions is at work in all true worshippers as they come to God through Jesus. In his light we see God's light (*2 Cor.* 4:6).

Jesus is still the Son of Man who has the authority to forgive sins (verse 24). When Jesus forgives he does so – fully (no sin is too shameful or unpardonable), permanently (God separates us from our sins forever), unconditionally (we cannot make ourselves worthy of his forgiveness), immediately (our sins are gone the moment we believe). What we need is a believing heart like the paralytic's four friends.

19

A Tax-Collector Called

> [27] *After this he went out and saw a tax collector named Levi,*
> *sitting at the tax booth. And he said to him, 'Follow me.'* [28] *And*
> *leaving everything, he rose and followed him.*
> [29] *And Levi made him a great feast in his house, and there was a*
> *large company of tax collectors and others reclining at table with*
> *them.* [30] *And the Pharisees and their scribes grumbled at his disciples,*
> *saying, 'Why do you eat and drink with tax collectors and sinners?'*
> [31] *And Jesus answered them, 'Those who are well have no need of a*
> *physician, but those who are sick.* [32] *I have not come to call the*
> *righteous but sinners to repentance.'* (Luke 5:27–32).

The third episode in this series concerns a tax-collector, representing the immoral elements of society. Jesus saw him as he walked out one day because Jesus saw people as individuals with potential and a future by his grace. He was called Levi. Tax-collectors were ostracised by their fellow Jews because they were seen as traitors to the Jewish nation; they were collaborators looking after their own profit.

That Jesus would choose to call a man like this was a revolutionary way of showing God's grace. A personal call from Jesus was a liberating experience. The authority and the attraction of Jesus showed in Levi's willingness to leave his lucrative trade and be with Jesus. But not before he organised a get-together for all his colleagues and cronies. For the new Levi this was an evangelistic dinner. See a similar change in Zacchaeus (*Luke* 19:1–10).

In spite of Jesus' manifest goodness the criticism of Jesus continued unabated. Now the Pharisees complain about the company

Jesus keeps. For them social contact with people like tax-collectors contracted ritual uncleanness. Jesus discredited himself by their norms. But their norms were wrong because they confused the outward life with the inward life as a way of justifying themselves. Jesus pronounced on their self-righteousness later (*Luke* 16:15).

They directed their criticisms at the disciples but Jesus defended them by declaring his mission as one of mercy to the sick and dying. Those like the Pharisees had no sense of need and so no need for Jesus. In fact they resented his interference in their field of responsibility. Health could only return to men and women through repentance so Jesus has come to make that known and to make that happen. He gives repentance and forgiveness of sins (*Acts* 5:31).

In his beatitudes (*Luke* 6:20–21) Jesus informs us that it is people dissatisfied with themselves that he can help. Others cut themselves off from him by pride and self-righteousness.

20

The Old Versus the New

33 *And they said to him, 'The disciples of John fast often and offer*
prayers, and so do the disciples of the Pharisees, but yours eat and
drink.' 34 *And Jesus said to them, 'Can you make wedding guests*
fast while the bridegroom is with them? 35 *The days will come when*
the bridegroom is taken away from them, and then they will fast
in those days.' 36 *He also told them a parable: 'No one tears a piece*
from a new garment and puts it on an old garment. If he does, he
will tear the new, and the piece from the new will not match the
old. 37 *And no one puts new wine into old wineskins. If he does, the*
new wine will burst the skins and it will be spilled, and the skins
will be destroyed. 38 *But new wine must be put into fresh wineskins.*
39 *And no one after drinking old wine desires new, for he says, "The*
old is good."' (Luke 5:33–39).

Jesus' critics did not give up so they bring another charge against him. Their disciples and those of John (whose ministry they had rejected) were known for their asceticism in prayer and fasting. Jesus' disciples by contrast were known for eating and drinking wherever they went. The critics directed their remarks at the disciples but they were intended for Jesus. He deflects their criticisms by making use of a number of everyday illustrations.

WEDDING CELEBRATIONS (verses 34–35)

The time of Jesus' ministry is like a wedding reception where everyone is jovial. The bridegroom (and his bride) create the mood. The disciples of Jesus are like the servants of the bridegroom who, in Jewish marriages, waited on him up to the day of his wedding, rejoicing at the coming celebrations. The kingdom of God is cause for celebration because it is a kingdom of justice and joy. It would be just as foolish for the attendants of the bridegroom to go around mourning as for Jesus' disciples to behave like killjoys.

In the background of Jesus' teaching lies the Old Testament imagery of the covenant betrothal of the Lord to Israel (*Isa.* 54:4–8, *Jer.* 2:2, *Hos.* 2:19–20). This gives Jesus' teaching greater point. He has come as her bridegroom to Israel but the leaders of the people fail to respond with love and fidelity to his affectionate advances. In fact they will do away with him before he reaches out to the whole world (*Luke* 24:46–47).

When Jesus is forcibly snatched away from the disciples – that will be the time for Jesus' disciples to fast and pray, but not so long as he is with them. John the Baptist belonged to the old religious order (the law and the prophets) before the coming of Jesus (*Luke* 16:16). By clinging to the older religious rituals (*Luke* 18:11–12) the Pharisees show that they lag behind the time of God's grace present in Jesus (*Luke* 4:21; 12:54–56). They were yesterday's people; Jesus belongs to today.

OLD AND NEW ITEMS (verses 36–39)

Jesus uses two more illustrations to season his teaching. No one mends an old garment with new cloth. Anyone who tries soon discovers that the new cloth shrinks when washed and tears the old material. In the same way no one pours new wine into old wineskins since the new wine will expand and rupture the old skins that have lost their elasticity. (Jewish wine was poured into skins, not bottles.) New wine is meant for new skins.

All this was Jesus' way of saying that he stood for a new day of God's truth and grace (*John* 1:17). This meant new concepts of God along with new ways of expressing these in serving and worshipping him. Jesus did not mean to replace everything in the Old Testament since Scripture is God's word and cannot be broken (*John* 10:34–35). Still, his coming does mean progress in God's ways with people, as the crowning act and last word of God (*Luke* 16:16, *Heb.* 1:1–2).

There is a sting to the tail of the parable (verse 36). In verse 39, he exposes the tendency of people to cling on to what they have been brought up with or have become comfortable with. Their secret thoughts tell them, 'What is old is better than anything new.' But if that is people's attitude then they will have no time for Jesus because he comes as a revolutionary leader to unsettle us in our comfort zones.

Ironically, in countries traditionally Christian Jesus' religion is being regarded as old and rejected for that reason. People in Western countries are making the very mistake Jesus exposes, only in reverse. 'What is new is better than anything old,' they say. Either way, Jesus' words penetrate to the heart of things. People live with their own prejudices and pay the penalty by missing God's best that is on offer in Jesus.

21

Two Sabbath Controversies

On a Sabbath, while he was going through the grainfields, his disciples plucked and ate some heads of grain, rubbing them in their hands. [2] *But some of the Pharisees said, 'Why are you doing what is not lawful to do on the Sabbath?'* [3] *And Jesus answered them, 'Have you not read what David did when he was hungry, he and those who were with him:* [4] *how he entered the house of God and took and ate the bread of the Presence, which is not lawful for any but the priests to eat, and also gave it to those with him?'* [5] *And he said to them, 'The Son of Man is lord of the Sabbath.'*
[6] *On another Sabbath, he entered the synagogue and was teaching, and a man was there whose right hand was withered.*
[7] *And the scribes and the Pharisees watched him, to see whether he would heal on the Sabbath, so that they might find a reason to accuse him.* [8] *But he knew their thoughts, and he said to the man with the withered hand, 'Come and stand here.' And he rose and stood there.* [9] *And Jesus said to them, 'I ask you, is it lawful on the Sabbath to do good or to do harm, to save life or to destroy it?'* [10] *And after looking around at them all he said to him, 'Stretch out your hand.' And he did so, and his hand was restored.*
[11] *But they were filled with fury and discussed with one another what they might do to Jesus* (Luke 6:1–11).

Luke brings to a close a series of confrontations between Jesus and the religious authorities (*Luke* 5:17–6:11). He records two separate incidents in doing so. Their common theme is the way the Jewish Sabbath commandment should be interpreted and applied, or more generally, the relationship between law and liberty.

Jesus did not go looking for controversy, rather it came to him. This was largely due to the critical attitudes of others who used God's law in a literalistic way that allowed no place for mercy or imagination when interpreting it. These sorts of attitudes are common to religious people the world over and are not exclusive to Jesus' opponents.

SAVING LIFE ON THE SABBATH (verses 1–5)

The Sabbath commandment, forbidding labour and enjoining rest on that day, was one of the Ten Commandments that made up God's law-covenant with Israel (*Exod.* 20:8–11). For this reason the Jewish teachers took the Sabbath regulation very seriously as a sign of national identity. In order to safeguard the Sabbath they had multiplied the practical regulations for keeping it. One such rule forbade the rubbing of grain in the hands since this could be construed as a kind of work and so a breach of the divine law. Actually Moses' law allowed people to pluck grain while walking through someone's field of standing-grain to satisfy their immediate needs (*Deut.* 23:25). Cutting the grain so as to sell it was a different kind of action and forbidden. The Jews of Jesus' day had confused the two types of action.

In response Jesus cites the precedent of David who broke the rules of the tabernacle by eating the Bread of the Presence that was so sacred that only the priests could eat it (*Lev.* 24:5–9, *1 Sam.* 21:1–6). That case did not involve the Sabbath but it did provide a parallel case where someone acted in technical breach of a divine commandment yet was morally innocent.

In giving this authoritative ruling Jesus claims to be the Lord of the Sabbath (verse 5). In doing so he is claiming not only to be the Messiah who has the right to interpret God's word for the people, but the Creator God who appointed the Sabbath in the first place for people and their good (*Gen.* 2:2–3, *Mark* 2:27). In itself the law of God is the law of liberty (*James* 2:12); because of our sin we have turned it into a regime of death (*Rom.* 7:9–10).

DOING GOOD ON THE SABBATH (verses 6–11)

It was another Sabbath day and Jesus was teaching again in one of the district synagogues. Present in the congregation was a man whose right hand was paralysed and twisted. The scribes and Pharisees immediately saw this as an opportunity to catch Jesus out in public. They were eager to learn whether Jesus would heal this man on the Sabbath day and so incriminate him for working on God's rest day.

As always Jesus knew the right thing to say and do in the circumstances. He was master of the situation and his critics. He took the initiative by posing them a question put in the form of a general moral principle. Not, 'Is it right to heal on the Sabbath day?' but, 'Is it right to do good on the Sabbath day?' or, 'Is it right to save life instead of destroying it, on the Sabbath day?'

By putting the argument in this form Jesus moved beyond the particular command about the Sabbath to the general moral principle behind all God's commands. This is human wellbeing and life (*Matt.* 19:17, *Rom.* 7:12). In practice this means preserving the life and welfare of other people made like us in the image of God. This first principle of moral action comes ahead of any thing else and is bound to be done for its own sake. What saves life is usually a good guide to what is right, unless it involves a sinful act to bring it about.

Unfortunately, the occasion of doing good to one man becomes an occasion of a new surge of wickedness for others (verse 11). Ironically, the Jewish leaders, in their too great zeal to honour the fourth commandment, made themselves guilty of breaking the sixth commandment. Their inner thoughts and passions were stirred up against Jesus and plotted revenge. We may learn from their case how a legalistic spirit in religion can typically be the source of two evils – people justify themselves in wrongdoing, at the same time showing themselves indifferent to the good of others.

22

Leaders of the Kingdom

> [12] *In these days he went out to the mountain to pray, and all*
> *night he continued in prayer to God.* [13] *And when day came, he*
> *called his disciples and chose from them twelve, whom he named*
> *apostles:* [14] *Simon, whom he named Peter, and Andrew his*
> *brother, and James and John, and Philip, and Bartholomew,* [15]
> *and Matthew, and Thomas, and James the son of Alphaeus, and*
> *Simon who was called the Zealot,* [16] *and Judas the son of James,*
> *and Judas Iscariot, who became a traitor* (Luke 6:12–16).

The rest of chapter 6 is concerned with Jesus setting up his kingdom of grace and righteousness (see also *Rom.* 14:17). First he appoints leaders for the future kingdom (verses 12–16), then he teaches about life in his kingdom (verses 17–49).

Choosing leaders for his kingdom is a defining moment in Jesus' strategy for the future. These men will carry on his work and mission after his departure (*Luke* 24:44–49). For this reason he spends a whole night in prayer to God before selecting them (verse 12); then he names them apostles (verse 13); finally Luke records their names (verses 14–16).

Several principles and lessons are present here:

- Jesus devoted himself to prayer and fasting before making his decision in choosing these individuals. Later his church will learn to proceed in the same way (*Acts* 13:1–3). The same pattern beckons the churches today faced with momentous decisions about policies, programmes, and personnel.
- Jesus chose twelve men as the core-group of his disciples. Obviously their number was meant to parallel the twelve fathers

of Israel. These men will be the fathers of the new Israel, the Christian church (*Rev.* 21:10–14). Christ's personal call invested them with a unique authority to act, speak and write in his name (*Eph.* 2:19–21; 3:1–7).

- Jesus called them 'apostles' because, like himself (*Luke* 4:43), they were 'sent out' (the meaning of the Greek word) by God to proclaim the message of the kingdom (*Heb.* 3:1). They were the original Christian missionaries. In a secondary, non-technical sense all believers are apostles of Jesus Christ sent out into the world as his witnesses.
- Jesus included in his chosen circle Judas who was going to sell him out to the authorities. In choosing him Jesus shows that he himself foreknew everything and acted to bring it about (*John* 6:70–71). This shows Jesus' perfect submission to the Father's determinate plan for him in becoming the human sacrifice for human sin.

The names of the Twelve are listed because they are individuals, chosen and called by Christ in person. Paul later included himself for this reason (*1 Cor.* 9:1; 15:8). Some of them, like Peter and John, have become household names; others remain largely unknown. Luke's list corresponds with others in the New Testament (*Matt.*10:2–4, *Mark* 3:16–19, *Acts* 1:13), that is, if we accept that persons often bore two names (so Bartholomew is usually identified with Nathaniel, Matthew with Levi and Judas, son of James with Thaddeus).

The Twelve are a motley crew, a cross-section of humanity, plucked out of first century Palestine. There are small businessmen (Peter, Andrew), a civil servant (Matthew), a political activist (Simon), brothers and hot-tempered individuals (John and James), a natural leader (Peter), a constitutional doubter (Thomas) and a sceptical believer (Nathaniel).

From this we may learn that –

- Jesus builds his church from people of different temperaments and backgrounds
- Jesus unites people who otherwise would be enemies
- Jesus calls unexpected and unlikely people to carry out his mission
- Jesus transforms people in the course of serving him

- Jesus equips those he calls to serve him
- Jesus brings out the best in those who serve with him
- Jesus allows for false individuals among those who claim to serve him.

Like the genealogy of Jesus (*Luke* 3:23c–38) the list of the Twelve is not without its practical and spiritual lessons. Every portion of Scripture is profitable (*2 Tim.* 3:16) when we read it with faith, prayer, and a teachable mind and heart.

23

Living in the Kingdom

[17] And he came down with them and stood on a level place, with
a great crowd of his disciples and a great multitude of people from
all Judea and Jerusalem and the seacoast of Tyre and Sidon,
[18] who came to hear him and to be healed of their diseases. And
those who were troubled with unclean spirits were cured. [19] And
all the crowd sought to touch him, for power came out from him
and healed them all.
[20] And he lifted up his eyes on his disciples, and said:
'Blessed are you who are poor, for yours is the kingdom of God.
[21] Blessed are you who are hungry now, for you shall be satisfied.
Blessed are you who weep now, for you shall laugh. [22] Blessed
are you when people hate you and when they exclude you and
revile you and spurn your name as evil, on account of the Son of
Man! [23] Rejoice in that day, and leap for joy, for behold, your
reward is great in heaven; for so their fathers did to the prophets.
[24] But woe to you who are rich, for you have received your
consolation.
[25] Woe to you who are full now, for you shall be hungry.
Woe to you who laugh now, for you shall mourn and weep.
[26] Woe to you, when all people speak well of you, for so their
fathers did to the false prophets.
[27] But I say to you who hear, Love your enemies, do good to those
who hate you, [28] bless those who curse you, pray for those who
abuse you.
[29] To one who strikes you on the cheek, offer the other also, and
from one who takes away your cloak do not withhold your tunic
either. [30] Give to everyone who begs from you, and from one who

takes away your goods do not demand them back. 31 And as you
wish that others would do to you, do so to them.
32 If you love those who love you, what benefit is that to you?
For even sinners love those who love them. 33 And if you do good
to those who do good to you, what benefit is that to you? For even
sinners do the same. 34 And if you lend to those from whom you
expect to receive, what credit is that to you? Even sinners lend
to sinners, to get back the same amount. 35 But love your enemies,
and do good, and lend, expecting nothing in return, and your
reward will be great, and you will be sons of the Most High, for
he is kind to the ungrateful and the evil. 36 Be merciful, even as
your Father is merciful. 37 Judge not, and you will not be judged;
condemn not, and you will not be condemned; forgive, and you
will be forgiven; 38 give, and it will be given to you. Good measure, pressed down, shaken together, running over, will be put into
your lap. For with the measure you use it will be measured back
to you.'
39 He also told them a parable: 'Can a blind man lead a blind
man? Will they not both fall into a pit? 40 A disciple is not above
his teacher, but everyone when he is fully trained will be like his
teacher. 41 Why do you see the speck that is in your brother's eye,
but do not notice the log that is in your own eye? 42 How can you
say to your brother, "Brother, let me take out the speck that is in
your eye," when you yourself do not see the log that is in your
own eye? You hypocrite, first take the log out of your own eye,
and then you will see clearly to take out the speck that is in your
brother's eye.
43 For no good tree bears bad fruit, nor again does a bad tree bear
good fruit, 44 for each tree is known by its own fruit. For figs are
not gathered from thornbushes, nor are grapes picked from a
bramble bush. 45 The good person out of the good treasure of his
heart produces good, and the evil person out of his evil treasure
produces evil, for out of the abundance of the heart his mouth
speaks.
46 Why do you call me "Lord, Lord," and not do what I tell you?
47 Everyone who comes to me and hears my words and does them,
I will show you what he is like: 48 he is like a man building a
house, who dug deep and laid the foundation on the rock. And

when a flood arose, the stream broke against that house and could not shake it, because it had been well built. [49] *But the one who hears and does not do them is like a man who built a house on the ground without a foundation. When the stream broke against it, immediately it fell, and the ruin of that house was great.'* (Luke 6:17–49).

Jesus came down from the mountain top (verse 12) where he had called and commissioned his twelve disciples. Coming down to a plateau he encountered one of the largest crowds that ever attended him. All his disciples were present along with a vast gathering of people from all over Palestine, as far away as Jerusalem and from the coastal communities of Tyre and Sidon. They had come to listen to Jesus, to experience his healing powers, even to touch him. As on other occasions, God's healing power was present in a special way through Jesus as the channel (*Luke* 5:17).

All these people groups provide the human setting for the discourse that follows.

It compares with a similar body of teaching in Matthew's Gospel (*Matt*. 5–7). Matthew's account is longer because Luke has broken up much of the same material and redistributed it to other parts of his Gospel. Luke's plain (verse 17) may have been part of the mountain (verse 12; *Matt*. 5:1). There are four major sections to the sermon.

BLESSINGS AND WOES (verses 20–26)

Unlike Matthew's Gospel Luke's sermon begins with beatitudes and woes (Matthew has only beatitudes, nine in number). Jesus' beatitudes and woes have an Old Testament background at the time of the renewing of God's covenant with Israel before entering the promised land. At that time Moses placed the Lord's blessings and curses before the people (*Deut*. 27:11–28:68). Beatitudes are words of divinely promised blessing. They are lined up with a number of woes, or words of divinely promised retribution. Again we pick up the principle of human reversal that is so much a part of life in Jesus' kingdom. The poor, the hungry, the weeping, and the hated are blessed; the rich, the satisfied, the laughing, and the popular are cursed!

Throughout these blessings and woes Jesus maintains a sharp contrast between what is happening to people now and what the future holds. Jesus indicates that the future he has in mind is life in the heavenly age (verse 23). True disciples willingly exchange present pleasures, gains, and popularity for the greater and more enduring gifts and pleasures of God's future kingdom. Everyone else, whatever their religious claims may be, lives for the present moment of personal advantage, worldly possessions, and enjoyments.

True disciples are motivated and supported by love and loyalty to the Son of Man, who is Jesus himself, so much so that they are willing to face animosity and scorn for his sake. Two lines of thought should sustain disciples living under such conditions. One is the belief in a heavenly reward, which is a genuine reward, though a matter of God's grace. The other is the memory of God's faithful and exemplary servants in the past (Jesus mentions the prophets), who have led the way in suffering for him.

Are you living for the future in the present, or for the present without a future? When did you last suffer for Jesus' sake?

BEING GENEROUS WITH EVERYONE (verses 27–36)

This section (verses 27–36) is bracketed by two statements about loving your enemies, but everything in between is about the same quality of love, in one shape or form. Love is a social disposition, so when Jesus speaks about loving he is talking about our attitudes to other people, enemies, those who ask for favours, friends, even strangers. Christ's kind of loving is meant to penetrate the whole range of our relationships without exception.

Nothing could show up better the difference living in Christ's kingdom makes than the command to love our enemies, because nothing is more uncommon or difficult in normal relationships. People naturally and easily keep up resentments and grudges, swearing that they will get even one day with those who have wronged them. Sadly, this can be true among Christians. But God's way of loving, unheard of amongst human beings, is wonderfully and lavishly displayed, at infinite cost, in Jesus himself and his crucifixion (*Rom.* 5:5–9).

To help us think about this love Jesus offers some examples, outrageous examples from daily living – asking for another punch from a mugger, or offering another item of clothing to a thief (verses 27–31)! What Jesus wants to establish in his hearers' minds is an attitude of generous dealing towards other people, one that honestly works towards their personal good. When other people are in a crisis, love means putting ourselves into their circumstances and emotions and acting as we would want them to do for us in the same situation (empathy and sympathy). Love is therefore imaginative, sensitive, outgoing, practical, sincere goodwill.

Love is non-discriminatory, not just responding to people of one's own class, background, age, sex, or culture (verses 32–34). Even non-Christians can do better than that. Jesus' kind of loving means seeking in practical and personal ways the lasting good of others, without calculating on any reward here or hereafter. From where does Jesus fetch this kind of human love? From the Most High, the heavenly Father, who distributes his largesse across his creation, to human and non-human beings, irrespective of people's record or character. This is the merciful mindset and behaviour that marks someone out as a genuine child of God.

We will never locate the secret of such qualities and behaviours within ourselves, but only out of a living, personal, thriving relationship to the Most High God as our own Father (verse 35–36). This kind of relationship can only be channelled through knowing and living for Jesus (verse 22). Knowing God and keeping his company is the only way to acting like him. Living Jesus' way is fed from the springs of personal faith and communion with him, now and forever.

APHORISMS OF THE KINGDOM (verses 37–45)

God will treat us the way we treat others is the message of verse 37. If we are hyper-critical of others, God will be so with us; if we are merciful and kind-hearted to others, he will be so to us. (Judging is not the same as using our common-sense or analytical powers of reason to evaluate circumstances; it is the spirit of the Pharisee in putting other people down in comparison with ourselves, *Luke* 18:9, 11). In other words, we set the terms and level of our everyday relationship to God by the way we treat other people in everyday life. Our relationship to him is determined by our relationship to them. We should not expect God to be loving, forgiving, and patient with us when we ourselves treat other people by a different set of standards. So if we want to get on with God better, we need to start treating other people better (*1 John* 4:20–21).

Jesus makes the same point in verse 38; generous people discover that God in his providence is generous to them. When we are stingy and cold to others our own quality of life suffers accordingly; when we are forgiving and hospitable, our own enjoyment of life and God grows too. The person who waters others will himself be watered; that is the spiritual law of Christ's kingdom (*Prov*. 11:24–25). The Lord will return in ample measure the generous acts of any of his people.

In Christ's kingdom no one can lead others until they have learned to be led, no one can correct others until they have first accepted correction. This is the thrust of Jesus' parable about blind people, disciples and teachers (verses 39–40). Christian leaders should be known for their humility not their arrogance, their teachability as well as their teaching. Unfortunately we all tend to magnify the faults of others, while excusing our own. Instead, we ought to start with our own faults. Religious teachers are particularly vulnerable to the self-deception that leads them to mistake position for practice and talking for walking. Pastors and teachers especially must be meek and gentle (*Gal*. 6:1).

The heart (not the physical organ but the spiritual core of our being) is all-important for living well in the kingdom of Christ (verses 43–45). Life fundamentally comes down to what we are rather than what we do and what we are comes down to whether we are good or bad characters. These are not natural differences but are determined by the relationship we have or do not have to God through Jesus. Every tree in an orchard produces its own kind of fruit, rotten or ripe. The human heart is like a bank vault, filled with treasures or trash. Either way it will show in our life, by the way we relate, the things we cherish, the values we live by, the goals we seek, the habits we form, the reactions we show and in a special way by the manner in whch we talk and the things we talk about.

FOUNDATIONS FOR LIVING (verses 46–49)

Jesus' teachings are like the foundation of the house of our lives (verses 46–49). Jesus tells the story of two buildings, one withstood the flood but the other was washed away. The difference was in the foundations, one was built into the rock, the other stood on sand. Our lives are built on Jesus' truth sayings or they are built on nothing. The floods of this life's experience of suffering, injustice and death will be enough to test our foundations, but Jesus has in mind the future judgement when our whole life story will come up before God (*Gal.* 6:7–8). After the judgement there will be no further opportunities to repair and rebuild our lives.

When the heavenly Judge examines us, he will be looking for the foundations on which our lives have been built. Will he find Christ and his truth at the centre of your existence? Did you take Jesus' words seriously, or only *call* him 'Lord'? Don't just sit there! Arise and build!

24

A Gentile Disciple

After he had finished all his sayings in the hearing of the people, he entered Capernaum. [2] Now a centurion had a servant who was sick and at the point of death, who was highly valued by him. [3] When the centurion heard about Jesus, he sent to him elders of the Jews, asking him to come and heal his servant. [4] And when they came to Jesus, they pleaded with him earnestly, saying, 'He is worthy to have you do this for him, [5] for he loves our nation, and he is the one who built us our synagogue.' [6] And Jesus went with them. When he was not far from the house, the centurion sent friends, saying to him, 'Lord, do not trouble yourself, for I am not worthy to have you come under my roof. [7] Therefore I did not presume to come to you. But say the word, and let my servant be healed. [8] For I too am a man set under authority, with soldiers under me: and I say to one, "Go," and he goes; and to another, "Come," and he comes; and to my servant, "Do this," and he does it.' [9] When Jesus heard these things, he marvelled at him, and turning to the crowd that followed him, said, 'I tell you, not even in Israel have I found such faith.' [10] And when those who had been sent returned to the house, they found the servant well (Luke 7:1–10).

In this chapter we see Luke's narrative theology at its best. He relates the truth about Jesus through the stories of four individuals. They represent the wider community, remain nameless, but show a common allegiance to Jesus. They are a soldier, a widow, a prophet, and a prostitute. Jesus possessed a magnetism that drew people to him because they sensed in him God's love, truth, and goodness that we all hunger for.

A SOLDIER AND HIS SERVANT (verses 1–5)

Following the sermon on the plain Jesus returned to his base at Capernaum. There he was met by a delegation of Jews speaking on behalf of a Roman centurion whose dear servant was on the point of dying. This soldier was known in the local synagogue as a Gentile God-fearer who had built the Jews a new synagogue. These grateful Jews assured Jesus of the good character of this soldier as good reason for healing his servant. Historians tell us that a company of Roman soldiers was billeted in Capernaum under Herod Antipas as a security force. The centurion himself never appears in his own story. Another centurion was to quit himself well at the cross of Jesus (*Luke* 23:47).

UNWORTHINESS AND AUTHORITY (verses 6–8)

Naturally Jesus set off to this man's home to heal his servant. As they approached his home Jesus is met by another delegation, this one made up of the centurion's friends who entreat Jesus to come no further. They give two reasons for this request.

First, the centurion does not believe that he is worthy of Jesus' company, either by Jesus coming into his home or by coming himself to meet Jesus. The Jewish elders had said, 'He is worthy'; the centurion says about himself, 'I am not worthy.' A sense of personal unworthiness in Jesus' presence is paradoxically the sign of genuine faith in Jesus as we see in John the Baptist (*Luke* 3:16) and Peter (*Luke* 5:8). It is a standard response of all sincere believers (*1 Cor*. 15:9–10).

Secondly, the centurion understood the principle of authority and how it works. He could tell his servants to come or go, to do this or that and they would immediately obey his words. In this way he had come to understand Jesus as an authority figure who could exercise a higher authority than he in the realms of the body and of the spirit.

The Roman would have heard of the remarkable feats of Jesus in healing the sick, casting out demons, and controlling the natural powers. His faith to some extent therefore rested on the facts of Jesus' life. Faith is never an irrational leap, but a personal commitment to Christ partly informed by the recorded facts about Jesus.

JESUS' SURPRISE (verses 9–10)

Jesus shows his real humanity in his astonishment and admiration at the centurion's faith. Here was a Gentile outshining the Jews in the realm of their specialisation – religion. In complimenting the centurion Jesus is faulting his peers for their lack of faith in him. Once again a reversal of fortunes takes place, the outsider winning God's approval, the sons of the kingdom excluding themselves.

That the centurion's faith was real appears from the curing of his servant at the very time Jesus responded to his trustful confidence (*Matt.* 8:13).

The story of the centurion's faith in Jesus has a two-fold reference. It illustrates the wide-ranging mission that Jesus outlined for himself at the beginning (*Luke* 4:24–27) and it prefigures the ingathering of the Gentile world through the mission of the apostles. It was another centurion, Cornelius, who was the first-fruits of the Gentile harvest (*Acts* 10).

25

Jesus, the Compassion of God

[11] Soon afterward he went to a town called Nain, and his disciples and a great crowd went with him. [12] As he drew near to the gate of the town, behold, a man who had died was being carried out, the only son of his mother, and she was a widow, and a considerable crowd from the town was with her. [13] And when the Lord saw her, he had compassion on her and said to her, 'Do not weep.' [14] Then he came up and touched the bier, and the bearers stood still. And he said, 'Young man, I say to you, arise.' [15] And the dead man sat up and began to speak, and Jesus gave him to his mother. [16] Fear seized them all, and they glorified God, saying, 'A great prophet has arisen among us!' and 'God has visited his people!' [17] And this report about him spread through the whole of Judea and all the surrounding country (Luke 7:11–17).

From Capernaum Jesus moved on to Nain, a township south of Nazareth. Jesus was in his usual mode of travel, surrounded by disciples and closely followed by a large crowd of spectators.

The scene is a vivid one. As Jesus and his entourage were approaching the outskirts of Nain another crowd of people came wending its way out of the town towards them. The second crowd was a very different one from the first. It was a funeral procession and a particularly tragic one at that. The corpse being taken out for burial was a young man, the only son of a woman who had already lost her husband. In a country without any social security, this woman faced a bleak future, without a bread-winner of any kind.

JESUS' GOD-LIKE LOVE (verses 11–15)

Jesus summed up the total situation and acted in perfect harmony with the will of God. Verse 13 is the climax of the event because it describes the reason for Jesus acting as he does. The word that Luke uses for Jesus' compassion is an earthy one that refers to the 'guts' of a human being. It gives the picture of someone sharing in another's grief and condition at the most elemental level. Responding in this way Jesus embodies the love of God in its mysterious depths. He will represent this same love again under the figure of a good Samaritan (*Luke* 10:33) and a compassionate father (*Luke* 15:20).

Unlike the gods of the Greco-Roman pantheon who indulged their own passions at the expense of human beings, Jesus shows a God whose very being is love, a love that reaches out to his creation in need and pain. Jesus in his incarnate loving-kindness is the glory of Christianity and its leading icon. In Jesus God shows his willingness to participate in and identify with this world's anguish and tragedies (*Psa.* 113:5–9). The world God has chosen to love is one that has no right to be loved, far less reconciled at personal cost to God (*Rom.* 5:5–8).

Jesus first comforts the widow, halts the funeral procession, then addresses the corpse. Since no faith-response was possible from the son and no mention is made of faith by the mother, Jesus must have acted here in sovereign grace. He commands the dead man to return to life, shown by the recovery of brain function, pulse, and breathing. But Jesus' life-restoring word is a sign and promise of that total life that belongs to the world to come. The Gospels call it eternal life or the life of the coming age received and lived here and now. The story of Lazarus illustrates this connection most clearly (*John* 11:25–26).

How deeply satisfied Jesus must have felt and how astonished the funeral party must have been, when the dead man sat up and began to speak with them! Jesus had halted the rule of death and raised a banner of hope for the future of humankind. Recalling the actions of another prophet of Israel (*1Kings* 17:23), with great dignity and humanity, 'Jesus gave him back to his mother' (verse 15). What a beautiful and fitting conclusion to a story of divine compassion. Jesus embodies the personal care of the Creator to heal his creation and banish the presence of death (*1 Cor.* 15:54–57).

THE AFTERMATH (verses 16–17)

What Jesus had done and the way he did it gripped the imagination of the people. Instinctively they responded with religious awe because they sensed in Jesus the very presence of the Holy. Trying to verbalize what they felt, there was a difference of opinion expressed.

Some said Jesus was a great prophet, recalling the time of Elijah when the Lord's servant had raised a dead son and given him back to his widowed mother (*1 Kings* 17:17–24). Others said Jesus was a sign that God was visiting his people again, in grace and saving power, just as he had promised to do in the latter days (*Luke* 1:68–79).

They were both right. The time of Jesus was the in-breaking of the era when God would speak his final word to the world through a special prophet (*Acts* 3:22–26). Since this prophet's message was one of salvation, God was visiting the world in mercy before judgement (*Acts* 13:38–48).

26

A Eulogy

18 *The disciples of John reported all these things to him. And John,*
19 *calling two of his disciples to him, sent them to the Lord, saying,*
'Are you the one who is to come, or shall we look for another?'
20 *And when the men had come to him, they said, 'John the*
Baptist has sent us to you, saying, "Are you the one who is to
come, or shall we look for another?"' 21 In that hour he healed
many people of diseases and plagues and evil spirits, and on many
who were blind he bestowed sight. 22 And he answered them, 'Go
and tell John what you have seen and heard: the blind receive
their sight, the lame walk, lepers are cleansed, and the deaf hear,
the dead are raised up, the poor have good news preached to them.
23 *And blessed is the one who is not offended by me.'*
24 *When John's messengers had gone, Jesus began to speak to the*
crowds concerning John: 'What did you go out into the wilder-
ness to see? f A reed shaken by the wind? 25 What then did you
go out to see? A man dressed in soft clothing? Behold, those who
are dressed in splendid clothing and live in luxury are in kings'
courts. 26 What then did you go out to see? A prophet? Yes, I tell
you, and more than a prophet. 27 This is he of whom it is written,
"Behold, I send my messenger before your face,
who will prepare your way before you."
28 *I tell you, among those born of women none is greater than*
John. Yet the one who is least in the kingdom of God is greater
than he.' 29 (When all the people heard this, and the tax collectors
too, they declared God just, having been baptized with the
baptism of John, 30 but the Pharisees and the lawyers rejected
the purpose of God for themselves, not having been baptized by
him.)

[31] *'To what then shall I compare the people of this generation, and what are they like?* [32] *They are like children sitting in the marketplace and calling to one another,*

"We played the flute for you, and you did not dance;
we sang a dirge, and you did not weep."

[33] *For John the Baptist has come eating no bread and drinking no wine, and you say, "He has a demon."* [34] *The Son of Man has come eating and drinking, and you say, "Look at him! A glutton and a drunkard, a friend of tax collectors and sinners!"*
[35] *Yet wisdom is justified by all her children.'* (Luke 7:18–35).

John the Baptist intersects the story of Jesus for the last time. He has already figured in the birth stories (chapter 1) and Jesus' baptism (chapter 3). Since then Herod Antipas had imprisoned John (*Luke* 3:18–20). From his lonely cell John communicates with Jesus about who Jesus really is. In reply Jesus gives a long discourse about John. There are three sections to Jesus' reply each ending with a memorable saying (verses 23, 28, 35).

A NEW BEATITUDE (verses 18–23)

John is the case of a believer suffering from doubts. He has fulfilled his ministry to the people faithfully, but now was waiting death at the hands of an angry and jealous king. John raised public hopes that Jesus was the Messianic Deliverer Israel had been waiting for (*John* 1:29–34). But the beginnings of Jesus' ministry seemed to contradict these hopes. Instead of bringing in God's endtime judgement (*Luke* 3:7–9, 15–18) Jesus had begun a quiet ministry of good works. Certainly some of his teaching was radical and he was stirring up the religious authorities against him. Yet nothing had happened to suggest that the end of the age was near. The time for John was short; he must know whether Jesus is the Messiah or not.

Jesus is not angry with John for doubting him, nor offended. Jesus tells John's messengers to report on all that they have witnessed – Jesus healing sick people, exorcising devils, raising the dead, and preaching the kingdom, especially to the poor. The signs of the messianic kingdom of liberty and grace (*Luke* 4:17–21) were there for all to see but only to those with the eyes of faith (*Isa.* 35).

Lastly, Jesus sends John a special beatitude – 'Blessed is the one who is not offended by me.' John could easily have given up his belief in Jesus through outward disappointment. The beatitude was especially crafted for John in his final hours. But it is equally suited to those who have served the Lord faithfully and suffered for him. Life moves on and the enthusiasm of young faith gives way to the constant pressures of routine service; setbacks and disappointments raise questions about the certainties of faith. But the Lord has nowhere promised to explain to us all that he allows or sends in our lives of service. He asks us simply to trust and obey. What we cannot understand now we will grasp hereafter.

WHAT DID YOU GO TO SEE? (verses 24–28)

After John's disciples had gone, Jesus eulogized John unashamedly. Three times he questions why the people had gone out to the desert to listen to John. They had not expected a weakling or a fop; they had gone out to meet a prophet. John was the greatest of all the prophets, even the greatest of men. His greatness was because of Jesus. Malachi had described John, in fact, as the Lord's messenger preparing the way of the coming Messiah (*Mal.* 3:1).

Jesus' second saying – 'the one who is least in the kingdom of God is greater than he' – means that, for all his greatness, John belonged to the old era that was passing away. Jesus stood for the new age of the kingdom of salvation (*Luke* 16:16). Between the two eras there is a chasm. Those who live on this side of Easter and Pentecost are more privileged, enlightened, and empowered than those who lived to see John's day. It is better to be part of Christ's new order than to belong to the old order of Jewish types, promises and ceremonies.

Do Christians live daily in the wonder of the incarnation and the cross? Are they living as new creatures in Christ? Do they always give thanks for what it means to be saved in the hope of the resurrection? When did you last thank God that you were born A.D. and not B.C.?

GOD IS VINDICATED (verses 29–35)

John's preaching and baptism were a litmus test for the Jewish people. The common people embraced John's word and work, the religious leaders rejected them. In going along with John's baptism the people were saying, 'God is right to pronounce judgement on us because we have lived without him in our hearts; he is gracious to call us to change our hearts and ways. Blessed be the name of the Lord!' The hardness of the religious leaders gives Jesus the opportunity to think aloud about the significance of John.

Jesus wants to make clear the obtuseness of the religious leaders. Because he is a keen observer of human life in all its stages, Jesus likens the leaders to the children he has seen playing in the public squares. Nothing pleases them. Some played music but the others refused to dance; some played dirges but the others refused to mourn! Just like uncooperative children the religious leaders had refused to dance to God's tune. John came in the austerity of the Old Covenant – the Pharisees and lawyers accused him of being demon-possessed; Jesus came in the freedom and celebration of the New Covenant – they accused him of having loose morals.

But God's wisdom, or God himself, the only wise God (*Rom.* 16:27), will have the final say. His methods are right for every time and place. Those who think they are smarter than God are sure to fall. God's 'children' here may be John and Jesus firstly, but also all those who respond to him in the longer view. True believers show how good and fitting the gospel really is.

The world in its wisdom has never known God, but the wisdom of God in Jesus makes us truly wise (*1 Cor.* 1:18–25). Men and women continue to follow the Pharisees in their limited view of truth; they refuse to open themselves to the liberating wisdom of Jesus. Do you have confidence in the wisdom of the world without God, or the wisdom of God without the world?

27

Jesus' Tabletalk (1)

36 One of the Pharisees asked him to eat with him, and he went
into the Pharisee's house and took his place at the table. 37 And
behold, a woman of the city, who was a sinner, when she learned
that he was reclining at table in the Pharisee's house, brought
an alabaster flask of ointment, 38 and standing behind him at his
feet, weeping, she began to wet his feet with her tears and wiped
them with the hair of her head and kissed his feet and anointed
them with the ointment. 39 Now when the Pharisee who had
invited him saw this, he said to himself, 'If this man were a
prophet, he would have known who and what sort of woman this
is who is touching him, for she is a sinner.' 40 And Jesus answering
said to him, 'Simon, I have something to say to you.' And he
answered, 'Say it, Teacher.'
41 'A certain moneylender had two debtors. One owed five hundred
denarii, and the other fifty. 42 When they could not pay, he
cancelled the debt of both. Now which of them will love him
more?' 43 Simon answered, 'The one, I suppose, for whom he
cancelled the larger debt.' And he said to him, 'You have judged
rightly.' 44 Then turning toward the woman he said to Simon,
'Do you see this woman? I entered your house; you gave me no
water for my feet, but she has wet my feet with her tears and
wiped them with her hair. 45 You gave me no kiss, but from the
time I came in she has not ceased to kiss my feet. 46 You did not
anoint my head with oil, but she has anointed my feet with
ointment. 47 Therefore I tell you, her sins, which are many, are
forgiven – for she loved much. But he who is forgiven little, loves
little.' 48 And he said to her, 'Your sins are forgiven.' 49 Then
those who were at table with him began to say among themselves,

'Who is this, who even forgives sins?' [50] *And he said to the woman, 'Your faith has saved you; go in peace.'* (Luke 7:36–50).

This incident is not the same as a similar one that came at the end of Jesus' life on earth (*Matt.* 26:6–13, *Mark* 14:3–9, *John* 12:1–8). In that one the disciples, especially Judas, figure prominently. This story illustrates several important themes of Luke's Gospel – different responses to Jesus, forgiveness in Christ's kingdom, and what salvation means.

A WOMAN GATECRASHES THE MEAL (verses 36–39)

Jesus never declined offers of friendship, even from Pharisees. Normally suspicious and critical of Jesus, they created an atmosphere on this occasion that was at least polite and outwardly friendly (unlike *Luke* 11:37–54).

The atmosphere became charged, however, when a woman gatecrashed the proceedings when all the guests were suitably placed. Probably a former prostitute, she came in as a woman changed by Jesus. The banquet was the one opportunity she could see to express publicly her overflowing love for Jesus as her Saviour and Lord (verses 47–48). The way she expressed herself was extravagant, weeping over Jesus' feet, drying them with her hair, pouring expensive ointment over them, and kissing them.

Not surprisingly, the Pharisee entertained negative and judgemental thoughts about the woman's actions and Jesus' patience with her. They knew the reports about him as a great prophet but in their view no prophet of God would allow a woman to touch him in this way. There are abiding lessons from this first part of the story. Firstly, Jesus' attitude to religion is one of the heart where interior principles like faith and love take priority over anything outward. For this very reason Jesus refused to restrain or rebuke this woman because he knew she acted out of love that issued from a purified heart, a good conscience, and unfeigned faith (*1 Tim.* 1:5). Secondly, the Pharisee illustrates how clinical, judgemental, and unfriendly a religion based on outward forms can be. How many seeking people have been offended and put off by the coldness, legalism, and self-righteousness of church-going people.

JESUS TELLS A PARABLE (verses 40–43)

Aware of all that was passing through the Pharisee's mind, Jesus invites him to hear a parable and then reach a verdict. There were two debtors owing the same creditor. But their debts could not be compared, one owing a tiny amount of money (about two months' wages), the other owing an enormous amount (about one and a half year's wages). Neither of the debtors could repay their debt. Yet the creditor in an amazing gesture of kindness and generosity wiped out their debts – they owed him nothing

Jesus' question is, 'Which of the two debtors would be / should be more grateful to the creditor so as to love him more?' To ask the question is to answer it. The Pharisee, called Simon, replied correctly, 'The second debtor.'

The parable is about God and his relations to every one of us. In the opinion of many Jews at that time as well as many people today, being a wrongdoer meant being guilty of certain kinds of behaviour such as murdering, raping, cheating, abusing children. The point of the parable, surely not lost on Simon, is that every single human being is a debtor to God. We have all incurred a huge debt over a lifetime that we cannot begin to repay to God. We have all sinned and come short of God's glory (*Rom.* 3:23). No one is exonerated from the charges against us (*Rom.* 3:9–19). The woman had incurred a catalogue of wrong deeds over many years but Simon was also a debtor to God because of his self-righteous and proud spirit. Like the emperor with no clothes each person persuades himself that he can appear righteous in the eyes of others. But not before God!

JESUS DEFENDS AND COMMENDS THE WOMAN (verses 44–50)

Now Jesus drives home the moral of the parable. The woman's lavish welcome of Jesus stands in stark contrast to Simon's cold reception. He was a poor host who had neglected his guest – a cardinal sin in middle-eastern culture. He provided no water for Jesus' feet, no kiss of welcome, no oil for Jesus' head – all the needs of a traveller. Simon was blameless of the woman's sexual misconduct but failed miserably the greatest test of spirituality – the test of love. On that score the woman was way ahead of him, his teacher by her example of unconditional love for Jesus the Son of God.

Perhaps the true state of our hearts is revealed more by what we fail to do and be than what we actually say and do. The Pharisee's religion was one of avoidance – of sinful objects and people; Jesus' religion is one of outreaching love to others in their need of God and his salvation. The woman was simply reciprocating the kind of love that Jesus had first shown her (*1 John* 4:10–11). Hers was truly a religion of grace.

Here two people meet and respond to Jesus in different ways. The woman's sins were many and gross but she was willing to face her personal failures, accept God's forgiveness, and live her life henceforth with gratitude and joy in God through Jesus. Simon was just as much a failure, only in a different way. In his case we could simply substitute pride for promiscuity and the point is clear. Unlike the woman he criticised he could not bring himself to believe that he had failed God and stood in need of his divine mercy and help. As a result his religious life was void of the love of God and the joy and freedom it gives

Before the woman left, Jesus with a personal word of absolution, assured her of her forgiven state (verse 48). He also deliberately drew attention to the reason for her life change – her faith in him (verse 50). The woman stood forgiven not because she loved much; rather she loved much because she was forgiven. There are no merit points with Jesus; he shares his merit points with us for our eternal gain.

Love generates love. We have learned to love God because he first has loved us (*1 John* 4:10). His love present in Jesus is the cause of any love by us for him and others. The more we access that fountain of love in God so much more will we love him and serve others in love. The greatest need of the world and of the church is gaining access to the God of love in Christ, displayed classically on the cross (*Rom.* 5:5–8). Only the Holy Spirit whose product is love can open the eyes of our understanding to the wonders of divine love (*Eph.* 1:15–18). He takes the things of Christ, including his love, and reveals them effectively to us (*John* 16:14). We love little because we do not grasp the wonder of forgiveness.

Here is love, vast as the ocean,
  Loving kindness as the flood,
When the Prince of life, our ransom,
  Shed for us his precious blood.
Who his love will not remember?
  Who can cease to sing his praise?
He can never be forgotten
  Throughout heaven's eternal days.
William Rees

Your love for Jesus can only grow by feeding on his love for you. This will only happen as you read, ponder and penetrate the Gospel story of Jesus and his love.

28

Helpful Women

Soon afterward he went on through cities and villages, proclaiming and bringing the good news of the kingdom of God. And the twelve were with him, [2] *and also some women who had been healed of evil spirits and infirmities: Mary, called Magdalene, from whom seven demons had gone out,* [3] *and Joanna, the wife of Chuza, Herod's household manager, and Susanna, and many others, who provided for them out of their means* (Luke 8:1–3).

These few verses picture Jesus travelling on the road like an itinerant rabbi, making the smaller and larger communities of Palestine his circuit. He proclaimed and evangelised as he made his way, asserting and explaining the crown rights of God his Father over men and women (the kingdom principle).

Sometimes Jesus chose to be alone, but during the daytime he was surrounded by crowds. Some of the people were curious, some were critical and others were well-disposed. In the last group was a noticeable number of women who owed to Jesus a new sense of worth, forgiveness, and liberty. From this entourage of women Luke selects three for special mention.

WOMEN SUPPORTERS (verses 2–3)

Jesus had rescued these women from either devils or disease (Luke makes this distinction). They were moved by a deep and lifelong loyalty to Jesus (*Luke* 7:36–50). The friendship of women is well illustrated by these individuals – they attended Jesus on his final journey to Jerusalem, stayed with him throughout the ordeal of the cross (*Luke* 23:49), and prepared perfumes for his entombed body (*Luke* 23:55–24:1).

- Mary from Magdala was a special case, from whom Jesus had exorcised no less than seven demons. She was foremost among those women who first reported to the disciples that Jesus had risen from his grave (*Luke* 24:9–10). Jesus also appeared privately to her in the garden of his tomb (*John* 20:11–18).
- Joanna was with Mary at the empty tomb of Jesus and when she reported to the disciple's about the resurrection. She was the wife of a top official in Herod's (Antipas, see *Acts* 13:1) palace staff.
- Susanna, the third woman named, is unknown beyond this reference.

These women explain how Jesus managed to live as a travelling teacher without a regular income. Some of them were sufficiently well-off to provide from their private means for Jesus and his disciples. The large number of these women attests the widespread appeal Jesus had to women, not in a sexual sense, but as a leader, friend, and teacher. The names and biographical details of these women show that Jesus appealed to a wide spectrum of women whose personal needs were very different. The material support these women gave to Jesus illustrates the practical ministry that women can excel at – services that are indispensable to the work of the kingdom of God.

Feminist writers often accuse the Bible of neglecting women but Luke makes them visible in the life and work of Jesus and the early churches.

29

Responding to Christ's Word

4 And when a great crowd was gathering and people from town
after town came to him, he said in a parable: 5 'A sower went out
to sow his seed. And as he sowed, some fell along the path and
was trampled underfoot, and the birds of the air devoured it. 6
And some fell on the rock, and as it grew up, it withered away,
because it had no moisture. 7 And some fell among thorns, and
the thorns grew up with it and choked it. 8 And some fell into
good soil and grew and yielded a hundredfold.' As he said these
things, he called out, 'He who has ears to hear, let him hear.'
9 And when his disciples asked him what this parable meant,
10 he said, 'To you it has been given to know the secrets of the
kingdom of God, but for others they are in parables, so that seeing
they may not see, and hearing they may not understand. 11 Now
the parable is this: The seed is the word of God. 12 The ones along
the path are those who have heard. Then the devil comes and takes
away the word from their hearts, so that they may not believe and
be saved. 13 And the ones on the rock are those who, when they hear
the word, receive it with joy. But these have no root; they believe
for a while, and in time of testing fall away. 14 And as for what fell
among the thorns, they are those who hear, but as they go on their
way they are choked by the cares and riches and pleasures of life,
and their fruit does not mature. 15 As for that in the good soil, they
are those who, hearing the word, hold it fast in an honest and good
heart, and bear fruit with patience' (Luke 8:4–15).

We are now reaching the later stages of Jesus' ministry in Galilee. A huge crowd of people was gathering around him from a wide region, so Jesus saw this as an opportunity to explain the terms of entry into the kingdom. For the first time we come to Jesus' parables. The word 'parable' suggests something laid alongside something else for comparison. In these stories from everyday life Jesus compares life in this world with life in his kingdom. The parables may contain a single point of comparison but sometimes, as here, the storyline is more complex and teaches several lessons.

THE PARABLE (verses 4–8)

Jesus tells the story of a typical Palestinian farmer scattering his seed by hand, as he walked the length and breadth of his field. Perhaps Jesus could actually see one as he spoke. A public path ran round the field, separated from the ploughed field by a border of stony ground where weeds grew unchecked. All this forms the visual frame of the parable and is essential for its understanding because the farmer's seed falls on all these four types of ground. The state of the ground in each case decides whether and how far the seed generates and grows.

Jesus gave some indication of the importance of his message by calling out the words, 'He who has ears to hear, let him hear!' (verse 8). This was an encoded way of saying, 'Pay close attention to this story, because it touches your deepest interests and you absolutely need to hear it.' This is still the case because the parable deals with the very basic issue of what happens when someone hears the word of Christ and how we should respond to it.

ITS PURPOSE (verses 9–10)

Alone with his disciples Jesus explains the purpose of the parables in general, since they were asking the meaning of this one. Understanding the parables is a spiritual matter and comes as a gift of God to those who hear his word. The disciples are an example of those who have received enlightenment and been empowered to grasp the mysteries of God's kingdom. This is a fixed point of the Scripture teaching, that spiritual enlightenment comes through the co-working of God's word and Spirit or, to be more precise, God's Spirit through the word (*John* 6:44–45, *1 John* 2:26–27; 5:20).

But there is also a judicial side to hearing God's word, carried over from the commissioning of Isaiah centuries before (*Isa*. 6:9–10). The prophet was sent by God to a generation of people who had long enjoyed hearing God's word outwardly but had inwardly closed their hearts to it. The Lord forewarned Isaiah that his preaching was meant to bring about the actual hardening of these people, resulting in their lasting rejection. In the same way Jesus was sent to a generation of Jews, the majority of whom had known God's word since childhood, but never surrendered to it (*Deut*. 29:4). Jesus' ministry was to these people a final opportunity to respond, but failing this, that same ministry would be the means of bringing down God's wrath on an unbelieving generation (*Luke* 11:29–32, *Acts* 2:40, *1 Thess*. 2:14–16).

So while Jesus' explanation of the parables has a lot to do with the special historical circumstances of his own messianic preaching, his explanation applies to other times and places. Hearing the word of God means coming into contact with his life-changing gospel. It also raises the question of how we respond to it in the long term. The parable tells us about a number of possible human responses to divine truth. These four responses are typical of audiences across the world. Jesus challenges us to read ourselves into the parable somewhere. To which group of hearers do you belong?

ITS EXPLANATION (verses 11–15)

Jesus explains the parable as being all about people (the soils) and their responses to his message (the seed). The parable need not only apply to a person's response the first time of hearing God's word. It also describes the continuing responses even believers can make at different times in their lives. Their spiritual condition can vary, sometimes tending towards the first three types of hearers more than the fourth. After all, true and fruitful hearing requires perseverance (verse 15), which means sincerity and persistence over a lifetime. Yet the primary reference of the story is to first-time hearers of the gospel.

There are four types of respondent.

Hearer A

The first sort of person (verse 12) listens to the Christian message carelessly and allows the word to slip away. Jesus explains that this does not happen randomly. There are dark spiritual powers (the devil) that are bent on stealing the word from people's hearts, so that they will not come to salvation (*2 Cor.* 4:3–4). Still, this person is responsible for his actions (this is what responsibility means) since believing for oneself is the one way to gain eternal life (*2 Tim.* 3:15).

Hearer B

The second kind of person (verse 13) shows a definite response but, because this is shallow, the word never roots in the heart. The heart is the spiritual centre of our being where we make our real choices and act accordingly. As a result 'faith' here is temporary. Suffering for Christ and godliness are the twin tests of whether real faith is present or not. The true disciple will always pass these tests, the impostor will not. Time and suffering are a full-proof check on all religious claims.

Hearer C

The third type of person (verse 14) never lets go the basic passions of life in the world – worry, greed, pleasure-seeking. This is a formidable triad that only divine grace can break. Left unchecked these primitive drives will choke off God's word from surviving in the heart. Because these passions are never surrendered to the Lord the word is never allowed to reach maturity. Real faith brings a real break with the world in its spiritual seduction and moral corruption (*Heb.* 11:24–27).

Hearer D

The final type of person (verse 15) becomes a true disciple by not only hearing but actually adopting God's word within. Like the good soil in the field that receives the seed, this person absorbs the word with its life-giving nutrients, so that the individual grows up to maturity in Christ. A process of spiritual growth takes place that is visible and public (*Mark* 4:28).

Notice how true hearers of the word show all the responses that were lacking in the other three types of people (verse 15). They hold on to God's Word (unlike hearer A), they welcome it into their hearts (unlike hearer B) and they carry it into their lives (unlike hearer C). These are the true believers who go on, over the years, to produce a rich harvest of good to others and the glory of Christ. Jesus himself is our supreme example of the one who truly hears God's word and serves him (*Heb.* 10:5–7).

30

More on God's Word

16 'No one after lighting a lamp covers it with a jar or puts it
under a bed, but puts it on a stand, so that those who enter may
see the light. 17 For nothing is hidden that will not be made
manifest, nor is anything secret that will not be known and come
to light. 18 Take care then how you hear, for to the one who has,
more will be given, and from the one who has not, even what he
thinks that he has will be taken away.'
19 Then his mother and his brothers came to him, but they could
not reach him because of the crowd. 20 And he was told, 'Your
mother and your brothers are standing outside, desiring to
see you.' 21 But he answered them, 'My mother and my brothers
are those who hear the word of God and do it.'
(Luke 8:16–21).

The word of God in the preaching of Jesus was the subject of the parable of the sower; it continues as the theme of Jesus' teaching. He resumes it in two forms. First, there is a set of sayings about the light of God's word (verses 16–18); then there is a real-life incident involving the family of Jesus that elicits certain truths about discipleship (verses 19–21).

The main point of this simple parable (verses 16–18) comes with verse 18a – 'Consider carefully how you listen to God's word!' The parable of the sower has already shown how differently people listen. Jesus gives us three further reasons why we ought to hear his word with care as a matter of conscience. The way we listen is just as important as what we listen to.

GOD'S WORD IS LIGHT FOR OUR DARKNESS (verse 16)

Christ's words are a lamp that enlightens our darkness (*Psa.*119:105). Palestinian homes were lit with oil lamps that members of the family carried into the rooms and set on a stand of some kind. In the same way Christ's words enter our minds bringing light to the inner self (*1 John* 2:11). Christ has come into the world as the Light of it; if we receive his words and act on them we will enjoy the light of life, breaking free of spiritual darkness (*John* 8:12). His is the true path of enlightenment. But first each of us must own our personal confusion and darkness.

GOD'S WORD WILL BRING EVERYTHING TO LIGHT (verse 17)

Another reason for paying close attention to Christ's words is their ability to unmask our secrets by bringing us into the light of God (*Heb*. 4:12–13). Many people live with pretence knowing at the same time how shameful they are inside. If we deny God's word entrance into our hearts then we will incur the shame of having the secrets of our lives exposed when Jesus comes (*1 Cor*. 4:5). Better far to submit to his word now that we may live in his light and enjoy his fellowship while experiencing the cleansing effects of his word in our conscience (*1 John* 1:7).

CHRIST'S WORD WILL LEAVE US RICHER OR POORER (verse 18)

Christ's words never leave us the same as when we hear them. When we listen carefully they lift us up, leaving us with a clearer faith and knowledge; when we treat them with indifference, they leave us worse than we had been. People think, 'I can respond to Christ and Christianity when I choose', only to discover too late that they have forfeited what they thought they could control (*Luke* 19:26).

What does it mean to listen carefully to God's word? It means taking Christ seriously in all that he says. We must hold on to the truth we have received and be open for more whatever the cost. Only in this way can anyone grow in knowledge of Christ and his grace (*2*

Pet. 3:18). See again the fourth kind of hearer in the parable of the sower (*Luke* 8:15).

BEING A MEMBER OF JESUS' FAMILY (verses 19–21)

Jesus was not the only child of Mary. He was her firstborn, but Mary went on to have other sons (at least four are named in *Mark* 6:3) and daughters some of whom are here with her, looking for Jesus. That Joseph is not mentioned could mean that he had already died. John tells us that his family had not yet believed in him (*John* 7:5). We are not told why they urgently wanted to speak with Jesus but people relayed their message to Jesus at the front of the crowd.

Ever the Master-Teacher Jesus saw in this contact with his family a teaching opportunity. He differentiated his biological family from his spiritual family consisting of all those who heard his words and did them. What these ones share with him is a determination to keep God's word. God will honour this on the last day (*Luke* 20:34–36).

Speaking in this way (verse 21) Jesus in no way meant to be judgemental about his natural family. After all, most of them became his disciples (*Acts* 1:14, *1 Cor.* 15:7). A historical connection with Jesus through a Christian family or a Christian church is never enough for salvation. What is needed are a mind and heart sympathetic to Jesus and his words. Only then can anyone claim to belong to him or expect Jesus to receive them into heaven.

What kind of relation to Jesus do you have? Is it a natural one, based on some contact with institutional Christianity? Or is it spiritual in nature, resulting from a personal knowledge and love of Jesus as Saviour, Master, and Friend?

31

He Holds the Cyclone in His Hand

[22] One day he got into a boat with his disciples, and he said to them, 'Let us go across to the other side of the lake.' So they set out, [23] and as they sailed he fell asleep. And a windstorm came down on the lake, and they were filling with water and were in danger.
[24] And they went and woke him, saying, 'Master, Master, we are perishing!' And he awoke and rebuked the wind and the raging waves, and they ceased, and there was a calm. [25] He said to them, 'Where is your faith?' And they were afraid, and they marvelled, saying to one another, 'Who then is this, that he commands even winds and water, and they obey him?' (Luke 8:22–25).

After the teaching of parables there comes a night incident which evokes fundamental questions about Jesus. Such questions have forced themselves on people ever since. Many people have rejected the Jesus of the Gospels in favour of their own theories about Jesus, God, and the world. Everyone must answer those questions with the help of the four Gospels of the New Testament.

DANGER (verses 22–24)

Being in Galilee meant that Jesus was often near the Sea of Galilee and sometimes sailed across it. On this occasion he suggested a trip with the disciples across to the other side. During the crossing Jesus fell asleep, due to the motion of the boat and his own exhaustion. What a marvellous proof of his full humanity! The everlasting God, the Creator of the ends of the earth, who never becomes weary (*Isa*. 40:28), the Lord the Keeper of Israel who never sleeps (*Psa*.

121:3–4), experienced both as the man Jesus. His first-hand experience of human weakness and limitations should be a source of endless encouragement to those who rely on him (*Heb.* 2:17–18).

While Jesus slept the weather turned ugly, a violent storm sprang up and lashed the lake. This kind of sudden change in the weather still happens on the Sea of Galilee due to the surrounding hills which channel the winds onto the surface of the lake. Conditions became so rough that the boat began to take in water and was threatening to capsize. In their terror the disciples turned to Jesus, still asleep in the prow and wakened him with the words, 'Master, we are perishing!' Jesus immediately took control, personally rebuking the wind and the waves. At once a great calm fell on the lake and the situation of the disciples was saved.

QUESTIONS (verse 25)

A series of questions follows, asked of the disciples and by them. Jesus wanted to know where their faith was since their heavenly Father was always in control and Jesus himself was there with them. As the perfect example of believing trust in God (*Heb.* 12:2) Jesus could not understand the panic of the disciples. For him it was as natural to sleep through a storm as to rest quietly in bed at night.

This story speaks to us about 'the storms of life'. Sadly, we can identify with the disciples rather than with Jesus. During such times of stress and testing we need to hold on to our faith in God and put it into service. Jesus did and he won through. This was not the first time Jesus rebuked the disciples for their little trust in God (*Matt.* 6:25–34). If our priorities were those of Jesus then life's troubles would take their proper place within the daily round of God's providential care and providing.

The Bible is full of inspiring examples of those who have trusted in God in the midst of their storms and achieved great things (*Heb.* 11:4–38). The hymn-writers help us to share this frame of mind.

Be still, my soul; your God does undertake
To guide the future as He has the past.
Your hope, your confidence let nothing shake;
All now mysterious shall be bright at last.

Be still, my soul; the waves and winds still know
His voice who ruled them while He dwelt below.
Katharina von Schlegel

Then it was the disciples' turn to ask a question. They asked themselves about Jesus. In face of such remarkable powers they were torn between the emotions of terror and wonder. Jesus himself was the mystery. 'Who then is this?' His falling asleep proved his real humanity, his ability to control the forces and laws of nature pointed to more than human authority.

We are faced with the same question as we read the story today. The mystery remains until we accept the double truth of who he is – God and Man in one person. The story is a lesson in Christology, that is, the truth about Jesus as the Christ. The whole of Luke's Gospel was written to help us to ask this question and answer it. We must allow ourselves to be questioned by the text of the story rather than rushing to our own conclusions about Jesus. Only by discovering who Jesus really is will we begin to understand who we are. Jesus our Creator is the key to the whole of our creaturely existence.

32

Jesus Restores a Lost Human Being

Then they sailed to the country of the Gerasenes, which is opposite
Galilee. 27 When Jesus had stepped out on land, there met him a
man from the city who had demons. For a long time he had worn
no clothes, and he had not lived in a house but among the tombs.
28 When he saw Jesus, he cried out and fell down before him and
said with a loud voice, 'What have you to do with me, Jesus,
Son of the Most High God? I beg you, do not torment me.' 29
For he had commanded the unclean spirit to come out of the man.
(For many a time it had seized him. He was kept under guard
and bound with chains and shackles, but he would break the bonds
and be driven by the demon into the desert.) 30 Jesus then asked
him, 'What is your name?' And he said, 'Legion,' for many
demons had entered him. 31 And they begged him not to command
them to depart into the abyss. 32 Now a large herd of pigs was
feeding there on the hillside, and they begged him to let them enter
these. So he gave them permission. 33 Then the demons came out
of the man and entered the pigs, and the herd rushed down the
steep bank into the lake and were drowned.

34 When the herdsmen saw what had happened, they fled and
told it in the city and in the country. 35 Then people went out to
see what had happened, and they came to Jesus and found the
man from whom the demons had gone, sitting at the feet of Jesus,
clothed and in his right mind, and they were afraid. 36 And those
who had seen it told them how the demon-possessed man had been
healed. 37 Then all the people of the surrounding country of the
Gerasenes asked him to depart from them, for they were seized
with great fear. So he got into the boat and returned. 38 The man
from whom the demons had gone begged that he might be with

him, but Jesus sent him away, saying, [39] *'Return to your home, and declare how much God has done for you.' And he went away, proclaiming throughout the whole city how much Jesus had done for him* (Luke 8:26–39).

Jesus moves from the sea to the land, from Jewish territory to a Gentile community, called sometimes Gerasenes, sometimes Gadarenes, after the names of two of the ten cities (the Decapolis) that made up a multi-racial confederacy on the east side of the Sea of Galilee. Having shown that he was Master of the natural world Jesus now proves that he can restore lost human beings.

CONFRONTATION (verses 26–28)

As soon as Jesus stepped from the boat he was confronted by a local man whose behaviour and appearance immediately signalled that he was a deeply disturbed individual. He came from the local graveyard, he wore no clothes and he had superhuman strength. He would make an interesting psychological study today but his need was deeper than the mind. His solitude, living in the necropolis, nakedness, and abnormal strength required a deeper diagnosis and Jesus gave it – he was demon-possessed. His own personality was submerged in that of the demon(s) who had taken control of him.

This man's captive state was obvious when he spoke as one of the demons inside him. Under the demon's compulsive power the man threw himself at Jesus' feet not as an act of personal surrender but because the demons are subject to Christ as Lord of creation (*Luke* 4:36). The demon spoke rationally enough to Jesus, recognising the gulf between them, calling him rightly Son of the Most High God. It begged him not to use his power to cast it into eternal torment. Although the demon knew Jesus this knowledge did it no good (*James* 2:19).

People in the western world and churches often play down the force of demonic evil or explain it away under another name. They may believe that science and psychology explain everything there is to know about strange behaviours. But missionaries in spiritually dark countries have come across the very same symptoms as this man showed, so the story is neither apocryphal nor dated.

We can go beyond the limits of Scripture by attributing too great knowledge and power to evil angels. Certainly they form a real and constant threat to Christians and their work (*1 Thess*. 2:18) but they are not supreme and God includes them in his eternal plan for good (*Rom*. 8:38–39). Christians must arm against them but not be paralysed by their attacks (*Eph*. 6:10–18).

DELIVERANCE (verses 29–37)

Jesus cures the man by asking his name. This was a means of breaking the grip of evil by appealing to the human individual within. By replying 'legion' the demon showed the extent to which the evil powers had taken up residence in this man. A Roman legion numbered thousands of soldiers. Now the demons in the man are agitated because they foresee what Jesus may do in casting them out of their human prey into the eternal abyss (*Matt*. 25:41). Jesus responds to their request for a reprieve by commanding them to transfer into a herd of swine – a sure sign of Gentile territory (*Luke* 15:13–16).

This part of the story brings to light a number of fundamental facts about the demonic world.

- demons are a real part of the creation of God.
- they are active in the world only by God's permission and patience.
- demons normally hide their presence though not always their activity.
- their final destruction is already certain (*Rev*. 12:12).
- Jesus uses his authority over their movements and their end.

The pigs now show some of the bizarre behaviour of the man. They rush headlong down a hillside and straight to their death by drowning in a lake.

Jesus' action in destroying the pigs has troubled some people because it raises an ethical issue. Apparently animals are expendable when it comes to defeating demons, glorifying God and saving humans. But this is no warrant for cruel experiments on animals or their wholesale slaughter. Here was a special event in the unique ministry of Jesus. At the same time, the incident with the pigs is a balanced reminder that animal existence is secondary to human survival and eternal salvation. Animal-loving Christians can be assured that in the new heavens and earth renewed creatures will have their place if the first creation is any guide (*Isa*.11:1–9, *Rom*. 8:19–22).

Local sentiment was aroused. The swineherds fled, reporting in town and country the astonishing events that they had witnessed. The curious inhabitants came out to see for themselves what had happened at the scene of the miracle. They reacted with fear when they saw the local outcast transformed from a wild animal into a respectable citizen and the herd of swine wiped out.

Instead of weighing the evidence in Jesus' favour the local people gave in to natural superstition and dread of the supernatural. They were blind to the moral meaning of what Jesus had done and the promise he gave of restoring other lives. They were more comfortable with the familiar than with the unexpected; the new thing that Jesus had done challenged their thinking in uncomfortable ways.

Many people prefer a busy or humdrum existence to any challenge to think for themselves and the change that Jesus brings. Talk of the gospel makes them uneasy; they refuse to venture beyond what is familiar and routine. Sadly, like the Gerasenes, Jesus may grant their desire and leave them to their world of sandcastles.

COMMISSIONING (verses 38–39)

There is a sequel to the story. Jesus' final words are to the man he has rescued. He has restored him to sanity and society, now he restores him to usefulness as Jesus' witness. Like any new convert the man wanted his new-found joy to go on forever. He wanted to be with Jesus for the rest of his life. But there was work for him to do so Jesus employs him in the service of the kingdom.

This means going back to his family and being Jesus' spokesperson there. He is to tell what wonderful changes God, through Jesus (notice the parallel in verse 39), has brought about in his life. In his zeal he evangelises the whole community in a foreshadowing of the great mission of the church to all people groups (*Luke* 24:46–48).

Jesus does not take his people out of the world, instead he sends them back into the world (*John* 17:15, 18). How can we be his witnesses otherwise? Witnessing means sharing with others what God has done for us because of Jesus. When did you last do this?

33

Saved by Faith Alone

Now when Jesus returned, the crowd welcomed him, for they were all waiting for him. [41] *And there came a man named Jairus, who was a ruler of the synagogue. And falling at Jesus' feet, he implored him to come to his house,* [42] *for he had an only daughter, about twelve years of age, and she was dying.*

As Jesus went, the people pressed around him. [43] *And there was a woman who had had a discharge of blood for twelve years, and though she had spent all her living on physicians, she could not be healed by anyone.* [44] *She came up behind him and touched the fringe of his garment, and immediately her discharge of blood ceased.* [45] *And Jesus said, 'Who was it that touched me?' When all denied it, Peter said, 'Master, the crowds surround you and are pressing in on you!'* [46] *But Jesus said, 'Someone touched me, for I perceive that power has gone out from me.'* [47] *And when the woman saw that she was not hidden, she came trembling, and falling down before him declared in the presence of all the people why she had touched him, and how she had been immediately healed.* [48] *And he said to her, 'Daughter, your faith has made you well; go in peace.'*

[49] *While he was still speaking, someone from the ruler's house came and said, 'Your daughter is dead; do not trouble the Teacher any more.'* [50] *But Jesus on hearing this answered him, 'Do not fear; only believe, and she will be well.'* [51] *And when he came to the house, he allowed no one to enter with him, except Peter and John and James, and the father and mother of the child.* [52] *And all were weeping and mourning for her, but he said, 'Do not weep, for she is not dead but sleeping.'* [53] *And they laughed at him, knowing that she was dead.* [54] *But taking her*

by the hand he called, saying, 'Child, arise.' [55] *And her spirit returned, and she got up at once. And he directed that something should be given her to eat.* [56] *And her parents were amazed, but he charged them to tell no one what had happened* (Luke 8:40–56).

Two biographies are interwoven here, the one a miracle of healing, the other a miracle of resurrection. They show vividly how very busy Jesus was, day after day, as people pressed him to answer their needs and fears. They show us how Jesus served the Father by serving men and women around him.

On this day, two individuals stood out, one, a woman who wanted to remain hidden, the other, a man who asked openly for Jesus' help. One is unnamed, a poor, shunned woman, possibly single; the other a man named Jairus, of some standing in the community as the synagogue ruler.

A HAEMORRHAGING WOMAN (verses 43–48)

The woman's story interrupts the story of Jairus and is contained within it. This gives it special prominence. The woman's condition was desperate and pitiable. She had suffered from a haemorrhage for twelve years and wasted her savings on ineffective medicine (*Mark* 5:26). Mosaic regulations declared her unclean as well as being a source of uncleanness to anyone she touched (*Lev*. 15:25–31). But she had heard of Jesus and his healing powers, so she came close to him in the crowd. Perhaps to avoid contaminating him she made contact with the border of his gown but she did so in the confidence that this would gain her a cure. Her faith, as Jesus explains, was her strongest attribute and what made the difference. Even a limited faith so long as it is genuinely focused on Jesus, is enough for God to work with.

Immediately Jesus was aware of someone touching him, so he asked who it was. Many around him denied any contact with him, while Peter stated the obvious, reminding Jesus that it was impossible for people not to be touching him in such a crowd. But Jesus had in mind a touch that was deliberate because the person was animated by confidence in his healing powers.

The woman's touch was different from the jostling and bumping of the crowd, because it drew healing power from Jesus in a way that he was conscious of (verse 46). Jesus was no magician because magic occurs without any rational explanation and not always for good. But personal confidence in Jesus, for a particular need, had helped to produce an immediate recovery for this woman.

In spite of being naturally afraid and embarrassed by what had happened, the woman came forward and told her story. Jesus asked the individual who had touched him to come forward for a number of reasons – so that she could be publicly restored to her community, so that the place of faith in Jesus could be explained, and so that the glory of God could be publicly displayed (verse 48).

Jesus draws attention to the principle of faith alone (verse 48, see next verse 50) that Paul will pick up and weave into the fabric of his gospel of God's grace to needy men and women. The letters to the Romans and Galatians illustrate this most clearly (see also *Eph*. 2:1–10). This woman became that day a living example of restored human life and so can we by following the example of her Christ-centred faith.

A DYING DAUGHTER (verses 40–42, 49–56)

The story of Jairus had already begun to unfold. He arrived first to accost Jesus with the news of his only daughter's fatal illness and to appeal for immediate help (*Luke* 7:12). Just as Jesus began to follow Jairus home the woman with the blood leakage interrupted Jesus, or distracted Jesus as it seemed to Jairus. Confirming Jairus' worst fears the delay proved fatal. A servant arrives with the tragic news that the daughter had died. There was no longer any need for Jesus to come (verse 49).

But 'Judge not the Lord by feeble sense, but trust him for his grace', is the lesson here. Jesus remained untroubled by the news and gave out the message, 'Don't be afraid, only believe!' (verse 50). With that attitude Jesus pressed on towards Jairus' family home to show what God could do in a humanly hopeless situation.

Arriving at the house Jesus put out everyone except the mother and father plus his three leading disciples. To the astonishment of the crowd of mourners Jesus announced that the girl was only asleep, not dead. Knowing that the girl had really died, they laughed in Jesus' face. But Jesus was about to show the power of God by giving life to the dead. Jesus is the resurrection and the life (*John* 11:25) who has come to bring life and immortality to light.

The girl had died, but in the presence of Jesus death had lost its sovereign power, instead becoming a pathway back to life. Jesus is Lord and death itself must give up its prey to him, at his command. This was no near-death experience, but a genuine return on the girl's part, from the realm of the departed to her former life on earth.

Combining tenderness with thoughtfulness Jesus requests something for her to eat. No wonder the family was astonished at what had just taken place under their roof.

Throughout this chapter Jesus has shown himself as the One who is really in control – over the ferocious powers of nature (*Luke* 8:22–25), the sinister powers of moral evil (verses 26–39), terminal illness (verses 43–48) and the power of death. Luke's four-fold witness to Jesus in a variety of human contexts is meant to awaken in those who read these stories a personal fascination with Jesus, leading on to personal confidence and commitment to him.

Our response should go something like this: if Jesus could control the forces of the natural world, the inner demons of a man's mind and body, an example of terminal illness, and even death itself, then surely he is Lord of all (*Acts* 10:36). In addition, we are meant to read ourselves into these four personal histories and discover Jesus as the Christ for us, the same yesterday, today, and for ever (*Heb.* 13:8).

34

The First Missionary Movement

> *And he called the twelve together and gave them power and authority over all demons and to cure diseases,* [2] *and he sent them out to proclaim the kingdom of God and to heal.* [3] *And he said to them, 'Take nothing for your journey, no staff, nor bag, nor bread, nor money; and do not have two tunics.* [4] *And whatever house you enter, stay there, and from there depart.* [5] *And wherever they do not receive you, when you leave that town shake off the dust from your feet as a testimony against them.'* [6] *And they departed and went through the villages, preaching the gospel and healing everywhere.*
>
> [7] *Now Herod the tetrarch heard about all that was happening, and he was perplexed, because it was said by some that John had been raised from the dead,* [8] *by some that Elijah had appeared, and by others that one of the prophets of old had risen.* [9] *Herod said, 'John I beheaded, but who is this about whom I hear such things?' And he sought to see him* (Luke 9:1–9).

Christianity is a missionary movement that Jesus himself inaugurated. Here he foreshadows the later work of world evangelisation by sending out the twelve as pioneer missionaries. In the next chapter (*Luke* 10:1–12) he will repeat the exercise with a larger number of disciples. The future conditions of world mission are replicated here by the disciples going ahead without the physical presence of their Master. In the meantime Jesus uses the disciples to extend his own mission among the peoples (*Matt*. 10:5–6).

Perhaps there is a case here for missionary training prior to service on the field. After the ascension things would be different. Jesus prepares them for mission by giving them a set of definite instructions that relate to the conditions they will encounter. Natural enthusiasm or giftedness are not enough, a period of training is needed so that the future missionaries can gain firsthand experience of what it means to serve Christ at the cutting-edge.

COMMISSIONING (verses 1–2)

The disciples can accomplish nothing without the help of Christ. So he shares with them, by direct communication, some of his messianic authority. This gives the disciples the right to order the demons to depart and to heal the sick. They will shortly discover what happens when they go without Christ's power (*Luke* 9:38–40).

This endowment of heavenly power matches their commission which is to proclaim the kingdom and to heal the sick. For the greater commission to disciple the nations Jesus will promise and give the Holy Spirit in power (*Luke* 24:45–49).

From these examples we learn the principle that the Lord's work can only be carried on in Christ's way, that is, on his terms. The work is spiritual and requires spiritual resources (*2 Cor*. 10:3–6).

MANDATING (verses 3–5)

Jesus impressed three things on the disciples before they set out.

- He taught them to travel lightly by not loading themselves with supplies or baggage. Instead they must trust God for their daily needs. So – no supplies of food, clothes, money beyond what they already took with them (verse 3). This is the principle of economy and simple faith in God.
- They must settle down immediately where they boarded without looking around for better accommodation. The urgency of the task demanded this so as not to waste time in looking for more comfortable quarters. This is the principle of contentment and a simple lifestyle (verse 4).
- They must be prepared for a mixed reception, even rejection by the local residents. This was Jesus' own experience (*Luke* 9:51–53). Without recrimination they must be ready to cut their ties with

that local community the way Jewish teachers did when leaving Gentile territories (*Acts* 13:44–52). This is the principle of prophetic integrity.

From these words of Jesus we can glean generic lessons. First, Christ's workers deserve a livelihood from those they serve. This is an apostolic principle of a worker deserving his wages (*Rom.* 15:25–27, *1 Cor.* 9:7–14, *1 Tim.* 5:17–18). Secondly, there may come a time to move on in anyone's ministry because of irreconcilable opposition in a particular congregation or community. Some people quit too soon, others stay too long. Jesus himself did not persist with recurring unbelievers, nor did his apostles (*Mark* 6:1–5, *Acts* 13:44–47).

QUESTIONING (verses 7–9)

The disciples went out at Christ's command on the strength of his delegated authority (verse 6). They were successful in preaching and healing and reported back to Jesus about this (verse 10). One of the sons of Herod the Great was tetrarch or ruler of that region of Palestine. News of the mission of Jesus and his disciples came to him and he enquired further about Jesus. His interest shows a mixture of curiosity and anxiety. He was haunted by the memory of John the Baptist whom he had beheaded in prison (*Luke* 3:19–20). Popular opinion fuelled Herod's fears by suggesting that John had perhaps come back to life. Others claimed Elijah had come as prophesied (*Isa.* 40:3, *Mal.* 3:1) or another of the prophets had risen. But Herod was sceptical, being a man of the world, knowing that John was dead but conceding that Jesus was attracting the same celebrity status. Only later would Herod face Jesus in person (*Luke* 23:6–12) without gaining any satisfaction from the interview.

Herod teaches us that conscience remains a real force in the memory of worldly people. Wealth and status are no shield against an evil conscience that operates on the basis of the facts of a person's past choices and acts. Only in Christ can we find peace of conscience because he underwent the death penalty for all our wrongs (*Heb.* 9:14; 10:22).

35

A Miracle of Feeding

> 10 *On their return the apostles told him all that they had done.*
> *And he took them and withdrew apart to a town called Bethsaida.*
> 11 *When the crowds learned it, they followed him, and he*
> *welcomed them and spoke to them of the kingdom of God and*
> *cured those who had need of healing.* 12 *Now the day began to*
> *wear away, and the twelve came and said to him, 'Send the crowd*
> *away to go into the surrounding villages and countryside to find*
> *lodging and get provisions, for we are here in a desolate place.'*
> 13 *But he said to them, 'You give them something to eat.' They*
> *said, 'We have no more than five loaves and two fish – unless*
> *we are to go and buy food for all these people.'* 14 *For there were*
> *about five thousand men. And he said to his disciples, 'Have them*
> *sit down in groups of about fifty each.'* 15 *And they did so, and*
> *had them all sit down.* 16 *And taking the five loaves and the two*
> *fish, he looked up to heaven and said a blessing over them. Then*
> *he broke the loaves and gave them to the disciples to set before*
> *the crowd.* 17 *And they all ate and were satisfied. And what was*
> *left over was picked up, twelve baskets of broken pieces* (Luke
> 9:10–17).

Jesus' miracle of feeding five thousand people in the desert is recorded by all four evangelists. This shows the importance that the early Christians attached to this particular miracle. Jesus himself gives the key to the true meaning of the miracle in John's Gospel (*John* 6:26–58). Miracles were acted parables with their own message about the nature of God's kingly rule over the world. Jesus is himself the bread that God supplies to feed the world's spiritual hunger. He gives life to the world by sacrificing his own life. Those who turn to him will receive his gift of new life.

THE SCENE SET (verses 10–14)

The disciples returned from their first missionary journey. They reported to Jesus who decided that they needed some time away together. As often happened the crowds learned of their whereabouts and immediately turned up. Characteristically Jesus welcomed them and set about meeting their needs by proclaiming the kingdom of God and healing their sick.

This work continued all day so that the evening overtook them all in a wilderness setting away from lodgings and food. Alert to this problem the disciples approach Jesus to send the people home or to purchase bread for them all. Jesus must have surprised the disciples when he commanded them to provide for the people's needs. Pressed on the matter the disciples admitted to having only a few loaves of bread and a couple of fish. Their only suggestion was to go to the nearest village and buy food.

In the light of the following miracle they were clearly thinking along natural lines and not using their faith in Jesus to help them solve the crisis.

THE MIRACLE PERFORMED (verses 14–17)

As always Jesus knew beforehand exactly what he would do. Having led his disciples to face the futility of their own position Jesus now took over and directed the action. He commanded the disciples to organise the crowd into groups of fifty persons. In addition they were to sit down to encourage patience and prevent disorder.

Jesus took the humble resources of the five loaves and two fish. From these he provided more than enough to satisfy the vast company. But first he acknowledged the spring of his power by looking up to heaven and giving thanks for the food available. Having broken the bread he gave it to the disciples who distributed it to the crowds. Even when everyone had been amply fed there were twelve baskets of left-overs, illustrating the limitless resources of Jesus.

THE MEANING EXPLAINED (verses 12–17)

What does the parable tell us?

First, the miracle is told with an economy of explanation. The simple facts are told without sensationalism. The miracle story calls on our belief but does not satisfy our natural curiosity. More information about what exactly Jesus did in performing the miracle would only divert our attention away from Jesus himself. As it stands the story leaves Jesus at the centre and forces readers to make some personal response for or against Jesus.

Secondly, the story points to the profound needs of humankind along with our inability to solve our crisis. The people along with the disciples are stranded in a desert remote from centres of help. Such is the spiritual landscape of every individual and of the whole human family. Like the disciples people make a number of suggestions or make attempts of one kind or another to resolve that deep spiritual hunger of the heart. Jesus Christ alone can meet the hunger of humankind for truth, meaning, peace, joy, and God. Throughout John's Gospel Jesus presents himself in absolute terms as the world's Light, Life, Saviour, Shepherd, Resurrection, Truth, and Way. These claims and offers remain as promises for today.

Thirdly, Jesus will make use of what we bring and sincerely offer to him in his service. John is the evangelist who tells us that a boy gave the five loaves and two fish (*John* 6:9). The disciples said, 'What is that among so many people?' failing to calculate what Jesus could do with even the smallest amount. In the same way he can take what his people offer him such as spiritual gifts, money, lives and opportunities and turn them to the greatest advantage for the good of many.

36

Jesus, the Cross and Resurrection

Now it happened that as he was praying alone, the disciples were with him. And he asked them, 'Who do the crowds say that I am?' [19] *And they answered, 'John the Baptist. But others say, Elijah, and others, that one of the prophets of old has risen.'*
[20] *Then he said to them, 'But who do you say that I am?' And Peter answered, 'The Christ of God.'*
[21] *And he strictly charged and commanded them to tell this to no one,* [22] *saying, 'The Son of Man must suffer many things and be rejected by the elders and chief priests and scribes, and be killed, and on the third day be raised.'* (Luke 9:18–22).

The ministry of Jesus in Galilee here reaches a turning-point over the issue of his messiahship and the kind of work he will do. The question of his identity had arisen before when Jesus calmed the storm (*Luke* 8:25) and when he performed miracles (*Luke* 9:9). Now Jesus faces his disciples directly with the same question before going on to explain about the direction of his messianic service at Jerusalem.

From all this we learn the necessity of coming to a clear understanding of who Jesus is and of linking who he is with what he did. The person and work of Christ are inter-connected.

THE OCCASION (verses 18–19)

As so often before an important stage in Jesus' relationship with his disciples, he was praying (*Luke* 6:12; 11:1). No doubt this prepared him for the impending interview. He was right in the time and place of God's appointing for asking this question of his disciples and instructing them further (*Matt.* 16:17).

Jesus astutely began with questions about the opinions of the people about him. The disciples had heard many views about Jesus when mingling with the crowds day by day. People saw Jesus on a par with some of the great figures of Israel's past. Some even believed that one of them had been brought back to life to prophesy again to the nation. But these sorts of explanations fell short of the answer Jesus wanted to hear.

QUESTION AND ANSWER (verse 20)

The time is ripe for the great enquiry and confession. Pointedly Jesus asks the disciples for their own opinion about him. Peter's reply is simply given, 'You are the Lord's Christ.' In saying this Peter was spokesman for the rest and in so saying he was claiming for Jesus a status above the greatest figures of the past. He was making a statement of faith in which he identified Jesus with the purposes of God for Israel's salvation. Jesus is the One spoken about by the prophets of Israel and prayed for by her psalmists and holy men and women.

Peter's faith and that of the other disciples was a simple one at this stage but it was enough for Jesus' purpose. They had only come to this conviction about their Master gradually on the basis of what he had said and done. In the same way the evidence that the Gospels give about Jesus should be enough for people to come to a simple but sufficient faith in him today.

When people listen to the biblical witness to Jesus they find that they are led beyond the limits of time and space, to the eternal and metaphysical world. They come to someone who is more than a Jewish rabbi, an example of what is most noble in human nature, or a social reformer. The truth about Jesus comes from the side of God and his saving plan for the whole world.

How delighted Jesus must have been to hear his leading disciple confess him in this way. He had not laboured with these men in vain, his prayers for them had come true. Having achieved this level of understanding about who Jesus is, Jesus now takes them deeper in understanding what he will do.

THE SEQUEL (verses 21–27)

Jesus surprises them by warning them to keep silent about him. We have already encountered this theme of secrecy in the Gospel history (*Luke* 4:35, 41; 5:14; 8:56). The reason for this strange demand is immediately clear. Jesus is not going to fulfil popular expectations of the Messiah by pleasing the people and placating their leaders. Instead he will take the lonely path of suffering, rejection, and death. Jesus is the glorious Son of Man who must suffer many ordeals at the hands of his enemies before being executed. But God will raise him from this undeserved death and vindicate him in heavenly splendour (verse 26).

Only a deep reading of the Scriptures can explain why Jesus must choose this path and no other. Suffering and death are connected with sin in all its aspects (*Gen.* 2:17). Jesus has come to be the One who removes the scourge of sin and death from human life by identifying totally with these destructive intruders. As the Son of Man he has become our human representative who substitutes himself for us in the place and time of judgement. The Jewish elders, chief priests and scribes will be the instruments of God's plan of redemption through the rejection of his Son. By treating Jesus as a criminal and handing him over to Pilate the human judge will fulfil the words of their own prophets (*Acts* 13:27).

But the travesty of Jesus' trial, rejection, and death will be followed by the great reversal of his resurrection three days later. Just as Jesus had to suffer in the way he did, so he must be raised from death soon afterwards. His personal resurrection is as necessary as his death. Only as he rises from death can he inaugurate the new age of the kingdom – one of justice, freedom and joy for all creation. Through rising his dying becomes effective for all nations (*Luke* 24:45–49). In the trauma of the crucifixion the disciples forgot this promise of rising again but the angels jolted their memories (*Luke* 24:6–7).

Only a suffering and dying Jesus will save us, for the simple reason that suffering and dying are the judicial consequences of our individual and collective guilt. No wonder Jesus declared that he *must* suffer and die (*Luke* 17:24–25; 24:6–7). This is the measure and the proof of his love, a love that has no boundaries because it is God's own love, the

One who is infinite, immense and free (*Eph.* 3:17–19). The cross is where God's love and justice meet (*Rom.* 3:23–26; 5:5–8).

Finally, Jesus imposed a virtual oath of silence on his disciples (verse 21). He did not wish the truth of his being the Messiah to reach the ears of the people, without further explanation and before accomplishing his mission of salvation. Otherwise the people would be only too ready to lionise him as another nationalist pretender to political hegemony over the Romans, or as a magician who would use his miraculous powers to gratify the raw cravings of the people (*John* 6:15, 26–27). Only after his death and resurrection would the disciples be ready to make him known on the basis of a sure understanding.

37

The Cost of Discipleship

And he said to all, 'If anyone would come after me, let him deny himself and take up his cross daily and follow me. [24] *For whoever would save his life will lose it, but whoever loses his life for my sake will save it.* [25] *For what does it profit a man if he gains the whole world and loses or forfeits himself?* [26] *For whoever is ashamed of me and of my words, of him will the Son of Man be ashamed when he comes in his glory and the glory of the Father and of the holy angels.* [27] *But I tell you truly, there are some standing here who will not taste death until they see the kingdom of God.'* (Luke 9:23–27).

No sooner has Jesus foretold his lonely path of suffering and future resurrection than he challenges his audience with the terms of true discipleship. These parallel the terms of his own messianic way just defined. Those who want to be on Jesus' side must be ready to follow him.

Go, labour on: spend and be spent,
  Your joy to do the Father's will;
It is the way the Master went;
  Should not the servant tread it still?
Horatius Bonar

TRUE DISCIPLESHIP (verses 23–24)

Jesus gave an open invitation to discipleship. A disciple was someone who committed himself to be with and learn from the one he wanted to follow as his mentor and authority. Jesus had no objection to this but wanted would-be followers to be clear at the start what this would mean. Jesus was never one to play down the terms of discipleship for anyone (*Luke* 18:18–23).

The way of Jesus was one of repeated self-denial. At the centre of human life there operates a principle of self-will on the basis of self-interest. Following Jesus means bringing our will into subordination to God's will. This is the cost of discipleship.

Nor should anyone imagine that there is a once-for-all crisis of surrender after which life will be naturally obedient. On the contrary, Jesus speaks of a cross that must be taken up and carried every day. People were put to death on crosses so what Jesus means is that there is a daily battle with self-will that must be fought and won again and again.

But who can live up to such high and holy demands? Jesus did and now he shares the virtue of his death and the power of his resurrection with all those who come to him so that we no longer live but Christ lives in us to do his will again through us (*Gal.* 2:20). Jesus is both the pattern and the power of discipleship. Paul is the one who interprets this mystery of union with Christ in his living, dying and rising as the power of discipleship and service (*Rom.* 6, *Gal.* 2:20, *Eph.* 4:17–24, *Col.* 3:1–17).

Jesus repeats his teaching. Either we protect ourselves – our own interests and fortunes – or we give them up for Someone better and bigger. This is the law of paradox at the heart of discipleship. Those people who live for their own interests will find they lose them; those who forfeit their interests for Christ's sake will find they gain them forever.

How does Jesus' teaching on self-denial differ from that of Buddha, the New Age, or natural morality? Jesus is the difference because he is the One who liberates us to live on a new plain and for a host of new reasons. Discipleship is 'for his sake' (verse 24).

PROFIT AND LOSS (verse 25)

Jesus now puts his teaching into a marketing idiom. There is profit and loss. Someone imagines they have had a great win only to discover later that the opposite is true. In the same way gaining world domination may look like the ultimate prize but again and again it has proved to be a destructive illusion. Not surprisingly the devil, the great deceiver, is the author of this universal dream (*Luke* 4:5–6).

All such thinking misses the point of human existence which is not about possessions, power or prestige but about knowing God in the service of others. Life is a summons to fellowship with God and serving our neighbour. In doing this we discover who we are and recover our true self. The natural inclination is to live for oneself but Christ teaches us the better way of love, by releasing us from the prison of the self through his death and resurrection (*2 Cor.* 5:14–15). Jesus' wisdom reverses the normal market values – earthly gain is loss and earthly loss is gain. In Christ's kingdom those who give rather than those who receive are the truly blessed (*Acts* 20:35).

FUTURE PROSPECTS (verses 26–27)

Finally, Jesus puts his message about discipleship in the future tense. He predicts the future in two ways. Jesus will return to the earth where he suffered and died. Then the whole world will have to confront the whole truth about him. He will appear as the glorious Son of Man who has passed beyond the reach of suffering, defeat or death. He will appear with a triple splendour – his messianic glory as the only Saviour of the world, his eternal glory as the only Son of the Father and his angelic glory as the Lord of the angels.

How is this future prospect connected with discipleship? The way we respond to Jesus and treat him now will in large measure decide his response to us and the way he treats us on the day he comes in his triple majesty. The key word is 'shame' (verse 26) – our shame over Jesus and his words and his shame over us at the end.

A test that any of us can apply has to do with Jesus' words (verse 26). Knowing and loving Jesus may appear too subjective and difficult to measure. But we cannot mistake his words as we have them in the Gospels. What we do with Jesus' words tell us what it is we have done with Jesus and how we stand with him because Jesus and his words are one (*John* 15:15, 21; 6:60, 66–69).

All that lies in the distant future. Jesus forecasts the immediate future for some of his disciples. In a saying clothed with mystery Jesus predicts that some of those standing with him there and then would not die until they had experienced in some way the kingdom of God coming in this world. Opinions have raged about who or what Jesus had in mind. Was he referring to his resurrection or to the day of Pentecost, both powerful events that most of the disciples witnessed for themselves?

Perhaps it is best to connect this prediction with what immediately follows. Peter was to write about it later as an unforgettable event, etched forever on his memory (*2 Pet.* 1:16–18).

38

We Saw His Glory

Now about eight days after these sayings he took with him Peter
and John and James and went up on the mountain to pray.
29 *And as he was praying, the appearance of his face was altered,*
and his clothing became dazzling white. 30 *And behold, two men*
were talking with him, Moses and Elijah, 31 *who appeared in*
glory and spoke of his departure, which he was about to accom-
plish at Jerusalem. 32 *Now Peter and those who were with him*
were heavy with sleep, but when they became fully awake they
saw his glory and the two men who stood with him. 33 *And as the*
men were parting from him, Peter said to Jesus, 'Master, it is
good that we are here. Let us make three tents, one for you and
one for Moses and one for Elijah' – not knowing what he said.
34 *As he was saying these things, a cloud came and overshadowed*
them, and they were afraid as they entered the cloud. 35 *And a*
voice came out of the cloud, saying, 'This is my Son, my Chosen
One; listen to him!' 36 *And when the voice had spoken, Jesus was*
found alone. And they kept silent and told no one in those days
anything of what they had seen (Luke 9:28–36).

That Luke introduces this event in the way he does in verse 27 (eight days after the sayings of verse 26) lends support to the view that Jesus was referring to this time and place when he spoke of the disciples seeing the kingdom of God.

WHAT THE DISCIPLES SAW (verses 29–31)

Accompanied by his leading disciples, Peter, James, and John, Jesus went up on a mountain to pray. During this prayer time a remarkable change came over Jesus. Normally his appearance attracted little attention. Now everything was different. Jesus' face and clothes were suddenly bathed in a heavenly light. This light came from within Jesus and transfigured his bodily presence. In the Bible light is often the sign of God's holy presence with humankind (*Matt.* 4:13–16, *Acts* 9:3, *1 Tim.* 6:16). Here was visible evidence of God's majesty and purity in Jesus (*1 John* 1:5).

Peter's confession (verse 20) showed that the disciples had glimpsed the truth about Jesus. Now the disciples could honestly say that they had seen the glory of a divine Person (*John* 1:14). Jesus had spoken of his glory when he will return (verse 26) but in these moments the disciples had a preview. We may learn from this transformation that Jesus normally refused to draw directly on his divine nature, choosing instead to live within the limits of his humble humanity. Here, for a few moments this order is reversed and the splendour of his deity overlays his humanity.

Nor was it only Jesus they saw transfigured before them for, as they gazed, they caught sight of two other figures deep in conversation with Jesus. By some means they were able to recognise these two as Moses and Elijah. They too appeared in glorious light as from another world. Together Moses and Elijah represented the whole line of prophets whom God had sent to Israel to speak his words. Moses was the first in that line and Elijah had restored Israel at a critical time in her national history. That they were talking with Jesus showed that they saw Jesus as the fulfilment and goal of their earthly hopes. Hebrews supports this view (*Heb.*1:1–2). So did Jesus (*Luke* 24:44–46). Jesus is the key to the whole Bible's outlook, forward and backward.

The topic of their conversation was Jesus' forthcoming death in Jerusalem. They called it his 'exodus' (outgoing, departure, march of liberty) clearly connecting it with the great liberating act of God when he set his people free from Egyptian captivity (the Exodus). For Moses and Elijah this was the great accomplishment of the earthly Jesus, the true liberation of humankind, setting his people free by dying and rising again.

The exodus or redemption from Egypt became possible when every family of Israel sacrificed a lamb in place of the firstborn son. When the angel of death passed over their homes and saw the blood of the lambs the angel of death spared the firstborn sons of Israel. Death had already been carried out on the lambs offered up in their place. So Jesus is the one true lamb, spotless in virtue and innocence, whose life-blood saves us from the death sentence of the law (*Heb*. 9:13–14, *1 Pet*. 1:18, *Rev*. 13:8).

Beyond this, we can say that the love of Christ in giving himself for us in incarnation, obedient life, servant-suffering and death will be the endless study and conversation of the citizens of heaven (*Eph*. 3:18–19). In the glory-land of Immanuel the saints will always behold Jesus as the Lamb put to death for them, his worthiness proclaimed throughout the new creation (*Rev*. 5:9–12; 21: 22–23).

WHAT THE DISCIPLES SAID (verses 32–33)

Out of tiredness and amazement the disciples responded to the scene in front of them. Again Peter spoke for the rest. Without thinking he blurted out to Jesus that it was good for them to be there and that it would be even better if they built some shelters for the three heavenly figures. His wish was to capture the moment of glory for ever. But this could never be if Jesus was to fulfil his destiny as the suffering Lamb of God who was going up to Jerusalem to be sacrificed (verse 22). Was Peter falling into the same error of judgement as before, by hindering Jesus from the way of the cross (*Matt*. 16:22–23)?

WHAT THE DISCIPLES HEARD (verses 34–36)

Just as the scene was about to break up another phenomenon overtook the wondering disciples. All of a sudden a cloud gathered around them and a voice came from its centre. Any Jew knew that a cloud like this could only signify one thing – God's near presence. So it was on the mountain of Sinai, in the tabernacle of Israel, throughout the desert wanderings and at the dedication of the temple (*Exod*. 33:7–11; 40:34–38, *Num*. 9:15–23, *Deut*. 5:22, *1 Kings* 8:10–13). But supposition was made certain by the heavenly voice because it addressed the disciples and told them what they needed to know and do.

A similar divine oracle had been heard at Jesus' baptism (*Luke* 3:22). But the difference between the two lay in the fact that the first spoke to Jesus about the Father's relation to him, the second to the disciples about their relation to Jesus ('You are my Son' and 'This is my Son'). The voice at the baptism assured Jesus, the voice on the mountain corrected the disciples. Peter never forgot the lesson and shared it before he died (*2 Pet*. 1:12–18).

- The heavenly voice spoke of Jesus as 'my Son'. In doing so God was owning Jesus as one in being and love with him, the way a father is intimate with his son. In the religious history of Israel God had never addressed any human person in this way, thus separating Jesus from all who had preceded him (so the argument of Hebrews 1:1–5). This is a proof-text for the eternal Sonship of Jesus since God welcomes and acknowledges him as an equal member of the divine family (*John* 1:1–2).
- The heavenly voice spoke of Jesus as God's 'chosen' pointing to him as the predestined servant of God. If 'Son' acclaimed Jesus as God, 'chosen one' acclaims him as Man. He was chosen and appointed by God before creation but was brought into the world at the appropriate time (*Eph*. 1:4, *1 Pet*. 1:20). This is a messianic description of Jesus in his historical person. The Chosen was Jewish short-hand for the long-awaited Messiah who would bring Israel into a golden age of salvation and blessing among the nations.
- The voice last of all commanded the disciples to listen to Jesus. This pointed to Jesus as possessing God's own authority, as the One who would speak the truth and whose words were life (*John* 6:63, 68). It also implies that the disciples needed to heed this lesson instead of being too quick to speak (as Peter had been).

James tells us to be slow to speak, quick to hear (*James* 1:19). This is always wise advice in the presence of Jesus.

The vision ended, the cloud dispersed and Jesus and the disciples were alone again. For a few moments the veil that normally separated the heavenly world from their own was lifted. We learn from this how close and all around us exists the world that faith makes real (*Heb*. 11:1; 12:1).

Unlike Paul who dared not describe what he had seen and heard in a heavenly state (*2 Cor*. 12:2–4) Peter later gave an independent record of the factual accuracy of this mountain experience. But in the meantime the disciples chose to keep quiet about such a frightening and sacred encounter. Now all readers of the Gospels have access to this private revelation of the personal glory of Jesus Christ.

39

Man's Inability, God's Sufficiency

On the next day, when they had come down from the mountain, a great crowd met him. [38] And behold, a man from the crowd cried out, 'Teacher, I beg you to look at my son, for he is my only child. [39] And behold, a spirit seizes him, and he suddenly cries out. It convulses him so that he foams at the mouth; and shatters him, and will hardly leave him. [40] And I begged your disciples to cast it out, but they could not.' [41] Jesus answered, 'O faithless and twisted generation, how long am I to be with you and bear with you? Bring your son here.' [42] While he was coming, the demon threw him to the ground and convulsed him. But Jesus rebuked the unclean spirit and healed the boy, and gave him back to his father. [43] And all were astonished at the majesty of God.
But while they were all marvelling at everything he was doing, Jesus said to his disciples, [44] 'Let these words sink into your ears: The Son of Man is about to be delivered into the hands of men.' [45] But they did not understand this saying, and it was concealed from them, so that they might not perceive it. And they were afraid to ask him about this saying (Luke 9:37–45).

By linking this story so closely with the previous one (verse 37, the very next day) Luke intends us to contrast the glory of Christ with the weakness of the disciples. But there is more because the power of Christ belongs to a pattern of suffering obedience. Only as the disciples learn to live by that same pattern of divine power in human weakness will they replicate Jesus' works.

HUMAN INABILITY (verses 38–40)

It does not take long for Jesus and his three disciples to make contact again with the real world of human pain and conflict. As soon as they appear at the bottom of the mountain a great crowd of people greets them. Out of the crowd a lone man cries to Jesus to look in pity on his sick son who is his only boy. This is not the first time Jesus has been appealed to for an only child (*Luke* 7:12). Perhaps the fact that he is himself an only Son (of God) strikes a chord within his heart that stirs his compassion.

The father informs Jesus about two important facts. First he describes the symptoms that his son displays – screaming, falling, foaming. Modern medicine would call this condition epilepsy but the father attributes the son's condition to an evil spirit. This does not mean that all epilepsy is due to evil spirits, nor that what the father called an evil spirit we should call epilepsy. An evil spirit could make use of physical disabilities for its own ends. Paul's thorn was a physical disability that Satan exploited (*2 Cor*. 12:7).

Secondly, the father informs Jesus that he had already appealed to the nine disciples who had remained behind. But the nine between them could not cure the boy's condition. Now he was repeating his appeal to Jesus ('beg' is the same term in verses 38, 40). Jesus showed he could do what his disciples could not. In the context of his teaching about discipleship (verses 22–24) their failure must be due to their failure to apply God's power by denying their own.

DIVINE REMEDY (verseS 41–42)

This announcement of the inability of the disciples draws from Jesus an outcry of his own. The whole scene was typical in his mind of the sad and shameful condition of the whole nation. Unbelief and hardness could be felt everywhere. Jesus was deeply distressed by this spiritual environment. It made him wistful for his heavenly home (*Luke* 12:49–50). More than any of us Jesus has known what it means to be lonely by being cut off from sympathy and the support of human company. Jesus was the pioneer and finisher of the life of faith (*Heb*. 12:2–3).

Jesus called for the boy. As he did so the evil spirit made one last assault on its poor victim, convulsing him to the ground. Jesus agrees that the son's problem is more than physical. The boy can only be healed as the spirit is cast out of him. The physical feeds off the spiritual.

Finally, Jesus was pleased to give the boy back to his father and bring closure to another family trauma (*Luke* 7:15). Jesus is the friend of families.

FAILURE IN UNDERSTANDING (verses 43–45)

In spite of their unbelieving hearts (verse 41) the people could not help experiencing awe in the presence of Jesus. What he had done and said channelled the strongest sense of God's greatness (*Luke* 4:36; 5:26; 7:16; 8:25). Being with Jesus was like being in God's presence, so at one was he with the being, the will, and the work of God (*John* 14:8–11).

A lesser person might have chosen to bask in the popularity and defer moving on. But even while the people were still applauding Jesus for all his mighty works he saw the need to challenge the disciples by forewarning them again about his forthcoming betrayal at Jerusalem.

As Luke tells it, this was no simple repetition of the first announcement (verse 22). There are several new features here.

- First, Jesus bids the disciples pay close attention to what he is about to tell them. This indicates how solemnly Jesus views these coming events as well as knowing how prone the disciples are to forget his words.
- Secondly, the focus this time is on the handing over of Jesus to the authorities. Slowly he is building up a picture of his final sufferings and trials, so preparing the disciples for what will also be their greatest test.
- Thirdly, Jesus states that he will be given into the hands of men for their disposal. Jesus reveals that his death will implicate and actively involve Gentiles as well as Jews. This paves the way for Jesus' message of the universal outreach of his death as a sacrifice for sinners to God.

Sadly, Jesus' fear that the disciples would miss his meaning was only too well placed. They heard his words but failed to grasp their meaning. Privately they still could not take in the possibility of a suffering and dying Messiah. This third announcement to them of his forthcoming trial and rejection still could not convince his slow-to-believe disciples (*Luke* 18:34).

Yet all was not lost because Luke indicates that a divine restraint was working in the disciples preventing them from understanding at this time what Jesus had said. This was not the first nor the last time such a divine over-ruling would be at work (*Luke* 24:16). At the appropriate time they would rejoice at the wise and gracious design of God. His resurrection was what finally unlocked the mystery of Jesus' death to all his followers (*Luke* 24:1–8). Even then they found it hard to let go their former thinking for the new thing that God had done (*Luke* 24:11, 25–26). We too are slow to believe, quick to forget.

The disciples suspected that Jesus was telling them something out of the ordinary because they were afraid to ask him for a fuller explanation. Perhaps they wanted to protect their pride by not admitting to him their confusion.

A lifetime and more is needed to grasp the height and depth and length and breadth of the love of Christ in dying for this fallen creation. But we can make a beginning now.

Come, let us join our cheerful songs
With angels round the throne;
Ten thousand thousand are their tongues,
But all their joys are one.
'Worthy the Lamb that died', they cry,
'To be exalted thus!'
'Worthy the Lamb', our lips reply,
'For he was slain for us!'
Jesus is worthy to receive
Honour and power divine;
And blessings, more than we can give,
Be, Lord, for ever Thine.

Isaac Watts

40

Greatness and Tolerance

An argument arose among them as to which of them was the greatest. [47] *But Jesus, knowing the reasoning of their hearts, took a child and put him by his side* [48] *and said to them, 'Whoever receives this child in my name receives me, and whoever receives me receives him who sent me. For he who is least among you all is the one who is great.'*
[49] *John answered, 'Master, we saw someone casting out demons in your name, and we tried to stop him, because he does not follow with us.'* [50] *But Jesus said to him, 'Do not stop him, for the one who is not against you is for you.'* (Luke 9:46–50).

With this passage Luke winds up the Galilean ministry of Jesus. From now on the shadow of the cross draws Jesus ever nearer to Jerusalem and the final conflict of his earthly life. The passage relates two deep-seated attitudes of the disciples that Jesus came to eradicate from all who follow him – pride and intolerance.

GREATNESS (verses 46–48)

The disciples were arguing about greatness and who of them should be counted the greatest. Coming right after the predictions of Jesus about his own sufferings and death there is something pathetic and perverse about this dispute among the disciples. How little they had grasped the meaning of his life! This craving for personal glory was to continue right up to the night when Jesus suffered and died (*Luke* 22:24).

Jesus saw into the dark recesses of their hearts. To challenge them Jesus brought a child and stood him at his side. What is Jesus' point?

That small is great in his kingdom. Children in Jesus' society had no voice in public life nor were they consulted when important decisions were made. Nor did they seek greatness or power themselves.

In terms of simplicity, insignificance, lowliness the child is a perfect symbol of Jesus as Jesus is of God. Jesus was present in the world as one who did not strive for attention, importance, or power. He was like a child, content to be and to serve. This is greatness – to be like him and to follow his example.

So when followers of Jesus welcome and serve the lowest members of society for Jesus' sake they find Jesus for he is present wherever meekness and openness predominate. In finding him we will find the God behind him, the holy and humble Father who dwells with the lowly and contrite person (*Isa.* 66:1–2).

How much Christian work is spoiled by the lust for power, prestige, or praise! How many encounters with Jesus we miss because we are too busy or proud to stop and stay for the sake of others who bear his name – or those who do not!

TOLERANCE (verses 49–50)

John (proudly?) relates to Jesus how he and other disciples had recently rebuked an individual because he was using the name of Jesus to cast out demons. They tried to stop him because he did not belong to the disciple group.

Expecting to earn Jesus' praise, how surprised they must have been when he rebuked them in turn! Jesus disapproved their being unwilling to recognise and welcome anyone but their own party. Anyone not against us ought to be treated as a supporter, says Jesus. (In Luke 11:23, because of a different set of circumstances, he reverses the axiom.) On this occasion Jesus wanted to encourage an open attitude to others who bore his name, not challenging their sincerity in doing so. Jesus' aim in this saying was to free the disciples from a narrow and judgemental spirit. They needed to understand and accept that there were true disciples outside the circle of the Twelve.

Modern disciples of Jesus can hold the same narrow frame of mind. One Christian group can ostracize another because they follow a different leader or do not agree with every point of doctrine or do not use the same methods. Christian maturity comes when we are able to embrace as equals in Christ those who may not see things or do things the way we do, without compromising the essential gospel. There is a wideness in God's mercies that we would do well to emulate on earth, for we will certainly find it in heaven.

41

The Final Journey and Its Lessons

> *When the days drew near for him to be taken up, he set his face to go to Jerusalem.* [52] *And he sent messengers ahead of him, who went and entered a village of the Samaritans, to make preparations for him.* [53] *But the people did not receive him, because his face was set toward Jerusalem.* [54] *And when his disciples James and John saw it, they said, 'Lord, do you want us to tell fire to come down from heaven and consume them?'* [55] *But he turned and rebuked them.* [56] *And they went on to another village* (Luke 9:51–56).

We stop at this point in the Gospel of Luke (verse 51) to note a new stage in Jesus' ministry. His work (Luke 4:14 to 9:50) in Galilee in the northern part of Palestine is now ended. In it he established his credentials as the Messiah of Israel through many miracles and teachings. He turns south to Jerusalem where he will meet his final destiny and accomplish his great work of atoning through death for the sins of his people. From this point onwards the shadow of the cross lies across the daily life of Jesus as the opposition to him hardens and he himself becomes more outspoken about the sins of the nation and its leaders.

The section from 9:51–18:14 tells us things about Jesus and what Jesus said that are not found in any of the other gospel writers. It consists of many of the best known and most loved parables and other sayings of Jesus. Throughout this section Jesus is making his way by a circuitous route to Jerusalem for the last time (*Luke* 13:31–35). At 18:15 Luke links up again with the records about Jesus in Matthew and Mark. This section has been called Luke's 'great insertion' in his gospel.

Luke speaks of Jesus being 'taken up' as the goal of this final journey. This refers to the ascension of Jesus which Luke, unlike Mark and Matthew, makes the point of transition between Jesus' earthly life (*Luke* 24:51) and heavenly ministry (*Acts* 1:9–11). Luke has got inside the mind of Jesus because the Lord could always see beyond the cross to the joy that was set before him when he would be enthroned in heaven (*Heb*. 12:2). As a result of the ascension Jesus was able to send down the Holy Spirit to carry on his work of evangelisation and teaching (*Acts* 1:1–2).

DOING JESUS' WORK IN JESUS' WAY

Jesus' way led through Samaria which lay between Galilee and Judea. The Samaritans were a mixed race as a result of local Jews marrying Gentile peoples transported to Palestine. Pure Jews regarded Samaritans as untouchables. This rivalry between the Jews and Samaritans was a live issue in Jesus' day.

The messengers that Jesus sent ahead of him reported that the Samaritans were disaffected as soon as they heard that Jesus' destination was Jerusalem, not Samaria with its alternative faith, worship, and traditions (*John* 4:19–20, 20). In reaction James and John wanted to take revenge. They asked Jesus for permission to bring down fire from heaven to destroy the Samaritans like the prophet Elijah (*2 Kings* 1:10, 12–14).

But Jesus was not impressed and rebuked the two disciples for their vindictive attitude. There is a longer ancient manuscript reading here [see KJV, NKJV] in which Jesus says, 'You do not know of what spirit you are. For the Son of Man did not come to destroy the lives of men but to save them.' Although these words may have been added by scribes in the process of writing up the gospel, they capture the intention of Jesus well.

The outburst of the disciples is in striking contrast to Jesus. He has deliberately chosen to face Jerusalem with all its personal horrors. He came to seek and to save the lost which included Samaritans (*John* 4). He calls all his followers to have the same mind, one directed in mercy to the salvation of human beings rather than their extinction. It is possible to preach Christ from wrong motives (*Phil*. 1:15–17), to offer people the law instead of the gospel, to proclaim the doctrines of grace ungraciously. We are to leave vengeance to God who alone can handle it justly; for our part we are to overcome evil with good (*Rom.* 12:18–21).

42

Some Tests of Discipleship

As they were going along the road, someone said to him, 'I will follow you wherever you go.' [58] *And Jesus said to him, 'Foxes have holes, and birds of the air have nests, but the Son of Man has nowhere to lay his head.'* [59] *To another he said, 'Follow me.' But he said, 'Lord, let me first go and bury my father.'* [60] *And Jesus said to him, 'Leave the dead to bury their own dead. But as for you, go and proclaim the kingdom of God.'*
[61] *Yet another said, 'I will follow you, Lord, but let me first say farewell to those at my home.'* [62] *Jesus said to him, 'No one who puts his hand to the plough and looks back is fit for the kingdom of God.'* (Luke 9:57–62).

The theme of discipleship is a recurrent one and reappears here in the form of three crisp conversations between Jesus and some would-be disciples. Jesus is on the way that will end for him in death; the three individuals are romantically attracted to the way of discipleship without understanding what is actually involved (verse 57).

In general terms we learn from these three cases how superficially people think about the nature of religious faith and its practical consequences. These cases involve a choice between an easy, comfortable following of Jesus and a once-for-all commitment to follow him whatever the cost, by putting him ahead of all our other loyalties.

ENTHUSIASM TESTED (verses 57–58)

The first individual greets Jesus with a fair promise that he will follow Jesus wherever he leads. This is easily said so Jesus tests this promise with a stark description of his own life-style. Though he is the heavenly Son of Man he has come to do God's will on earth and this means for him the loss of home comforts, normal family life and personal possessions. The wild animals and the birds live more comfortably than he; they have homes to go to at night but Jesus lives from day to day dependent on his heavenly Father for providing his needs. Is this man ready for this level of commitment?

Imitating Jesus' physical circumstances will not make us true disciples as some imagine who have renounced marriage or embraced poverty. Jesus commends family life and approves home ownership. What Jesus wants is a new set of values within – a willingness to give up everything if Jesus requires it. How relevant and searching that test is in a consumerist and narcissistic culture!

FAMILY LOYALTIES TESTED (verses 59–62)

The second and third individuals want to follow Jesus but make this conditional on first attending to family duties. Jesus opens the conversation by telling the first man to follow him anyway. Perhaps Jesus detected in this man's attitude a lack of resolve. The second man promises publicly to follow Jesus. But both share a prior commitment to their families that keeps Jesus in second place (notice the use of 'first' in verses 59 and 61).

The first man wants to go and bury his father. In Jewish culture (and many others today) filial loyalties and rituals are of primary importance (for example the Confucian tradition that affects Asian cultures). This man would not be considered a respectful son were he to neglect the burial of his father. Yet Jesus challenges even this sacred relationship and duty in the interests of carrying out the higher and more urgent duties of the kingdom of God. Jesus repeated this lesson (*Luke* 14:26).

Jesus indicates the different sets of loyalties involved by speaking of living people as 'dead' in a spiritual sense (verse 60), hence the greater urgency and demand of proclaiming the message of hope and new life in Jesus. The rituals of burial can be taken care of by someone else but not everyone who is spiritually dead may hear of the kingdom of God. Even family ties and loyalties must not stand in the way of the kingdom and its advancement in the world (*Matt.*

6:33). Even the family can become an idol that keeps us from the Father above. We must always obey God rather than humans.

The second man requests time to say farewell his family. A harmless request, one might think, but Jesus detects in this man's heart an unwillingness to cut all his ties with his past and begin life anew with Jesus. It is like a farmer who keeps looking behind him as he ploughs his field. The result is a very crooked furrow that is useless for sowing crops. Christ's servant the apostle Paul uses the very same language as Jesus when he expresses his own understanding of what it means to approach and live the Christian life (*Phil.* 3:13–14). Jesus is insistent and consistent in his subordination of family ties (sacred as they are) to the higher and prior demands of the Father and his kingdom (*Luke* 14:26).

No other attitude makes us worthy of the kingdom of heaven. Jesus wants to be the treasure and the pleasure of our hearts, otherwise we will never serve him effectively (*Psa.* 73:25). The lack of joy and freedom among many Christians may be due in part to a failure to take his words in verse 62 seriously. We may spend many years holding on to aspects of the world that we ought to have surrendered when first we believed (*James* 4:1–10). But it is never too late with Jesus.

43

Principles of Christian Mission

After this the Lord appointed seventy-two others and sent them
on ahead of him, two by two, into every town and place where
he himself was about to go. 2 *And he said to them, 'The harvest*
is plentiful, but the labourers are few. Therefore pray earnestly
to the Lord of the harvest to send out labourers into his harvest.
3 *Go your way; behold, I am sending you out as lambs in the*
midst of wolves. 4 *Carry no moneybag, no knapsack, no sandals,*
and greet no one on the road. 5 *Whatever house you enter, first*
say, "Peace be to this house!"
6 *And if a son of peace is there, your peace will rest upon him.*
But if not, it will return to you. 7 *And remain in the same house,*
eating and drinking what they provide, for the labourer deserves
his wages. Do not go from house to house. 8 *Whenever you enter*
a town and they receive you, eat what is set before you. 9 *Heal*
the sick in it and say to them, "The kingdom of God has come
near to you." 10 *But whenever you enter a town and they do not*
receive you, go into its streets and say, 11 *"Even the dust of your*
town that clings to our feet we wipe off against you. Nevertheless
know this, that the kingdom of God has come near." 12 *I tell you,*
it will be more bearable on that day for Sodom than for that
town.' (Luke 10:1–12).

The sending of seventy or seventy-two (the manuscripts vary slightly) disciples recalls the first commissioning of the Twelve (*Luke* 9:1–6). The Lord wanted more of his followers to experience firsthand what it was like to act and speak in his name. It also reminds us that the band of disciples following Jesus at any one time was far in excess of twelve.

The number seventy (if we accept that reading) is very specific and may be meant to recall the seventy elders Moses appointed to help him rule Israel (*Exod.* 24:1, *Num.* 11:16, 24–25). Just as they extended Moses' rule so the seventy disciples enable Jesus to be in several places at one time, speaking and acting with authority.

This was a more temporary mission than that of the Twelve (*Luke* 9:1–6), since Jesus was coming behind them and would confirm their efforts (verse 1). But human company is necessary too, so Jesus sent them out in pairs for their mutual encouragement. Western individualism struggles with this concept but we all need human and divine company if we are to complete the work that the Lord has given us to do (*Col.* 4:17). A husband and wife team can fulfil the terms of Jesus' mission admirably and often has (*Acts* 18:26).

INSTRUCTIONS (verses 2–12)

Jesus gives a number of instructions to his disciples as they leave. These contain some permanent principles for mission work.

- The disciples are to pray for workers (verse 2). There are four reasons for such a request. First, God is the Lord of the harvest and so controls the harvest. Secondly, the harvest is plentiful. The disciples have only to look around and see men and women ready for ingathering into God's kingdom. Thirdly, the harvesters are relatively few and more are needed if the harvest is to be gathered in. Fourthly, the Lord is able to call them up and send them out.
- They are to be off on their journey (verse 3). But they should know that they are vulnerable to the attacks of men just like lambs facing wolves. Their trust must be in God alone.
- They are to travel lightly and not be distracted from their work (verse 4). For the disciples this meant taking no extra baggage and not stopping to talk idly to people on the road. They are to concentrate 100% on the work before them until it is finished.
- They are to be peace-makers (verses 5 and 6). Their message is one of peace just as they speak and act for a God of peace. In Jesus God was reconciling the world to himself. As his spokespersons, the disciples are to offer that peace even where it may not be accepted.

- They are to be content with their provisions (verse 7). They are not to keep changing houses in the hope of better accommodation but gratefully receive the food and shelter that they have earned.
- They are to do all the good they can in towns that welcome them (verses 8 and 9). This means accepting their hospitality, healing their sick, and proclaiming to the citizens the nearness of God's kingdom.
- The disciples are to disown publicly the towns that reject them (verses 10–12). This means pronouncing the word of judgement against them and yet assuring them that the kingdom of God has come near to them. Jesus adds his weight to this judgement by asserting that in the day of judgement inhospitable and immoral Sodom (*Gen.* 19) will fare better than these towns.

Invaluable lessons reside in these mission mandates. Translating these mandates into contemporary terms we may say that they mean –

- praying the Lord for missionaries to gather in the extensive harvest
- going out, trusting in divine protection from physical and verbal attacks from people
- giving priority to the Lord's work over all other considerations
- living out and speaking out God's peace to all we meet or live with
- accepting wages for spiritual work well done, as a matter of principle
- doing all the good we can to those who are receptive
- accepting the justice of the judgement against those who defame Christ's words

We do not find a whole theology or methodology of missions here yet there are invaluable reminders of some of the fundamental principles and goals of missionary procedures in any culture or period of history.

44

Judgement and Joy

'Woe to you, Chorazin! Woe to you, Bethsaida! For if the mighty works done in you had been done in Tyre and Sidon, they would have repented long ago, sitting in sackcloth and ashes. 14 But it will be more bearable in the judgment for Tyre and Sidon than for you. 15 And you, Capernaum, will you be exalted to heaven? You shall be brought down to Hades.

16 The one who hears you hears me, and the one who rejects you rejects me, and the one who rejects me rejects him who sent me.'

17 The seventy-two returned with joy, saying, 'Lord, even the demons are subject to us in your name!' 18 And he said to them, 'I saw Satan fall like lightning from heaven. 19 Behold, I have given you authority to tread on serpents and scorpions, and over all the power of the enemy, and nothing shall hurt you. 20 Nevertheless, do not rejoice in this, that the spirits are subject to you, but rejoice that your names are written in heaven.'

21 In that same hour he rejoiced in the Holy Spirit and said, 'I thank you, Father, Lord of heaven and earth, that you have hidden these things from the wise and understanding and revealed them to little children; yes, Father, for such was your gracious will. 22 All things have been handed over to me by my Father, and no one knows who the Son is except the Father, or who the Father is except the Son and anyone to whom the Son chooses to reveal him.'

23 Then turning to the disciples he said privately, 'Blessed are the eyes that see what you see! 24 For I tell you that many prophets and kings desired to see what you see, and did not see it, and to hear what you hear, and did not hear it.' (Luke 10:13–24).

Mention of Sodom (verse twelve) prompts Jesus to say more on the subject. After this the seventy disciples return and Jesus rejoices with them in their successful mission. Judgement followed by joy are the themes of this section.

PROPHETIC WOES (verses 13–16)

Jesus utters a number of woes that form a part of the prophetic tradition in Israel (*Deut.* 27:11–26). Jesus is responding to the woeful unbelief of his generation the way his predecessors in the prophetic office did in theirs (*Isa.* 5:8–23, *Jer.* 23:1–5). So inexcusable is their non-response to Jesus' words and works (especially the works here) that Jesus holds out more hope for wicked Sodom and Gomorrah and pagan Tyre and Sidon on the day of judgement. By comparison the local towns like Chorazin, Bethsaida, Capernaum (physically elevated, with a spiritual pride to match) were being favoured with Jesus' presence and his many miracles to validate his claims. Yet they refused to change their mind and heart in returning to God (repentance is the focus here). Had the coastal cities and the cities of the plain, already mentioned, had half this opportunity presented to them they would have repented long ago.

A number of truths jostle for attention here:

- there is such a thing as community sin. Jesus addresses these towns in the singular (the old 'thou') since every community is a kind of corporate personality. This communal way of thinking is foreign to western individualism but reflects God's appointment of our lives in social networks such as families, local communities, churches, nations. Christians have a special vocation to raise awareness of this collective responsibility.
- Jesus shows that he knows the different contingencies of the future. Contrary to the belief in some circles that the future is open and unknown to God as well as us, Jesus declares certainties about that future. He knows what would have happened if other things had been true. This is supernatural knowledge of all possible permutations of events and reveals the absolute knowledge God has of future events.

- contrary to moral relativism and the loss of individual accountability for one's actions that goes with it Jesus declares that there is a final, future judgement of human actions. This future judgement in no way conflicts with the love of God since God's love has been presented in Jesus. He is God's appointed way for any of us to avoid future judgement by accepting Jesus' judgement in our place (*2 Cor*. 5:18–21).
- only the breaking off of practices and dispositions offensive to God will satisfy the judgement (*Rom*. 2:4). The Jewish communities mentioned by Jesus knew the truth but did not keep it from the heart. Real repentance is always a deeply personal response targeting particular issues.
- God's judgement will be based on the opportunities people had for changing their lives and whether they responded to these or not (*Rom*. 2:1–16). The townspeople of the Galilean settlements had met Jesus in person; their opportunities were unsurpassed. The pagan townships had lacked these opportunities so their failure was less. See further Luke 12:47–48.

Finally, Jesus prepares the way for the disciples' return by stating that a direct line of command runs from the Father through the Son to those who officially speak for him. Consequently, the type of response people give to Christ's spokesmen is actually their response to Christ and his Father. His spokesmen speak with his authority (*2 Cor*. 5:20). When we listen to living preachers of Christ let us remember that they do not stand or speak alone, for Christ himself and the living Father are by their side and in their mouths.

THE DISCIPLES' JOY (verses 17–20)

The seventy disciples returned brimming with joy from the amazing successes of their mission work. They were especially excited by the way the demons were subject to their commands in Jesus' name. This was more to them than proclaiming the kingdom message or healing the sick.

In reply Jesus shares some truths for their encouragement and further enlightenment.

- Their mission had coincided with a fall of Satan. Jesus likens it to lightning crashing to the earth. By his initial conflict with Satan in the desert (*Luke* 4:1–13), Jesus had established a bridgehead against the kingdom of darkness. Jesus' death and resurrection would make the victory complete. In the meantime his disciples were able to enjoy the fruits of Jesus' mission (verse 18).
- Their success was due to the delegated authority of Jesus himself (verse 19). Jesus repeats the promise of his power over all the resistance of the enemy. He likens this to trampling on serpents and scorpions, two of the creatures used in biblical symbolism for Satan and his crew (*Gen.* 3:1, *Rev.* 9:1–6). Both are loathsome and dangerous creatures usually fatal in their bite. Jesus has destroyed their power by drawing their sting in his own dying on the cross (*1 Cor.* 15:54–57).
- There is a hierarchy of joys for the followers of Christ (verse 20). The disciples were overjoyed because the demons obeyed them. Jesus alerts the disciples to a deeper and more secure joy, that of having their names enrolled in heaven. Heavenly citizenship is the ultimate prize (*Phil.* 3:20), greater even than a lifetime of Christian service and achievement (*Phil.* 4:3). Heaven will bring them into the presence of God their chiefest joy (*Psa.* 16:11).

Here, then, we learn that –

- through Christ believers can break down Satan's strongholds (verse 18)
- Christ guarantees spiritual safety to his followers (verse 19)
- the prospect of heaven should be the cause of greatest joy to Christians (verse 20).

JESUS' JOY (verses 21–24)

Now it was time for Jesus to rejoice. The fact that he did so 'at that time' means that his joy came from the success of his disciples and the downfall of Satan, God's enemy in the life of the world. Joy is the fruit of the Holy Spirit (*Gal.* 5:22) both in Christ the man and in those who belong to him. This mention of the Holy Spirit in the life of Jesus is a reference to his humanness in which he was always dependent on the Spirit to empower, sanctify and lead him. It also shows that the Holy Spirit replenished the human spirit of Jesus with all his own virtues and graces. Jesus set about his public work with the Spirit's help and so he continued to the end (*Luke* 4:1,14). He shares this holy joy through the same Holy Spirit with all those who commit themselves to him (*Luke* 24:52, *Acts* 16:30–34).

The Spirit also causes Jesus to delight in his heavenly Father whom he confesses as Lord of heaven and earth. This is none other than the God of Israel, the Creator of the ends of the earth in Isaiah's preaching (*Isa*. 40:28). He is supreme in all things but noticeably in the realm and experience of salvation. In this realm the Lord shows himself free and undetermined by human factors. He reveals himself through his Son to whom he chooses. Humility and wonder befit the chosen of God.

The Father was pleased for his own glory in this matter to keep 'these things' (presumably the things of his saving kingdom in Jesus his Son) from the humanly wise and clever, revealing them unsolicited instead to 'little children'. These terms are code for the religious leaders on the one hand and the ordinary disciples on the other. God is glorified through using human weakness as his channel, rather than human greatness that can always claim the glory for itself. Paul expresses this principle emphatically (*1 Cor*. 1:26–31). Saving knowledge of God in Christ always comes back to a personal instruction by the Father in heaven. Peter had already experienced and known this (*Matt*. 16:15–17).

Jesus speaks of the Father revealing the truth of the kingdom to individuals (verse 21). Now he develops this further by carrying it home to the heart and life of the triune Godhead. Revelation comes down to knowing persons, in this case the divine Persons of the Father and the Son. This is salvation and life, to know them, or the Father through the historical and humanised Son (*John* 17:3). Just as the Father and the Son know one another perfectly and eternally so the Father has appointed and entrusted it to the Son to make them known to whom he chooses.

With this utterance about the inner relations of the Father and the Son our minds go immediately to the Gospel of John. There Jesus speaks consistently in this exalted language of inner divine relations and his own consciousness of that relationship even on earth as the

Son of the Father. To have it here in the heart of Luke's Gospel with its strong attachment to the historical facts of Jesus' earthly career only helps us to integrate the Jesus of the first three Gospels – the historical Jesus – with that of the fourth – the heavenly Son of God. Together they show the depth and mystery of the complex and unique Person of Jesus Christ, both Man and God for our salvation, instruction and representation.

Salvation is both a once-for-all accomplishment by Jesus on the cross and an individual experience when that truth of his Person and work illumine the heart of an individual. Paul reaches back to creation for his analogy to this inner light as nothing less than an act of new creation in the core of our being when God calls us from darkness into his wonderful and life-giving light (*2 Cor.* 4:6). Jesus' speech here in prayer to the Father focuses everything on the inner light of revelation flowing from and grounded in the truth of his historical life and work. Believers are the true *illuminati* of the world (*Heb.* 10:32). This saving knowledge about God and of God personally is a recurring theme of Luke's Gospel (*Luke* 2:49; 3:22; 9:35).

To close, Jesus turns deliberately to his disciples to impress upon them the privilege that is theirs and the blessedness they are living under in seeing and hearing the Messiah. The prophets and kings of the ancient order of Israel had longed to experience what was theirs daily to enjoy. These kings and prophets had typified Christ and spoken in prophetic mode about him, but none had met him in the flesh. Theirs was an era of promise and hope without the reality.

Jesus pronounced a similar blessing on those of us who have believed in him, his words and deeds, without having seen him (*John* 20:29). To know Christ by faith on the evidence of his word, is the greatest honour and the truest wealth. Without him life is meaningless, with him all things are ours. The least believer under the new order of grace and truth in Jesus Christ is greater and higher than the greatest under the former order (*Luke* 7:28). What a privilege to be a Christian!

So ends the second disciple mission (*Luke* 10:1–24), on a note of satisfaction for work well done and of thankful joy for the Father's sovereign grace. Both the mission of Jesus and that of his disciples flow from the generous heart of God, the Father of world mission.

45

Loving Our Neighbour

And behold, a lawyer stood up to put him to the test, saying,
'Teacher, what shall I do to inherit eternal life?' 26 *He said to*
him, 'What is written in the Law? How do you read it?' 27 *And*
he answered, 'You shall love the Lord your God with all your
heart and with all your soul and with all your strength and with
all your mind, and your neighbour as yourself.' 28 *And he said*
to him, 'You have answered correctly; do this, and you will live.'
29 *But he, desiring to justify himself, said to Jesus, 'And who is*
my neighbour?' 30 *Jesus replied, 'A man was going down from*
Jerusalem to Jericho, and he fell among robbers, who stripped
him and beat him and departed, leaving him half dead. 31 *Now*
by chance a priest was going down that road, and when he saw
him he passed by on the other side. 32 *So likewise a Levite, when*
he came to the place and saw him, passed by on the other side.
33 *But a Samaritan, as he journeyed, came to where he was, and*
when he saw him, he had compassion. 34 *He went to him and*
bound up his wounds, pouring on oil and wine. Then he set him
on his own animal and brought him to an inn and took care of
him. 35 *And the next day he took out two denarii and gave them*
to the innkeeper, saying, "Take care of him, and whatever more
you spend, I will repay you when I come back." 36 *Which of these*
three, do you think, proved to be a neighbor to the man who fell
among the robbers?' 37 *He said, 'The one who showed him mercy.'*
And Jesus said to him, 'You go, and do likewise.' (Luke 10:25–
37).

On another occasion a Jewish teacher of the Law (lawyer) put to Jesus a question that deeply troubled many Jews, 'What must

I do to inherit eternal life?' (*Luke* 18:18). In spite of all their knowledge and traditions going back to Moses many Jews lacked assurance of their own salvation. This was because they had turned the covenant laws into a condition of salvation and so could never be sure of whether they had done enough good over wrong to merit God's approval. This question prompted one of Jesus' own that in turn provoked another from the professional rabbi (verse 29). Unfortunately the man's motives in asking his questions were not the best since he was suspicious of Jesus and wanted to justify himself. Characteristically Jesus turned this possible confrontation into a valuable teaching opportunity.

THE TWO COMMANDMENTS OF LOVE (verses 25–28)

Since the revelation of God to Israel was a written one Jesus asked this man what it was that he read in God's word. By 'the law' Jesus had in mind the first five books of the Old Testament in which God's covenant-making with Israel is fully recorded. His covenant took the form of a body of teaching (torah) that showed Israel how to live as God's special people (*Exod.* 19:3–6; 20:1–17).

The rabbi picks out from this great body of moral teaching two commandments that both speak of love (*Deut.* 6:5, *Lev.* 19:18). The first of these asks for total love for the Lord as the God of the covenant, with every part of a person's being; the second asks for love for other people (neighbour) as being on a par with the kind of love that everyone shows himself. So love is the key to the religious and moral life.

Jesus praised truth wherever he found it so he commended the teacher for answering correctly. This was Jesus' own view of the matter (*Mark* 12:28–31). Keeping God's commandments as a way of life is the way to life more abundant. This was clear from God's covenant with Israel (*Deut.* 5:28–33).

From the beginning obedience to God's word has been the way of eternal life for humankind as God's moral partner in creation. For Adam and Eve this was focussed in the single command to keep away from the tree of the knowledge of good and evil (*Gen.* 2:15–17). For Israel later it was enshrined in the ten words of the commandments at the heart of the covenant (*Deut.* 10:3–5). For every member of humankind the essentials of this law have been written on the tablets of our hearts with conscience as God's witness to their truth claims (*Rom.* 2:14–15).

The central demand of God's covenant law is love, as this lawyer had come to see. This means that moral obedience is more than outward actions, it is a matter of the inner dispositions of the heart. Love is all about our attitudes to God in the first place and to other human beings secondly. The love God demands for himself is absolute since he is our Creator God; the love he demands towards other people is egalitarian since we are all God's creatures bearing his image (*Gen.* 1:26). Our love for God is worshipful, our love for others is ministerial.

Love is goodwill (benevolence), so love will check every evil against a neighbour (*Rom.* 13:10). The parable of the Good Samaritan that follows illustrates the benevolence of love in a story of practical action. By following the dictates of love Jesus assures us we will discover the fullness of life and living and what it means to be fully human ('You will live'). But love begins with God the Lord otherwise our love of humanity may become self-serving and idolatrous (humanist). Love is the paramount Christian virtue, highlighted in all the apostles' writings (*Rom.* 12:9, *1 Cor.* 13:1–7, *Col.* 3:14, *Heb.* 13:1, *1 Pet.* 1:22, *1 John* 4:7–12, *Rev.* 2:4).

WHAT LOVING A NEIGHBOUR MEANS (verses 29–37)

Asking the right question can show as much intelligence as giving the right answer in a public debate. So wanting to keep himself in a good light the lawyer presses another question, 'And who is my neighbour?' In response Jesus relates one of his best known (but least understood or practised?) stories but in doing so he also changes the question. He identifies the neighbour as anyone we come across in need but also places the onus on each of us as a moral agent with a responsibility to love and give aid.

Jesus draws the details of his story from the familiar world of his hearers. The road down from Jerusalem to Jericho was a sharply descending one running through fissured hill country where robbers hid out and made strikes on travellers. In Jesus' narrative one such luckless traveller has fallen into the hands of thieves who have mugged him to within an inch of his life, leaving him beaten up by the road-side, stripped of everything. Here is a neighbour in a crisis of need.

Two religious professionals from the temple pass by this man, one a priest the other a Levite. Neither stops to help although they see the man in his plight. They are either too busy in their religious duties or are more anxious to preserve their own ritual purity than help a fellow human being. By the test of practical love their religion is hollow, driven by self-love not neighbour-love (*1 Cor*. 13:1–3).

A third man, a Samaritan, comes down the road and immediately gives aid. In fact he goes beyond the call of duty because he is motivated by the kind of love that Jesus is speaking about. He tends the man's wounds, takes him to the nearest hospital, pays for his medical expenses and returns to take him home. His is an extravagant and generous love that goes to great lengths to meet the real needs of another person who crossed his path.

That the hero of Jesus' story was a Samaritan would have added shock value to Jesus' tale. They were accustomed to think of neighbour as confined to fellow Jews. In this story Jesus forces them to think outside the square. That the example of neighbour love in Jesus' story is provided by a Samaritan is like a good Iraqi helping and defending an American GI in one of the Gulf Wars. Yet this is the way of God's love in loving us as his enemies (*Rom*. 5:6–8).

This is the heart of the parable because it brings us face to face with the costly and practical caring of all true love. Many people and religions praise love but fail to show it. Christians can be sound in their beliefs but short on love in practice. Congregations can become routine in their activities because they have lost their first love (*Rev*. 2:2–4). Christ values love in his people (*1 John* 3:17–18).

JUST DO IT! (verses 36–37)

The lawyer's original question was, 'Who is my neighbour?' or the person I should love. Jesus has answered that from the story of the individual in need. At the same time he has answered in advance another question that he now puts to the lawyer, 'Who was the neighbour?' or 'What does it mean to be neighbourly?' The answer is clear, 'The one who showed mercy.' This gives Jesus the platform he needs to drive home the final lesson, 'You go and do likewise!' Love acts first and asks questions afterwards. Faith without works, especially works of love, is dead.

We who have listened to Jesus' parable are included in his mandate for action. He is calling all of us to go and live in a different way, with openness and honesty, with generosity and practical readiness to aid our fellow human beings, just for their own sake because they matter to Christ and should matter to us. This is the Gospel in action, a winsome apologetic for the truth claims of Jesus.

At a still deeper level the Samaritan's love is a mirror of Christ's love for us, in taking the dangerous and lonely road into the far country of this wicked and violent world. He chose to serve our needs at infinite cost to himself through his own serving and suffering, culminating in the cross. Jesus knew that by his stripes we would be healed. What we are and hope to be we owe solely to the love of Christ. This extravagant love of Christ should inspire us to love God and serve others (*2 Cor.* 5:13–15).

Ultimately Jesus is the Good Samaritan, who loved us with a neighbour's love and by his overcoming has set us free to love in turn (*1 John* 4:10–11). This is why the parable is more than good advice – it is the Gospel ethic of freely loving others as Christ has loved us.

46

Sisterly Lessons

Now as they went on their way, Jesus entered a village. And a woman named Martha welcomed him into her house. [39] *And she had a sister called Mary, who sat at the Lord's feet and listened to his teaching.* [40] *But Martha was distracted with much serving. And she went up to him and said, 'Lord, do you not care that my sister has left me to serve alone? Tell her then to help me.'* [41] *But the Lord answered her, 'Martha, Martha, you are anxious and troubled about many things,* [42] *but one thing is necessary. Mary has chosen the good portion, which will not be taken away from her.'* (Luke 10:38–42).

Jesus was a family man, having a number of siblings (*Mark* 6:3). Being single he found in the family of Martha, Mary, and Lazarus a home where he could relax and enjoy hospitality. The story is about the two sisters, without any mention of Lazarus and is recorded by Luke alone. The sisters were different by temperament, which has a lot to do with their different responses to Jesus (see further John 11:20–32). Martha was full of energy and organised the details of Jesus' visit; Mary was more contemplative and took time out to sit with Jesus and hear his word.

MARTHA'S COMPLAINT (verse 40)

Under pressure from what may have been an unexpected visit, Martha immediately went into action, setting up a lavish meal for Jesus. This created a bustling background for what took place next. Meantime Mary was sitting at Jesus' feet absorbed in his teaching, seeming not to notice or care about Martha's stress. At last, Martha could restrain herself no longer, chiding even Jesus for failing to tell Mary to come and help her.

Was Martha wrong to be so anxious and busy for Jesus' visit? Jesus' reply to her in verse forty-one indicates that she was not wrong to take trouble for Jesus. Her mistake was in going beyond what was necessary in the circumstances when only one thing (a meal) was necessary. Her response was not measured by the wishes or needs of her guest so much as by her own desire to host something grand. Martha ought to have been more taken up with Jesus and less with herself.

Active, organisational people may do the Lord's work for the wrong reasons or busy themselves in ways that may not promote the real work of Christ's kingdom. Christ needs and uses practical people, but he wants them to serve him for his sake and in his ways, not their own. Usually, active people need to be more contemplative.

MARY'S CHOICE (verses 41–42)

Jesus, as always, knew how to respond to everyone. He reassures Martha of his appreciation of her part, calling her twice by name. He turns Martha's impatience and self-pity to good use by opening up the real issue for her. Martha was wrong in placing her own activity ahead of her relationship to Jesus, a relationship that could only be developed through being with him and listening to his words. Mary had perceived the importance of personal communion with Jesus and had deliberately chosen this. This should not and would not be taken from her.

There are many activities that Jesus' followers can engage in but among them all one is essential. Mary's example serves to show that whatever work we do for Christ the primary need is for time spent with him and hearing his word. This is not something for contemplative Christians only. By daily communing with Christ through his word, both kinds of people will flourish: contemplatives will find that they can be more practically useful, activists will find that their activities become more spiritual and satisfying. Whatever our temperament we need to be attending to the one thing needful – knowing and loving our Jesus better (*Phil.* 3:8–16).

Incidentally, Jesus seems to commend a diversity of roles for believing women: Martha for her domestic skills and home-based hospitality; Mary for her learning in the school of Christ.

47

A Teaching Module on Prayer

Now Jesus was praying in a certain place, and when he finished,
one of his disciples said to him, 'Lord, teach us to pray, as John
taught his disciples.' 2 *And he said to them, 'When you pray, say:*
"Father, hallowed be your name.
Your kingdom come.
3 *Give us each day our daily bread,*
4 *and forgive us our sins,*
for we ourselves forgive everyone who is indebted to us.
And lead us not into temptation."'
5 *And he said to them, 'Which of you who has a friend will go to*
him at midnight and say to him, "Friend, lend me three loaves,
6 *for a friend of mine has arrived on a journey, and I have nothing*
to set before him"; 7 *and he will answer from within, "Do not*
bother me; the door is now shut, and my children are with me in
bed. I cannot get up and give you anything"? 8 *I tell you, though*
he will not get up and give him anything because he is his friend,
yet because of his impudence he will rise and give him whatever
he needs. 9 *And I tell you, ask, and it will be given to you; seek,*
and you will find; knock, and it will be opened to you. 10 *For*
everyone who asks receives, and the one who seeks finds, and to
the one who knocks it will be opened. 11 *What father among you,*
if his son asks for a fish, will instead of a fish give him a serpent;
12 *or if he asks for an egg, will give him a scorpion?* 13 *If you then,*
who are evil, know how to give good gifts to your children, how
much more will the heavenly Father give the Holy Spirit to those
who ask him!' (Luke 11:1–13).

Praying is one of Luke's favourite themes, in the example and teaching of Jesus and for disciples of his. This section consists of Jesus' example of praying, a model prayer, a parable about praying, and an everyday illustration. No one finds it easy to pray. What better way to learn than from the example and words of Jesus, the praying Christ.

PRAYING MEANS FOLLOWING JESUS' EXAMPLE (verse 1)

Jesus' teaching lesson was a response to the disciples' request for some instruction which was itself a response to Jesus' practice of praying. They remind Jesus that John had taught his disciples to pray. In every authentic religious movement in history prayer has always figured prominently. As a man Jesus shows us how integral to ordinary human life prayer is. Human fallenness is nowhere more clearly seen than in the reluctance of people to pray to God and praise him under ordinary circumstances. For Jesus prayer was the most natural thing in the world and the natural order of every day (*Luke* 4:42a). Jesus' human habits are a guide for our own.

PRAYING MEANS BEING A CHILD OF GOD (verse 2)

In his guide to praying Jesus first mentions the filial relation that is ours with God through Jesus. Everything in our earthly life follows from having and knowing God as our heavenly Father. It is through Jesus sharing with those who follow him his filial relation with God that this can be so. Many recite the Lord's Prayer but know nothing of the author!

Jesus teaches us to pray 'our Father' which reminds us that praying means being a member of the family of God in Jesus and cannot be restricted to private prayer. This is a needed corrective in an age of excessive individualism. The first Christians devoted themselves to corporate prayers (*Acts* 2:42). Nearly every great spiritual awakening and missionary movement in the long history of the church has begun and continued with cells of praying Christians.

Praying like this means being intimate with God. This is the wonder and privilege of Jesus' prayer. The word 'Father' is based on an Aramaic one (Jesus' original language) that comes close to the affectionate yet respectful term 'Dad'. Although prayer to Jesus is not unknown in the Bible (e.g. *Acts* 7:59, *Rev.* 22:20) the usual pattern is for believers to pray to the Father as the Author of all our good, through Jesus the Son as the Mediator who has reconciled us to God, with the help of the Spirit in forming desires and requests (*Eph.* 2:18).

PRAYING MEANS PUTTING GOD'S INTERESTS BEFORE OUR OWN (verses 2–4)

The Lord's Prayer, as we call these verses, should not be used as a mantra but as a guide to the kind of praying that pleases God and keeps us in the right frame of mind. Because of our relation to God as Father and because we have learned to love and fear him, his interests and desires come ahead of our own. Surely one of the most common mistakes in public and private praying is our failure to begin with God's interests, rushing instead into our own. Jesus' list teaches us the right order. When we have seriously considered God's interests in the world we will better understand our own.

- Pray that God's name will be honoured. God's name stands for all that he is, has done, and has said. We should wish for the truth about him to spread throughout the world to dispel the falsehood and ignorance that clouds his glory and deprives him of rightful worship.
- Pray for the arrival of his kingdom. This is the social order where men and women not only call God Lord but do his will heartily. The appearance of this order is the goal of present history. It began to come with Jesus and it will finally be established when he returns. In the meantime we can help answer this request by our own efforts at mission.
- Pray for God's will to be done on the earth. Moral decadence and self-will are the evidence of what sin has done to the world. The standard is the heavenly world where angels delight to honour God by doing his will at all times. Pray that the lives and

gatherings of Christians everywhere will reflect this order of obedience to the authority of God through Jesus.

- Pray for daily bread. This is the first request that we may offer for our own needs. Daily bread is more than a meal on the table. It stands for all our legitimate bodily and material needs. Jesus has promised to provide these for those who put him first (*Matt.* 6:25–34, especially verse 33).
- Pray for the Father's forgiveness of our many failures. The word for sins here means debts because we fail to live up to our calling in Christ and so incur daily debts. Our sins as Christians are often omissions and just as calamitous as sins of commission (*James* 4:17). But other people / Christians let us down in the same ways we let God down. This should help us to be merciful and forgiving in turn. Jesus told a parable to help us practice such forgiveness by showing that the failures of others towards us do not begin to compare with our failures towards God (*Matt.* 18:21–35).
- Pray to be kept strong in the test with evil. Because Satan is our deadly enemy he will tempt us, like he tempted Jesus, to choose the easier way of self-indulgence and compromise. Jesus teaches us to pray not for escape from the testing with evil but to be kept from the devil's snares (*John* 17:15). Jesus' vicarious victory is our starting-point in every conflict with evil (*Luke* 4:1–13; 22:39–46).

PRAYING MEANS PERSISTING (verses 5–8)

Jesus tells a delightful parable about three friends. Friend A is the host, Friend B is a visitor and Friend C lives next door. The parable is told from the point of view of the friend next door. A traveller calls unexpectedly and late at night for help. The host has nothing to set before him so appeals to his friend next door. What should Friend C do? At first he rebuffs Friend A because he is already in bed with the family and getting up would be troublesome to them all. But what friendship could not achieve persistence did. Friend A's persistent calls finally win over Friend C who provides what is necessary for the needs of Friend B.

In the culture of Jesus hospitality was a golden rule; any breach of hospitality was a grave offence, especially in an emergency. It is also shameful to embarrass a friend by persistent requests for then both may lose face. Yet Jesus encourages this attitude of persistence to the point of rudeness in his teaching on prayer. The point is not the reluctance of God to help and hear us – remember God is our heavenly Father! Rather the point is the test that he may give us to learn our determination and belief in what we are asking for.

How we approach God may be just as important as what we ask for. Praying depends on right attitudes as well as right requests. The inner life of the child of God is an integral part of the praying process. God, after all, searches the hearts. Many prayers may be lost due to wrong asking or persistence of the wrong kind (*James* 4:1–10).

PRAYING MEANS ASKING, SEEKING, AND KNOCKING (verses 9–10)

Next, Jesus matches three sorts of prayer actions with three promises. If we ask we will receive; if we seek we will find; if we knock it will be opened. Jesus speaks in present continuous time and so is thinking of regular asking, seeking and knocking. So the lesson of persistence from the parable carries over here.

But Jesus wants to teach that there is more to praying than asking. It involves our active participation (seeking and knocking). Praying means looking out for the answers (seeking) and doing what we can responsibly to discover God's answers (knocking). How often we ask for something but forget to wait or work for the answer. Instead Jesus urges us to remember what we have asked for and to follow up our requests by knocking at closed doors to discover where God may be leading us. This is the spirit of determination God honours. Without it praying becomes a formality; with it praying becomes an ongoing conversation and relationship with God that is always fresh and open to new things from God.

PRAYING MEANS TRUSTING IN THE FATHER'S GOODNESS (verses 11–13)

Jesus taught by using earthly life to illustrate heavenly life. For his final lesson on prayer he appeals to the universal habit of fathers to grant what their children ask for (for example, something to eat). Good fathers do not cheat on their children by tormenting them with hollow or dangerous gifts. How much less will God exploit us as his children in Christ; how much more will he give us what we need and more.

The reason Jesus can promise this is because of the nature of true fatherhood as seen in God the archetypal Father (*Eph.* 3:14–15). Incidentally, Jesus' illustration not only reflects the place of fathers in Jewish society as bread-winners but of all fathers in the human family. How essential are fathers and how important that they establish relations of affection based on trust with their children. On the other hand, how unnatural for fathers to abuse or cheat their children. From what God is like and does as Father we have a guide for earthly fatherhood.

Jesus sums up the supreme good that the Father will give his children as the Holy Spirit. Through the Spirit people come to know the Father and the Son (*John* 14:23); through the Spirit we understand experientially all the good things graciously bestowed on us from God (*1 Cor.* 2:12); by the Spirit within we come to enjoy the love of God in Jesus Christ for us (*Rom.* 5:5).

Jesus thus encourages us to ask specifically for the Holy Spirit. The time of the verb (present continuous) again suggests that this is an appropriate request throughout our lives. Nothing pleases the Father more than to give his Spirit and we never can say that we have outgrown the need for more of the Spirit's influences.

After this seminar on praying from Jesus, who is not for prayer?

48

Jesus and the Evil Powers

Now he was casting out a demon that was mute. When the demon had gone out, the mute man spoke, and the people marvelled.
[15] *But some of them said, 'He casts out demons by Beelzebul, the prince of demons,'* [16] *while others, to test him, kept seeking from him a sign from heaven.* [17] *But he, knowing their thoughts, said to them, 'Every kingdom divided against itself is laid waste, and a divided household falls.* [18] *And if Satan also is divided against himself, how will his kingdom stand? For you say that I cast out demons by Beelzebul.* [19] *And if I cast out demons by Beelzebul, by whom do your sons cast them out? Therefore they will be your judges.* [20] *But if it is by the finger of God that I cast out demons, then the kingdom of God has come upon you.* [21] *When a strong man, fully armed, guards his own palace, his goods are safe;* [22] *but when one stronger than he attacks him and overcomes him, he takes away his armour in which he trusted and divides his spoil.* [23] *Whoever is not with me is against me, and whoever does not gather with me scatters.*
[24] *When the unclean spirit has gone out of a person, it passes through waterless places seeking rest, and finding none it says, "I will return to my house from which I came."* [25] *And when it comes, it finds the house swept and put in order.* [26] *Then it goes and brings seven other spirits more evil than itself, and they enter and dwell there. And the last state of that person is worse than the first.'* (Luke 11:14–26).

A new sub-section begins here that runs on to the end of chapter 14. Jesus is engaged in an ever-growing controversy with the

Jewish leaders who intensify their opposition to him. Under these pressures Jesus speaks like a true prophet of God. He sets everything in the light of a future judgement, unmasks falsehood and summons people to a radical new beginning. At the end of this section the way to the cross lies open before Jesus.

A DIVIDED KINGDOM (verses 14–23)

Once again Jesus' act of kindness in setting someone free provokes his critics. He has cured a man of dumbness by expelling an evil spirit. The crowds were amazed and duly impressed but the religious leaders were thoroughly sceptical. The way they explained what Jesus had done was by ascribing it all to the devil's agency. They used the name of an ancient demon called Beelzebul (popularly thought of as Satan, the ring-leader of evil in the world). At the same time they demanded that Jesus perform a great sign that would prove that he was a prophet of the Lord (*Deut.* 13:1–5). As if Jesus had not performed enough signs for those who wanted to believe!

Jesus meets their audacity head on by showing the inconsistency of their thinking by means of an extended apologetic. First, there is the general principle that any kingdom divided within itself will fall. Then there is the application to Satan's kingdom (notice that Jesus does not deny the devil's power in the world). If Jesus casts devils out by the devil's power then the devil's kingdom is undermined from within and will collapse. This being so, there must be another explanation for Jesus' power over the demons. That can point only in one direction. Lastly, why do his critics not make the same complaints against their own disciples who claim to cast out demons the way Jesus does (*Acts* 19:13)? They will witness against their mentors in the day of judgement for their foolishness and unbelief.

The true explanation of Jesus' acts (verse 20), because it is the only one that explains the facts, is that God's Spirit ('the finger of God'), is at work through Jesus, giving evidence of the arrival of the kingdom of God (*Matt.*12:28). This is a reminder of what happened formerly at Mount Sinai when God's Spirit was active in revelatory ministry (*Deut.* 9:10). For this reason Paul teaches that the things of God are spiritually discerned and cannot be understood by natural reason (*1 Cor.* 2:12–16). Christianity is throughout a supernatural revelation both in its historical presence in Jesus and in its subjective apprehension by faith. To experience both the Spirit of God is necessary.

Jesus has one more illustration. It concerns a local prince who wants to protect his castle and his goods. A rival king arrives who challenges his citadel and holdings. If the rival wins then he will immediately disarm his opponent and despoil his goods. In the same way Jesus has arrived in history to challenge the god of this world (*2 Cor.* 4:4), by disarming him and spoiling his kingdom of evil. Jesus' acts of exorcism are examples of the latter, the cross and resurrection will achieve the former (*John* 12:31–33).

In this conflict between Satan and Jesus there is no place for neutrality (verse 23). The nature of the conflict demands that every individual makes a choice for or against Jesus. Those who claim to be undecided about Jesus are really casting a 'no' vote against him. Under different circumstances Jesus could state the opposite view (*Luke* 9:49–50).

From this passage we learn that Jesus was a realist when it came to the existence of evil and evil as personalized in the devil. Evil is masterminded throughout history and across the cultures of the world (*Luke* 4:5–6). Evil is networked into a kingdom of darkness (*Eph.* 6:10–12). Many churches in the West have given up belief in a personal devil under the naturalistic theories of modern psychology and science. The explanations of Jesus never become obsolete because he knows the secrets of the spiritual world. Nor can the cross-work of Jesus be fully understood without a belief in moral darkness and its hold over humankind (*Heb.* 2:14–15).

AN EMPTY HOUSE (verses 24–26)

Jesus adds a codicil to his earlier teaching. Vacuums are just as dangerous in the spiritual world as in the physical – they always get filled. The evil powers live parasitically off the rest of God's creation, especially human beings who bear his image. By plaguing men and women the devils can wreak their vengeance against God.

The point of Jesus' story is the hopelessness of moral reformation without spiritual regeneration. Turning over a new leaf in a person's life without the indwelling of the Holy Spirit may only result in deeper bondage and darkness in the end. The evil powers may depart for a time but they can easily overcome human resolution and take possession in greater numbers. In the story the demon that departed returned with seven demons worse than itself.

Mere morality is no match for the powers of evil and temptation. Jesus alone gives deliverance from moral addiction and weakness. Human beings need more than moral education, they need spiritual regeneration. Our fallen nature is plagued from within by moral weakness, a tendency to the dark side, and final despair. Where Christ enters in he reclaims the whole person for God and righteousness. He brings peace, power and purity on an increasing scale.

49

An Assortment of Sayings

As he said these things, a woman in the crowd raised her voice
and said to him, 'Blessed is the womb that bore you, and the
breasts at which you nursed!' 28 *But he said, 'Blessed rather are*
those who hear the word of God and keep it!'
29 *When the crowds were increasing, he began to say, 'This*
generation is an evil generation. It seeks for a sign, but no sign
will be given to it except the sign of Jonah. 30 *For as Jonah became*
a sign to the people of Nineveh, so will the Son of Man be to this
generation. 31 *The queen of the South will rise up at the judgment*
with the men of this generation and condemn them, for she came
from the ends of the earth to hear the wisdom of Solomon, and
behold, something greater than Solomon is here. 32 *The men of*
Nineveh will rise up at the judgment with this generation and
condemn it, for they repented at the preaching of Jonah, and
behold, something greater than Jonah is here.
33 *No one after lighting a lamp puts it in a cellar or under a*
basket, but on a stand, so that those who enter may see the light.
34 *Your eye is the lamp of your body. When your eye is healthy,*
your whole body is full of light, but when it is bad, your body is
full of darkness. 35 *Therefore be careful lest the light in you be*
darkness. 36 *If then your whole body is full of light, having no*
part dark, it will be wholly bright, as when a lamp with its rays
gives you light.' (Luke 11:27–36).

An assortment of sayings follows. What holds them together is Jesus' concern to make plain the terms of discipleship. He was rightly anxious that people should not follow him for the wrong reasons or with a misunderstanding of what it meant to live under the kingly rule of God (see again Luke 9:57–62).

A MOTHER'S CRY (verses 27–28)

Jesus' handling of his critics in the Beelzebul controversy clearly impressed some of the crowd. A mother cried out how blessed Jesus' mother must have been to bear him and wean him. She was seeing Jesus as a man through the eyes of a mother. But Jesus corrected this perspective (*Luke* 8:19–21). His point is that a physical tie with Jesus is inconsequential if a spiritual one is missing. Doing God's will from the heart is much more important than knowing about Jesus historically. In replying Jesus hands out one of his less known beatitudes (*Acts* 20:35).

Throughout history many people have had contact with Jesus through the church, its sacraments, or the Bible. They know something about the Christian faith or Jesus but they have taken it no further. They may be relying on this outward contact to get them into heaven. But Jesus insists that only the moral test of a life lived for him by faith, will speak for them in that day (*Matt.* 7:21–23).

JESUS THE GREAT SIGN (verses 29–32)

As the crowds increased so did Jesus' anxiety for their spiritual knowledge. For this reason he spoke out against their ingrained unbelief. A critical condition calls for shock-treatment. Jesus condemns his generation of Jews for always wanting another sign to authenticate him publicly. In Israel's history true believers and godly people asked God for signs and God granted them (*Jud.* 6:36–40, *Isa.* 7:10–11) so what is the difference with the Jews of Jesus' day?

Jesus himself was the supreme sign of God's wisdom, grace, and power through the miraculous events of his conception, life, teachings and miracles (*John* 10:31–39). No one had ever acted, spoken, or lived the way Jesus did. The evidences for the truth of his being God's eternal Son and the human Messiah of Israel were and are overwhelming. By repeatedly asking for signs and more signs (*Luke* 11:16), the Jews were putting off a choice they did not want to make (see the similar case of the pagan ruler Felix in Acts 24:24–25).

In a sensational age in which image is everything, the churches can err by reflecting the general culture and its values. So Christianity becomes identified with miraculous cures, prophecies and personalities. This hyper-interest in the miraculous in human experience can obliterate the grand miracle which is Jesus himself. Not only are his miracles greater than any today but he himself is the incarnate miracle of God dwelling with humankind and showing his glory (*John* 1:14). Christians need to prioritise God's miracles by beginning with Jesus himself, his cross and resurrection, as the only miracle that actually saves (*1 Cor*. 15:1–8).

Jesus appeals above all to his forthcoming resurrection. For this he uses the story of Jonah whose time in the stomach of a sea creature foreshadows the entombment of the Son of God before his deliverance in resurrection (*Jonah* 1:15–2:10, *Matt*. 12:40). Jesus' resurrection continues to this day as the strongest reason for trusting in him as the one trustworthy Saviour (*1 Cor*. 15:3–28).

Jesus follows this up with two well-known stories from the Old Testament. The queen of Sheba took the trouble to visit Jerusalem to listen to Solomon (*1 Kings* 10:1–13). She responded to Solomon's wisdom better than Jesus' hearers responded to him. Yet Solomon bears no comparison to Jesus. In the same way the pagan people of Nineveh repented at Jonah's preaching (*Jonah* 3). Jonah did not compare with Jesus yet Jesus' hearers refused to repent at his words. In the judgement the queen of Sheba and the people of Nineveh will both alike rise up to condemn the Jews of Jesus' day for their inexcusable hardness.

As at Nazareth when he signalled the kind of ministry he would conduct (*Luke* 4:21–27), Jesus picked out examples of non-Israelites. They responded to God's offer of mercy more quickly than the historical people of God. The church's evangelists would experience the same phenomenon in taking the gospel to Jews and Gentiles (*Acts* 13:42–52). As then so now. Those who have known most and enjoyed the greatest religious opportunities are often overtaken, bypassed and replaced by those who have known nothing before their first encounter with Christ (*1 Cor*. 1:26–31).

'The first will be last and the last first' is a pattern of human reversal in Christ's kingdom and Luke's theology. This way satisfies both God's grace and his justice.

Religious connections mean nothing if people close their hearts to Christ. Throughout the Christian era since Jesus came, people have had access to a complete Bible. If people will not believe the Scriptures that point to Christ, no amount of miracles will change them (*Luke* 16:31).

THE LIGHT OF LIFE (verses 33–36)

This section begins and ends with the picture of a Palestinian lamp, hand-held, fuelled with oil and burning through a narrow spout. These lamps were the means of lighting homes and could be taken from room to room, the kind of scenario that Jesus imagines here. A lamp is for illuminating, not for being hidden, for scattering darkness, not prolonging it.

Jesus now explains his parable. He likens the human eye to an aperture, not for letting light out, but for letting it in – to the whole body. So if a person's eye is clear, so will his whole body be; but if the eye is faulty it will prevent light from passing through to the body within.

The physiology is simple but the spiritual truth is profound. Through our senses (including sight) we take in images and impressions that transfer to the brain where they are organised and result in responses favourable or negative. Our knowledge of the world and our behaviour are deeply affected by our bodily experiences. Jesus wants us to think about the images our brains process from our eyes. The outer eye can be immediately decisive for the inner eye of conscience or understanding. Paul speaks of the 'eyes of your understanding being enlightened' (*Eph.* 1:15–17). In the same way the Jews saw Jesus as physically present, heard his voice and observed his miracles, yet they closed their eyes to him inwardly. They refused to allow the light of his truth to instruct their conscience and lead them to a change of mind.

When anyone reads or hears God's Word they receive images about Jesus in their mind's eye. If they choose to close their eyes to him, then they deepen their inner darkness; if they open their eyes to him then they will become filled with the light of his knowledge (*2 Cor.* 4:3–6). Christians should live in the light of God, mirror that light to a world in darkness and cultivate more and more of the light of true knowledge (*1 John* 1:5–7, *2 Pet.* 1:5–9).

50

Six Prophetic Woes

*While Jesus was speaking, a Pharisee asked him to dine with him,
so he went in and reclined at table. [38] The Pharisee was astonished
to see that he did not first wash before dinner. [39] And the Lord
said to him, 'Now you Pharisees cleanse the outside of the cup
and of the dish, but inside you are full of greed and wickedness.
[40] You fools! Did not he who made the outside make the inside
also? [41] But give as alms those things that are within, and behold,
everything is clean for you.*
*[42] But woe to you Pharisees! For you tithe mint and rue and every
herb, and neglect justice and the love of God. These you ought
to have done, without neglecting the others. [43] Woe to you
Pharisees! For you love the best seat in the synagogues and
greetings in the marketplaces. [44] Woe to you! For you are like
unmarked graves, and people walk over them without knowing
it.'*
*[45] One of the lawyers answered him, 'Teacher, in saying these
things you insult us also.' [46] And he said, 'Woe to you lawyers
also! For you load people with burdens hard to bear, and you
yourselves do not touch the burdens with one of your fingers.
[47] Woe to you! For you build the tombs of the prophets whom your
fathers killed. [48] So you are witnesses and you consent to the deeds
of your fathers, for they killed them, and you build their tombs.
[49] Therefore also the Wisdom of God said, "I will send them
prophets and apostles, some of whom they will kill and persecute,"
[50] so that the blood of all the prophets, shed from the foundation
of the world, may be charged against this generation, [51] from the
blood of Abel to the blood of Zechariah, who perished between
the altar and the sanctuary. Yes, I tell you, it will be required of*

this generation. [52] *Woe to you lawyers! For you have taken away the key of knowledge. You did not enter yourselves, and you hindered those who were entering.'*

[53] *As he went away from there, the scribes and the Pharisees began to press him hard and to provoke him to speak about many things,*
[54] *lying in wait for him, to catch him in something he might say* (Luke 11:37–54).

Jesus was never unresponsive in his social relations so when a Pharisee invited him to eat with him he agreed to go along (also *Luke* 14:1–24). The party was made up largely of Pharisees, the zealous practitioners of the law and the scribes, the literalistic interpreters of it. When Jesus failed to wash his hands before eating he aroused the astonishment of the Pharisees (see *Mark* 7:1–4). The Pharisees practised a strict regime of washing before eating, not only for reasons of hygiene but for religious reasons. Otherwise, they believed, they would contract ritual uncleanness that would render them unholy before God and discredited in his service.

When Jesus neglected to engage in these washings they judged him by their principles. But this caused Jesus to launch into a fiery censure of their leading beliefs and practices, first of the Pharisees (verses 39–44), then of the scribes (verses 46–52). This he did not out of personal annoyance but in the service of the truth. By pronouncing blessings and curses in the Lord's name on the Lord's people (*Isa.* 5:8–25) Jesus was coming from the prophetic tradition (*Deut.* 27–28) and showed himself the last of the classical prophets (*Mal.* 3:1–5).

AGAINST THE PHARISEES (verses 39–44)

The underlying error of the worst of the Pharisees was an attachment to outward acts without the devotion of the heart to God. They passed judgement about washing utensils, but at the same time their hearts were controlled by greed and other kinds of wickedness (verse 39). They were fools who had failed to see that the God who made us outwardly had also made us inwardly and both for his glory (verse 40). True charity begins with giving the heart to God through

Jesus; then the rest of religious faith in practice will be acceptable and praiseworthy (verse 41).

The Lord demands my soul, my life, my all. There ought to be no 'off-limits' part of our life before God. When the heart is right with him the rest of the life will be acceptable to him (*Rom.* 12:1–2). Jesus was incensed by the persistent double-standards of the Pharisees. Against their brazen inconsistencies Jesus pronounces three woes.

- First woe (verse 42). The Pharisees were living with muddled priorities. In obedience to God's law they conscientiously practised the tithe (*Deut.* 14:22–29), including the whole range of garden produce. But while they were being so particular over tithing they neglected to be just in their treatment of others and to love God sincerely. They majored on minor matters of the law and minored on major ones. Jesus advocates the reverse order of giving first place to loving God and serving people, then giving a proportion of our income to God.
- Second woe (verse 43). The Pharisees were vain and conceited. They loved to be the centre of attention in public gatherings. If they were in the synagogue they loved having the front seats reserved for dignitaries; if in the market-place they loved being greeted effusively because of their professional status. Jesus' religion is about humility (not the same as low self-esteem) and self-giving following his own example.
- Third woe (verse 44). The Pharisees saw themselves as the holy men of Israel whose sanctity made atonement for the sin of the nation. Actually they were like unmarked graves whose lives and example contaminated those who made contact with them. Their inner uncleanness defiled those around them without their knowing it (*Num.* 19:16). Jesus imparts purity of heart to those who come to him.

AGAINST THE SCRIBES (verses 45–54)

The scribes, who had been listening to Jesus' diatribe against the Pharisees, unwisely got involved (verse 45). They felt implicated in what Jesus had been saying and wanted to clear their reputation. The scribes fair no better than the Pharisees in Jesus' estimation. He censures them for faults peculiar to their legal practice in explaining the meaning of the law in everyday living.

- Fourth woe (verse 46). The scribes made hard rulings for the people from the law of Moses. Their interpretations did not make clear the fundamental framework of grace for all God's commandments, so people felt crushed by a religion of regulations (do's and don'ts). The scribes failed to mix mercy with the just demands of the law. Like all legalists (conservative or liberal) these people neglected love (of God and for God) as the key to a virtuous life (*Luke* 6:27–36; 10:25–37). Jesus summed up the whole of biblical morality as a double standard of love (*Matt*. 22:34–40).
- Fifth woe (verses 47–51). The scribes believed in religious monuments as reminders of Israel's leaders of the past. They adorned the tombs of the prophets. But Jesus put a different spin on their actions. Their real predecessors were those who murdered the prophets. The actions of their descendants in renovating these tombs could be seen as a way of acclaiming what their fathers had done! Good riddance to those troublesome prophets who spoke God's word so freely!

Jesus recalls the bloody history of the prophets, starting with righteous Abel (*Gen*. 4:1–8) and coming down to Zechariah (*2 Chron*. 24:20–21, *Zech*. 1:1). Jesus' quotation from 'the wisdom of God', or 'the God of wisdom', is meant to sum up the way the Israelites repeatedly treated those sent to them by God (for example, Elijah (*1 Kings* 19:10, 14) and Jeremiah (*Jer*. 25–26; 20:1–2). The correctness of Jesus' interpretation is borne out by the way these religious guides are treating him – in exactly the way their fathers treated the prophets before him. In murdering Jesus the Jews of his generation would cap all those wicked acts of persecution and bring upon their children the just judgement of God (*Luke* 21:20–24; *1 Thess*. 2:14–16).

- Sixth woe (verse 52). The scribes had the advantage of knowing the Scriptures. Jesus likens their knowledge to a key that could have and should have opened the door of the kingdom both to

> themselves and to the people entrusted to their care. Instead they had refused both and were doubly guilty. Better never to have known the truth than to have known it and to have abused it. Jesus trusts us to make use of the knowledge we receive from him for our own betterment and that of others. Freely we have received, freely give!

Predictably his enemies were incensed against Jesus. In their anger they lost self-control, beginning to bait him openly in the hope of catching him out and having grounds for a legal process. But Jesus never lost control, even under fire and so was well able to evade their plots and go on his way.

Jesus kept his sharpest polemic for those who offended in the religious sphere. Our Lord detested the religious hypocrisy that was rooted in spiritual arrogance, self-righteousness and a failure of sympathy towards others in need. The Pharisees were the type of those people in every age and in many religious circles and institutions who pride themselves on their religious faith but who react vigorously to the demand for personal repentance. This they may brand as 'fundamentalist' religion. To all such Jesus reiterates the principle, 'to obey is better than sacrifice' (*1 Sam.* 15:22).

51

Double-Standards, Fear and Confession

> *In the meantime, when so many thousands of the people had gathered together that they were trampling one another, he began to say to his disciples first, 'Beware of the leaven of the Pharisees, which is hypocrisy. 2 Nothing is covered up that will not be revealed, or hidden that will not be known. 3 Therefore whatever you have said in the dark shall be heard in the light, and what you have whispered in private rooms shall be proclaimed on the housetops.*
>
> *4 I tell you, my friends, do not fear those who kill the body, and after that have nothing more that they can do. 5 But I will warn you whom to fear: fear him who, after he has killed, has authority to cast into hell. Yes, I tell you, fear him! 6 Are not five sparrows sold for two pennies? And not one of them is forgotten before God. 7 Why, even the hairs of your head are all numbered. Fear not; you are of more value than many sparrows.*
>
> *8 And I tell you, everyone who acknowledges me before men, the Son of Man also will acknowledge before the angels of God, 9 but the one who denies me before men will be denied before the angels of God. 10 And everyone who speaks a word against the Son of Man will be forgiven, but the one who blasphemes against the Holy Spirit will not be forgiven. 11 And when they bring you before the synagogues and the rulers and the authorities, do not be anxious about how you should defend yourself or what you should say, 12 for the Holy Spirit will teach you in that very hour what you ought to say.'* (Luke 12:1–12).

The key to this chapter lies in verse 56 about interpreting the times in the light of Christ's being present in the world. This momentous development changes everything and calls for a change of viewpoint and behaviour in every area of life. The time between the two comings of Jesus is a new day of salvation in which all human values are revalued. Jesus is the true revolutionary and prophet of the modern age, not Nietzsche or Mohammed.

This is *not* the time for double standards (verses 1–3), the fear of man (verses 4–7); it *is* the time for confessing Jesus in the power of the Spirit (verses 8–12); it is *not* the time for amassing earthly wealth (verses 13–21) or being anxious about such matters (verses 22–34); it *is* the time for alert and faithful service for Christ as Master (verses 35–48), for accepting division as a fact of discipleship (verses 49–53), for interpreting all events in the light of Christ's presence at the second advent (verses 54–56) and for being reconciled urgently with God (verses 57–59).

DOULE-STANDARDS (verses 1–3)

Because of the vast crowds that he had attracted Jesus began to warn his disciples, as future leaders, against the wrongful example of Israel's current leaders. He likens their behaviour to leaven since leaven corrupts or changes the substance it is mingled with. In the Bible leaven is often, though not always (*Matt.* 13:33), used to illustrate bad influences (*1 Cor.* 5:6–8, *Gal.* 5:7–12). In the same way the Pharisees affect people for worse because they misrepresent the kingdom of God and harden people's hearts against the truth.

The religious leaders were masters of the art of deception in covering up the real motives and goals of their actions. They acted from self-interest and at the very time gave the impression of acting in God's (*Matt.* 6:1–2, 5, 16). Jesus has already faced them with this charge (*Luke* 11:37–54). A partition between the inner life and public life has always been a subtle deception for religious people.

Jesus' main reason for giving this warning is that at the judgement the whole truth about everyone will come to light. God, through Jesus, will judge everyone according to their true story. His judgement is founded on the whole truth and nothing but the truth about us all. He is the all-knowing One.

This will include secrets whispered in private to another person. Jesus applies the criterion of double-standards to what we say because it is above all in our words, spoken to and about others, that self-deception can take control. One person may speak sweetly to another's face but destroy the same person with their words behind their back (*Psa.* 28:3). Words are power for good or evil. By our tongues we will all be judged (*James* 3:1–12).

WRONG AND RIGHT FEAR (verses 4–7)

Jesus calls his disciples 'my friends'. Shortly he will call them 'little flock' (verse 32). These are terms of endearment that assure us of the love of Christ that passes knowledge (*Eph.* 3:17 – 19). In this way he differentiates his true disciples from those who followed him out of curiosity or self-interest.

Fear is one of the most powerful of human emotions. Fear can paralyse, even destroy people. Jesus is speaking about religious suffering, where his followers may be threatened with torture or death. This experience is a daily one for many Christians around the world in the twenty-first century; no one should exempt themselves from this possibility.

In the hands of one's enemies it is natural to fear what they may do to you. But Jesus prepares his followers for such an eventuality. He reminds his disciples of the limitations of human power. Human beings do not control the ultimate destiny of other people. They can inflict pain on the body and mind but their powers do not reach beyond death. They are not therefore proper objects of fear.

On the other hand, God has all power; he does control life beyond death and can inflict the penalty of eternal death in hell (*Rev.* 20:14). Fearing God is a different kind of fear to that of fearing humankind. Human fear is rooted in dread and self-protection; fearing God means loving God, giving him his due and opening ourselves to him. Such fear grows out of faith and is not alien to knowing Christ (*Psa.* 19:9, *Prov.* 1:7, *2 Cor.* 7:1, *Eph.* 5:21). The answer to the fear of man is the fear of the Lord. His perfect love casts out servile fear (*1 John* 4:18).

To all this Jesus adds the delightful thought that God values his people far beyond the care that he holds for the humble house sparrow. Five of these are sold in the market place for a pittance yet God knows every one of them and cares about them. If God so cares for the common sparrow how much more must he love us who bear his very image and for whom Christ died?

To make his meaning doubly clear Jesus assures his disciples that the very hairs of their head are numbered by God their Father. This is no exaggeration, so exhaustive is God's knowledge of us. In the hands of such a Deity how can any be afraid what other mortals may do to us! Anything they do accomplish against us can only be by God's permission and will somehow promote our eternal good in Christ (*Rom.* 8:28, 35–39).

CONFESSING JESUS (verses 8–12)

Continuing the thought of public persecution Jesus assures and warns his disciples.

- First, he connects the earthly world with the heavenly as though organised like two courts. What takes place in the lower one (on earth) will be acted out in the higher one (in heaven). When his disciples confess him openly before men on earth Jesus will confess them openly in heaven, with the angels as witnesses. The reverse is equally true. When someone denies Jesus in the lower court on earth Jesus will deny that he knows that person in the court of heaven. This means that when anyone takes a stand for Jesus on earth, whatever their earthly critics or judges may say, Jesus registers that act in the records of heaven. Who would not have the Son of Man as their advocate in heaven!
- Secondly, Jesus makes a difficult pronouncement about the Holy Spirit (verse 10). Jesus sets the Holy Spirit above himself by declaring that sins of utterance against Jesus himself (the Son of Man) will be forgiven but that such sins against the Holy Spirit amount to blasphemy and cannot be forgiven. How are we to understand this puzzling statement?

  The Spirit is the divine witness to the truth about Jesus, both in his full Godhead and his full manhood, hence he is known as the Spirit of truth (*John* 15:26). If someone persistently and deliberately rejects this witness then he cuts himself off from all hope of salvation and renders himself guilty of an eternal sin. In the nature of things the sin against the Holy Spirit will not be forgiven because it cannot be forgiven – it is the final refusal of the only forgiveness there is, through Christ.

This outrage against the Spirit of grace (*Heb.* 10:29) should be contrasted with the periodic, temporary failure of a Christian through grieving or quenching the Holy Spirit within them (*Eph.* 4:30, *1 Thess.* 5:19). This is far removed from the condition of the Pharisees in calling Jesus' life and ministry the devil's work (*Mark* 3:28–30). The Christian will always return in remorse to the God he has offended and loves. Peter's case is the proof of this. Anxiety over this sin is frequently experienced during times of intense spiritual experience. A person anxious about this sin should take comfort that such concern is incompatible with this sin. This is because this sin, as the case of the Pharisees shows, results in spiritual insensitivity forever.

- Thirdly, Jesus promises the Spirit's extraordinary help in extra-ordinary times of need or danger (verses 11 and 12). When Christians are brought before human tribunals they will be naturally anxious to say the right thing. Here the temptation is anxiety rather than fear. Don't be anxious, says Jesus, because you should not rely on yourselves. The Holy Spirit is the great witness and will supply you with the reasons and the words you need. The apostles would prove the truth of this promise (*Acts* 4:5–12; 5:32; 6:10) but so have many Christians in the modern world.

52

Life Is More, Not Less

*Someone in the crowd said to him, ‘Teacher, tell my brother to
divide the inheritance with me.’ 14 But he said to him, ‘Man, who
made me a judge or arbitrator over you?’ 15 And he said to them,
‘Take care, and be on your guard against all covetousness, for
one’s life does not consist in the abundance of his possessions.’
16 And he told them a parable, saying, ‘The land of a rich man
produced plentifully, 17 and he thought to himself, “What shall
I do, for I have nowhere to store my crops?” 18 And he said, “I
will do this: I will tear down my barns and build larger ones,
and there I will store all my grain and my goods. 19 And I will
say to my soul, Soul, you have ample goods laid up for many
years; relax, eat, drink, be merry.” 20 But God said to him,
“Fool! This night your soul is required of you, and the things
you have prepared, whose will they be?” 21 So is the one who lays
up treasure for himself and is not rich toward God.’
22 And he said to his disciples, ‘Therefore I tell you, do not be
anxious about your life, what you will eat, nor about your body,
what you will put on. 23 For life is more than food, and the body
more than clothing. 24 Consider the ravens: they neither sow nor
reap, they have neither storehouse nor barn, and yet God feeds
them. Of how much more value are you than the birds! 25 And
which of you by being anxious can add a single hour to his span of
life? 26 If then you are not able to do as small a thing as that, why
are you anxious about the rest? 27 Consider the lilies, how they
grow: they neither toil nor spin, yet I tell you, even Solomon in
all his glory was not arrayed like one of these. 28 But if God so
clothes the grass, which is alive in the field today, and tomorrow is
thrown into the oven, how much more will he clothe you, O you of*

little faith! [29] And do not seek what you are to eat and what you are to drink, nor be worried. [30] For all the nations of the world seek after these things, and your Father knows that you need them. [31] Instead, seek his kingdom, and these things will be added to you. [32] Fear not, little flock, for it is your Father's good pleasure to give you the kingdom. [33] Sell your possessions, and give to the needy. Provide yourselves with moneybags that do not grow old, with a treasure in the heavens that does not fail, where no thief approaches and no moth destroys. [34] For where your treasure is, there will your heart be also.' (Luke 12:13–34).

As must have happened often to Jesus in public, someone from the crowd called out to him. A complete stranger requested Jesus to adjudicate between him and his brother over the family property. In doing this he was treating Jesus as a rabbi with expertise in deciding legal cases. He also hoped Jesus would lend his considerable prestige to his side of the dispute.

But Jesus refuses this role because he is more concerned about the underlying moral and spiritual condition of the man. Jesus did not come as a jurist to decide property issues but as a Saviour from sin and all its works. As with the rich young ruler (*Luke* 18:22) Jesus lays bare a deeper problem than the one the individual started from. In this case the problem was a spirit of greed that drove this man to Jesus as a way of acquiring his share of the property. The issue was not justice but greed. How many social and inter-personal disputes go back to personal failings in moral character?

The principal fallacy of greed is the belief that life consists in possessions and acquiring wealth. Greed is idolatry because it worships the goddess of wealth (*Col.* 3:5). Unless greed is restrained it has the potential to ruin personal and family life (*1 Tim.* 6:9–10). Jesus repeats a warning about the ever-present danger of greed (verse 15).

A STORY (verseS 16–20)

Jesus turns the moment into an opportunity for telling a story. A parable is an imaginary story placed alongside real life for the sake of comparison(s). From this comparison one or more principles about living in the kingdom of God emerges. This is meant to bring about a change of focus and so of behaviour.

This story is about a wealthy landowner whose ground produced a bumper crop. This forced him to think about rebuilding his sheds to accommodate his harvest and to enlarge his properties. In addition he chose a life of pleasure and leisure, presuming that he would live for many years enjoying his new-found wealth (*Isa*. 22:13, *1 Cor*. 15:32).

He made one fatal error – he failed to reckon with God. In doing that he also denied life's accountability and the finality of death. The landowner died that very night, was called to give an explanation of his life on earth and to surrender everything he owned to people who came after him (*Eccles*. 2:18–19). The farmer is shown to be short-sighted and a hopeless manager of his life.

THE LESSON (verse 21)

Jesus draws the lesson of the story just as he had set it up beforehand (verse 15). The cause of the landowner's wasted life was selfishness. He lived for himself, only thought about his own interests and in doing so failed to reckon with heavenly, eternal realities. Here was someone who thought and spoke exclusively in the first person singular (verses 17–19; see also *Luke* 18:11–12). There was no place for God or other people in his plans.

Here is the secular mindset and lifestyle, based on the assumption that this is the only life and that it is one-dimensional. Jesus' story is a warning against all forms of consumerism (*Luke* 9:25). Following Jesus means being lifted out of a self-centred, imprisoned existence, to live for heavenly truth and goods (*2 Cor*. 4:18).

Moses sets us the example here by renouncing the pleasures and treasures of this world, choosing instead the sufferings of God's people and the disgrace of Christ, reckoning the latter the true wealth of the world (*Heb*. 11:24–26). Jesus' disciples are those who amass heavenly treasures rather than earthly fortunes, because that is where their hearts are (*Matt*. 6:19–21). Where is your heart?

DON'T WORRY! (verses 22–31)

How often people give this advice to one another without being able to make it happen! Jesus tells us the secret of conquering our anxieties, as well as telling us not to worry. He does this by setting our human needs within the larger framework of God's Fatherly care.

'Therefore' (verse 22) shows a logical connection with the parable Jesus told. Here are the practical lessons from it. People worry about the future and about whether they can make ends meet. Jesus gives the examples of finding food and buying clothes. This can be true in all kinds of economies. Jesus answers the problem of anxiety by presenting five interlocking arguments that are meant to change the way we see things by turning us in a new direction.

- The first argument appeals to the 'more-ness' of human existence (verse 23). The problem with worry is that it narrows the meaning of life. But real existence finds its meaning beyond such concerns. Jesus does not say what the 'more than' consists in but we can guess that he had in mind our primary relationship to God. The chief end of human existence is knowing God and being known by him and to glorify and enjoy him.
- The second argument (verse 24) is the high value God places on human beings over other living creatures. Ravens are scavengers that make no provision for their future by sowing, reaping or storing food but God still feeds them. If God cares about birds of the scrap-heaps how much more will he make sure that his own image-bearers (*Gen.* 1:26) are properly provided for!
- Jesus' third argument (verses 25–26) points out how futile worry is; it adds nothing to life, either in time or pleasure. Adding an hour to life makes more sense here than adding a cubit to one's height. Worry only detracts from the quality of life, as well as preventing us from making a worthwhile contribution to the world we live in.
- In his fourth argument (verses 27–28) Jesus appeals to the wild flowers of the Palestinian landscape. How they grow, yet they don't engage in human skills like spinning to produce their beauty! Even King Solomon, for all his wealth, could not dress so finely as those wild flowers. Yet God is the artist who decks them with their

colours and textures. In addition, those wild flowers were exposed to the burning sun of the desert lands; they blossom one day and are shrivelled up the next. As with the ravens, Jesus reasons from the lesser to the greater – God's care for his own children who are so much more valuable to him than all his creatures.

In passing, Jesus pinpoints the root of worry (verse 28). This is nothing less than unbelief or under-developed faith. Like Peter, people who worry are looking at the threatening waves rather than the Lord, the master of the storm (*Matt.* 14:25–31). When people worry they are living by sight, not faith; when people trust God they are living by faith, not sight. We need to trust God more, our senses less (*Luke* 11:3–4, *2 Cor*. 4:16–18).

- Fifthly (verses 29–30), worrying about the needs of this life is a pagan activity rather than a Christian one. Pagans, ancient and modern, spend most of their lives frantically chasing wealth and all it can buy, before life runs out at death. How different are Jesus' values and goals! The main point is that disciples should know their heavenly Father knows what they need (not what they want) and is more than willing to give it.

Finally, Jesus reveals the one sure antidote to worry – be anxious about God's kingdom instead (verse 31)! Make heavenly matters your primary concern and trust God for your material needs. By so saying Jesus means to help people prioritise their lives so that they have a clear agenda in which God and his interests come ahead of their own. Once people settle that issue they may be confident that the matters they worried about will be added, sometimes in surplus.

GET BY GIVING (verses 32–34)

Fear is another name for worry, so Jesus vetoes the one as well as the other. Disciples of Christ are like a little flock of sheep that their heavenly Shepherd cares for (*John* 10:2–4). He is going to prove his love and fidelity by laying down his life for them at the cross (*John* 10:11–16). But even before this, the Father has been delighted to grant them all a share in his eternal and heavenly kingdom (*1 Thess.*

2:12). It is the Father's nature to give and this he has done right royally in Jesus and the kingdom. What need of fear or worry, then?

The logic of the believer's situation as a citizen of a heavenly city (*Phil.* 3:20) must be to let go earthly possessions out of his heart, instead sharing freely his earthly goods. Only the vaults of heaven are safe from fraudulent dealing. It is a matter of the heart and its desires. What people value most is where their hearts lie. Christ himself is the wealth we should aim for since he alone has true wealth to give (*Rev.* 3:18).

53

Be Ready and Responsible

*'Stay dressed for action and keep your lamps burning, [36] and be
like men who are waiting for their master to come home from
the wedding feast, so that they may open the door to him at once
when he comes and knocks. [37] Blessed are those servants whom
the master finds awake when he comes. Truly, I say to you, he
will dress himself for service and have them recline at table, and
he will come and serve them. [38] If he comes in the second watch,
or in the third, and finds them awake, blessed are those servants!
[39] But know this, that if the master of the house had known at
what hour the thief was coming, he would not have left his house
to be broken into. [40] You also must be ready, for the Son of Man
is coming at an hour you do not expect.'
[41] Peter said, 'Lord, are you telling this parable for us or for all?'
[42] And the Lord said, 'Who then is the faithful and wise manager,
whom his master will set over his household, to give them their
portion of food at the proper time? [43] Blessed is that servant whom
his master will find so doing when he comes. [44] Truly, I say to
you, he will set him over all his possessions. [45] But if that servant
says to himself, "My master is delayed in coming," and begins
to beat the male and female servants, and to eat and drink and
get drunk, [46] the master of that servant will come on a day when
he does not expect him and at an hour he does not know, and
will cut him in pieces and put him with the unfaithful. [47] And
that servant who knew his master's will but did not get ready or
act according to his will, will receive a severe beating. [48] But the
one who did not know, and did what deserved a beating, will
receive a light beating. Everyone to whom much was given, of*

him much will be required, and from him to whom they entrusted much, they will demand the more.' (Luke 12:35–48).

In this section Jesus gives out encouragements and warnings to disciples in the light of his future return. Throughout these verses he likens his followers to servants, firstly as ordinary house servants (verses 35–38), then managerial servants with authority over the other servants (verses 42–46), lastly as servants of any kind (verses 47–48). Throughout these short parables Jesus himself is the master in question who will call his servants to account (verse 41).

ENCOURAGEMENTS (verses 35–40)

Jesus compares his disciples to servants ready, awake and dressed for the knock of their master on the door, who wants to be let in after attending a wedding banquet. For the servants to be ready they must have their night lamps burning and be mentally alert for their master's arrival so as to open the door to him. Jesus pronounces his blessing on servants who are like this, when he comes. Their being ready and alert at any time showed their minds were focussed on him and not on themselves (unlike the servant in the next section, verse 45). This is the inner secret of spiritual vigilance, being centred on the master and his return.

The master himself will reward these servants in a kind of role reversal. Normally the master would expect the servant to wait on him, but here the master will do the serving (*Luke* 17:7–10)! No wonder Jesus says that it will be good (literally 'blessed', verses 37, 38) for those servants when the master comes back! No matter when they lived in the long history of the church (the hours between nightfall and dawn were divided into watches, verse 38) Christ's servants will have been alike in this – their readiness for their master's return.

Jesus changes his metaphor. The house-owner would have waited up to intercept the burglar if he had received forewarning. But disciples have been forewarned and so have no excuse for forgetfulness, careless or worldliness during their serving time. That Jesus left no precise information about the time of his return is used by

Peter as a reason why Christians should always be clear-minded, alert and self-controlled (*1 Pet.* 4:7). Otherwise they will be ashamed when Jesus comes, for their careless living and unproductive lives (*1 John* 2:28–3:3).

To heighten the effect Jesus calls himself the Son of Man, a glorious and God-like figure (*Dan.* 7:13–14). The Son of Man receives from the Most High a kingdom that brings the whole of humankind into his service, a service that will never end. Such is the Master we serve now by faith; such is the Master to whom we will give an account when he comes.

DIFFERENT KINDS OF SERVANTS (verses 41–48)

Peter interrupts Jesus with a question about the intended audience of Jesus. Is he speaking to the disciples or for everyone within earshot? Without answering directly Jesus relates another parable that has two parts. This parable is starker than the first because it sets up the two options of those who claim to serve him. In the first part the servants take their responsibilities seriously by looking after their fellow-servants and apportioning the master's resources (verses 42–44). As a reward the master will promote these servants by placing them over all his possessions.

In the second part of this parable (verses 45–46) Jesus imagines the case of a servant who made the delay of his master's return an excuse for indulging his selfish and sinful passions – he oppressed the other servants and lived a dissipated life. Because this servant's heart is preoccupied with his own enjoyment of power the master will return when the servant has virtually forgotten about him. The servant's end will be swift and sure. The master will execute his displeasure on him and place him with his enemies.

Jesus takes his hearers further with yet another set of comparisons. This time he compares servants who have known his will but failed to do it with those who never knew his will and so could not be blamed for failing to keep it. Neither of these two sorts of servants, however, is wholly without blame because neither was wholly ignorant of the master. The first servants were more blame-worthy than the second because they knew more. The master was right to expect more from them. As a result the first servants will receive a more severe judgement. But even the second servants had some knowledge, though less. As a result they too will be judged, though less severely than the first servants.

Jesus explains the principle at work here as being one of regulated accountability (verse 48b). More privilege means greater accountability; greater privilege means greater penalty, where the privilege is abused. The Lord will expect more from those who have received more knowledge. This applies both to natural as well as to spiritual gifts since everyone is a steward of the gifts and opportunities God freely bestows. No one is exempted from a relationship of a kind to God, either as Creator or Saviour or both (*Rom.* 14:7–9). This is the reason for a universal judgement of every individual (*Rom.* 2:6–11).

The conclusion from these parables is that there are three classes of people. The servants who act responsibly are true believers who embrace warmly the promise of Christ's return (verses 35–40); the servants who act irresponsibly, who knew his will but never did it, are nominal Christians who appear religious but whose lives show none of the telling signs of grace (verses 42–46); the last group of servants who did not know the master's will, are people who live and die beyond the reach of the gospel but who are still answerable to God through natural law and creation (verses 47–48).

Every person fits into one of these categories. Only by knowing and serving the Master by faith, in love and gratitude, can any one face the judgement with a calm mind and a good conscience. How a person thinks of Christ's return and whether it makes a difference to the way he lives, is a good guide to where he stands in relation to him.

54

Causing Division, Interpreting the Times and Being Reconciled

'I came to cast fire on the earth, and would that it were already
kindled! [50] *I have a baptism to be baptized with, and how great*
is my distress until it is accomplished! [51] *Do you think that I have*
come to give peace on earth? No, I tell you, but rather division.
[52] *For from now on in one house there will be five divided, three*
against two and two against three. [53] *They will be divided, father*
against son and son against father, mother against daughter and
daughter against mother, mother-in-law against her daughter-
in-law and daughter-in-law against mother-in-law.'
[54] *He also said to the crowds, 'When you see a cloud rising in the*
west, you say at once, "A shower is coming." And so it happens.
[55] *And when you see the south wind blowing, you say, "There*
will be scorching heat," and it happens. [56] *You hypocrites! You*
know how to interpret the appearance of earth and sky, but why
do you not know how to interpret the present time?
[57] *And why do you not judge for yourselves what is right?* [58] *As*
you go with your accuser before the magistrate, make an effort
to settle with him on the way, lest he drag you to the judge, and
the judge hand you over to the officer, and the officer put you in
prison. [59] *I tell you, you will never get out until you have paid*
the very last penny.' (Luke 12:49–59).

Three pieces from Jesus' preaching make up the last section of Luke 12. What makes these pieces so memorable is the artful way Jesus is able to weave his pictures and lines from the everyday world of Palestine. He appeals to the same sort of common sense his listeners would have used in making everyday decisions, in order to sort out the more vital matters of eternal life and the kingdom of heaven.

CAUSING DIVISIONS (verses 49–53)

We have seen repeatedly in this gospel how Jesus belongs to the tradition of the prophets who brought a radical message from God. Here also Jesus speaks of the fire of God's judgement and of his own involvement in it. John spoke of Jesus' ministry as offering a baptism in the refining fire of the Holy Spirit (*Luke* 3:16). In our passage, because of the context of judgement, the fire must refer to the consuming fire of God's holiness against the world of persistent sinners. Christ longs for that time to arrive because it will mean the removal of all evil from the world.

In the meantime he must himself undergo his own form of judgement. He likens it to a baptism or inundation of suffering, leading to death. In doing so Jesus makes use of common Old Testament imagery (see *Isa*. 53:4–6; *Psa*. 69:1–2, 14–15; 88:7, 17; 124:1–5). This is the penal suffering of the cross ending in death that he came to accomplish for his people. Jesus speaks freely of the intense pressure of that prospect, until he achieves it (see also the struggle in the garden, Luke 22:39–46 and on the cross, Mark 15:34).

In the popular imagination Jesus stands for love, forgiveness and peaceful co-existence. Certainly, his primary reason for coming into the world was to create new harmonies between God and human beings and among human beings themselves. For this reason his death was an act of reconciliation and amnesty (*2 Cor*. 5:16–21; *Eph*. 2:11–22). Yet because of who he is and what he asks from those who follow him there is another side to Jesus' advent ('from now on'). He stirs deep emotions and reactions in people's hearts, even within the same family circle that otherwise sticks together (*Luke* 2:34–35). Jesus imagines a family where two are divided against three and three against two, because of him. He quotes from the prophet Micah (7:6) who lived in a time of social and spiritual distress, like the one that will follow Jesus' demise. Fathers and sons, mothers and daughters, mothers-in-law and daughters-in-law will all be against each other because of different estimates of Jesus.

The primary reason for Jesus Christ coming into the world was the salvific one of reconciling the world to God (*John* 3:15–16; *2 Cor*. 5:18–21; *1 Tim*. 1:15). But because of human freedom to reject him, his coming carries another side, that is, to judge sinners for their failure to respond favourably to him. This is the dark, inevitable side of the gospel of God's grace in Jesus Christ.

INTERPRETING THE TIMES (verses 54–56)

Jesus now turns to the crowd around him, on the same or another occasion. He recognises their skill in reading weather patterns. When the winds blew in from the Mediterranean Sea, the western seaboard of Palestine, the people rightly expected rain; when the winds blew in from the southern deserts people knew that hot weather is on the way. In other words, they could interpret the weather patterns and confidently predict conditions for the next days, weeks, or months.

How is it, Jesus asks, that you can interpret the weather but not the seasons of God's mercy and judgement present in Jesus' ministry? How hypocritical, to be able to do the one but not the other, when both are a matter of interpreting the visible evidence. To make things worse, interpreting the time of Jesus in history is so much more important in itself than reading the weather-map. Temporal issues do not compare with eternal ones.

The word that Luke uses for 'this present time' (*kairos*) is one that suggests a time in history appointed by God, for revealing and carrying out his special purposes. From a human point of view it is a time of special opportunity for seeking and finding God in mercy and grace. Such was the time of Jesus who embodied in his personal presence in the world the mercies and the judgements of God.

The time of Jesus in history is the measure and judge of all other times. Jesus' presence in world-history, because he is the eternal Son of God, transforms the historical experience for individuals and nations. He is the judgement of the world and the hope of the world's future. The world cannot remain the same since he has come. His coming is the beginning of the new age of God's kingly rule over all things.

Many people around the world, even within churches, live as though God had never intervened in history through Jesus. They can predict horse races and read share markets; they may rely on horoscopes for future guidance. Yet they do not consider the gigantic meaning for the world and for their own future of Jesus' coming into the world from God. They are no better than the people of Jesus' day who read the weather patterns but failed completely to understand the change in the times brought about by the person and work of Jesus Christ.

BEING RECONCILED WHILE THERE IS TIME (verses 57–59)

The urgency of the human situation comes out in Jesus' third picture of life in Palestine. A local individual has been accused of theft or dishonesty, with the result that his creditor is dragging him off to court. Knowing that he has nothing to pay with and that he will surely lose the case, what should he do? The answer is obvious: settle immediately with your adversary on the way to court before the court sits, otherwise you will be liable to the full penalty of the law. This could lead to penury and years in prison.

In the same way, Jesus implies, settle with your divine adversary while you have time, before the day of final reckoning arrives. God is our adversary because of debts we owe him through many acts and attitudes of wilfulness. In no way can anyone pay this debt (*Matt.* 18:23–25). Through Jesus' intervention on our behalf in coming into the world the judgement is deferred, so that we have the opportunity to straighten things out with God. God's patience becomes the world's salvation. In other words, 'Be reconciled to God here and now', since God has reckoned the guilt and shame of your sin to Christ, to reckon his righteousness freely to you' (*2 Cor.* 5:18–21). How unbelievably short-sighted for anyone to ignore God's offer of amnesty and freedom from debt forever!

55

The Moral Lessons of Tragedy

There were some present at that very time who told him about the Galileans whose blood Pilate had mingled with their sacrifices. [2] And he answered them, 'Do you think that these Galileans were worse sinners than all the other Galileans, because they suffered in this way? [3] No, I tell you; but unless you repent, you will all likewise perish. [4] Or those eighteen on whom the tower in Siloam fell and killed them: do you think that they were worse offenders than all the others who lived in Jerusalem? [5] No, I tell you; but unless you repent, you will all likewise perish.' (Luke 13:1–5).

People often ask moral questions about human tragedies that involve loss of human lives. Sometimes the scale of human suffering is so great that life seems to be without meaning. Although Jesus does not answer the philosophical side of the question, he does throw some light on the general moral lessons that such tragic events bring out.

Some of those around Jesus reported to him one day about a number of Galileans who had lost their lives while offering their sacrifices in the temple at Jerusalem. The Roman provincial governor Pilate, who was later to try Jesus, was held responsible for this slaughter. Jesus himself draws attention to another tragic example of human loss of life that had occurred recently. Part of the old wall of Jerusalem had fallen on eighteen innocent bystanders, killing them all.

Jesus then repeats a question that some Jews, due to their sense of divine justice, might be asking – was the tragedy of those people somehow tied up with the lives they had lived? Did they suffer because they had done wrong (*John* 9:1–3)? This was the case put to Job by some of his 'friends' (*Job* 8, 11, 15, 18, 22). Some modern people who believe in reincarnation hold that sufferings in this life are due to bad karma in a previous one.

Jesus will have none of this. He makes several observations: we are all wrongdoers in relation to God; suffering has somehow to do with wrongdoing; but individuals do not suffer on a scale determined by their wrongdoing. Jesus chooses to turn tragedy into wisdom by warning the living as a result of these deaths. The suffering of others is an opportunity for self-examination. In particular, bad times call for individual repentance towards God and a change of heart. Otherwise our fate will be worse than that of those who suffer tragedy. Jesus implies by this remark that the eternal suffering of post-judgement existence is a hopeless state (*Luke* 16:19–31).

Jesus teaches two precious lessons. Firstly, public tragedies are God's call to consider ultimate issues such as the meaning of life and its proper goals. Eternal issues well up unsolicited at such times and summon people to seek the living God. Secondly, personal repentance (a leading theme of Luke) is the response most appropriate at such times. Repentance means changing the centre of life from self to God in Christ. Only Jesus can save people from the greater tragedy of perishing eternally.

56

The Patience of the Lord

And he told this parable: 'A man had a fig tree planted in his vineyard, and he came seeking fruit on it and found none. [7] *And he said to the vinedresser, "Look, for three years now I have come seeking fruit on this fig tree, and I find none. Cut it down. Why should it use up the ground?"* [8] *And he answered him, "Sir, let it alone this year also, until I dig around it and put on manure.* [9] *Then if it should bear fruit next year, well and good; but if not, you can cut it down."'* (Luke 13:6–9).

Jesus continues the theme of judgement with a parable aimed at his own generation. Likening Israel to a vineyard of the Lord's planting was popular Old Testament imagery (*Psa*. 80:8–18; *Isa*. 5:1–7; 27:2–4) which was also in Jesus' teaching (*Luke* 20:9–19). The thrust of Jesus' parable could not have been missed by his hearers. They were the unfruitful tree of Jesus' story.

Jesus' parable is about a single fig-tree planted in an owner's vineyard. Understandably the owner looked for fruit from his fig tree, but found none. He shared his concern with the workman in charge. For the past three years he had patiently waited for fruit to appear. His first inclination was to cut down the fig-tree because it was using valuable ground yet producing nothing. The vineyard worker, however, pleads for one more year in which he will do everything possible to make the tree fruitful. After that, if there is still no fruit, he will chop the tree down.

This simple story has allegorical features. It tells the story of the Lord's patience with the Israelites, especially during the years of Jesus' ministry among them. Even now he could see little evidence of national repentance or of turning to him as their Messiah-King.

How tempted Jesus must have been to call for God's wrath upon his recalcitrant people! But he decides to continue with them and postpone his judgements. One more chance will be extended to them to produce the fruits of repentance (*Luke* 19:28–44). Then the Lord will turn away from Israel to the Gentile world with the offer of his kingdom. From now on Israel is living on borrowed time.

This parable is more than about Israel in Jesus' day. It tells of God's exceptional patience in spite of the fact that people delay responding to his amazing offer of mercy in Christ. He deliberately chooses to delay the judgement, so giving the world more time to come to salvation (*2 Pet*. 3:9, 15). Yet the parable also reveals that God's patience while excessive is not infinite. The Lord is slow to anger but he will not forgive the persistently impenitent. The slowness of his anger is no excuse for continuing in sin.

57

A Woman Released, Satan Defeated and God Glorified

Now he was teaching in one of the synagogues on the Sabbath.
[11] And there was a woman who had had a disabling spirit for
eighteen years. She was bent over and could not fully straighten
herself. [12] When Jesus saw her, he called her over and said to her,
'Woman, you are freed from your disability.' [13] And he laid his
hands on her, and immediately she was made straight, and she
glorified God. [14] But the ruler of the synagogue, indignant because
Jesus had healed on the Sabbath, said to the people, 'There are
six days in which work ought to be done. Come on those days and
be healed, and not on the Sabbath day.' [15] Then the Lord answered
him, 'You hypocrites! Does not each of you on the Sabbath untie
his ox or his donkey from the manger and lead it away to water it?
[16] And ought not this woman, a daughter of Abraham whom Satan
bound for eighteen years, be loosed from this bond on the Sabbath
day?' [17] As he said these things, all his adversaries were put to
shame, and all the people rejoiced at all the glorious things that
were done by him (Luke 13:10–17).

It was another Sabbath day and Jesus was teaching in one of the local synagogues. In the crowd was a woman who had been physically twisted for eighteen years. The cause was demonic and not only physical, according to Jesus (verse 16). As well as preaching the message of the kingdom Jesus healed people as a way of displaying the saving powers of the kingdom.

Jesus called the woman forward, which was itself a test of her faith. In response to her faith Jesus told her that she was freed from her infirmity. Finally, he laid his hands on her, at which point the condition ceased and she was able to stand straight for the first time in years. Jesus' opponents may not have appreciated what Jesus had said and done but the common people were delighted with the outcome. Jesus shows his deep compassion for suffering humanity by his caring response to this woman's plight. Naturally she was full of the praise of God whom she recognised as the real author of the miracle of healing. Jesus' miracles always led people to know God better because he was the Lord's servant and not his own.

Once again, Luke traces a particular physical condition to a spiritual cause, without confusing the two. At other times he separates them clearly (*Luke* 4:40–41). Because Luke was an observant doctor, thoroughly familiar with medical diagnoses, we ought not to question his allocation of the problem and the cure to more than physical causes. Human beings are more than the sum of their physical parts.

We would have expected everyone to rejoice at such a wonderful release for this poor woman but the ruler of the synagogue objected to someone being healed on the Sabbath. Healing was a form of work and should be performed on the other days of the week. The Sabbath laws required rest from normal labour. Perhaps because he wanted to avoid confronting Jesus directly the ruler criticised the crowds for coming for healing on the Sabbath, rather than Jesus for performing a cure.

Jesus objected to the ruler's negative and carping spirit and said so, putting forward a number of irrefutable reasons in doing so. Firstly, the ruler and others like him 'worked' on the Sabbath themselves, when they watered their animals. Secondly the woman was a daughter of Abraham, who deserved her freedom from Satan's bondage. Thirdly the ruler had failed to show pity to a fellow human being enslaved and broken for eighteen years. Finally the ruler failed to understand the proper nature and purpose of the Sabbath day which was to celebrate the works of God, in creating the world and now setting it free in Jesus.

Jesus is openly opposed to those who turn religion into a set of rules that stifle the human spirit, yet who turn a blind eye to their own inconsistencies. Jesus' religion is one of deliverance from oppressive legalisms and the setting free of the human spirit to serve and praise God in him.

58

Two Snapshots of the Kingdom

He said therefore, 'What is the kingdom of God like? And to what shall I compare it? [19] It is like a grain of mustard seed that a man took and sowed in his garden, and it grew and became a tree, and the birds of the air made nests in its branches.' [20] And again he said, 'To what shall I compare the kingdom of God? [21] It is like leaven that a woman took and hid in three measures of flour, until it was all leavened' (Luke 13: 18–21).

Jesus is known for his parables – stories from real life that draw comparisons with life in his kingdom. We have already studied a number of his parables (*Luke* 8:4–18; 10:22–37; 11:5–8); most of them are longer and more complex than the present two.

Jesus admits to the difficulty he finds in describing the world of God's kingdom rule (verses 18, 20). This is largely due to the novelty and grandeur of the world of the kingdom compared with anything we know here and now. Living under the rule of God as heavenly Father shifts the focus of life entirely and lifts our experience onto higher ground.

Jesus himself embodies the truth and power of the kingdom as God's chosen ambassador on earth clothed with the Father's authority. Jesus has planted the Father's rule on earth, as a seed sown through his chosen disciples, then grown fuller through his churches across the world. His final return will perfect the kingdom he has established, when the earth will be filled with the knowledge of God as the waters cover the sea.

PARABLE 1 – KINGDOM GROWTH (verse 19)

A farmer threw seed into his ground where it grew into a tree that gave shelter to the birds. In the same way the kingdom begins small in the world at large or in a person's life, but over time it grows to become a mighty power that results in good things for many people. The size of the seed is no index of its final form. The birds of the air are code for the peoples of the world (*Dan.* 4:20–22), so Jesus is here predicting the worldwide growth of his kingdom and church. People from all nations will continually find shelter and nourishment within its confines (*Luke* 24:46–47; *Acts* 1:8). The kingdom grows through the preaching of Christ and the working of his Spirit.

PARABLE 2 – KINGDOM HIDDENNESS (verse 21)

A woman takes some yeast and mixes it with a large quantity of flour until the whole batch of dough is leavened. In the same way the forces of the kingdom work unseen, yet irresistibly, in world-history and human experience until the time comes when the whole of creation will be completely under God's rule. God will then be all in all (*1 Cor.* 15:28).

Jesus' teaching about the future triumph of the kingdom has nothing to do with the secular philosophy of progress in history or the idea that the kingdom will gradually Christianise the world through human efforts or organisation. The kingdom is spiritual and mighty through God to the pulling down of human pride residing in fallacious and audacious arguments against the rule of Christ (*2 Cor.* 10:3–5).

What an incentive these parables are to Christ's workers to abound in his work even when the results seem poor, slow in coming, or non-existent! God's rule spreads in every generation though hidden from the world's eyes and sometimes our own. We are to labour in faith not always by sight. The kingdom has a life of its own because the life of God is in it. We are his workers; he gives the life and the growth through us (*1 Cor.* 3:5–9). We may always be optimistic.

59

The First Shall Be Last

He went on his way through towns and villages, teaching and journeying toward Jerusalem. [23] *And someone said to him, 'Lord, will those who are saved be few?' And he said to them,* [24] *'Strive to enter through the narrow door. For many, I tell you, will seek to enter and will not be able.* [25] *When once the master of the house has risen and shut the door, and you begin to stand outside and to knock at the door, saying, "Lord, open to us," then he will answer you, "I do not know where you come from."* [26] *Then you will begin to say, "We ate and drank in your presence, and you taught in our streets."* [27] *But he will say, "I tell you, I do not know where you come from. Depart from me, all you workers of evil!"* [28] *In that place there will be weeping and gnashing of teeth, when you see Abraham and Isaac and Jacob and all the prophets in the kingdom of God but you yourselves cast out.* [29] *And people will come from east and west, and from north and south, and recline at table in the kingdom of God.* [30] *And behold, some are last who will be first, and some are first who will be last'* (Luke 13:22–30).

Luke continues to set Jesus' teaching within the overall framework of his long, last journey to Jerusalem (verse 22; see *Luke* 9:51; 13:34; 18:31–32). His destiny lay in Jerusalem as the city of the great king where people stoned to death God's witnesses. Without his final sufferings that led to the cross nothing that Jesus said or did would have any lasting value. His cross-work is his great work.

AGONIZING OVER THE KINGDOM (verses 22–24)

Jesus replies to a question from the crowd. Perhaps impressed by the high standards of Jesus' view of discipleship an individual asks whether only a few people will be saved. (This is not the only time people had this reaction to Jesus' teaching, Luke 18:24–27)). But Jesus never answered hypothetical questions. He was more interested in the issues of the present and what people should do at that moment. Such is the urgency of the kingdom as Jesus understood it.

Jesus turns the question into a command. 'Don't worry about the number of the saved, make sure *you* are saved!' And the only way to make sure of that is by pressing through the narrow entrance to the kingdom, whatever it takes. The fact is that many (not the same as an overall majority) will make the attempt, but fail. 'Don't be among the "many"!' Jesus gives no reason for this failure but presumably the same sorts of reasons come into play here as Jesus gave in the parable of the sower (*Luke* 8:5–7, 11–14). Salvation is not for the half-hearted but for the single-minded (*Phil.* 3:13–14).

MAKING THE KINGDOM AN URGENT MATTER (verse 25–28)

Jesus relates the story of a band of travellers arriving late at night at a road-side inn, only to find the doors closed and the owner in bed. Trading on their claim to know the inn-keeper they appeal to him to let them in. To their astonishment and dismay the inn-keeper replies that he knows nothing of them and commands them to depart as evil-workers.

There is nothing subtle about the details of the story. They address directly the plight and falsehood of the people of Jesus' generation. They had no qualms about the judgement because they had known Jesus' presence in their streets and gatherings. Surely such a social contact with the Lord's Messiah would stand for them in the great day.

On the contrary, says Jesus, their spiritual apathy and disbelief in him made them the equivalent of open wrong-doers. They would receive no mercy in the day, but be cast out of his presence eternally.

They had chosen not to know Christ in his lifetime and so he would disown them.

The words of Jesus are a sober warning to make friends with him while we may. The nature of that relationship is all important. The way Jesus tells this episode also informs us that there is no further place for amendment of life beyond this life. The doors of the kingdom will finally be shut to impenitents, however much knowledge of a religious kind people may have had. It is not religion that will save us in that day but Jesus himself, known to us, and we to him, in this life.

BEING EXCLUDED FROM THE KINGDOM (verses 28–30)

Jesus depicts the kingdom as a vast congregation made up of people from the beginning of history and including people from every part of the inhabited world. Jesus discriminates sharply among the guests by naming the patriarchs and the prophets while excluding his immediate audience. Jesus does not mince his words which was his right as the Son of God. How shocking and utterly offensive his utterances must have been! Once again the divine reversal of human expectations is in evidence – the first will be last and the last first. Human pride is humbled and the humble poor believe, as Mary explained at the beginning (*Luke* 1:46–55).

But Jesus' words have a universal relevance. In his graphic description of the anguish of the eternal state of those excluded from his kingdom he speaks to all humankind. No one knew and spoke of the glories of heaven and the anguish and shame of hell more pointedly and poignantly than Jesus. He knew because he has seen them both.

Jesus' teaching is totally opposed to the religious relativism of the modern world where all religious faiths are equal and none must make exclusive claims to truth. But Jesus is the way, the truth and the life; no one can come to the Father except through him (*John* 14:6).

60

Jerusalem! Jerusalem!

At that very hour some Pharisees came and said to him, 'Get away from here, for Herod wants to kill you.' [32] *And he said to them, 'Go and tell that fox, "Behold, I cast out demons and perform cures today and tomorrow, and the third day I finish my course.* [33] *Nevertheless, I must go on my way today and tomorrow and the day following, for it cannot be that a prophet should perish away from Jerusalem."* [34] *O Jerusalem, Jerusalem, the city that kills the prophets and stones those who are sent to it! How often would I have gathered your children together as a hen gathers her brood under her wings, and you would not!* [35] *Behold, your house is forsaken. And I tell you, you will not see me until you say, "Blessed is he who comes in the name of the Lord!"'* (Luke 13:31–35).

The theme of this section is Jerusalem. It is both the goal of Jesus' journey (verses 31–33) and the subject of his lament (verses 34–35). The way Jesus focuses on Jerusalem teaches us that Jesus never lost sight of his destiny as the suffering Messiah and Servant-King of Israel.

WARNINGS AND FOREBODINGS (verses 31–33)

The chapter ends the way it began with people coming to Jesus to inform him of local events. The fact that Pharisees report to him makes unclear whether they want to save Jesus or to unsettle him. They warn Jesus about Herod's (Antipas, subject-ruler of northern Palestine) murderous intentions against Jesus. Unfazed, Jesus sends a reply. Herod is a fox in Jesus' estimation, treacherous and cowardly.

Jesus has a divine timetable to fulfil and will not be deflected from completing it, even in the face of death-threats (*John* 4:34). The reference to the 'third' day should not be taken here in relation to Jesus' resurrection but as a part of his figure of speech about a timetable to fulfil.

Jesus was profoundly conscious of a divine plan that bound him to act in certain ways and to visit certain places. In particular, he was bound to go to Jerusalem since that was the God-ordained place of execution of all his prophets and Jesus was one of them (*Matt*. 23:34–37).

I OFTEN WANTED TO ... BUT YOU WOULD NOT (verses 34–35)

True to that prophetic office Jesus utters a lament for the city of his destiny. He expresses the longing he has often had of drawing the people of Israel to himself, the way a mother hen gathers her chicks under her wings for protection and warmth (*Ezek*. 33:10–11). This is an unforgettable metaphor for the tenderness and compassion it conveys of the divine yearning for the salvation of the Jews and, by extension, for all humankind. By speaking in this way Jesus identifies himself in person as well as in sympathy with the God of Israel, the Creator of the ends of the earth.

This is one of the Bible's feminine metaphors for God, which tells us that God possesses and shares all that is most tender and caring in a mother's love. The Bible nowhere addresses God with feminine names or titles although it uses feminine metaphors as Jesus does here. God is beyond gender though the dominant images and titles for God are masculine (Father, Son). The ordering of the genders is an ontological one that expresses the riches of God's own being which is love and truth.

Jesus' words authenticate the double truth of divine and human freedom. Beyond this they teach the mystery of the divine freedom whereby God wishes something that he does not will. He longs for the salvation of the Jews yet he has not willed it in every case. The truth of human liberty to resist the expressed will of God is real. This is not the same as the traditional Calvinist-Arminian debate. Jesus' words carry us beyond the entrenched positions of that divide into the mystery of his relation to his human creatures.

One thing is clear – the strength of his passionate love for his lost creatures that they would return to him for their own eternal good. Jesus' words of longing are further spoken in the face of Israel's persistent rejection of the Lord and his messengers. This would include Jesus himself in the coming days, when the nation would crown their history of rejection by crucifying their anointed King.

Jesus' words have a special context in the history of Israel but by analogy we may apply them to the other cities and communities of the world. All are dear to him who has appointed their boundaries and their periods of prosperity (*Amos* 9:7, *Acts* 17:26–27). God has no pleasure in the death of the wicked anywhere, especially because their death is a self-inflicted punishment contrary to his express desire and invitation that they should live and not die (*Ezek*. 33:10–11).

Jesus' parting word is a promise (rather than a conditional prophecy). For the present Israel will be forsaken by God for her rejection of Jesus. Like an empty mansion the people of the Jews will live in isolation outside the blessings of the kingdom. In the future, however, God will revisit Israel who will welcome their Messiah in proper form. Centuries of divine rejection and human suffering will work a change of heart (*Deut*. 30:1–10).

Paul appears to pick up this theme of a spiritual restoration of Israel in the course of his argument in Romans chapter 11, although his words are open to a different interpretation. Jesus' words here are consistent with such a prospect of future spiritual regeneration for the Jewish people as a whole, sometime before the coming of Jesus. At that time the Jewish people will sing the words of Psalm 118 with evangelical fervour and faith, having come to know Jesus as their promised Messiah and Saviour.

Non-Jewish people may make the same mistake as the Jews of Jesus' day by insisting on their own free will, independently of God The most tragic human life is one that is empty of God's presence when it might have been otherwise. Yet still the Saviour waits, and where there is life there is hope through Christ.

61

Jesus' Tabletalk (2)

*One Sabbath, when he went to dine at the house of a ruler of the
Pharisees, they were watching him carefully. [2] And behold, there
was a man before him who had dropsy. [3] And Jesus responded to
the lawyers and Pharisees, saying, 'Is it lawful to heal on the
Sabbath, or not?' [4] But they remained silent. Then he took him
and healed him and sent him away. [5] And he said to them, 'Which
of you, having a son or an ox that has fallen into a well on a
Sabbath day, will not immediately pull him out?' [6] And they
could not reply to these things.*

*[7] Now he told a parable to those who were invited, when he
noticed how they chose the places of honour, saying to them,
[8] 'When you are invited by someone to a wedding feast, do not
sit down in a place of honour, lest someone more distinguished
than you be invited by him, [9] and he who invited you both will
come and say to you, "Give your place to this person," and then
you will begin with shame to take the lowest place. [10] But when
you are invited, go and sit in the lowest place, so that when your
host comes he may say to you, "Friend, move up higher." Then
you will be honoured in the presence of all who sit at table with
you. [11] For everyone who exalts himself will be humbled, and he
who humbles himself will be exalted.'*

*[12] He said also to the man who had invited him, 'When you give
a dinner or a banquet, do not invite your friends or your brothers
or your relatives or rich neighbours, lest they also invite you in
return and you be repaid. [13] But when you give a feast, invite
the poor, the crippled, the lame, the blind, [14] and you will be
blessed, because they cannot repay you. You will be repaid at
the resurrection of the just.'*

[15] When one of those who reclined at table with him heard these
things, he said to him, 'Blessed is everyone who will eat bread in
the kingdom of God!' [16] But he said to him, 'A man once gave a
great banquet and invited many. [17] And at the time for the
banquet he sent his servant to say to those who had been invited,
"Come, for everything is now ready." [18] But they all alike began
to make excuses. The first said to him, 'I have bought a field,
and I must go out and see it. Please have me excused.'
[19] And another said, "I have bought five yoke of oxen, and I go
to examine them. Please have me excused." [20] And another said,
"I have married a wife, and therefore I cannot come." [21] So the
servant came and reported these things to his master. Then the
master of the house became angry and said to his servant, "Go
out quickly to the streets and lanes of the city, and bring in the
poor and crippled and blind and lame." [22] And the servant said,
"Sir, what you commanded has been done, and still there is
room." [23] And the master said to the servant, "Go out to the
highways and hedges and compel people to come in, that my house
may be filled. [24] For I tell you, none of those men who were invited
shall taste my banquet'" (Luke 14:1–24).

Jesus was no recluse. Even when one of the leaders of the Pharisees (verse 1) invited him to dinner, he accepted and went. After all, they too needed to hear the message of the kingdom. Luke picks out four cameos from the dinner-party that would have lasted some hours. There is first of all a healing (verses 1–6), then a parable to the guests (verses 7–11), followed by a word to the host (verses 12–14), rounded off by another parable about being invited to the heavenly banquet (verses 15–24). The context that links all these pieces is a social gathering.

A HEALING (verses 1–6)

Jesus was always under scrutiny (verse 1). The religious rulers and their henchmen acted like not-so-secret police in a totalitarian state. They were desperate to maintain their control over the people by enforcing the strict rules of their legalistic interpretations. Theirs was an oppressive theocracy in which the Sabbath day was highly regulated; acts of healing were treated as work that transgressed the commandment.

Suddenly Jesus came face to face with a man suffering from excess fluid in his body. Whether this man was planted by the Pharisees or not they sat in judgement on Jesus anyway. But Jesus seized the initiative by asking them the first of two questions. He goes straight to the heart of the matter – is it lawful to heal or not on the Sabbath day? Either the Pharisees lacked the courage of their convictions, or they wanted Jesus to incriminate himself, so they chose not to answer.

Jesus healed the man and then sent him away. Now Jesus posed his second question to his opponents. Did they not, on the Sabbath day, pull a child or a beast of burden out of a well if it had fallen in there? Of course they did, because in a situation of need they did not hesitate to help. In the same way Jesus was helping someone in need of healing that he could give.

Jesus showed his lordship over human lives by never losing control of the situation; he exposed the inconsistency of the Pharisees by showing that they practised one thing but demanded something different from Jesus; he appealed to natural morality rooted in human decency for guidance in a moral conflict situation. It can never be wrong to do good especially when it is in a person's power to help another person. It would be wrong to refuse (*James* 4:17).

ADVICE AND GUESTS (verses 7–11)

Jesus was a keen observer of human beings. In Jewish banquets the guests were arranged in positions that put them nearer or further away from the host, depending on their social status or the honour shown them by the host. By choosing the higher positions for themselves, without being placed there by the host, the guests showed they thought this was the honourable position they deserved or that this was how they wanted others to see them.

Jesus points out the unnecessary risk that they took in doing so, because someone more important than they might arrive and be given their position near the host. Then they would lose face by having to get up and take a position lower down the line of guests. It is far better to be publicly honoured by being called to a higher position than the reverse.

In giving this example from real life Jesus is not encouraging people to be falsely humble. Jesus' point is the virtue of humility, a leading attitude in his kingdom where the childlike and the humble are honoured and the proudly self-righteous shut out (*Luke* 16:15; 18:16–17; 22:24–27). Those who have been too proud to humble themselves before Christ will be publicly humbled by God and those whom the world has treated with disdain for Christ's sake will be publicly exalted (verse 11, see again Luke 13:29–30).

ADVICE FOR THE HOST (verses 12–14)

Having addressed the guests Jesus turns now to the host. He too had acted poorly. How relatively easy and tempting to give a dinner for close friends, family members, or rich neighbours! Guests like these are quite capable of returning the favour. How much more costly and genuine, says Jesus, to invite people with no social connections, the poor, disadvantaged and ordinary! They cannot pay back in kind, so they are the real test of a person's generosity.

Once more Jesus opens up the underlying issue – what motivates a person's actions? People make use of other people for their own ends instead of making themselves available for them? Jesus is not discouraging acts of hospitality towards influential or well-to-do friends. The ethics of the kingdom is all about serving others in love (*Gal.* 5:13–14), whoever the other may be. This is the heart of the gospel rooted squarely in Jesus' own example who served us in love all the way to the cross and back again (*Mark* 10:43–45, *Rom.* 15:2–3, 8).

Jesus assures those who lose themselves in his service that they will be rewarded by his Father at the resurrection (verse 14). This is meant as a back-up reason for persisting in goodness since a calculating spirit is exactly what Jesus opposes here. Goodness should be voluntary to be good. But Jesus wants us to know that the heavenly Father notices every effort made for him, which he will lavishly reward at the resurrection. Nothing done for Jesus will ever be lost (read Luke 16:9 for the same lesson).

ANOTHER PARABLE (verses 15–24)

The final part of this banquet cycle contains another parable. Jesus mentioning the resurrection triggers a pious remark from one of the guests (verse 15). Whether this remark was sincere or an attempt to win praise is unclear. Either way, it draws from Jesus a highly developed parable about the kingdom of God.

The kingdom is like a great banquet to which many people are invited. Sadly, those first invited find other things to do, so the nobleman urges his servants to carry invitations throughout the town so that his hall may be filled. When this still leaves room he commissions his servants to go out again, this time into the rural parts to compel people to join the great man's feast.

In the context of Jesus' ministry the parable is a potted history of the kingdom and how it fares in this world. The first guests are the Jews of Jesus' day who refuse his invitation to come in. When the Jews refuse the kingdom the Lord turns it over to the Gentile peoples of all ranks and places so that his hall may be alive with laughter and friendship.

The overriding impression is the large heartedness of the nobleman who above everything else wants his hall to be filled. He welcomes all who are willing to come, without discriminating on the ground of class, age, gender, or nationality. This is a great parable about God's mission to the world motivated by infinite love and longing for the salvation of people everywhere. The parable also supports the idea of enthusiastic even aggressive mission by those who have already entered the kingdom and enjoy the gospel feast.

The parable suggests a number of related truths.

- The guests are invited to come as they are because everything is ready (verse 17). They do not have to make any preparations but simply respond positively to the invitation. In the same way God has reconciled the world to himself in Christ so that people need only respond in person to that great event (*2 Cor.* 5:18–21)
- The kingdom invitation is turned down by many people who are invited (verses 18–20). They offer face-saving excuses but not one of them is valid in view of the nobleman's kindness. In the same way unbelief is never justified but earns God's wrath (*John* 3:36).

- All kinds of people are included in the gospel invitation (verse 21). Modern societies are no longer homogeneous but composed of many communities based on differences. Yet Christ is the great unifier who reaches out to every human group because he alone can meet their deepest needs (*Luke* 15:1–2).
- The man is committed to filling his banquet hall (verses 22–23). In the same way God has loved the whole world desiring that people everywhere should come to know the truth and be saved (*1 Tim.* 2:3–4; *2 Pet.* 3:9). We dare put no restrictions on his desire for people to be saved (*John* 3:16).
- The kingdom invitation may be refused (verse 24). When a person rejects the gospel offer others receive the invitation instead. Rejecting the gospel-invitation is such a short-sighted response that people will live to regret it (*Heb.* 12:15–17).

The parable of the great banquet publishes God's gracious intention of saving men and women. He does this through the efforts of those who have already accepted the gospel invitation. The parable is a missionary one that encourages Christ's followers to entertain the highest hopes in evangelistic work. The heavenly Father is content with nothing less than the filling of his house with repentant and believing men and women. What an incentive this parable is to untiring missionary outreach in every generation and to every people-group on earth!

62

What Will It Cost to Follow Jesus?

Now great crowds accompanied him, and he turned and said to them, [26] 'If anyone comes to me and does not hate his own father and mother and wife and children and brothers and sisters, yes, and even his own life, he cannot be my disciple. [27] Whoever does not bear his own cross and come after me cannot be my disciple. [28] For which of you, desiring to build a tower, does not first sit down and count the cost, whether he has enough to complete it? [29] Otherwise, when he has laid a foundation and is not able to finish, all who see it begin to mock him, [30] saying, "This man began to build and was not able to finish." [31] Or what king, going out to encounter another king in war, will not sit down first and deliberate whether he is able with ten thousand to meet him who comes against him with twenty thousand? [32] And if not, while the other is yet a great way off, he sends a delegation and asks for terms of peace. [33] So therefore, any one of you who does not renounce all that he has cannot be my disciple.
[34] Salt is good, but if salt has lost its taste, how shall its saltiness be restored? [35] It is of no use either for the soil or for the manure pile. It is thrown away. He who has ears to hear, let him hear' (Luke 14:25–35).

Luke leaves the banquet scene and returns to the crowds in the open air. Jesus chooses to make crystal clear what following him entails. The passage ends where it begins, with the uncompromising terms of absolute loyalty to Jesus himself (verses 26 and 33).

HOLY HATRED (verses 26–27)

Jesus wants to shock would-be followers into a sober acceptance of what discipleship demands. He deliberately uses the language of exaggeration (hyperbole) to produce this effect (see Matthew 5:38–42 for another example). If people take Jesus' words literally they will find themselves in conflict with biblical teaching elsewhere (*Eph.* 6:1–2), as well as Jesus' own teaching about universal love (*Luke* 6:27–36). What Jesus means is that those who follow him must place him far above even the most dear, natural human relationships. Our attitude to family must be like 'hate', compared to the primary love that we give to him. In biblical usage 'loving' when contrasted with 'hating' is a way of expressing preference for one person over another, not actual hatred (*Mal.* 1:2–3).

In the same way, just to enforce the point, Jesus speaks of the necessity of cross-bearing. His own way of life consisted of unashamed witness to the truth and service for the kingdom of God, even when that brought him into conflict with the authorities and led to misunderstanding. People must commit to the same goals in following him; they must take up their own cross every day and be faithful to him (*Luke* 9:23–26).

Speaking in these terms Jesus is claiming the same total allegiance to himself that God requires (*Luke* 10:26–27). This is an implicit claim to be God and equal with God. If anyone else said this it would be blasphemy, satanic pride. But from Jesus' lips these words come naturally, confirming the rest of the truth about him. Only a man who is God could honestly make these claims and expect them to be met. Of all others Jesus could say, 'You are from below; you are from this world.' But of himself he said, 'I am from above; I am not of this world' (*John* 8:23).

TWO ILLUSTRATIONS (verses 28–32)

Jesus was a great artist with words, taking his illustrations from everyday life in first century Palestine. He paints two pictures, first from building work, then from the art of war. In the first story a man decides to build a tower (for storage of some kind or protection). He calculates first whether he can afford the project. Otherwise he faces public humiliation by always being remembered and referred to as the man who began but could not finish. In the second story Jesus imagines a local chieftain engaging an enemy's army. First he calculates his chances of winning. Otherwise he will immediately open peace talks to secure a settlement.

In the same way, those who want to set out on a life of discipleship ought first to calculate whether they have the stamina and commitment for such an undertaking. Many have started off on this path only to become casualties (*Luke* 8:13–14).

HANDING EVERYTHING OVER (verse 33)

Finally, Jesus repeats his demands for all or nothing. Following Jesus means being willing, if need be, to lose everything we possess for his sake. Jesus does not intend people to sell or give away all they own to take a vow of self-imposed poverty. What he requires is a deep attitude of detachment from material wealth, so as to possess an inner freedom to love him unreservedly.

> All to Jesus I surrender,
> All to him I freely give;
> I will ever love and trust him,
> In his presence daily live.
> All to Jesus I surrender,
> Lord, I give myself to thee;
> Fill me with thy love and power,
> Let thy blessings fall on me.
>
> *J. W. Van de Venter*

KEEPING FRESH (verses 34–35)

In the hot, desert climate of Jesus' homeland salt was sprinkled on food to keep it fresh and pure. In the same way disciples of Jesus need to keep themselves fresh and pure in the spiritual and moral climate around them if they are going to have a wholesome and redemptive influence on the world. Otherwise disciples may bear the name without living by the reality. People must do the truth as well as know it. A Christian who has lost the freshness of a daily lived faith is virtually good for nothing (*Mark* 9:50–51).

There is only one way to keep or regain personal integrity and usefulness. This is by keeping close to Jesus himself, the sole source of spiritual vitality (*Luke* 12:35–44).

63

God's Joy at Finding Lost Things

Now the tax collectors and sinners were all drawing near to hear him. [2] *And the Pharisees and the scribes grumbled, saying, 'This man receives sinners and eats with them.'*
[3] *So he told them this parable:* [4] *'What man of you, having a hundred sheep, if he has lost one of them, does not leave the ninety-nine in the open country, and go after the one that is lost, until he finds it?* [5] *And when he has found it, he lays it on his shoulders, rejoicing.* [6] *And when he comes home, he calls together his friends and his neighbours, saying to them, "Rejoice with me, for I have found my sheep that was lost."* [7] *Just so, I tell you, there will be more joy in heaven over one sinner who repents than over ninety-nine righteous persons who need no repentance.*
[8] *Or what woman, having ten silver coins, if she loses one coin, does not light a lamp and sweep the house and seek diligently until she finds it?* [9] *And when she has found it, she calls together her friends and neighbours, saying, "Rejoice with me, for I have found the coin that I had lost."* [10] *Just so, I tell you, there is joy before the angels of God over one sinner who repents'* (Luke 15:1–10).

Luke 15 must be one of the best known parts of the teaching of Jesus. The chapter is made up of three stories, the first two making way for the third, which is more developed. The first two parables are quite alike in their length, story-line, and lessons, while the third can stand by itself. Because of this similarity we will take the first two stories together as one.

LOST AND FOUND (verses 1–10)

Luke tells us why Jesus was telling these stories (verses 1–2). The Jewish leaders had been faulting him for socialising with people they considered ritually and morally unclean, mainly promiscuous women and tax-collectors. The truth of the matter was that these kinds of people actively sought Jesus out and were the most responsive to his message. They could tell that Jesus was authentic, that he knew what he was talking about, and that he really cared about them. They sensed none of these things in their religious leaders.

The religious leaders, on the other hand, had mentally divided society up into two groups – the sinful and, people like themselves, the righteous. In doing this they had become insufferably proud of their religious faith, being of the opinion that they were superior to other people (*Luke* 18:9–14). What they had failed to see was that in God's eyes there are no naturally holy people; everyone needs to become humble by turning to God with moral sorrow and trusting in God's mercies in Jesus.

There are four valuable lessons from these two parables.

BEING LOST (verses 4, 8)

Firstly, there is the condition of being lost. A sheep was lost and so was a coin. In each case something had lost its bearings. This resulted in the sheep being in danger and cut off from the security of the fold; it resulted in the coin being missed and unused. In both cases Jesus was illustrating how God sees our condition as men and women made in his image but living decentred lives, outside the security of his reconciling love. In the same way the prophet Isaiah described the human condition (*Isa*. 53:6); more candidly Paul informs us that human lives are lived without God in alienation and foolishness (*Eph*. 4:18).

THE SEEKING GOD (verses 4, 8)

Secondly, there is the seeking God. The shepherd goes out alone into the desert to seek and find the one lost sheep; the woman turns her house upside down to retrieve the one coin lost. In similar fashion the God of creation and Lord of history has come into the world in Jesus to seek and to save the lost men and women (*Luke* 19:10). This is what he promised he would do, ages before (*Ezek*. 34:11–24). At infinite cost he has undertaken a personal rescue mission. The Lord God seeks for us as individuals, as the story of Zacchaeus makes so clear, for each of us is unique and precious to God. He knows us and calls us by name (*1 Tim*. 1:15).

PERSONAL REPENTANCE (verses 7, 10)

Thirdly, there is the need for repentance. In these two parables, unlike the third, human repentance is overshadowed by divine searching, through God acting in love in Christ. Repentance is highlighted at the close of each of the two parables. Repentance is about a change of mind and heart in relation to God and being sorrowful for sins done against God and for a sinning heart. Normally Luke links repentance with forgiveness, most clearly shown in the third story where the son repents and the father forgives (verses 17–24). In the mystery of God's grace, repentance awakens a belief in pardon, while pardon awakens true repentance (*Luke* 24:47).

THE JOY OF SALVATION (verses 6–7, 9–10)

Fourthly, there is the joy of someone being found and forgiven. This is another of Luke's major themes, an indispensable sign of salvation in Christ. But whose is the joy? Certainly the one found and forgiven experiences a heavenly joy, something that flows from loving, trusting and expecting Christ (*1 Pet*. 1:8). But remarkably, the joy expressed in these parables is the joy of heaven, of angels and of God, at the recovery of a single human being to the fold and enfold of the Father's care. Nothing could signal more clearly and movingly how important to God and the citizens of heaven, is the recovery of fallen men and women. Heaven will be and already is, a community of joy-filled people who have come to know the treasures of God's grace and the wonders of his love in Jesus.

Jesus managed to mix with the people of the world without condoning their sin, or being contaminated by it. Too often his supporters have moved with the wrong crowd, among the religious hierarchy, instead of among the needy, lost and seeking.

Do you share God's joy and that of the angels, in seeking and seeing lost people finding and being found by him? You can only do this as you share first in his generous love for them as precious individuals.

64

The Man with Two Sons

And he said, 'There was a man who had two sons. [12] And the younger of them said to his father, "Father, give me the share of property that is coming to me." And he divided his property between them. [13] Not many days later, the younger son gathered all he had and took a journey into a far country, and there he squandered his property in reckless living. [14] And when he had spent everything, a severe famine arose in that country, and he began to be in need. [15] So he went and hired himself out to one of the citizens of that country, who sent him into his fields to feed pigs. [16] And he was longing to be fed with the pods that the pigs ate, and no one gave him anything.

[17] But when he came to himself, he said, "How many of my father's hired servants have more than enough bread, but I perish here with hunger! [18] I will arise and go to my father, and I will say to him, 'Father, I have sinned against heaven and before you. [19] I am no longer worthy to be called your son. Treat me as one of your hired servants.'" [20] And he arose and came to his father. But while he was still a long way off, his father saw him and felt compassion, and ran and embraced him and kissed him. [21] And the son said to him, "Father, I have sinned against heaven and before you. I am no longer worthy to be called your son."

[22] But the father said to his servants, "Bring quickly the best robe, and put it on him, and put a ring on his hand, and shoes on his feet. [23] And bring the fattened calf and kill it, and let us eat and celebrate. [24] For this my son was dead, and is alive again; he was lost, and is found." And they began to celebrate.

25 Now his older son was in the field, and as he came and drew
near to the house, he heard music and dancing. 26 And he called
one of the servants and asked what these things meant. 27 And
he said to him, "Your brother has come, and your father has killed
the fattened calf, because he has received him back safe and
sound." 28 But he was angry and refused to go in. His father came
out and entreated him, 29 but he answered his father, "Look, these
many years I have served you, and I never disobeyed your
command, yet you never gave me a young goat, that I might
celebrate with my friends. 30 But when this son of yours came,
who has devoured your property with prostitutes, you killed the
fattened calf for him!" 31 And he said to him, "Son, you are
always with me, and all that is mine is yours. 32 It was fitting to
celebrate and be glad, for this your brother was dead, and is alive;
he was lost, and is found.'" (Luke 15:11–32).

The third parable Jesus told is the best known of all three. Throughout the church's history it has been admired and found helpful by countless people, even being the subject of religious art. It is full of profound insights into human beings and the way repentance and salvation work in human experience. It proves that Jesus was a master story-teller and perfectly understood the entire human condition. Although the parable has been strongly connected with one son ('the parable of the prodigal son') it is more accurately called the parable of the father who had two sons.

THE YOUNGER SON (verses 11–19)

There was a father with two sons. Normally Jewish sons would stay with their father and serve under him in the family business, waiting until he died before inheriting a share of the family assets. In this story the younger son brought forward his claim on his inheritance, no doubt deeply wounding the father in doing so. His attitude showed that he cared more about his inheritance than about his father. Nor did he choose to work his part of the property. Instead he asked for it to be realised as capital, then immediately left home. How broken the heart of the father must have been in the face of his son's selfishness and insensitivity! Already there are spiritual lessons for us in considering our dominant attitude to God our Creator – one no less selfish and ungrateful than that of the prodigal (*Rom.* 1:21, 25).

The younger son put as much distance between himself and the father as possible, by travelling to a country far away from home. By choosing a far country the younger son was choosing the life of paganism over the privileges of the covenant people, like any rebellious Christian young person (*2 Chron.* 6:32–33). To begin with he enjoyed himself in the far country with its bright lights and entertainment, spending his money freely, indulging his senses to the full (verse 30). Generally he was glad to be free of the restraints and service of living with his father.

But times changed. The son burned up his whole inheritance just at a time that economic recession was falling on that country. Jobs were scarce and none of his former friends, so ready to share his fortune when he was rich and generous, would help him now that he was the one in need. In crisis mode he hired himself out to a local farmer to do the most menial jobs, like feeding pigs. As a Jew this would have been distasteful and ritually defiling work, reminding him every day how low he had fallen. He even reached the point where he envied the beasts because they were eating while he went hungry.

How attractive the far country of the world appears when first people set out for it, often when they are young, in pursuit of its dreams and virtual pleasures. They begin by celebrating with other kindred spirits, exhilarating in the freedom of being their own person and following their own illusions, free from the moral restraints of serious religion. Many young people in the West today share in the relativistic outlook and behaviour of the prodigal son, keen to choose their own paths by experiencing the options that the world offers. But boom times never last, dreams fade, friends desert and people discover for themselves the painful realities of a fallen world. The prodigal son's is everyone's story to some degree, whether we have lived far away from God or not.

But a turning-point is reached – the younger son came to himself when he remembered his father and his true home and realised that all he had aspired to had left him empty. He compared his current situation with that of his father's servants and knew which was better. No longer gripped by self-interest he accepted the need for change. He faced his responsibilities, expressed himself eager and willing to make amends to his father and to God. He decided there and then that he would go back and throw himself on his father's kindness. He would offer to be a servant of his father instead of a son. In this way he hoped to get his life together again by rediscovering his roots in his father's home.

In a similar way sin has decentred us from God and our 'home' in him. We can only reorientate ourselves when we return to God our Creator and Father in Christ. And this will only happen when we face up to our life story of disobedience as empty of purpose and centred on self.

THE FATHER (verses 20–24)

Just as the younger son represents the wanderlust of sin in every heart, the father represents the God and Father of Jesus in his patience and love to lost men and women. In view of the son's rebellion, the father would have been within his rights to disinherit him forthwith, saying, 'I knew it would come to this!', or 'You have had your share and you can expect nothing more!' On the contrary, the father had never forgotten his erring son. As a result, the day his son appeared on the horizon the father immediately ran to welcome him back, not in reproachful coldness but with the warmest reunion. In spite of the son's humble protestations that he should be taken on as a hired servant, having forfeited his sonship, the father calls for a celebration. He kits out his son in the best clothes, sends out an invitation to friends and relations and organises a banquet. The father is ecstatic about the occasion – the wanderer has returned, the son feared dead has come back to life!

This is a truly wonderful representation of the love of God for the world and especially for all who come home again to him. Even before we begin to think about him we learn that he has always been thinking about us; in returning to him we discover that he has already begun the journey to meet us; in confessing our sinfulness he covers us with his love, forgiveness and generosity through Jesus. He refuses to disown us; instead he bestows on us a new kind of sonship; he gives himself to us in an eternal covenant of friendship and love; and in him we find our eternal home, true joy and freedom, the end of the search for truth and reality, personal purity and a future hope. Being dead we come alive (*Eph.* 2:5, *Col.* 2:13). Saving us this way in Christ, his mercy triumphs gloriously over judgement at the cross (*James* 2:13, *1 John* 4:10–16)).

THE OLDER SON AND BROTHER (verses 25–32)

But all is not well on the father's farm. There is another son and brother, who enters the story for the first time, just as his younger brother returns. He has been working in the fields, just as he had done every day for all the time his younger brother has been away from home. Music from the house catches his attention as he makes his way home at the end of another working day. He asks a servant what is going on, only to learn that his younger brother has returned and his father is celebrating the event and spoiling his long lost son.

This is more than the elder brother can stomach, so he angrily refuses to go in and join the celebrations. The father goes out for him, just as he had gone out earlier for his younger son. The father's invitation to join the festivities sparks an outburst of pent-up resentment against his father and his younger brother. He boasts his own record of loyal service over many years, a record unblemished by insubordination. He criticises his father because in all those years the father had never thrown a party for him or his friends, yet as soon as this wandering and profligate son of the father (verse 30, 'this son of yours') returns, no expense is too great to celebrate the occasion.

Mildly the father reminds his older son of two important truths. Firstly, everything now belonged to the elder son. This was because the younger son had forced a distribution of the property before the father died. So the elder son was in possession of his inheritance no less than his younger brother. Secondly, all along the elder son had access to the father's presence, because he was always there with him. In truth, it was the elder son's fault if he had never availed himself of this wonderful opportunity of the father's company. The younger son had denied himself the pleasure of his father's love, but now had discovered it at great personal cost. It was right for the father to celebrate the prodigal's return, because it was like a resurrection of a member of the family.

The story tells itself, but what is its lasting theme and meaning? When Jesus told it the two sons represented symbolically (the younger son) the morally loose and marginalised people of Jewish society, such as the sexually promiscuous and the traitorous tax-collectors and (the elder brother) the religiously correct, such as the religious leaders and their legal experts (verses 1 and 2). Those who had lived like the younger son, also like him, responded to Jesus' presence and his invitation to return to the Father's house. Those who lived like the elder brother, also like him, took offence at Jesus' message and ministry by refusing to rejoice at the return of the prodigals of society, choosing to remain aloof from the arrival of God's kingdom. They preferred to lose everything rather than to admit that they were wrong.

What of the parable today? There are two classes of people still, right across societies, the many who live their lives self-indulgently, determined to get everything from life while they can. 'Let us eat, drink and be merry, because tomorrow we die' is their slogan. The others live more moral lives, respecting some code of practice and often taking some pride in doing so; they think of themselves as being good enough.

As in the parable it is often individuals from the first group that respond more readily to the invitation and claims of Jesus. Those from the second group are deceived into believing in their own moral respectability and worth, denying their need of repentance for the heavenly Father's blessing.

Perhaps we might take note of a third group, represented by the younger son in the return stage of his journey – penitent, reconciled and restored to his father's love and service At that stage he represents every true disciple of Jesus, who has come to experience new life, purpose and power for living from God in Jesus Christ.

Where do you see yourself in Jesus' parable?

65

Learning from the World

He also said to the disciples, 'There was a rich man who had a
manager, and charges were brought to him that this man was
wasting his possessions. [2] *And he called him and said to him,*
"What is this that I hear about you? Turn in the account of your
management, for you can no longer be manager." [3] *And the*
manager said to himself, "What shall I do, since my master is
taking the management away from me? I am not strong enough
to dig, and I am ashamed to beg. [4] *I have decided what to do, so*
that when I am removed from management, people may receive
me into their houses." [5] *So, summoning his master's debtors one*
by one, he said to the first, "How much do you owe my master?"
[6] *He said, "A hundred measures of oil." He said to him, "Take*
your bill, and sit down quickly and write fifty." [7] *Then he said*
to another, "And how much do you owe?" He said, "A hundred
measures of wheat." He said to him, "Take your bill, and write
eighty." [8] *The master commended the dishonest manager for his*
shrewdness. For the sons of this world are more shrewd in dealing
with their own generation than the sons of light. [9] *And I tell you,*
make friends for yourselves by means of unrighteous wealth, so
that when it fails they may receive you into the eternal dwellings.
[10] *One who is faithful in a very little is also faithful in much, and*
one who is dishonest in a very little is also dishonest in much. [11] *If*
then you have not been faithful in the unrighteous wealth, who will
entrust to you the true riches? [12] *And if you have not been faithful in*
that which is another's, who will give you that which is your own?
[13] *No servant can serve two masters, for either he will hate the one*
and love the other, or he will be devoted to the one and despise the
other. You cannot serve God and money' (Luke 16:1–13).

In this chapter Jesus' special interest in wealth comes up in the form of two major parables. Not all the details are clear in their meaning and there are many interpretations of these parables available, but the main line of each is clear. It is always easier to understand Jesus' parables than to apply them honestly to people's lives, yet he always told his parables with a view to changing people's attitudes, values and behaviour (e.g. Luke 10:37).

THE SHREWD MANAGER (verses 1–7)

The first parable is about a manager of the estate of a wealthy landowner. In running his master's business the steward enjoys a fair degree of discretionary power. He is going to put this to good use. A complaint, however, is brought against this man, whether rightly or unfairly we are not told. Unfortunately for him his master believes the report, summons his manager, tells him he is dismissed and requires him, before leaving, to draw up the books.

Now follows a soliloquy in which the manager discusses with himself what course of action he will follow (verses 3–4). He is not trained as a labourer and he is above begging. So he uses those discretionary powers to ingratiate himself with his lord's debtors, with a view to securing his own future.

This is the point in the story where many readers run into difficulty – the action of the manager in reducing the sums of debt owed to his master seems fraudulent. Perhaps the best way round this difficulty is to understand that on top of the amounts owed in cases of public debt managers had the liberty to add their own commission. If that is the case here, the action of the manager can be read in a new light. He is not so much cheating his master as disadvantaging himself. In the first case he cancels his own commission that amounted to fifty per cent, in the second case twenty per cent. By acting in this way the manager cleverly created a win-win situation in which he helped his master's debtors clear their debts and did himself a favour by putting them in his debt.

On this reading of the story we can understand why Jesus could commend the manager for his shrewdness but not any dishonesty he might have been guilty of.

THE MAIN POINT (verses 8–9)

It is possible to close the parable in the middle of verse 8, understanding 'the lord' as referring to the lord in the parable. It is perhaps preferable to take this as referring to the Lord Jesus (e.g. *Luke* 10:1) who now begins to take over from the parable.

There are three things the story is not saying. Firstly, the Lord Jesus does not condemn in itself the profit motive and margin in business practice. This does not make him a modern capitalist, however. Secondly, Jesus says nothing that would excuse dishonest dealings in business or advertising. He commends the manager for being foresighted not unethical (although he is called 'dishonest' in verse 8 this may only be harking back to the unfounded report about him in verse 1). Thirdly, Jesus is not recommending selfish motives under the guise of generous trade practices. He teaches a principled use of money that will incidentally also serve a Christian's own interests (*Matt.* 19:21).

So what is the main lesson? – that believers in Jesus (the children of light) should learn from the world (the children of this age) that money should be wisely invested. For worldly people this means investing wealth for short-term interests; for believers this should mean investing wealth for long-term interests. Jesus' parable is an indictment of any of his followers who use their investments the way the world does – for private needs, comforts and enjoyments only. Wealth falls under the demands of discipleship (verse 33). Jesus wants his followers to rejoice when he comes, at the way they handled this world's goods – for the kingdom, not only for themselves.

Quite literally disciples can achieve what the shrewd manager did, by using their wealth to make friends who will testify on their behalf when Jesus returns (*3 John* 5–6). In this way there will be richly provided for them an entrance into the eternal kingdom (*2 Pet.* 1:10–11). The assumption is that the Lord will reward personally all who were generous donors for his sake.

Will there be those who will come forward in that day to thank God for your investment of money in their interests – such as setting up trusts, making regular donations, funding Bible translation and distribution, paying travel, financing seminars, conferences and international speakers, helping provide a local pastor's livelihood, giving Christian literature, donating to the poor and so on?

FURTHER EXPLANATIONS (verses 10–13)

Jesus clarifies his meaning further through a simple principle (verse 10), a pair of rhetorical questions (verse 11–12) and a general statement (verse 13).

- (Verse 10) The test of character is often in little things. A reliable and organized person will be so in small business as well as big; so will a dishonest, self-serving person. In the context of the parable 'the very little things' stand for material wealth while the 'much' is the higher wealth of the post-resurrection world. The quality of a believer's service here will have a bearing on the type of service he will be entrusted with then (*Luke* 19:12–19).
- (Verses 11 and 12) Money and its use is a test of spiritual character. If people cannot manage earthly resources why would God entrust them with heavenly riches? And if they could not manage the wealth that God gave them here and now why would he give them possessions of their own in the future kingdom?
- (Verse 13) Jesus warns against a divided heart in this matter of money. Just as a servant cannot be loyal to two masters at the same time so his followers cannot love God and wealth together (*Matt.* 6:24). Either God or money will have first place in their hearts, whatever they tell themselves or pretend otherwise.

Luke's Gospel has a lot to say about wealth and its management, but Jesus nowhere denounces wealth in itself. Instead he constantly puts people on their guard against its corrosive effects on their moral values and priorities in living (*1 Tim.* 6:6–10, 17–19). In Jesus' parable wealth is an opportunity for investment for the kingdom now and our own interests in the day of Christ's coming (*Matt.* 25: 37–40).

66

The Law and the Kingdom

The Pharisees, who were lovers of money, heard all these things,
and they ridiculed him. [15] *And he said to them, 'You are those*
who justify yourselves before men, but God knows your hearts.
For what is exalted among men is an abomination in the sight of
God.
[16] *The Law and the Prophets were until John; since then the good*
news of the kingdom of God is preached, and everyone forces his
way into it. [17] *But it is easier for heaven and earth to pass away*
than for one dot of the Law to become void.
[18] *Everyone who divorces his wife and marries another commits*
adultery, and he who marries a woman divorced from her
husband commits adultery' (Luke 16:14–18).

These verses contain miscellaneous sayings of Jesus. Verse fourteen provides the context in which these sayings should be understood. The Pharisees who loved money reacted against all that Jesus had just taught (verses 1–13). Because Jesus did not affirm them the Pharisees strongly disliked him (verse 14, see *Luke* 23:35 for the use of the same word expressing a violent reaction).

Because the Pharisees stood for a religion that held firmly to the letter of the Old Testament and went beyond it, Jesus here deftly handles a number of relevant topics such as self-righteousness, the passing of the old era with the coming of the new, and divorce.

RELIGION OF THE HEART (verses 14–15)

Jesus exposes the false bottom on which the Pharisees built their religious faith in practice. They were so convinced of their own acceptability that they despised other people without any pangs of conscience (*Luke* 18:11–12). Their righteousness was built around their disciplined performance of external rituals but Jesus exposes the emptiness and uncleanness of their hearts within. What they made much of, God thought little of; what he said was important they neglected (*Luke* 11:37–44). The Pharisees could impress people but never God who saw them for what they were – stiff and proud sinners.

Biblical religion starts with forgiveness and inaugurates a new heart and life regime. Without this there can be no pleasing God (*1 Sam*. 15:22). Christianity is about love that springs from a pure heart, sincere faith and a good conscience (*1 Tim*. 1:5). Only in Jesus can we find these and maintain them.

THE OLD AND THE NEW (verse 16)

The Pharisees were entrenched in the teaching of Moses and the Prophets that was inscribed in the Old Testament and interpreted in their oral tradition. They were not open to God's new revelation and salvation act. They were prisoners of their traditions and prejudices. Jesus opened a new account by establishing the kingdom of God (*Mark* 1:14–5). The kingdom does not allow people to remain in their settled ideas or behaviour. On the contrary the kingdom in Jesus requires people to make every effort to enter it. At the same time, the kingdom affirms the word of God written in the Old Testament. 'The new lies concealed in the old; the old lies open in the new' (Augustine). Christians ought not to disparage their Jewish roots, nor should they claim that Christianity is a wholly new religion. Jesus qualifies and adds to the old without replacing it.

DIVORCE AND ADULTERY (verse 18)

As an example of the way in which the new order of Jesus connects with the old, Jesus cites the case of divorce. According to Deuteronomy 24 (verses 1–4) a man could divorce his wife but never remarry her after she had married another. The grounds of such divorce are not made clear but the woman must receive a bill of divorce as protection at law. Elsewhere Jesus explains that the law of divorce was a divine concession in a sinful world (*Matt.* 19:3–9).

But divorce was not part of God's original plan and this is Jesus' point. Elsewhere Jesus allows for divorce in the case of sexual infidelity leading up to, or after, marriage (*Matt.* 5:31–32; 19:9. See further the case of Joseph and Mary (*Matt.* 1:18–20). But here he states the matter starkly – divorcing without warrant and marrying again, means adultery. Marrying someone improperly divorced has the same result.

Marriage, as an exclusive and life-long union between a man and a woman, is the moral principle Jesus upholds. Jesus' own example of love for the church (*Eph.* 5:21–33) should inspire and empower all married or engaged couples to avoid divorce by making a weak relationship stronger and a good marriage better.

67

Rich Man, Poor Man

'There was a rich man who was clothed in purple and fine linen and who feasted sumptuously every day. [20] And at his gate was laid a poor man named Lazarus, covered with sores, [21] who desired to be fed with what fell from the rich man's table. Moreover, even the dogs came and licked his sores. [22] The poor man died and was carried by the angels to Abraham's side. The rich man also died and was buried, [23] and in Hades, being in torment, he lifted up his eyes and saw Abraham far off and Lazarus at his side. [24] And he called out, "Father Abraham, have mercy on me, and send Lazarus to dip the end of his finger in water and cool my tongue, for I am in anguish in this flame." [25] But Abraham said, "Child, remember that you in your lifetime received your good things, and Lazarus in like manner bad things; but now he is comforted here, and you are in anguish. [26] And besides all this, between us and you a great chasm has been fixed, in order that those who would pass from here to you may not do so, and none may cross from there to us." [27] And he said, "Then I beg you, father, to send him to my father's house – [28] for I have five brothers – so that he may warn them, lest they also come into this place of torment." [29] But Abraham said, "They have Moses and the Prophets; let them hear them." [30] And he said, "No, father Abraham, but if someone goes to them from the dead, they will repent." [31] He said to him, "If they do not hear Moses and the Prophets, neither will they be convinced if someone should rise from the dead"'(Luke 16: 19–31).

After the parable about the shrewd manager Jesus told another parable about wealth. Again, this parable teaches that a person's attitude to wealth carries consequences beyond the grave. One man worships wealth instead of God and loses himself forever; another man trusts in the Lord in poverty and gains everything eternally.

The parable uses the traditional Jewish imagery of the afterlife, rooted in the Old Testament. Not everything in the parable should be taken at face value (for example, being with Abraham is a picture of the restful and secure state of heaven), but everything in the parable should be taken seriously. Only Jesus could speak with this level of authority about the world beyond death.

A RICH MAN AND HIS NEIGHBOUR (verses 19–21)

Two men are described, who could hardly be more different, one extremely rich, the other extremely poor. The rich man's wealth is displayed in his designer clothes and his consumption of gourmet foods. The poor man is given a name – Lazarus, which means 'the Lord helps', suggesting a religious faith that is vindicated when the beggar dies. Like the prodigal son in his extremity (*Luke* 15:16), but for very different reasons, Lazarus longed to satisfy the gnawing pains of an empty stomach. Like the prodigal too, his companions were unclean animals – the scavenger dogs of the streets that came and licked his ulcerated body.

Though the two men are neighbours, they never actually meet. The onus is on the wealthy man who must have seen the beggar man every time he drove from his mansion, but with no results. The rich man goes on regardless, dressing in the latest fashions, sampling the most exotic foods, wholly absorbed in his own pursuits.

Jesus has already shown how loving God means serving those around us, especially when they are in pain or need (*Luke* 10:25–37). Faith always expresses itself through love (*Gal.* 5:6) and without it faith is suspect. Religion and relationships should feed off one another (*1 John* 4:20–21).

Once again Luke shows Jesus' interest in wealth and poverty. In the Old Testament the real people of God are often 'the poor and needy' and so it is here. This is either because the believing people of God do not make wealth their aim in life or because they are not willing to acquire it by unethical means. There is no support in this parable for the promise that God will always bless his people with health and / or wealth. The rich man represents those who have made wealth their goal in life and live to enjoy the good things wealth can buy.

AND THEY DIED (verse 22)

Verse 22 is the flashpoint of the parable because it reveals the great reversal that death brings to people (*Luke* 1:51–53; 6:20–26; 7:30). The poor man who suffered extremely now finds happiness and eternal rest in God; the rich man who knew only material pleasure now experiences the ultimate pain of being shut out from God.

We must be careful not to make a virtue of Lazarus' poverty as though being poor guarantees a place in God's heaven. His hope stems from his personal trust in God who names him as his child. In the same way, we must be careful not to damn the rich for being rich. The rich man loses everything because he did not believe he needed God.

The way Jesus tells this story gives no support for believing in anything like soul-sleep or annihilation at death. Death brings a new awareness of a spiritual kind, where individual destiny is immediately fixed. What decides that destiny is the life lived on earth, whether good or evil (*Rom*. 2:11–16). Immediately on dying every individual experiences either the joyful life of heaven or the personal anguish of hell-fire. There is no middle state that offers hope for future improvement.

A LOST SOUL (verses 23–26)

An imaginary conversation takes place between Abraham, the father of believers and the wealthy man, now experiencing the dreadful anguish of a personal hell. Part of his agony is due to seeing Lazarus enjoying the bliss of heaven, while he himself bears the pain of Hades (not here the realm of the dead, but rather the place of punishment for those who die without repenting). The rich man pleads with Abraham to send Lazarus to cool his tongue by dipping his finger in water. In this he shows the same imperious manner that he lived by on earth. But Abraham raises two objections. Firstly, it would be unfair, because the wealthy man had already received many good gifts from God, whereas Lazarus was only now experiencing some of his. Secondly, it was impossible, because the two men inhabited two worlds that were forever separated.

The fire that burns the rich man is a fire that consumes without purifying. It communicates a direct sense of the holy anger of God against a person's sinfulness, past, present, and future. It will burn eternally in the consciousness of the deceased (*Mark* 9:44–48). How awesome are Jesus' words!

THE POWER OF THE SCRIPTURES (verses 27–31)

The rich man now knows that his own condition is hopeless but not so his five brothers still alive on the other side of death's threshold. Again he requests Abraham to send Lazarus on an errand, this time to his brothers. He believes that a visit from a dead person will change their views and save them from his fate. But Abraham protests that his brothers have the Scriptures of the Old Testament which are sufficient for showing them the way to God. In fact, Abraham argues, the Scriptures are more persuasive then even a resurrection miracle. God's word (in this case the Old Testament) is the means appointed for bringing people to repentance and to God (*2 Tim.* 3:15–17). At best miracles may help to confirm the authority of Scripture but can never replace God's written and preached word as the way to truth or spiritual renewal. Faith needs a personal and historical foundation to rest on if people are truly to repent and know God. Jesus himself built his public ministry on the preaching of the word rather than the performance of miracles. He himself is the grand miracle (*Luke* 11:29–32).

Finally, Jesus teaches that personal repentance is the only way to gain an assurance of heaven when we die. Repentance means a change of heart that leads to a change of life. Only Jesus can give us the repentance we need and the forgiveness that goes with it (*Acts* 5:31). But we need to seek him for it with all our heart.

68

A Second Assortment of Sayings

*And he said to his disciples, 'Temptations to sin are sure to come,
but woe to the one through whom they come! [2] It would be better
for him if a millstone were hung around his neck and he were
cast into the sea than that he should cause one of these little ones
to sin. [3] Pay attention to yourselves! If your brother sins, rebuke
him, and if he repents, forgive him, [4] and if he sins against you
seven times in the day, and turns to you seven times, saying, "I
repent," you must forgive him.'*
*[5] The apostles said to the Lord, 'Increase our faith!' [6] And the
Lord said, 'If you had faith like a grain of mustard seed, you
could say to this mulberry tree, "Be uprooted and planted in the
sea," and it would obey you.*
*[7] Will any one of you who has a servant ploughing or keeping
sheep say to him when he has come in from the field, "Come at
once and sit down at table"? [8] Will he not rather say to him,
"Prepare supper for me, and dress properly, and serve me while
I eat and drink, and afterward you will eat and drink"? [9] Does
he thank the servant because he did what was commanded? [10]
So you also, when you have done all that you were commanded,
say, "We are unworthy servants; we have only done what was
our duty."'* (Luke 17:1–10).

In these verses Luke has linked together a number of sayings of Jesus. Some people have tried to find a common theme running through them, such as life in the believing community, but perhaps it is better to treat them as unrelated sayings. Taken together or separately they deliver up some priceless lessons and principles about living in God's kingdom. There are four in number: sinning (verses 1–2), forgiving (verses 3–4), believing (verses 5–6), serving (verses 7–10).

CAUSING OTHERS TO SIN (verses 1–2)

These are solemn words about sinning within the human community. Sin is unavoidable in a fallen world but this is no excuse for getting entangled in sinning ourselves and involving other people with us. Occasions of temptation come to everyone, but woe to those persons who facilitate the sinning of third parties. This is particularly the case when the third party is a weak Christian ('one of these little ones').

To make his point Jesus pictures someone having a millstone tied to his neck and being cast into the sea! That would be preferable to the fate awaiting the person who deliberately leads one of Christ's people into sin by their own sordid example or some evil passion such as the profit motive (*1 Tim.* 6:9–10; *Heb.* 12:15). In a culture that glamorises all sorts of sinful behaviour for selfish gains it is not difficult to find points of contact for Jesus' solemn warning.

SINNING, REPENTING, FORGIVING (verses 3–4)

Sin remains in the Christian after regeneration so believers will sometimes have cause for complaint and conflict among themselves. This calls for caution and vigilance lest sin gains the advantage over us or over fellow-believers within the fellowship of the church family ('your brother'). In the case of serious sin (Paul gives examples of how we might measure this [*1 Cor.* 5:9–13]) one Christian needs to take action towards another. If this action fails to produce confession and amendment then further steps may be taken (*Matt.* 18:15–17). Where repentance is forthcoming and sincere (showing the fruits, *Luke* 3:8, forgiveness must be equally forthcoming and sincere. Even if a fellow Christian repeats the offence many times, but repents as often, forgiveness and restoration of fellowship must keep in step.

What if a fellow Christian rejects the charges and refuses to admit to anything? Must forgiveness still be given? The willingness to forgive and the desire and prayer for reconciliation must be present.

However, forgiveness cannot operate without repentance since fellowship and reconciliation involve two parties. In the same way God is ready to forgive even the worst offender against him but repentance is necessary if forgiveness is to take effect and be effective. The evangelistic task and message involve both, on the basis of Christ's death and resurrection (*Luke* 24:45–47).

INCREASING FAITH (verses 5–6)

That 'the apostles' spoke to 'the Lord' means that this third saying has particular relevance for leaders in his church. Sensing the weakness of their faith and knowing Jesus to be a great believer in God (*Heb.* 12:2) and the one who gives faith, they ask him for more faith than they consciously possess. They can see that without more faith their efforts will be greatly hampered.

He replies to their request with a conditional saying about how faith operates. Since faith is a living and growing principle in the heart, Jesus likens its working to a tiny grain of seed that can grow up and accomplish great results. There are several subsidiary points to learn here.

- Without faith no work can be done for God. The work of Christian service can only be done through faith that instils us with vision and determination to reach our goals (*1 Thess.* 1:3).
- Jesus is speaking about the special gift of faith here as Paul's use of the same language indicates (*1 Cor.* 13:2). This faith is over and above the universal gift of saving faith that all Christians possess through grace.
- Through this spiritual gift great changes can come about, difficulties can be overcome, and God's work be given new beginnings. This is not due to faith in itself (the common idea of having faith in yourself or even having faith in faith) but because faith works with a great God who can do wonderful things.
- Christian leaders and pioneers in new works of mission should pray for such faith and its increase. Then we can pray for, look for and work for great things from God (William Carey). Mountains will move, the spiritual landscape will change and Christ's kingdom will advance.

UNWORTHY SERVANTS (verses 7–10)

Jesus had a mind for the obvious as well as the ridiculous. Here he relates a typical story of a master and a servant who was employed by him to work the property and carry out household chores. Imagine, says Jesus, the master telling his servant to rest and eat at table before the master has done so; imagine the master thanking the servant for doing what he is employed and paid to do! No more can any one of us expect Christ our lord to praise us for doing what is only our duty when serving him in doing his work. No one can ever put Christ in debt or claim that they have done more than they needed to do (the whole idea of merit as found in certain religious traditions is foreign to the teaching of Christ). We are unworthy servants at the best of times because we all fail to live up to what Jesus requires in the first place (*Rom.* 3:23).

69

Then There Was One

On the way to Jerusalem he was passing along between Samaria and Galilee. [12] *And as he entered a village, he was met by ten lepers, who stood at a distance* [13] *and lifted up their voices, saying, 'Jesus, Master, have mercy on us.'* [14] *When he saw them he said to them, 'Go and show yourselves to the priests.' And as they went they were cleansed.* [15] *Then one of them, when he saw that he was healed, turned back, praising God with a loud voice;* [16] *and he fell on his face at Jesus' feet, giving him thanks. Now he was a Samaritan.* [17] *Then Jesus answered, 'Were not ten cleansed? Where are the nine?* [18] *Was no one found to return and give praise to God except this foreigner?'* [19] *And he said to him, 'Rise and go your way; your faith has made you well'* (Luke 17:11–19).

As Jesus made his last trip to Jerusalem, the route took him along the border between Samaria and Judea. The Samaritans were half-breeds yet proud of their national history. Jesus had already visited this forbidden territory with mixed results (*Luke* 9:51–56). He had also shocked public opinion by making a Samaritan the hero of one of his parables (*Luke* 10:29–37). Now he is drawn into contact with them again with surprising results.

TEN LEPERS (verses 12–14)

Lepers were not uncommon in Jesus' day, living alone or in groups, but always on the outskirts of society. Lepers were required by law to proclaim their approach, as a public health measure (*Lev*. 13:45–46). In the spirit of this legal requirement the ten lepers kept their distance from Jesus, while calling out to him to help them. All that they could do was to appeal to his mercy, since they had nothing to offer him. Perhaps they had heard about the leper who appealed to Jesus and was cleansed (*Luke* 5:12–16).

Jesus responded to their appeal in a different way, not by touching them, but by telling them to do something. They were to go immediately and show themselves to the local priest, who acted as a kind of health officer, who could verify that their leprosy was gone (*Lev.* 13:49). In the very act of going the lepers were healed.

Leprosy was and is a loathsome disease with no absolute cure. In the same way, our sinful human condition is a loathsome one with no human cure. Like leprosy our sin separates us from our fellows and isolates us psychologically and morally. Only Jesus Christ in the exercise of his mercy can cure anyone of the deeper malady of sin.

ONE LEPER (verses 15–19)

The ten lepers looked like a homogenous group, but one broke ranks and showed his independence. For him it was not enough to be healed, he must go back to thank his benefactor. In his gratitude he falls at Jesus' feet. Surprisingly, he was a Samaritan, an outcast who lacked the privileges of the Jewish people (*John* 4:9). But God is undiscriminating in his love by choosing the unlikely and the unlovely. Again we have an example in life of the way the wisdom of God reverses the wisdom of the world (*Luke* 1:46–55; *1 Cor.* 1:26–31).

The Samaritan's return prompts Jesus to reflect on the absence of the nine, since all ten were cleansed. The ethnic status of the one who returned only intensifies Jesus' disappointment that no more than ten per cent of those cured could find it in themselves to come back to say 'thank you' to God. To encourage the one who came back, Jesus picks out his faith as the channel through which he had received salvation from Jesus. By isolating faith in this way Jesus draws attention to himself as the only proper object of trust, and faith as the sole medium of salvation. In principle this is the later theological formula of 'faith alone in Christ alone'.

There are two lessons from this story, one historical, the other personal.

- God promised Abraham that one of his descendants would become a blessing to all the world's families (*Gen.* 12:1–3). Jesus is Abraham's promised descendant and this Samaritan is a standing tribute to God's universal promise. Unfortunately, Jesus' fellow Jews had grown familiar with Israel's special privileges and had become proudly complacent.
- When people turn truly to Jesus they show this by thankfulness to God for his salvation. Christ is our principal benefactor to whom we owe all that we are (*1 Cor.* 15:10). Expressed gratitude is a Christian virtue (*Phil.* 4:6, *1 Thess.* 5:18), just as rank ingratitude is the mark of the unbeliever (*Rom.* 1:21).

70

The Coming of the King

*Being asked by the Pharisees when the kingdom of God would
come, he answered them, 'The kingdom of God is not coming with
signs to be observed, 21 nor will they say, "Look, here it is!" or
"There!" for behold, the kingdom of God is in the midst of you.'
22 And he said to the disciples, 'The days are coming when you
will desire to see one of the days of the Son of Man, and you will
not see it. 23 And they will say to you, "Look, there!" or "Look,
here!" Do not go out or follow them. 24 For as the lightning flashes
and lights up the sky from one side to the other, so will the Son
of Man be in his day. 25 But first he must suffer many things and
be rejected by this generation. 26 Just as it was in the days of
Noah, so will it be in the days of the Son of Man. 27 They were
eating and drinking and marrying and being given in marriage,
until the day when Noah entered the ark, and the flood came
and destroyed them all. 28 Likewise, just as it was in the days of
Lot – they were eating and drinking, buying and selling, planting
and building, 29 but on the day when Lot went out from Sodom,
fire and sulphur rained from heaven and destroyed them all –
30 so will it be on the day when the Son of Man is revealed. 31 On
that day, let the one who is on the housetop, with his goods in the
house, not come down to take them away, and likewise let the
one who is in the field not turn back. 32 Remember Lot's wife.
33 Whoever seeks to preserve his life will lose it, but whoever loses
his life will keep it. 34 I tell you, in that night there will be two in
one bed. One will be taken and the other left. 35 There will be
two women grinding together. One will be taken and the other
left. 36 Two men will be in the field; one will be taken and the
other left.' [verse 36 added from footnote].*

> 37 *And they said to him, 'Where, Lord?' He said to them, 'Where the corpse is, there the vultures will gather.'* (Luke 17:20–37).

The present discourse could stand alone in the absence of any chronological markers. Asked by the Pharisees about the time of the arrival of God's kingdom Jesus quite typically both answers the question in an unexpected way and goes beyond the question to bring further truth to light. The present passage only appears in Luke, though with some similarities to passages in the other Gospels (Matthew 24, Mark 13 and Luke 21). Jesus speaks of his future return and describes how the world will be and how we should be, when he comes. This is futuristic prophecy.

THE PRESENCE OF THE KINGDOM (verses 20–21)

Some Pharisees asked Jesus about the time of the coming kingdom. First Jesus clears away confusion about the subject. The kingdom (in its present form before his final return) is not a public spectacle that people can point to and say, 'There it is!' On the contrary, the kingdom is 'within' or 'among' you (either meaning is possible). Jesus thus highlights the spiritual nature of the kingdom. He could mean that the kingdom is a matter of the heart, the self within; he could mean that he himself is the kingdom present in their midst. Perhaps the contrast with the kingdom as a public spectacle favours the first of these two possible meanings. This would harmonise with his emphasis elsewhere on such inner gifts and experiences as forgiveness, love, the Holy Spirit, thankfulness, and so on. Paul's definition supports this reading (*Rom.* 14:17). On the other hand, in what follows, the coming of the kingdom is the coming of Jesus, the Son of Man.

THE FUTURE OF THE KINGDOM (verses 22–37)

Yet the kingdom is also a future event that will transform the shape of the earth and every human relationship. This double perspective on the kingdom as present and yet also future, as already now but not yet completed, became normative for the outlook of Jesus' disciples in writing their epistles. It is the key to understanding the eschatological stance of the whole New Testament.

From these statements of Jesus we may notice a number of lessons about the coming of the future kingdom of God.

- Disciples of Jesus naturally long for the coming of the King (verse 22). Jesus predicts that there will be many times when his apostles will wish they could go back to the days when Jesus was still with them. But all disciples of Jesus must look forward rather than backward when they pine for Christ's physical presence (*Rev*. 22:20).
- The coming of the King will be a global event (verses 23–24). In contrast to some people's claim that the kingdom has come to them as an elite group (verse 23) the real event of the kingdom will be awesome in its trans-world reach – like an electric storm that illumines the whole landscape. No one can possibly miss the return of Jesus Christ (*Rev*. 1:7).
- Before the kingdom comes the King must die (verse 25). Without his sufferings and death there can be no kingdom of grace and glory for his disciples. This is because their salvation is a matter of satisfying certain divine principles of moral governance. Only his sufferings and death can match the moral demands of divine justice, goodness, and truth. This is why Jesus must suffer 'first' and why he 'must' suffer at all.
- The King will come when the world is preoccupied (verses 26–30). Two other periods of biblical history help illustrate what Jesus means. The flood came in Noah's days and the fire fell in the days of Sodom and Gomorrah when men and women were eating, drinking, marrying, buying, selling, planting, and building. What is wrong with these activities and interests? Nothing – except when they stand in the way of God and his kingdom in our lives. Then they become an idol and take us away from God, our first love (*Rom*. 1:25).
- The coming of the King will test where our hearts lie (verses 31–33). Those whose hearts are in the world will want to go back and retrieve their possessions; Christ's people will leave everything behind to be with him forever. Jesus already stated the first principle of discipleship – leaving everything for his sake (*Luke*

14:25–33). Jesus recalls another biblical story – Lot and his wife (*Gen.* 19:15–26). She looked back on what she was leaving and missed the rescue of her husband and family. In just the same way Jesus' sudden return will disclose the secrets of people's hearts and decide their eternal state.

- The arrival of the King will separate people forever (verses 34–35/36). There is some doubt whether verse 36 belongs to Luke's original writing (what it says has really been said in the previous two verses). Whether people are sleeping during the night or working together during the day Christ's advent will immediately and permanently separate them. Here the judgement takes place in the blink of an eye but Jesus elsewhere describes it as a process (*Matt.* 25:31–32). Both aspects are true.
- The King's arrival will lead to judgement for many (verse 37). The final word of Jesus is not easy to explain. Those who are left behind at the Lord's return will be handed over to judgement, just like corpses left to the vultures. It is a grim reminder of the seriousness of the issues involved. How blind and foolish to imagine that death is the end or that there are further chances after death through reincarnation or some other purificatory process (*Heb.* 9:27)!

71

Keep On Praying!

And he told them a parable to the effect that they ought always to pray and not lose heart. [2] *He said, 'In a certain city there was a judge who neither feared God nor respected man.* [3] *And there was a widow in that city who kept coming to him and saying, "Give me justice against my adversary."* [4] *For a while he refused, but afterward he said to himself, 'Though I neither fear God nor respect man,* [5] *yet because this widow keeps bothering me, I will give her justice, so that she will not beat me down by her continual coming.'"* [6] *And the Lord said, 'Hear what the unrighteous judge says.* [7] *And will not God give justice to his elect, who cry to him day and night? Will he delay long over them?* [8] *I tell you, he will give justice to them speedily. Nevertheless, when the Son of Man comes, will he find faith on earth?'* (Luke 18:1–8).

Having spoken about his coming again Jesus now turns to the practice of praying – the two are related (verses 7 and 8). To help his teaching he offers another story (parable) that is only found in Luke. The main lesson of the parable is stated beforehand but there is a twist to the parable at the end.

THE STORY-LINE (verses 2–5)

An unscrupulous judge is running a legal practice in a community. He is practically an atheist and quite without morals in dispensing justice. A widow who has been wronged in a suit comes to him for legal representation but the judge puts her off. However, she is persistent and refuses to take 'no' for an answer. Widows were dependent on a fair justice system if they were to survive. So strong is the Greek that it suggests the possibility of the woman coming to blows with the judge if he continues to prevaricate. As a result the judge decides to take up her case, contrary to his usual practice. For purely selfish reasons and neither for the sake of the woman nor of justice, he yields to her persistent coming and vindicates her appeal.

THE LESSONS (verses 6–8a)

Jesus helps his hearers out when it comes to the message of the story. The key is found in the words of the unscrupulous lawyer. Jesus reasons from the lesser case of the unscrupulous lawyer to the higher case of God the just judge of all his people. If an irreligious and immoral lawyer can act on behalf of a needy client, how much more can we expect God to act on behalf of those who belong to him when they suffer injustice?

Several points are made about this higher relationship.

- Believers should remember that whenever they cry to God they are in a secure and privileged relationship with him through Christ. They are God's chosen ones for whom he works everything together for their eternal good in Christ (*Rom.* 8:28).
- God may sometimes appear to put his children off by not immediately answering them. It is as though he neither hears nor cares about their cries. God's delays are a test of his people's commitment to the justice they crave. In the face of such testing the natural response is to give up but this is not the way to go. This is exactly the lesson the widow's case is meant to teach. Behind God's frowning providence he hides a smiling face. He likes to be entreated (*Luke* 24:28–29).
- When God does answer the cries of his people he answers speedily and appropriately. The time of waiting and suffering may seem long but in the light of Christ's coming again all time in this world is shortened (*1 Cor.* 7:29–32) and puts a new perspective on everything people experience.
- Many will give up on God and prayer because of the seeming silence of God. When Jesus returns to the earth he predicts it will be a desert of unbelief where little praying takes place.

Whatever the uncertainty of verse 8 may be, the main lesson of the parable is clear enough – that people must train themselves to persist in their praying and not give up in the face of the most daunting events. God cares, hears, and will answer in his own sure time. When he does there will be no reason for complaint from those who hope in him.

72

Self-centred and God-centred Religion

He also told this parable to some who trusted in themselves that they were righteous, and treated others with contempt:
[10] *'Two men went up into the temple to pray, one a Pharisee and the other a tax collector.* [11] *The Pharisee, standing by himself, prayed thus: "God, I thank you that I am not like other men, extortioners, unjust, adulterers, or even like this tax collector.* [12] *I fast twice a week; I give tithes of all that I get."*
[13] *But the tax collector, standing far off, would not even lift up his eyes to heaven, but beat his breast, saying, "God, be merciful to me, a sinner!"* [14] *I tell you, this man went down to his house justified, rather than the other. For everyone who exalts himself will be humbled, but the one who humbles himself will be exalted'* (Luke 18:9–14).

The theme of prayer continues. To illustrate his teaching Jesus compares two kinds of people. The characters are sharply drawn so as to make his main point unmistakable. This is supplied in Luke's introduction (verse 9). It is that people ought not to think self-righteously about themselves and, as a result, inevitably look down on others for being less good.

THE SELF-CENTRED PHARISEE (verses 10–12)

Although Jesus makes use of a Pharisee for his first example we should remember that not all Pharisees were as bad and blatant as this (*Mark* 12:32–34; however, see also Luke 11:37–44; 16:14–15). Also it is not just Pharisees that were or are like this. If people are honest most will admit that there is something of the Pharisee in them that makes them think, judge and speak in the same way.

When people pray they reveal what they are really like. Judged by that standard the Pharisee showed himself egoistical and smug. He calls on God's name but he worships himself; he does not thank God for what he (God) is but for what he (the Pharisee) is; he praises himself at the expense of other people; he lists the outstanding faults of others but mentions none of his own; he boasts to God about his religious achievements (as though God needed to be reminded); he talks endlessly about himself in the first person singular ('I'); he is a thorough egoist who knows nothing of humility, repentance, or love for others; his prayer is a soliloquy not a dialogue; his relationship to God consists of one-way traffic, from himself to God, because he has no sense of needing anything from God. Such is the spirituality of man-centred religions, ancient and modern. Man is the measure and self is the centre. God is present but only as an audience, not a leader or Lord of religion.

THE GOD-CENTRED TAX-COLLECTOR (verse 13)

The contrast could hardly be sharper. The tax-collector's body-language tells the story of his life and the state of his heart. He positions himself, unlike the Pharisee, in a remote corner of the temple where only God can see him. Even there he cannot get himself to look up to heaven because of an overwhelming sense of uncleanness in the pure presence of the holy Other. For the same reason he beats his breast in remorse and deep feeling.

His prayer could not differ more from that of the Pharisee either. If prayer shows who we really are then the second prayer is just as revealing as the first. Like the Pharisee he addresses God by name but after that the similarities cease. The first word he pronounces after the divine name is 'mercy', in a plea that mercy might be shown to him. The next word is 'sinner', applied to himself and not to others. The tax-collector has turned the Pharisee's prayer on its head, by exalting God and abasing himself. In doing so he expresses spiritual praying at its best. Not that his prayer should be used as a formula. Precisely the opposite, for it is the spirit of the tax-collector's prayer and worship that underlie his words that matters.

FINALE (verse 14)

Jesus has the final say and draws the main lesson of the story. Once again we meet the reversal pattern in Luke's Gospel. God sees and judges people and their actions differently from the way people do themselves (*Luke* 16:15). The tax-collector went home, his relationship with God restored (justification); the Pharisee came to the temple imagining that his relationship was already intact. The one received righteousness from God as a gift, the other thought to bring it to God as an achievement. One came to the temple a self-confessed sinner and went home justified; the other came up to the temple virtuous and went home condemned. Jesus here teaches the principle of righteousness by faith in God alone through grace. Paul describes and defends this principle in his letters to the Romans and Galatians.

If people hold on to the belief that they are good enough for God then they receive nothing; if people face their faults and failures and confess to God they receive everything (*Luke* 1:50–53).

73

Learning from Children

Now they were bringing even infants to him that he might touch them. And when the disciples saw it, they rebuked them. [16] But Jesus called them to him, saying, 'Let the children come to me, and do not hinder them, for to such belongs the kingdom of God. [17] Truly, I say to you, whoever does not receive the kingdom of God like a child shall not enter it.' (Luke 18:15–17).

Learning from children follows quite naturally the story of the proud publican and the humble tax-collector. Little children open up the way and the terms of salvation in Christ's kingdom.

Concerned parents were bringing their little children to Jesus for blessing through his physical contact. Perhaps the story of the woman who received healing through simply touching Jesus (*Luke* 8:42–48) was well known. They seem to have believed that this would secure the blessing of God on them without more ado. Thus there was something superstitious in their approach to Jesus. But this did not cause Jesus to abandon them, nor should his followers today forsake those with a mixed understanding of what Christianity is about.

That 'even' the children (verse 15) were brought to him says a great deal about the way people saw Jesus – as a man of broad sympathies and ready charity. Their expectations of Jesus were high and not disappointed in this case. But the disciples thought otherwise because they had a lower view of children than Jesus did, so they drove them away. How often the behaviour of Christians has hindered simple seekers from finding Jesus!

Jesus welcomed the children literally with open arms, along with the words, 'Let the little children come to me and do not forbid them.' In so saying Jesus says that the kingdom of his heavenly Father is open to children just as much as to other social groups. This is an encouragement to family Bible reading, child evangelism, parental prayers for their children, and belief in child conversion. The history of revivals records many examples of sound child conversions with spiritual insight of a high order and godly practice. Jesus is here speaking of children and to children as persons in their own right worthy of his time and attention. How different his treatment of children from a world that exploits, abuses, and enslaves them!

Then he adds words of larger reference when he says, '... f or to such the kingdom of God belongs'. The words of the next verse (17) explain what Jesus has in mind. Whether as children or adults we must all receive the kingdom as a divine gift that we have not earned and can never merit or repay. Let us be thankful simply to receive! This is the quality in children that Jesus picks out, their simplicity and straightforwardness in receiving gifts. He was not blind to their other sides (*Luke* 7:31–32).

So see yourself as a child in relation to God. Let him love you and bestow on you the inestimable gift of his Son, Jesus! Those who receive him have eternal life here and now and always. God wants to save us as a result of his grace alone (*Eph*. 2:8–9). He is not open to bargaining.

74

The Rich Man Who Went Away Poor and the Poor Disciples Who Will be Rich

And a ruler asked him, 'Good Teacher, what must I do to inherit eternal life?' [19] *And Jesus said to him, 'Why do you call me good? No one is good except God alone.* [20] *You know the commandments: "Do not commit adultery, Do not murder, Do not steal, Do not bear false witness, Honour your father and mother."'* [21] *And he said, 'All these I have kept from my youth.'* [22] *When Jesus heard this, he said to him, 'One thing you still lack. Sell all that you have and distribute to the poor, and you will have treasure in heaven; and come, follow me.'* [23] *But when he heard these things, he became very sad, for he was extremely rich.* [24] *Jesus, looking at him with sadness, said, 'How difficult it is for those who have wealth to enter the kingdom of God!* [25] *For it is easier for a camel to go through the eye of a needle than for a rich person to enter the kingdom of God.'* [26] *Those who heard it said, 'Then who can be saved?'* [27] *But he said, 'What is impossible with men is possible with God.'* [28] *And Peter said, 'See, we have left our homes and followed you.'* [29] *And he said to them, 'Truly, I say to you, there is no one who has left house or wife or brothers or parents or children, for the sake of the kingdom of God,* [30] *who will not receive many times more in this time, and in the age to come eternal life'* (Luke 18:18–30).

The theme of salvation continues (*Luke* 9:57–62; 14:25–33). What begins as a simple conversation between Jesus and a young aristocrat turns (verses 18–23) into a wider discussion with the crowds around him (verses 24–30). Jesus begins by talking about the obstacle wealth can be to gaining eternal life; he ends by promising rewards for those who put wealth aside for the sake of Jesus and his kingdom.

A RICH YOUNG MAN AND JESUS (verses 18–23)

The young man accosts Jesus with the title, 'Good Teacher!' Whether he meant to flatter Jesus and so make him sympathetic, is not clear. This form of address gave Jesus the opening he needed to teach his basic lesson – no one is good except God. Was Jesus denying his own moral goodness by this remark? No, Jesus could see that his questioner had a shallow view of goodness (like many in the world today). Only as he began to compare himself with God would he become aware of his own innate lack of goodness. By God's law that sets him forth, comes the knowledge of sin (*Rom.* 3:10–12).

To the young man's question, 'What must I do to inherit eternal life?' Jesus lists some of the great moral commandments of God's covenant law. Eternal life is on the basis of obedience. This was shown in paradise when the man and woman were forbidden the tree of knowledge (*Gen.* 2:8–9, 15–17); it was apparent again in Israel when God's blessings were united with their obedience and his curses with their unfaithfulness (*Deut.* 30:15–20).

The young man had grown up in a devout Jewish home where he had learned the commandments from childhood without understanding their connection with a future Messiah who would secure through his own obedience the blessings of God for his people (*2 Tim.* 3:15). He showed this ignorance by claiming to have kept all God's commands! Yet how could he, when he was asking Jesus the way to eternal life! He was searching still for personal peace and spiritual assurance, in spite of his obedience. How many are doing the same in our highly spiritualised world! What matters is not the amount of religion people engage in, but its kind.

There was one thing missing and Jesus placed his finger on it. He was in love with himself more than God. His money was his god and he lived for it. Asked to choose between his money and Jesus he chose his wealth. He wanted eternal life but on his own terms. He was willing to live a moral life but not to give his heart to God. His discipleship was conditional and Jesus would have none of it.

Jesus calls everyone who comes to him to a life of poverty in his name – poverty of spirit (*Matt.* 5:3) and poverty of possessions, by sharing them and leaving them if asked (*1 Tim.* 6:17–19).

When we walk with the Lord,
  In the light of his Word,
What a glory He sheds on our way!
  While we do His good will
He abides with us still,
  And with all who will trust and obey.

But we never can prove
  The delights of his love
Until all on the altar we lay;
  For the favour He shows,
And the joy He bestows
  Are for those who will trust and obey.

John H. Sammis

The young man was saddened by Jesus' reply because he was extremely rich. The terms of eternal life were too high. He is not the first nor will he be the last person to lose his soul in the love and pursuit of wealth. How much better to be rich toward God and to lay up wealth in heaven through serving Jesus (*Matt.* 6:19–21).

THE CROWDS AND JESUS (verses 24–30)

Jesus speaks his thoughts aloud about wealthy people and the kingdom of God. He states the difficulty rich people have of ever entering God's kingdom. Quite literally Jesus declares it is easier for a camel with its hump to squeeze through the fine eye of a needle than for a rich person to get into God's kingdom. Yet wealth is what so many people want and pursue in the belief that wealth can solve all their problems and bring them happiness. See the wiser prayer of the man of wisdom (*Prov.* 30:7–9).

The crowds draw breath at Jesus' words by asking the obvious, 'Who then can be saved?' In Jewish society wealth was widely seen as a sign of God's favour. So how could Jesus say that wealth kept people out of God's kingdom? Jesus' sayings turned their beliefs upside down.

But Jesus understands the issues and knows the answer. 'What is impossible with men is possible with God'. Only a God of grace can set people free from the inner bondage of desire that shackles them to wealth and its pleasures. It is not wealth that is the problem but the man or woman of wealth who cannot live without it because it acts like a drug.

Long my imprisoned spirit lay
  Fast bound in sin and nature's night;
Thine eye diffused a quickening ray,
  I woke, the dungeon flamed with light;
My chains fell off, my heart was free,
  I rose, went forth and followed Thee.
Charles Wesley

PETER AND JESUS (verses 28–30)

It was always difficult for Peter to remain silent so now he has his say, by reminding Jesus that he and his fellow-disciples have left everything to be with him. To this Jesus gives the generous assurance that God will more than make up what people have given away for Christ. He does this through the new family of brothers and sisters that make up his people, new homes that friendly believers open up to others, possessions that they can enjoy that others may share with them. The kingdom blessings are here and now as well as in the future when Jesus comes. Even now believers can experience the joy of sacrifice for Jesus (*Luke* 24:52–53), as a foretaste of that joy that will make heaven their home (*Luke* 15:7,10).

When upon the storms of life
  You're tossed about,
When you are discouraged,
  And begin to doubt,

The Rich Man Who Went Away Poor

Count your many blessings,
  Name them one by one,
And it will surprise you
  What the Lord has done.

When you look at others
  With their lands and gold,
Think that Christ has promised you
  His wealth untold;
Count your many blessings,
  Money cannot buy
Your reward in heaven,
  And your home on high.

J. Oatman

75

Going Up To Jerusalem

And taking the twelve, he said to them, 'See, we are going up to Jerusalem, and everything that is written about the Son of Man by the prophets will be accomplished. [32] *For he will be delivered over to the Gentiles and will be mocked and shamefully treated and spat upon.* [33] *And after flogging him, they will kill him, and on the third day he will rise.'* [34] *But they understood none of these things. This saying was hidden from them, and they did not grasp what was said* (Luke 18:31–34)

For a third and last time Jesus speaks about his forthcoming death in Jerusalem (*Luke* 9:21–22, 44–45). This shows us how focused Jesus was on reaching this goal where he was to accomplish the work God gave him to do. This repeated emphasis by Jesus on his death and resurrection also teaches how pivotal these two events are for understanding his saving work.

Luke's third account of Jesus' prediction of his passion (or suffering) contains three main elements.

1. Jesus sees his death as the completion of the Scriptures. The final visit to Jerusalem where he will suffer to death is a matter of fulfilling all that the prophetic Scriptures have said about the Messiah. The Scriptures, as God's Word, have outlined the way in which the Messiah should bring in salvation for God's people among the nations. Jesus took his cue from the written Word of God as the road-map of his obedient life even when it entailed death by crucifixion.

2. Jesus presents his death as a physical ordeal at the hands of the Gentiles. Jesus endured the wrath of God against human sin in his own body on the tree (*1 Pet.* 2:24). We ought not to overlook the sheer physical ordeal of Christ in the interests of establishing the spiritual nature of his atonement. He presented himself in his whole personal being to God on our behalf.

   Jesus speaks of four types of suffering that he will face in his ordeal. There will be:

   - mocking of his claims to be the Messiah and of his innocence. The authorities charged him with crimes against God and the empire.
   - loss of face through the public humiliation heaped on him.
   - spitting on his face and body as a sign of utter rejection and hatred.
   - flogging that broke a prisoner's resolve as well as his body. Jesus was spared none of the usual indignities and brutality meted out to criminals.

   All this will happen to the glorious Son of Man because he was to be handed over to his enemies (verse 32). Historically this took place through the human agency first of Judas, then of the religious authorities representing the Jews and finally of Pilate representing the Gentile world. But with the human agency there was a divine agency supervising everything to do with Jesus so that he died according to the will of God (*Acts* 2:22–23).

3. The disciples failed to grasp the message of Jesus about his dreadful death and his certain resurrection. Nor was this only a matter of their slowness to learn, it was actively hidden from them by God. Afterwards they understood and recalled what Jesus had said to them (e.g. *Luke* 24:8). The resurrection event and the coming of the Holy Spirit taught the disciples what they needed to know, in order to proclaim a triumphant Saviour to the world. For now, Jesus must be left alone to accomplish his strange work of suffering unto death for the sin of his people.

76

Your Faith Has Saved You

> *As he drew near to Jericho, a blind man was sitting by the roadside begging.* [36] *And hearing a crowd going by, he inquired what this meant.* [37] *They told him, 'Jesus of Nazareth is passing by.'* [38] *And he cried out, 'Jesus, Son of David, have mercy on me!'* [39] *And those who were in front rebuked him, telling him to be silent. But he cried out all the more, 'Son of David, have mercy on me!'* [40] *And Jesus stopped and commanded him to be brought to him. And when he came near, he asked him,* [41] *'What do you want me to do for you?' He said, 'Lord, let me recover my sight.'* [42] *And Jesus said to him, 'Recover your sight; your faith has made you well.'* [43] *And immediately he recovered his sight and followed him, glorifying God. And all the people, when they saw it, gave praise to God* (Luke 18:35–43).

There is some disagreement among the Gospel writers where the next incident took place, either before Jesus entered Jericho (Luke) or after Jesus left Jericho (*Matt.* 20:29; *Mark* 10:46). Jericho was near Jerusalem but there was historically an old and a new Jericho, so that in leaving the one Jesus could have been entering the other. In this way both accounts in the Gospels could be correct.

The incident involves a blind man who was a beggar because of his blindness. There were no anti-discrimination laws in those days. But this gave Jesus the opportunity to show in action the non-discriminatory love of God.

Jesus' presence always created a stir. Blind people often have their other faculties developed to compensate for their loss of sight. As a result Bartimaeus enquired what was going on (*Mark* 10:46). When told it was Jesus of Nazareth he cried out in the hope of being heard by him.

Bartimaeus showed true knowledge of faith in two ways. First, he called on Jesus by his messianic name, 'Son of David' (not 'Jesus of Nazareth' his local name); secondly, he appealed to him for mercy (*Luke* 18:13). By calling him Son of David he showed that he believed that Jesus fulfilled the promises that God gave to David about a future son of his who would rule the world (*2 Sam*. 7:12–13). By calling on Jesus for mercy the blind man showed he understood his blindness was more than physical and that only God's mercy through Jesus could cure him of an inner blindness.

Jesus gave himself to people as individuals and to individuals whom others overlooked. This was the case with Bartimaeus for the people urged him to be silent (verse 15).

Undaunted, the blind man repeated his cry. Jesus not only stopped but commanded that the man be brought to him. Knowing he had faith Jesus wanted to make that faith more visible so he asked him what he wanted from him. The man believed that Jesus could restore his sight so he asked for nothing less. Jesus responded favourably with a word of authority ('Recover your sight') and an explanation ('Your faith is what has saved you'). By singling out his faith Jesus was confirming the rightness of his request for mercy. Overlooking his inability to heal himself the man trusted Jesus to restore him.

The blind man illustrates the only way back to God. This is the way of confiding in Jesus alone. People can be hindered both by a sense of their own unfitness as well as by a sense of their own rightness (*Luke* 18:11–12). The blind man could have let his blindness stop him appealing to Jesus but he surmounted what he was in himself and sued Jesus for mercy alone (*Luke* 18:13). This is the meaning of true faith.

The outcome of the incident was what Jesus always aimed for – the glory of God. Bartimaeus led the way because he had most to praise God for. But the people joined in because they shared his joy and wonder. God is glorified in Jesus because he consistently showed the compassion of God to human beings in their sinfulness and helplessness (*Matt*. 20:34) or God's power used in man's service.

77

The Heart of the Gospel

> *He entered Jericho and was passing through.* [2] *And there was a man named Zacchaeus. He was a chief tax collector and was rich.* [3] *And he was seeking to see who Jesus was, but on account of the crowd he could not, because he was small of stature.* [4] *So he ran on ahead and climbed up into a sycamore tree to see him, for he was about to pass that way.* [5] *And when Jesus came to the place, he looked up and said to him, 'Zacchaeus, hurry and come down, for I must stay at your house today.'* [6] *So he hurried and came down and received him joyfully.* [7] *And when they saw it, they all grumbled, 'He has gone in to be the guest of a man who is a sinner.'* [8] *And Zacchaeus stood and said to the Lord, 'Behold, Lord, the half of my goods I give to the poor. And if I have defrauded anyone of anything, I restore it fourfold.'* [9] *And Jesus said to him, 'Today salvation has come to this house, since he also is a son of Abraham.* [10] *For the Son of Man came to seek and to save the lost.'* (Luke 19:1–10).

Many see this story as the heart of Luke's presentation of the things recently accomplished through Jesus (*Luke* 1:1). Many of Luke's favourite themes are present here such as the compassion of God, sin, repentance, and human recovery. The whole story makes engrossing reading, all the more so because it is true. Jesus appears here in his most attractive role as the gracious Redeemer of lost men and women.

The story is simply told. A very rich (by professional profiteering?) tax-collector named Zacchaeus (related to Zechariah which means 'the Lord is righteous') had heard that Jesus from

Nazareth was heading through Jericho. Intrigued by what he had heard about this travelling rabbi Zacchaeus ran ahead of the crowd and climbed a sycamore tree (an easy task because of its low branches). Zacchaeus was a small man and wanted a vantage point to see Jesus. To his and everyone's surprise Jesus halted right under where Zacchaeus was watching and invited him down so that he could entertain Jesus at his house.

Gladly Zacchaeus opened his home and hospitality to Jesus. The visit of Jesus was the occasion of deep soul-searching and change of heart for Zacchaeus. He used the occasion to confess his past corruption in his professional work and to make a clean start by promising compensations to those he had wronged. Jesus responded in kind by declaring that God's salvation had come to Zacchaeus' household. Zacchaeus was an example of those lost men and women Jesus as the Son of Man had come to seek and save.

Surely this is one of the best loved and most moving stories of the Gospel of Luke which is crowded with so many memorable characters and incidents. It sums up many of the most valuable lessons of salvation and the kingdom.

- In their lostness Jesus presents a figure of great interest and attraction to people (verses 1 to 3). Business can harden people's hearts. Zacchaeus had made a good living out of tax-collecting yet he was conscious of a deep need that wealth could not satisfy. He chose to find out about Jesus for himself. Jesus continues to attract the interest of many men and women who are seeking for answers to life's deepest questions and dilemmas.
- The end of human questioning comes when Jesus makes himself known (verses 4 and 5). Jesus took the initiative with Zacchaeus as he does still with others. This is what being saved by grace means – God seeking us when we did not yet seek for him. God pursues us in his love for us through Jesus.
- Receiving Jesus into heart and home is a moment of great joy (verse 6). Only joy can express what it means to be caught up in Christ's salvation (*Luke* 15:6–7). Joy is something Jesus brought into the world from God and the world has been a more joyful place ever since (*Luke* 2:10–11).

- Jesus was not afraid to challenge the religious establishment with his own new brand of orthodoxy. He did this, among other ways, by approaching, calling, and blessing those the establishment discounted (verse 7), represented in our story by Zacchaeus who belonged to the despised tax-collectors. They were generally despised by the people because of their job in taking taxes from their fellow-Jews for the occupying power of Rome. In choosing such people God shows how unpredictable he is in distributing his grace.
- The proof of genuine conversion is personal and particular repentance (verse 8). Zacchaeus had something the rich young ruler lacked – a willingness to part with his wealth. Zacchaeus' heart now belonged to Jesus. As a result he could unashamedly redistribute his wealth for the benefit of others around him. He made a public vow to donate half his wealth to the poor and promised fourfold compensation (well beyond the legal requirements) to those he had wronged through tax-collecting. A person's use of money is a good barometer of how seriously they are following Jesus as Lord.
- Salvation is shown in a new set of attitudes and relationships (verse 9a). Zacchaeus' change of heart and public confession for Jesus was the sign of salvation. (Verse 8 does not mean Zacchaeus was a righteous man who needed no change of heart). The change in Zacchaeus' attitude to money was indicative of a deeper change of heart towards God and other people's needs.
- In the salvation of someone like Zacchaeus God shows the mystery of his secret choice of people for salvation. Jesus refers to this when describing Zacchaeus as a son of Abraham (verse 9). Zacchaeus was biologically a child of Abraham the forefather of the Jews. Now he had become one of his promised children who would share his faith in the promises of God (*Gen.* 15:6; *Luke* 13:16).
- The whole mission of Jesus was and is that of seeking and saving lost men and women (verse 10). Like the prodigal son Zacchaeus symbolizes all lost men and women whose lives are alienated from God. Salvation means the centring of our lives again in God but this comes about through Jesus Christ and his earthly mission of suffering and obedience for us.

78

The Kingdom? Not Yet!

*As they heard these things, he proceeded to tell a parable, because
he was near to Jerusalem, and because they supposed that the
kingdom of God was to appear immediately. 12 He said therefore,
'A nobleman went into a far country to receive for himself a
kingdom and then return. 13 Calling ten of his servants, he gave
them ten minas, and said to them, "Engage in business until I
come." 14 But his citizens hated him and sent a delegation after
him, saying, "We do not want this man to reign over us."
15 When he returned, having received the kingdom, he ordered
these servants to whom he had given the money to be called to
him, that he might know what they had gained by doing business.
16 The first came before him, saying, "Lord, your mina has made
ten minas more." 17 And he said to him, "Well done, good servant!
Because you have been faithful in a very little, you shall have
authority over ten cities." 18 And the second came, saying, "Lord,
your mina has made five minas." 19 And he said to him, "And
you are to be over five cities." 20 Then another came, saying,
"Lord, here is your mina, which I kept laid away in a hand-
kerchief; 21 for I was afraid of you, because you are a severe man.
You take what you did not deposit, and reap what you did not
sow." 22 He said to him, "I will condemn you with your own
words, you wicked servant! You knew that I was a severe man,
taking what I did not deposit and reaping what I did not sow? 23
Why then did you not put my money in the bank, and at my
coming I might have collected it with interest?" 24 And he said
to those who stood by, "Take the mina from him, and give it to
the one who has the ten minas." 25 And they said to him, "Lord,*

he has ten minas!" [26] *"I tell you that to everyone who has, more will be given, but from the one who has not, even what he has will be taken away.* [27] *But as for these enemies of mine, who did not want me to reign over them, bring them here and slaughter them before me.'"* (Luke 19:11–27).

The disciples had just seen Jesus bring salvation to Zacchaeus, on his final journey to Jerusalem He had shown great determination to get there (*Luke* 9:51; 13:22, 33; 18:31). Everything seemed to point to the imminent arrival of the kingdom of God. But Jesus knew and taught otherwise. Surely, thought the disciples and the crowds around Jesus, the kingdom of God is imminent. Anytime now Jesus will enter the holy city, claim his kingly power and begin to reign. Not so, said Jesus, and he told a parable that has its parallel (though with differences) in Matthew 25:14–30. The kingdom has arrived in Jesus but has a provisional form until he returns. Then the King will square all his accounts and establish his kingdom forever.

Four groups of people (a nobleman, citizens, and two different kinds of servants) contribute something important to the plot of the story. The plot is more complex than some other of Jesus' parables and involves some allegory. The challenge of the parable for the reader lies in finding where he or she fits into it.

THE NOBLEMAN (verse 12)

The parable begins and ends with a nobleman who inherits a kingdom, travels away from home to receive it, then returns in possession of it. Absentee landlords were not uncommon in Jesus' day and the parable may be based upon one.

Not too much imagination is needed to see that this nobleman represents Jesus himself in his progress as future King from earth to heaven and back again to earth. The parable focuses on the interim period from his ascension to his return in glory. Verse 12 sums this up neatly. The nobleman's absence sets the scene for the behaviour of the citizens and the servants. That the nobleman journeyed 'far away' (verse 12, see Luke 15:13) suggests both distance and delay before he returns, exactly the point Jesus wanted to register (verse 11).

That the central figure is a nobleman teaches that Jesus is inherently regal; everyone is and will be accountable to him; he will succeed against all his enemies; and his personal return will be cataclysmic for the world.

THE CITIZENS (verses 14, 27)

This part of the parable may be based on local history, when Archelaus, the son of Herod the Great, inherited parts of Palestine. Before he could take control, Archelaus had to travel to Rome to secure his kingdom, since Palestine was a part of the Roman Empire. His future subjects, the Jews, had experienced enough of his father not to want to live under another Herod, so they sent a delegation to Rome to plead against his investiture. The delegation was unsuccessful and Herod returned to claim his kingdom against his citizens.

The 'citizens' remind us that people are naturally subject to God as their Creator and Judge. Sin has awakened hostility in the human heart towards God so that there can be no willing submission to his rightful authority (*Rom.* 8:7–8). Only a repentance towards God that changes the heart's desires can save people from the dreadful consequences of their resistance to God's claims on their lives (verse 27, *Rom.* 2:6–11). The slaughter of the citizens (verse 27) may seem ruthless but it is Jesus' picture of the terrible reality of God's justice when it comes into full operation. The execution of the citizens is part of the story and should not be taken as support for a belief in annihilation of the damned. Jesus elsewhere clearly teaches a doctrine of eternal and conscious punishment of the wicked who die without remorse for the lives they have lived (*Luke* 16:19–31).

THE SERVANTS (verses 13–26)

The body of the parable pays attention to the servants and their different histories. Jesus wanted his hearers then and now to think seriously about the responses people make to him and the quality of their service for him. Ten servants are mentioned but only three receive attention, a sufficient number for Jesus' purpose in telling the parable.

Before leaving for his overseas journey the nobleman summons his servants and entrusts his property / capital to them. Each receives the same amount – a single mina or roughly three months' wages (in Matthew they receive different amounts). Each servant is told to trade with what he has received. How each servant does this is left to his own imagination and initiative because the nobleman wants each servant to develop his potential as he sees best. Neither does the Lord Jesus restrict those whom he calls and commissions in his service, in and through the churches. This is the main point of the parable: each servant begins the same but the ends are different due to the individual initiative, enterprise and work of each servant.

What are we to understand by the capital that the nobleman entrusted to those servants? Probably the reader is meant to understand by this concept natural and spiritual gifts entrusted to each one, including the opportunities that life brings to develop and use them in the service of others and for the glory of God. Such gifts are intended for the common good, both within the church and within the state (*1 Cor.* 12:7). The challenge of the Lucan parable is about the extent to which each individual deploys the gift(s) each has received.

There are two types of servant.

1. *Faithful Servants* (verses 15–19). When the nobleman returns from his journey he calls his servants to account to learn about their relative successes in individual enterprise. The first two servants have worked hard and made good returns on their lord's capital though these returns differ. The nobleman commends them both and entrusts them with greater responsibilities that correspond to their individual successes. Here the master shows both his generosity and his fairness, since the servants all received the same amount of capital to trade with, yet some have worked harder than others.

We learn from this what experience confirms, that Christians make different responses to their God-given gifts and opportunities throughout their lives (*Matt.* 13:23). There are many factors at work here such as upbringing, natural abilities, spiritual experience, personality and personal circumstances. In the final analysis, only Christ can and will reveal the worth of our individual service for him (*1 Cor.* 4:1–5). In the meantime we should assess the worth of our service soberly, remembering that each Christian will be responsible for his or her own work (*Gal.* 6:3–5).

All Christians will be saved by Christ, yet their work for Christ is another matter, it may pass muster or suffer loss in the fire of Christ's testing examination (*1 Cor.* 3:11–15). Their special responsibilities in the future kingdom will depend in some way on the quality of their service for Christ in the present kingdom. Here is a spur to action for half-hearted and compromising Christians. Far better to give everything for him now that we may have a rich entrance into his heavenly kingdom at last (*2 Pet.* 1:5–11).

Yet everything is a matter of grace in Christ's household, for two reasons.

- No servant deserves to be in Christ's employment; everything is due to Christ's pity and generosity (*Matt.* 20:1–16).
- No servant deserves a reward since no one ever lives up to what Christ has the right to ask of us (*Luke* 17:7–10).

2. *Useless Servants* (verses 20–23). The third servant stands apart from the other two. Instead of engaging in productive activity he kept his master's gift as it was, wrapping it up and hiding it away. His defence consists of excuses in which he virtually blames his master for his own failures. Believing that his master was a ruthless and inconsiderate man who looked for something from nothing, the third servant did nothing at all. While his fellow-servants were busy in their master's service this servant remained paralysed with fear and self-pity.

Naturally the master is unimpressed and vents his anger upon him by calling him wicked and irresponsible, questioning why he did not at least invest the money in a bank for interest. He strips the servant of his one mina and, by giving it to the first servant displays how generous and kind-hearted he actually is, contrary to the third servant's accusations.

The third servant stands for all those people throughout Christendom who have enjoyed an outward relationship to the church and the gospel. Yet these individuals have never made any return on these privileges and opportunities by trusting, loving and serving Christ personally. They are like land that has received the fructifying rain, but only produces thorns and weeds. As a result they are fit only to be uprooted and discarded (*Heb.* 6:4–8). In the judgement Christ will strip them of those very opportunities, privileges, and gifts that they have neglected.

The third servant failed to act because he had a wrong mental picture of his master. In the same way, many people bear no fruit for Christ because they entertain wrong ideas of God. Either they see him as authoritarian and judgemental or as indulgent and all-forgiving. Either way they never attain to a well-grounded knowledge of God that is essential for fruitful labour and God-pleasing service. Nothing is as consequential as a person's mental image of God.

So the parable is about being responsible and hardworking servants in the interval between Jesus' ascension and his return. Then everyone who names him will be accountable for services rendered. Those who have served him faithfully in loving obedience will receive a generous reward and new responsibilities in Christ's kingdom; those who have pretended to serve him will lose what they once had and experience the displeasure of their offended Lord. For each type of servant and their respective ends, see again Luke 12:41–47.

79

Three Messianic Signs

*And when he had said these things, he went on ahead, going up
to Jerusalem.* [29] *When he drew near to Bethphage and Bethany,
at the mount that is called Olivet, he sent two of the disciples,*
[30] *saying, 'Go into the village in front of you, where on entering
you will find a colt tied, on which no one has ever yet sat. Untie
it and bring it here.* [31] *If anyone asks you, "Why are you untying
it?" you shall say this: "The Lord has need of it."'* [32] *So those
who were sent went away and found it just as he had told them.*
[33] *And as they were untying the colt, its owners said to them,
'Why are you untying the colt?'* [34] *And they said, 'The Lord has
need of it.'* [35] *And they brought it to Jesus, and throwing their
cloaks on the colt, they set Jesus on it.* [36] *And as he rode along,
they spread their cloaks on the road.* [37] *As he was drawing near
– already on the way down the Mount of Olives – the whole
multitude of his disciples began to rejoice and praise God with a
loud voice for all the mighty works that they had seen,* [38] *saying,
'Blessed is the King who comes in the name of the Lord! Peace
in heaven and glory in the highest!'* [39] *And some of the Pharisees
in the crowd said to him, 'Teacher, rebuke your disciples.'* [40] *He
answered, 'I tell you, if these were silent, the very stones would
cry out.'*

[41] *And when he drew near and saw the city, he wept over it,*
[42] *saying, 'Would that you, even you, had known on this day the
things that make for peace! But now they are hidden from your
eyes.* [43] *For the days will come upon you, when your enemies will
set up a barricade around you and surround you and hem you in
on every side* [44] *and tear you down to the ground, you and your*

children within you. And they will not leave one stone upon another in you, because you did not know the time of your visitation.'

45 And he entered the temple and began to drive out those who sold, 46 saying to them, 'It is written, "My house shall be a house of prayer," but you have made it a den of robbers.'

47 And he was teaching daily in the temple. The chief priests and the scribes and the principal men of the people were seeking to destroy him, 48 but they did not find anything they could do, for all the people were hanging on his words (Luke 19:28–48).

The Gospel narrative here catches up with itself (*Luke* 9:51). Jesus has reached his final destination. At this dramatic moment in his ministry Jesus engages in three symbolic acts: he rides into the city on a donkey, he weeps over the city, and he cleanses the temple. Each of those acts witnesses in a special way to his messianic claims and hopes.

THE TRIUMPHANT ENTRY (verses 28–40)

Jesus enters the city on the back of a donkey. The background here is the prophecy of Zechariah (*Zech*. 9:9–10) where the future Messiah rides into Jerusalem on a donkey as a gesture of peace to the nation. In doing so he claims to be the King of Israel. Jesus himself organises the circumstances for the prophecy to come about. He sends two of his disciples into the village Bethphage which was next on their route to Jerusalem. There they would find a donkey. They were to explain to its owners that the Lord had need of it. This was enough to secure it for Jesus' service.

This took place as he said, showing again Jesus' foreknowledge of events. Far from being uncertain of the future Jesus is the one who foreknows it in its details. Appropriately for the sinless Son of God no one had ridden the donkey before him so that it was unspoilt (see *Luke* 1:34; 23:53 for other examples of this principle).

The disciples knew what Jesus wanted to do so they set him on the donkey and walked beside him as a band of pilgrims bound for the holy city. The disciples found themselves breaking out into a spontaneous song of praise. It was as if those moments and movements possessed a life of their own that overtook the disciples (this seems to be Jesus' meaning in verse 40). Such is every movement of God's free Spirit.

The words of Psalm 118 (verse 26) came instinctively to mind, which tell of the great Messiah-King who comes in the Lord's name. The people recognise that the coming of Jesus as the King makes way for the peace and glory of God in heaven (verse 38b). Jesus brings heaven near and reveals the heart of God. The hymn-writer captured that moment and its deeper meaning:

> Ride on, ride on in majesty!
> In lowly pomp ride on to die;
> O Christ, Your triumphs now begin
> O'er captive death and conquered sin.
> Ride on, ride on in majesty!
> The angel armies of the sky
> Look down with sad and wondering eyes
> To see the approaching sacrifice.
> Ride on, ride on in majesty!
> Your last and fiercest strife is near:
> The Father on his sapphire throne
> Awaits his own anointed Son.
> Ride on, ride on in majesty!
> In lowly pomp ride on to die;
> Bow your meek head to mortal pain,
> Then take, O God, your power and reign.
>
> *Henry Hart Milman*

How different the scene at the same location, the valley of the Mount of Olives, hundreds of years before! David the ancestral king of Jesus' family, walked barefoot from the city in personal failure and public humiliation and rode down the same ravine weeping (*2 Sam.* 15:30). Now his descendant, Jesus the promised Messiah, takes the very same journey in reverse, in personal obedience and public acclamation. Jesus is great David's greater son who has come to rule over the house of Jacob forever and of whose kingdom there will be no end (*Luke* 1:31–33).

A few Pharisees in the crowd (they spied on Jesus everywhere) called on Jesus to rebuke the disciples for using the words of the Psalm about him. But Jesus rebuts their objection with a plea of his own. If the disciples were silent the very stones of the city and temple would find voice to praise him. This is a defining moment in the history of the nation but the authorities are blind to what is taking place in front of their own eyes. Their hearts are spiritually as lifeless as the stones that could at least cry out in praise of Jesus.

Riding on a donkey was itself a public statement, one that showed that he was claiming to be a King. Yet Jesus was and is a King with a difference, meek and lowly at heart, riding a lowly donkey to prove it. He is not a King who commands squadrons of armed horsemen, because his kingdom is not from this world (*John* 18:36). His kingdom is about the truth of God and his glory, so he conquers by the persuasive force of God's own truth and the irresistible bonds of God's own love. Even the praise he receives is not for acts of brute force (verse 37) but for powerful acts of mercy leading to human rehabilitation.

Jesus is the King of creation, so when the religious rulers complain that the disciples are worshipping him, he declares that the very stones will cry out if the disciples fall silent. Now is the time for the hills to dance, for the trees to clap their hands, for the seas to roar, for the whole of creation to burst forth in universal homage to her Creator King! Can you hear the music; do you join the chorus?

JESUS WEEPS OVER THE CITY (verses 41–44)

Jesus weeps over the city before he enters it. Normally Luke does not tell us much about the emotions of Jesus, surprisingly since he was a doctor. But on this occasion he chooses to mention that Jesus wept (see also John 11:35). The reason for his grief is explained. He was about to enter the city as the proper King of the Jews (verse 38) but they were not going to welcome him (*John* 1:11). He weeps for them, not for himself, because their rejection will expose them to the just judgement of God. This actually happened in A.D.66–70 when the Romans besieged and sacked the city amidst great atrocities. Josephus the Jewish historian records these facts. The stones of the city that would have cried out in adoration of Jesus (verse 40) will then be thrown down as a sign of God's outrage against the people

There are several lessons contained in this episode.

- Christ sincerely weeps over the hardness and unbelief of lost men and women. Jesus would rather the people had known and received him, for then they would have received God's everlasting blessing (verse 41–42). In the same way he grieves for the hardness of men and women in the twenty-first century, who shut him out of their world. Since Jesus is the man who was God those who have seen and heard him have seen and heard God (*John* 14:8–9). The grief of Jesus is God's grief too, expressed long ago through his prophet (*Ezek*. 33:11). Any theology that leaves Christians indifferent or unfeeling towards the plight of the unconverted is fatally flawed.
- People ought not to procrastinate when it comes to hearing and receiving Jesus. Such postponing can prove fatal for those who engage in it as the case of the Jewish people shows. The message of salvation in Christ is not theirs for people to dispose of as they choose. The message is God's and he may choose to remove it from those who spurn it so that it becomes 'hidden' from them (verse 42).
- Jesus is the place and time where and when God visited the world (verse 44). Zechariah had recognised this at the beginning of the Gospel (*Luke* 1:76–79). Normally 'visitation' has a favourable sense in the Bible referring to times when God draws near, not in judgement but in mercy (*Acts* 15:14; *1 Pet*. 2:12). Jesus himself is the place to begin to draw near to God, that he may draw near to you; he is the one reliable path of enlightenment, the way to life, love, and happiness.

JESUS CLEANSES THE TEMPLE (verses 45–48)

Jesus enters the temple where he drives out those who were trading in the temple precincts. The first part of the background here is the prophecy of Malachi (*Mal*. 3:1–4) who predicted the coming of the Lord to his temple. But first he must cleanse the temple of its accumulated rubbish as a refiner of silver. Only then can worshippers offer pure sacrifices to God and be pleasing. By acting in this way Jesus lays claim to the temple as his rightful home where he, his Father and his people are one. The religious leaders had lost sight of the spiritual nature of worship and the true meaning of the temple building. By his dramatic action Jesus' life was coming full circle, from the time he visited the temple as an infant (*Luke* 1:8–23; 2:21–40) and as a young man (*Luke* 2:41–51) to this his final visit as the true Messiah.

The second part of the biblical background here is from two of the major prophets. Jesus quotes Isaiah (*Isa.* 56:7) by referring to the temple as God's 'house of prayer'. Inexcusably the Jews have turned it into an emporium. By joining this quotation with one from Jeremiah (*Jer.* 7:11) and calling it 'a den of robbers' Jesus lines up his generation of Jews with that of Jeremiah's, when full-scale apostasy reigned in the land. Jesus was accusing his contemporaries of robbing God of his legitimate worship and of using the temple as a cover for all kinds of lawless behaviour. How often state religion has gone hand in hand with worldly living!

In characteristic mode Jesus settled into a daily routine of teaching ministry using the temple as his base. Then as now the ordinary rank and file were more willing to believe Jesus than the religious establishment. How often it has been the theologians, scholars, bureaucrats, and leaders of the churches who have opposed the Jesus of the Gospels, at the very time that ordinary people inside and outside the churches have taken him at his word!

Just because of his popularity the authorities could do nothing openly against Jesus. But it was only a matter of time before their ruthless hands of jealousy and betrayal took hold of Jesus to dispense with him once for all. Yet this was the very way that God was going to advance his cause of the world's redemption, at the proper moment and in the correct circumstances (*Acts* 4:27–28).

80

By Whose Authority?

One day, as Jesus was teaching the people in the temple and preaching the gospel, the chief priests and the scribes with the elders came up [2] *and said to him, 'Tell us by what authority you do these things, or who it is that gave you this authority.'* [3] *He answered them, 'I also will ask you a question. Now tell me,* [4] *Was the baptism of John from heaven or from man?'* [5] *And they discussed it with one another, saying, 'If we say, "From heaven," he will say, "Why did you not believe him?"* [6] *But if we say, "From man," all the people will stone us to death, for they are convinced that John was a prophet.'* [7] *So they answered that they did not know where it came from.* [8] *And Jesus said to them, 'Neither will I tell you by what authority I do these things.'* (Luke 20:1–8).

At this point in the Gospel (*Luke* 20:1–21:4) Jesus engages in a series of public debates with the religious leaders that exposes their prejudices and shocking ignorance. Every round of this contest goes to Jesus but at great personal cost because their public humiliation only fuels their fury and hastens their decision to do away with Jesus.

The first question that arises is the very basic one of authority. 'How can Jesus act as he does?' they ask. 'By what authority does he work?' Their authority was a human construct, in spite of their claims to the rabbinical tradition. Jesus' authority was from heaven, directly bestowed on the banks of the Jordan river by God through the Holy Spirit. Appealing to two different sources of authority meant that the two groups could never agree about the most important things such as the truth of Scripture, the will of God, the nature of God's kingdom, and the way of salvation. Today, the same issue of authority divides religious and secular people alike.

Refusing to answer their question Jesus asked a counter-question that was intended to force them to face up to their own falsehood. By taking them back to John the Baptist's ministry Jesus was reminding them of their first mistake that all their subsequent acts of defiance against Jesus had only compounded. Unless and until they acknowledged the truth of John's ministry they could never understand Jesus, about whom John spoke. Since birth, John and Jesus had shared a common destiny (Luke 1–2).

The leaders were taken aback, caught on the horns of a dilemma that they could not avoid. If they praised John's ministry as from God then why had they never submitted to it? If they rejected John's ministry, then they would lose face with the people who held him a prophet. Actually, the people had more spiritual awareness than their religious teachers. The leaders amazingly chose to plead ignorance rather than lose face by climbing down about John. Jesus leaves them impaled on the horns of their dilemma by refusing to explain the source of his authority. They knew enough about John and even more about Jesus, to acknowledge them both as prophets of the Lord.

Jesus taught his disciples that there are times when they must safeguard the truth rather than broadcast it freely (*Matt.* 7:6). Not everyone's questions are sincere enquiries after truth. On the one hand Christians are always to be ready to give an answer for the hope they have (*1 Pet.* 3:15); on the other they must be wise as serpents (*Matt.* 10:16).

The short debate reveals the importance of starting points in human reasoning. These may be man-centred or God-centred, biblically-based or contrary to Scripture teaching. Whichever they are, conclusions are largely determined by assumptions. By addressing the false assumptions underlying their bad behaviour and attitudes Jesus teaches by example one way of refuting the challenges of critics of Christianity.

81

Jesus the Key to the History of Salvation

And he began to tell the people this parable: 'A man planted a
vineyard and let it out to tenants and went into another country
for a long while. 10 When the time came, he sent a servant to the
tenants, so that they would give him some of the fruit of the
vineyard. But the tenants beat him and sent him away empty-
handed. 11 And he sent another servant. But they also beat and
treated him shamefully, and sent him away empty-handed.
12 And he sent yet a third. This one also they wounded and cast
out. 13 Then the owner of the vineyard said, "What shall I do?
I will send my beloved son; perhaps they will respect him."
14 But when the tenants saw him, they said to themselves, "This
is the heir. Let us kill him, so that the inheritance may be ours."
15 And they threw him out of the vineyard and killed him. What
then will the owner of the vineyard do to them? 16 He will come
and destroy those tenants and give the vineyard to others.' When
they heard this, they said, 'Surely not!' 17 But he looked directly
at them and said, 'What then is this that is written:
"The stone that the builders rejected
has become the cornerstone"?
18 Everyone who falls on that stone will be broken to pieces, and
when it falls on anyone, it will crush him.'
19 The scribes and the chief priests sought to lay hands on him at
that very hour, for they perceived that he had told this parable
against them, but they feared the people (Luke 20:9–19).

For the second of these public debates Jesus takes the initiative by staking out his debating ground in the form of a parable.

There are several points to the parable that deserve mentioning. First, the parable covers the whole of Luke's theology about the history of salvation for Jews and Gentiles. Secondly, the parable obviously contains some allegorical elements that call for comment at the appropriate place. Thirdly, the parable reflects some social and economic practices of Jesus' day but its main principles apply across cultures.

THE STORY-LINE (verses 9–15a)

A landowner hired out a vineyard he had planted, to a number of tenants. He had a legal right to expect a share of the harvest when it came. For this purpose he sent a series of messengers who were all shamefully treated by the tenants and sent back empty-handed. Finally the owner decided to send his son, whom he loved dearly, in the belief they would respect him. Unfortunately they treated him the most violently of all because they knew he was the heir and believed wrongly that they would inherit the vineyard in his place.

The real-life applications of the parable are just as relevant for modern readers as they were for the first audience (verse 19). The Lord as Israel's God is the owner of the vineyard; the tenants are the Israelite people represented by their leaders; the vineyard is God's kingdom with all its material and spiritual favours (*Isa*. 5:1–7); the messengers stand for the prophets; Jesus Christ is the beloved son; his death outside Jerusalem (*Heb*. 13:11–12) is described as the climax of the story. In this way the parable represents the biblical history of salvation across the Testaments, touching Israel, Jesus and the transfer of the kingdom of salvation to the Gentile peoples.

Jesus appears as the last of the prophets but a prophet with a difference because he is the cherished Son of God. This is a pointer to his fully divine status (*Luke* 3:22; see also 9:35). The most significant thing that happened to him in his turbulent short life was the way he died. His life was climaxed in his death when he was treated as a reject (verse 17), fit only to be executed like a criminal outside the precincts of the holy city. In this way Jesus actually fulfilled the saving plan of God which was to make his beloved Son the atoning sacrifice for the sin of his people scattered throughout the world (*John* 11:49–52). Jesus is the chosen yet rejected stone of God's building (*Isa*. 28:16; *1 Pet*. 2:6).

THE SEQUEL (verses 15b–19)

Jesus follows up the parable with a question plus a prophecy about himself. The tenants will not succeed – the owner will destroy them because of their wicked treatment of his son. The vineyard they imagined was their own, will be handed over to new tenants. In this final piece of interpretation Jesus predicts the virtual end of Israel as a theocracy and the emergence of the Gentile world as the new location of God's kingdom. Any suspicions of anti-Semitism here on Luke's part are more than quashed by the feeling way in which Jesus tells the tragic story of Israel's unbelief and by his being the only Evangelist who holds out any hope for Israel in Jesus' eschatological teaching (*Luke* 21:24).

The Jewish leaders claim to be shocked either by the suggestion that they might be unfaithful to God's intentions or that they would lose control of the vineyard. Either way Jesus presses home his advantage by quoting the messianic words of Psalm 118 (verse 22). The psalm speaks of a stone that is first of all rejected for building purposes but later selected by God and made the key stone of the building (the cornerstone aligned the walls and so gave the whole building alignment and stability). Here again Luke's theme of reversal of fortunes appears: God's wisdom and ways overturning those of the world.

Jesus adds a final prediction that this stone of God's appointing and their rejecting will one day crush them to powder. The Jewish leaders are representative of all those everywhere who have rejected the self-witness of Jesus. Their fate will be the same, everlasting dismissal from the comforting presence of the Lord.

These are some of the most awesome words that Jesus ever spoke and show the fallacy of the postmodern virtue of universal tolerance. The Bible judges human unbelief in face of the self-attesting evidence for Jesus as a kind of private crucifying of the Son of God (*Heb*. 6:4–6) for which there can be no remedy. Paul (*Rom*. 11:17–24) applies the sad case of unbelieving Israel to the Gentile peoples as a cautionary tale. The Gentile nations will go the same way as Israel unless they continue in the faith of the gospel; otherwise they too will be cut off. Is not this the pattern of spiritual experience that the once Christian nations of the West are now exhibiting? The vineyard is being handed over again, this time to responsible tenants among the nations of the developing world.

The parable incited the religious leaders all the more against Jesus. They would have arrested him on the spot if they had been able, but they were political creatures at heart and feared a public backlash against any rash move. False church leaders act from the same motives of self-preservation.

82

God and Caesar

So they watched him and sent spies, who pretended to be sincere, that they might catch him in something he said, so as to deliver him up to the authority and jurisdiction of the governor. [21] *So they asked him, 'Teacher, we know that you speak and teach rightly, and show no partiality, but truly teach the way of God.'* [23] *But he perceived their craftiness, and said to them,* [24] *'Show me a denarius. Whose likeness and inscription does it have?' They said, 'Caesar's.'* [25] *He said to them, 'Then render to Caesar the things that are Caesar's, and to God the things that are God's.'* [26] *And they were not able in the presence of the people to catch him in what he said, but marvelling at his answer they became silent* (Luke 20:20–26).

In the third exchange it is a measure of their frustration with Jesus that the religious authorities stay home and send spies to speak to him. Their method was entrapment of Jesus through flattery. Their hope was that they could get him to incriminate himself so that they could use this in court against him. But just as in the first encounter (*Luke* 20:1–8) Jesus turned the tables on his opponents by asking them questions that exposed their double-standards and insincerity. The front men are no more successful against Jesus than their masters.

They raise with Jesus the vexed question of paying taxes to the occupying power of Rome, represented by Caesar. Opinions were divided, some Jews resenting the Roman presence with all its political demands; others chose to go along with Rome's rigorous demands so as to save the nation. Jesus responds by asking for a denarius coin because it bore on one side a likeness of the emperor's head. Having established from his opponents that it was Caesar's face Jesus made the coin the basis of a legitimate claim to power by the Romans in Palestine. At the same time Jesus reminds his hearers of another King, God, who has legitimate and higher claims on the hearts and lives of the people. Jesus' answer was so original and penetrating that the spies asked him no more questions.

Jesus' reply raises the larger question of the limits of human authority and the claims of the state. Human governments are God's institution for guarding public morals and restraining evil in society (*Rom.* 13:1–7). But God's claims are primary because they are absolute. Where God and Caesar compete for people's loyalty or worship God must always be first (*Acts* 5:29). God alone is Lord of the conscience, though human groups or individuals may have a legitimate claim on conscience.

The relation between the kingdom of God and citizenship is like two concentric circles rather than two circles alongside one another. The inside circle is civil power, the outside circle is the rule of God that qualifies all human loyalties by overshadowing them. This is how Jesus explained the subject (*John* 19:9–11).

83

If There Is No Resurrection ...

There came to him some Sadducees, those who deny that there
is a resurrection, 28 and they asked him a question, saying,
'Teacher, Moses wrote for us that if a man's brother dies,
having a wife but no children, the man must take the widow
and raise up offspring for his brother. 29 Now there were seven
brothers. The first took a wife, and died without children.
30 And the second 31 and the third took her, and likewise all seven
left no children and died. 32 Afterward the woman also died. 33
In the resurrection, therefore, whose wife will the woman be? For
the seven had her as wife.'
34 And Jesus said to them, 'The sons of this age marry and are
given in marriage, 35 but those who are considered worthy to
attain to that age and to the resurrection from the dead neither
marry nor are given in marriage, 36 for they cannot die anymore,
because they are equal to angels and are sons of God, being sons
of the resurrection. 37 But that the dead are raised, even Moses
showed, in the passage about the bush, where he calls the Lord
the God of Abraham and the God of Isaac and the God of Jacob.
38 Now he is not God of the dead, but of the living, for all live to
him.' 39 Then some of the scribes answered, 'Teacher, you have
spoken well.' 40 For they no longer dared to ask him any question
(Luke 20:27–40).

Now it was the turn of the Sadducees to ply Jesus with questions. The Sadducees came from aristocratic Jewish families and carried great influence in political circles. Theologically they were liberals who rejected the supernatural by denying the existence of angels and a bodily resurrection (*Acts* 23:8).

It was about the latter that they chose to test Jesus, so they concocted an unlikely story about a woman who married seven brothers in turn. The Mosaic law advocated levirate (from Latin for a brother-in-law) marriage which required the brother of a man who had died childless to marry his widow in the hope of producing a son and heir to his late brother (*Gen*. 38:8; *Deut*. 25:5–6). The Sadducees wanted to know whose wife this woman would be if there was a resurrection! Obviously they wanted to reduce belief in a resurrection to ridicule.

Jesus' reply has two parts – how the resurrection differs from bodily life now (verses 34–36) and the case for the resurrection of the body (verses 37–38). By this means he moves from the particular to the general in a logical way.

JESUS' FIRST ANSWER (verses 34–36)

Jesus speaks about the resurrection with the same authority and clarity that he brings to every subject he addresses. The resurrection will mean changes to our present form of existence. Because resurrection bodies will lack reproductive organs the question of whose wife the woman would be is based on a fundamental ignorance about the nature of the resurrection. Humans will become like angels in their changeless state because as God's redeemed children they will never die. Marriage and reproduction are therefore unnecessary in the post-resurrection world.

The Sadducees assumed that, if there was a resurrection, the human body would be the same after it as before. In fact, the resurrection means change, some things remaining the same, others becoming new. Paul develops this belief in continuity and discontinuity in the resurrection (1 *Cor*. 15:35–57; also *Phil*. 3:20–21). Whatever the changes and whatever remains the same the resurrection will mean the final and complete defeat of death in God's creation. What will trigger the resurrection is Jesus' personal return in glory (*1 Cor*. 15:22–23; *1 Thess*. 4:14–17).

Jesus' teaching about the sexless condition of the resurrection need not mean that the gender difference between men and women will not continue after the resurrection in a recognisable form. Nor does it mean that family members will not experience the same close ties of earthly life. All this is predicated on the belief that each person will know themselves in the resurrection (Jesus advertised himself as the same person who had died on the cross) and that we will recognise one another, but now freed from sin and like Christ.

JESUS' SECOND ANSWER (verses 37–38)

Jesus refutes the scepticism of the Sadducees by appealing to the Pentateuch (the first five books of the Old Testament) which they held was the only Scripture. He cites the passage where the Lord makes himself known to Moses as the God of Abraham, Isaac and Jacob (*Exod.* 3:6). Although these patriarchs had been dead for hundreds of years Jesus takes the Lord's reply in the present tense (*I* am *the God of* ...) as meaning tha t they were alive in God's presence as he spoke and destined for resurrection.

But Jesus goes one step further and states how everyone who dies is alive in God's presence since he has a relationship with people that transcends death. At death the disembodied spirit immediately appears before God (*Eccles.* 12:7) for private judgement (*Heb.* 9:27).

Paul gives a Christian turn to this thinking by claiming that all live and die to the Lord Jesus Christ (*Rom.* 14:7–9). Through dying and rising again Jesus has become the rightful Lord of all human beings whether in life, at death, or thereafter. Everyone will appear before Christ to receive his verdict on their lives as a whole (*Rom.* 14:10–12). This means that there will be a resurrection of both the righteous and the wicked (*John* 5:28–29). There is no suggestion of annihilationism in Jesus' prospective teaching.

The only way to be informed and ready for the resurrection is by believing what the Scriptures teach on this and other subjects. Belief in a general resurrection is part of a larger belief in the supernatural power of God whereby he is able to overturn the present regularities of the physical world by introducing new ones. Their failure to believe this led the Sadducees astray as it also does many in the scientific community today (*Matt.* 22:29). Jesus has the power and the right to reconstruct the universe (*Phil.* 3:20–21).

Perhaps the Pharisees felt that they needed to redeem their battered image so they applaud Jesus in his public rebuttal of the Sadducees (verse 39). The Pharisees were in agreement with Jesus on the resurrection but they were not risking any more questions to him (verse 40). Jesus had now effectively silenced all his critics by winning every public debate. How thankful we are that they did debate Jesus on these subjects because we know things now that otherwise we might have remained in ignorance about!

84

Is Jesus a Son?

[41] But he said to them, 'How can they say that the Christ is
David's son? [42] For David himself says in the Book of Psalms,
"The Lord said to my Lord,
Sit at my right hand,
[43] until I make your enemies your footstool."
[44] David thus calls him Lord, so how is he his son?'

(Luke 20:41–44).

The Pharisees congratulated Jesus on his success in answering the Sadducees with whom the Pharisees also disagreed about a number of things. But Jesus has no wish to cosy up with the Pharisees so he directs a question at them. The traditional belief was that the messiah would be born of King David's line since many biblical passages taught this (*2 Sam.* 7:11–13; *Psa.* 89:19–37, *Isa.* 11:1–5; *Ezek.* 34:23–24). The expectation was that this national deliverer would appear in the latter days.

Psalm 110 celebrates the kingship of the Messiah but David, the author of the Psalm, calls the Messiah his Lord. By looking up to his son to call him Lord, David created a theological problem since normally descendants admire their ancestors, not the reverse. How could the Messiah both be David's son and his Lord, at the same time descended from him yet exalted over him? Jesus does not answer his own question but leaves his audience to work it out for themselves (often the best means of teaching).

A clue to this puzzle is provided in verse 1 of the psalm where the Lord takes David's son, the Messiah, up into his own presence to share the rule with him over time and space. Clearly the Messiah is more than man, though belonging to David's house historically.

He is God's partner in government because he is God's equal in being. In Jesus the religious authorities were confronting God's mystery, the unique individual who is both God and Man.

At his birth angels told how he would be David's biological son but also the eternal Son of God Most High (*Luke* 1:32–35). Jesus is here witnessing to the mysterious truth of his double generation, from God in God's eternity and from David in human history. Jesus is everything we are, apart from our sinfulness; and everything the Father and the Holy Spirit are, except their personality. Because the Son of God is now eternally human as well as fully divine, he has been raised as Man to the same position that Adam had over the first creation. Jesus is exalted over the new age which will encompass, after the resurrection, the new heaven and earth, the second creation (*Heb*. 2:5–9). His status as glorified man corresponds to his eternal glory as God (*John* 17:5). No wonder all God's angels worship him (*Heb*. 1:6)!

85

Beware – Theologians at Work!

And in the hearing of all the people he said to his disciples,
46 'Beware of the scribes, who like to walk around in long robes,
and love greetings in the marketplaces and the best seats in the
synagogues and the places of honour at feasts, 47 who devour
widows' houses and for a pretence make long prayers. They will
receive the greater condemnation.' (Luke 20:45–47).

The chapter ends with a short warning against the scribes of the Pharisees, who were their official theologians. Jesus had already spoken against them to their faces (*Luke* 11:45–52). Now he warns his disciples against them and in doing so tells us four truths about them that give the lie to what they seemed to be.

First, their affections were fixed on earthly things. For example, they loved the robes that brought them acclaim and status in public life. They loved deferential greetings, the most prominent seats in synagogue worship, and top-table placings at banquets. Paul encountered religious spokespersons with the same earth-bound minds (*Phil.* 3:18–19). They proliferate in any age of religious exploration because they see religion as an opportunity for making money (*1 Tim.* 6:3–5).

Secondly, they were ruled by dark passions such as greed and intolerance. They had no scruples about seizing widows' properties as soon as they died, to make themselves wealthy (*Luke* 16:14); and while these same widows were alive the scribes imposed burdensome regulations that no one could keep, even themselves (*Luke* 11:46). Religious claims may often camouflage unholy motives.

Thirdly, their religion consisted in public performance, such as making long prayers that gave the impression of great spirituality.

The scribes are a standing lesson on how necessary it is to live out religious faith. Religious professionals, above all, need to be accountable by not living a double life, publicly one thing but privately another. Jesus calls for the surrender of the inner life to God (*Luke* 11:39–41).

Fourthly, their life of double standards, cloaked by religion, will mean a greater punishment in the day of Jesus' judgement. They knew more than most yet performed worse. Jesus' judgement will be measured by a person's knowledge and the opportunity for improvement that was had. By this measure the scribes will fair badly because they had the key of religious knowledge but never used it for themselves or others (*Luke* 11:52). How many will be like them in Jesus' day!

Jesus reminds us of the danger of a religion of the head and/or of public appearance, without a change of heart and right motives. A religious faith that consisted in outward rites and moral habits will never save when the individual stands before Christ in judgement. He will want to know not what a person knew, but what he did with what he knew (*Luke* 13:24–30).

86

Generous Giving

Jesus looked up and saw the rich putting their gifts into the offering box, [2] *and he saw a poor widow put in two small copper coins.* [3] *And he said, 'Truly, I tell you, this poor widow has put in more than all of them.* [4] *For they all contributed out of their abundance, but she out of her poverty put in all she had to live on.'* (Luke 21:1–4).

Chapter 21 ends Jesus' public teaching ministry where it began (*Luke* 2:46–49) – in the temple in Jerusalem. This section began with his triumphant entry into the city (*Luke* 19:28–48); it concludes with Jesus prophetically foretelling world events leading up to his triumphal return to the world.

At work in the temple one day Jesus caught sight of a poor widow casting her meagre earnings into one of the receptacles for the donations of worshippers, that lined one wall of the temple. Jesus turns human estimates upside down by pronouncing a blessing on the widow and bypassing the rich people who gave great amounts. Most widows were poor because their men-folk had died, leaving them without a livelihood. On three counts she was despised by the religious establishment that saw poverty as a sign of God's rejection, widowhood as a cause for exploitation, and being a woman as being a second-class citizen. But God's ways are not our ways, nor his thoughts our thoughts (*Isa*. 55:8–9).

Measured in quantity the widow's offering did not begin to compare with the vast amounts cast in by the rich. But measured in quality of giving their gifts did not begin to compare with hers. This was because of the degree of sacrifice involved in her giving. She gave away all that she had so that her giving was costly to her. What the rich gave involved no sacrifice and would never be missed. Such are God's values in deciding the worth of what people give to him. What she did stands for all time as a guide to giving in Christ's kingdom. Like the woman who anointed Jesus the widow's praise will go wherever the gospel goes because she was inspired by evangelical faith and love.

A similar case of people giving generously out of their poverty in a spirit of real sacrifice arose in one of Paul's churches (*2 Cor.* 8:1–7). From their example he drew out lessons of cheerfulness and generosity if Christian giving is in any way to match God's giving in Jesus. In his incarnational coming in Jesus, the Son renounced the wealth of his heavenly existence, choosing instead the poverty of our human condition. This was to make us rich through his self-imposed poverty (verse 9). The sacrificial coming, living and dying of Jesus will always be the measure of what giving means in Christian practice.

The question we should always ask ourselves in the matter of Christian giving is not, 'How much did I give?' but, 'How much did it cost me to give?'

87

The End of the World

*And while some were speaking of the temple, how it was adorned
with noble stones and offerings, he said, 6 'As for these things that
you see, the days will come when there will not be left here one
stone upon another that will not be thrown down.' 7 And they
asked him, 'Teacher, when will these things be, and what will be
the sign when these things are about to take place?' 8 And he said,
'See that you are not led astray. For many will come in my name,
saying, "I am he!" and, "The time is at hand!" Do not go after
them. 9 And when you hear of wars and tumults, do not be
terrified, for these things must first take place, but the end will
not be at once.'*

*10 Then he said to them, 'Nation will rise against nation, and
kingdom against kingdom. 11 There will be great earthquakes,
and in various places famines and pestilences. And there will be
terrors and great signs from heaven. 12 But before all this they
will lay their hands on you and persecute you, delivering you up
to the synagogues and prisons, and you will be brought before
kings and governors for my name's sake. 13 This will be your
opportunity to bear witness. 14 Settle it therefore in your minds
not to meditate beforehand how to answer, 15 for I will give you
a mouth and wisdom, which none of your adversaries will be able
to withstand or contradict. 16 You will be delivered up even by
parents and brothers and relatives and friends, and some of you
they will put to death. 17 You will be hated by all for my name's
sake. 18 But not a hair of your head will perish. 19 By your
endurance you will gain your lives.*

*20 But when you see Jerusalem surrounded by armies, then know
that its desolation has come near. 21 Then let those who are in*

Judea flee to the mountains, and let those who are inside the city
depart, and let not those who are out in the country enter it,
[22] *for these are days of vengeance, to fulfill all that is written.*
[23] *Alas for women who are pregnant and for those who are nursing*
infants in those days! For there will be great distress upon the
earth and wrath against this people. [24] *They will fall by the edge*
of the sword and be led captive among all nations, and Jerusalem
will be trampled underfoot by the Gentiles, until the times of the
Gentiles are fulfilled.
[25] *And there will be signs in sun and moon and stars, and on the*
earth distress of nations in perplexity because of the roaring of
the sea and the waves, [26] *people fainting with fear and with*
foreboding of what is coming on the world. For the powers of the
heavens will be shaken. [27] *And then they will see the Son of Man*
coming in a cloud with power and great glory. [28] *Now when these*
things begin to take place, straighten up and raise your heads,
because your redemption is drawing near.'
[29] *And he told them a parable: 'Look at the fig tree, and all the*
trees. [30] *As soon as they come out in leaf, you see for yourselves*
and know that the summer is already near. [31] *So also, when you*
see these things taking place, you know that the kingdom of God
is near. [32] *Truly, I say to you, this generation will not pass away*
until all has taken place. [33] *Heaven and earth will pass away,*
but my words will not pass away.
[34] *But watch yourselves lest your hearts be weighed down with*
dissipation and drunkenness and cares of this life, and that day
come upon you suddenly like a trap. [35] *For it will come upon all*
who dwell on the face of the whole earth. [36] *But stay awake at all*
times, praying that you may have strength to escape all these things
that are going to take place, and to stand before the Son of Man.'
[37] *And every day he was teaching in the temple, but at night he*
went out and lodged on the mount called Olivet. [38] *And early in*
the morning all the people came to him in the temple to hear him
(Luke 21:5–38).

This is Jesus' final public teaching before his betrayal, trial, and death. He fulfils his role as God's end-time prophet (*Heb.* 1:1–2).

Very fittingly he makes pronouncements about the immediate future of the Jewish people, as well as about the future of this planet which will be radically changed at the coming of the Son of Man.

Luke's arrangement of Jesus' last discourse is easier to sort out since it is more clearly arranged into groups of sayings, than Mark's (*Mark* 13) or Matthew's (*Matt.* 24) accounts. It falls into a number of sub-divisions.

OCCASION (verses 5–8)

The whole discourse is sparked by the surroundings of the temple precincts. The Jerusalem temple was still being built in Jesus' day, the work having begun around 20 B.C. at the initiative of Herod the Great with no expense being spared on the work. It was not to be finished until 63 A.D., just in time for the Romans to destroy it in the Jewish War seven years later, as Jesus predicts (verse 20).

No doubt the disciples were still thinking like Jews long conditioned to the externals of religion, while missing its inner meaning (*Rom.* 2:28–29). Later Peter was to see that God's real temple is his believing people, wherever they worship. The church as God's end-time temple is built together as a spiritual house around the corner-stone of Jesus Christ who gives his people all their unity, foundation, and beauty (1 *Peter* 2:4–10 following *Luke* 20:17–18).

The disciples' expressions of admiration for the magnificence of the temple sparks Jesus' announcement that the whole work is in vain, because it will all be undone in the next generation. Stunned by this pronouncement the disciples ask for more information. When will this happen and what signs will precede it? Jesus chooses not to satisfy their curiosity about dates but answers instead in personal terms. Yet one thing he does reveal, that many religious figures will claim the kind of future knowledge that Jesus refuses to give to the disciples. More important than futurology is being ready oneself for the future, however it works out. So, 'Beware that you are not led astray!'

Predictive prophecy and conspiracy theories have been popular in recent times due to the dramatic changes in the modern world. People experience fear, insecurity, and a feeling of helplessness.

Obsession with eschatology (the study of the end times), or being dogmatic about it, can be a kind of spiritual sickness that takes our focus away from Jesus himself. Jesus' words set limits to our knowledge of the future; he also stresses the practical use of a proper study of biblical prophecy. If it does not make us better people and more ready for his coming then it is useless.

WORLD SITUATION (verses 9–11)

Jesus turns the disciples' question about the destruction of the temple into an opportunity to speak about the world at large and the end of history as a whole (verse 9, 'the end'). This quick transition from nearer to further horizons in time is not uncommon in biblical prophecy. Clearly Jesus' remarks refer to more than the local Palestinian politics of his day.

The world will continue to be torn by wars and conflicts. The physical world will add to this state of fear and suffering through natural disasters like earthquakes, drought, diseases, and disturbances in outer space that will threaten terrible possibilities. The natural reaction to these sorts of events is fear. But Jesus speaks against being terrified since these very developments are part of God's plan, a prelude to the world's end. Yet contrary to natural expectations these frightful events by themselves do not mean the end of the world. Here again we meet the 'delay motif' in relation to the coming of the kingdom of God (*Luke* 19:11).

The twentieth century was one of unprecedented carnage through two world wars and genocidal pogroms in several countries. The later part of the century was marked by earthquakes, famines, and disease (new and older ones once thought to have been eradicated) across the world. As our knowledge of the physical universe increases so will our awareness of dangers and changes threatening the earth from inside and outside. All such developments are in line with Jesus' words and should strengthen our confidence in him as the church's Prophet (*Acts* 3:22–26). Jesus assures us that frightening as these developments may be they are all part of God's means for bringing in his kingdom through the return of Jesus his Son in glory (verse 28).

DISCIPLES OF JESUS (verses 12–19)

What should followers of Jesus expect in the future of the world? Jesus paints a dark picture of persecutions by religious and political authorities, of public trials and imprisonment, betrayal by family members and friends, even death itself. Just as the twentieth century was notorious for its destruction of human life through genocide and war so it was infamous for the high number of its martyrs for Jesus. As the Western countries that have known so much of the social and political benefits of Christ's gospel throw off the last vestiges of that religious legacy, we can expect a more openly hostile environment to live and work in.

Into this dark picture of the future Jesus speaks two words of unspeakable comfort. These are that when Christians are put on trial they need not feel alone. Jesus through his Spirit will himself be with them to give them courage to speak boldly for him. Further, by adhering to the faith Christians will eventually win through to the eternal salvation that Christ has promised (verse 18 need not mean being saved from death).

Along with these two great promises go two conditions. One is that we see any public trial in a positive way, as an opportunity for testifying to Christ. The other is the need for endurance because only those who persevere to the end will be saved (*Heb.* 10:36–39). Only saving faith in Christ can accomplish this double feat of turning danger into opportunity and of holding up through suffering. We ought to make sure that we are among the number of those who have a living faith, one that works out in the testing times of life, just as Jesus' faith did (*Heb.* 12:2–3).

THE JEWISH WAR (verses 20–24)

Jesus changes tack again by foretelling the traumatic events of the Jewish War (66–70 A.D.) when Jerusalem was encircled by Roman armies and eventually sacked. Josephus the Jewish historian writes graphically of life in the besieged city during those days and confirms Jesus' words about the unimaginable sufferings of its inhabitants. Some scholars of the Gospels explain the accuracy of Jesus' words by claiming that they were put into his mouth by Christian editors who lived to see the real events. But this way of explaining Jesus' prophetic powers rests on the prior philosophical assumption that Jesus was limited like other men and could not know the future any more than we can. The fact that Jesus had genuine prophetic powers fits in with everything else that we learn about him as the God-man filled with the Holy Spirit (see *Luke* 13:31–35; 17:22–36). It is the absence of such prophetic powers that would be problematical, an inexplicable defect that would undermine Jesus' claims.

Jesus makes three comments on the fall of Jerusalem:

- The fall of the city would be no isolated event but rather the culmination of generations of rejecting the Lord's witness (*Luke* 13:34–35a). The mills of God grind slowly but they grind exceeding small (*Hos*. 1:4–5). The rejection of Jesus as Messiah was going to be the finale of Israel's denial of the God of their salvation. There could be no more patience and mercy; instead God's invoking of the curses of a broken covenant (*Deut*. 28:15–68; *Luke* 13:6–9; 20:9–18; *1 Thess*. 2:14–16).
- Future believers, living in Jerusalem, are forewarned to flee the city to escape the cauldron of suffering and devastation that would engulf its inhabitants. This in fact did happen resulting in the formation of the early Jewish Ebionite churches made up of the poor (the meaning of 'ebionite') believers from Jewish society.
- Jesus appears to limit the period in which Israel will be subject to Gentile overlords following the sack of Jerusalem. Jesus' words (verse 24c), like those on another occasion (*Luke* 13:35), give hope of a future restoration of Israel, a prospect that Paul appears to endorse in his overview of religious history (*Rom*. 11:11–32). Does Jesus hold out an end-time promise of saving mercy to bring Israel into the fullness of the blessings of the gospel (possibly in Galatians 6:16)?

FINAL REDEMPTION (verses 25–28)

The last times of this age will be notable for tragic events on a global scale such as disturbances in the heavenly bodies in the solar system and natural changes on the earth connected with the oceans, resulting in confusion and terror among the world's inhabitants. In those future generations people's hearts will fail them from fear of what is coming on the earth, bringing closure to human civilisation.

Into the midst of this final apocalypse of disorder and terror Jesus will appear as the triumphant Son of Man whose lordly power extends over the whole creation. His appearance will be marked by heavenly splendour and unimaginable power. Jesus commands believers alive immediately prior to his coming to lift up their heads amidst the surrounding gloom and doom, because his arrival will bring their final salvation.

By referring to certain global signs of the coming of the kingdom Jesus is not contradicting his habit of refusing to give signs, on other occasions (*Luke* 17:20–21). There Jesus was checking the sceptical scribes who shut their eyes to the evidence of Jesus' public ministry (*Luke* 11:29–32); here Jesus is aiming to forearm those followers of his who will face the rigours and terrors of the last days. They will need the strength and security that these words of Jesus will give (*John* 16:4).

In an age of global warming, ecological destruction, and greater awareness of the dangers from outer space (e.g. meteorites hitting the earth) the conditions Jesus predicts in this apocalyptic discourse are not inconceivable in a foreseeable future time.

A PARABLE (verses 29–33)

A parable works on a comparison between things that differ in a number of ways but have one important thing in common. Leaves appearing on Palestinian trees and shrubs were a sure sign that summer was approaching. In the same way the appearance of the sorts of events Jesus has outlined is a sign of the imminence of the kingdom of God and the close of the present age. One thing points to another both in the natural world and the historical-spiritual one.

Of course, throughout history there have been famines, earthquakes, and strange signs in the heavens. So how will Christians know when the end of history has arrived? Jesus implies that these sorts of events will accelerate and multiply and this is what will make them signs of the very end time. The close of history will disclose its own meaning to the discerning.

To this parable Jesus adds two words of wisdom.

First, Jesus says famously that 'this generation will not disappear until all these things come to pass'. These words cannot be taken literally since it is now two thousand years since Jesus uttered them. A number of difficulties face us here. If we could translate 'generation' as 'people' the main difficulty would disappear since the Jews remain until today, but 'generation' normally means just that and no more (a period of twenty-five years). Then come the words 'all these things'. There is no way in which all that Jesus has said in his discourse could be fulfilled in the generation of Jews to whom he was speaking.

This leads us to the last possibility and that is to translate 'come to pass' in a beginning sense (which is grammatically possible). It would then read as 'begin to come to pass'. This is possibly the best option so that Jesus now says, 'Assuredly I tell you, this generation will not disappear until all these things begin to come to pass.' This would tender the message that God's judgements were going to start falling on the Jewish people very shortly but that they would not be exhausted in one generation. This explanation fits in well with the general structure of New Testament eschatology that encloses the first parts of the future age in the present age.

The second saying is more straightforward (verse 33). Jesus claims absolute authority for his teaching and his individual sayings. Since only the Creator can survive the meltdown of creation, Jesus here identifies himself with God. Those who have followed the gospel story so far will not be surprised or offended by Jesus' claim here. This is all in keeping with what people have come to believe about him. They know that he is speaking the truth when he speaks like this (see *Heb.* 1:8–12).

PRACTICAL LESSONS (verses 34–36)

All this teaching about the end of the age stays in the realm of speculation unless it impacts on life in the real world. Jesus now shows the difference this belief of the future should and can make. The main lesson is a call to constant watchfulness, combined with prayerfulness. These two responses are mutually fulfilling. The reason for vigilance and the content of praying are both stated. Disciples are to be on their guard against spiritual entrapment from the sensuality and worldliness that are rife in the culture that surrounds them. These unsavoury influences produce a spirit of heaviness in which the human spirit is weighed down, preventing disciples from enjoying the proper joy and liberty that come with living in Christ's kingdom. As a result the day of Christ's return for judgement will come suddenly like a trap that is triggered without warning. In actual fact Christ has warned his disciples plenty, but self-indulgence dulls the hearing and erodes moral character (*Mark* 9:50).

Incidentally, Jesus makes it clear that his advent is no secret coming before or after death, some private encounter in the spirit realm. Instead, his coming will overtake the whole international community then alive on earth and he will summon the dead from the after-life for judgement (*John* 5:28–29).

Specifically, disciples should pray to escape those terrible events of the end-time. In saying this Jesus does not mean that people should ask to be removed from the earth, as in some rapture experience. After all, there will be believers alive on the earth when Jesus returns (*1 Thess.* 4:15). No, what he means is that Christians should ask to be kept from the corrupting temptations, sins and anxieties of those times, so that they may be able to stand before Christ in judgement without shame or fear (*1 John* 4:17–18).

There is a real sense in which every generation faces these pressures. Jesus is reminding his followers everywhere that they are all too easily affected by the fallen aspects of the culture in which they live. Immediately prior to his coming at the end of this age Christians will find the moral and spiritual climate of the world increasingly suffocating (*Luke* 18:8).

Jesus at the same time holds out the promise that he will preserve his own in the worst of times, as a proof of his power and faithfulness (*Luke* 22:31–32; *1 Pet.* 1:4–5). Purity of heart is something to pray for, receive strength and work for, through Christ's grace.

The whole chapter ends with a description of Christ's daily teaching activity in the temple, his habit of withdrawing to the Mount of Olives by night (shades of events to come) and how he was always a drawcard for the people. From this point on events take a sinister turn in the private sector and they move quickly. Jesus' public teaching ministry is effectively over.

88

The Beginning of the End

Now the Feast of Unleavened Bread drew near, which is called the Passover. [2] *And the chief priests and the scribes were seeking how to put him to death, for they feared the people.*
[3] *Then Satan entered into Judas called Iscariot, who was of the number of the twelve.* [4] *He went away and conferred with the chief priests and officers how he might betray him to them.* [5] *And they were glad, and agreed to give him money.* [6] *So he consented and sought an opportunity to betray him to them in the absence of a crowd* (Luke 22:1–6).

The last stage of Jesus' earthly journey begins here. Scholars like to call it the 'Passion Narrative' based on the Latin word that means suffering. The occasion was the Jewish Passover festival when lambs were killed by Jewish people, as a way of remembering and participating symbolically in the momentous event of the Exodus. This was in keeping with the Lord's command to sacrifice lambs by shedding and daubing their blood (*Exod.* 12). The symbolism for Jesus was striking and intentional. By offering up his own life to God Jesus wanted to become our Passover Lamb once for all offered to set us free (*1 Cor.* 5:7). Passover was followed by the seven days of Unleavened Bread, an essential part of the whole celebration (*Exod.* 12:15–20).

Wherever Jesus went he had one of two effects on people. Either he aroused deep-seated hostility or he elicited heart-felt praise. As his life-story moves toward its climax the forces of darkness and hostility make their final move. Three players dominate the scene. These are the religious teachers, Judas, and Satan. They make a strange trio but are united in a shameless conspiracy against the Son of God. One restraining factor was fear of the people who might protest violently against any mistreatment of Jesus. Satan stirred Judas up and he and the religious authorities fed off one another in their shared resentment of Jesus.

DECEPTION AND BETRAYAL

So far the Pharisees have been playing a cat and mouse game with Jesus. Now it was the turn of the priestly families and the experts in legal interpretation, representing the brains behind the operation. They were already trying to work out some plan to be rid of Jesus when Judas came to their aid. His arrival provided them with the perfect alibi for achieving their end. However, as we read through the whole narrative we should remember that everything that was happening was according to the perfect will of God for Jesus and for us, even to the finest detail. Evildoers never catch God out or put him under pressure; they can only advance his glory (*Acts* 4:24–28).

What was shocking was the fact that all this plotting and deception was being practised by those who claimed to be God's representatives. Jesus saw through their pretence and turned his holy outrage against them (*Luke* 11:45–52). So often since Jesus' day professional theologians and church leaders have been the greatest enemies of the Lord's people by undermining evangelical truth and working for its marginalisation.

Not surprisingly the powers of darkness (Satan) were also stirred up against Jesus the Son of God. In fact, Satan was the real instigator of the scheme to remove Jesus whose coming into the world was a direct threat to his universal rule (*Luke* 4:33–37; *2 Cor*. 4:4; *Eph*. 2:1–2). Jesus likened his incarnate ministry to the binding of a strong man before spoiling his possessions (*Luke* 11:20–22).

How Satan influences human hearts and human events remains a mystery but there can be no doubt about the reality of it as the present case shows. Satan is an intelligent spirit who responds to the movement of the times and helps influence them. So he entered into Judas. This is a strong expression that stands for more than just sowing an evil thought (*John* 13:2; *Acts* 5:3). Judas, in effect, became demon-possessed. After all, his act of betraying Jesus compares only with the original sin of Adam, surpassing it for sheer evil. Only a demon-possessed man could receive a food-morsel from the Son of God one moment, then the next go out and sell him secretly into the hands of his enemies (*John* 13:27). Judas had known the Son of God intimately yet chose finally to sell him for the price of a slave (*Exod.* 21:32). No wonder Jesus declared that it would have been better for Judas never to have existed (*Matt.* 26:24)!

Judas went on his own initiative to the religious leaders to fix a deal whereby he would hand Jesus over to them and they would pay him for the trouble. We get a further glimpse into the real state of the hearts of these religious men when we read how they delighted at the turn of events in their favour. They showed none of that love that does not rejoice at evil but rejoices at the truth (*1 Cor.* 13:6). They were religious terrorists, hell-bent on a crusade of destruction in the name of religion.

For Judas there was no turning back. He was being driven by the evil powers to whom he had surrendered. Having entered into a contract of evil with the religious authorities he was on the prowl for the opportunity to pounce on Jesus to destroy him. Unfortunately for both parties the Son of God could not be disposed of so easily, in fact, not at all.

The resurrection of Jesus just a few days later was going to demonstrate how indestructible Jesus is. This lesson deserves to be noted well by every generation that works to crucify Jesus on its own account. It cannot be done; he will not return to death; he is alive now for ever more; he is ready to come as Judge of the living and the dead (*Acts* 17:31; *Rev.* 1:7).

89

The Last Supper

Then came the day of Unleavened Bread, on which the Passover lamb had to be sacrificed. [8] *So Jesus sent Peter and John, saying, 'Go and prepare the Passover for us, that we may eat it.'* [9] *They said to him, 'Where will you have us prepare it?'* [10] *He said to them, 'Behold, when you have entered the city, a man carrying a jar of water will meet you. Follow him into the house that he enters* [11] *and tell the master of the house, 'The Teacher says to you, Where is the guest room, where I may eat the Passover with my disciples?'* [12] *And he will show you a large upper room furnished; prepare it there.'* [13] *And they went and found it just as he had told them, and they prepared the Passover.* [14] *And when the hour came, he reclined at table, and the apostles with him.* [15] *And he said to them, 'I have earnestly desired to eat this Passover with you before I suffer.* [16] *For I tell you I will not eat it until it is fulfilled in the kingdom of God.'* [17] *And he took a cup, and when he had given thanks he said, 'Take this, and divide it among yourselves.* [18] *For I tell you that from now on I will not drink of the fruit of the vine until the kingdom of God comes.'* [19] *And he took bread, and when he had given thanks, he broke it and gave it to them, saying, 'This is my body, which is given for you. Do this in remembrance of me.'* [20] *And likewise the cup after they had eaten, saying, 'This cup that is poured out for you is the new covenant in my blood.'* (Luke 22:7–20).

The scene has now been set for playing out the final acts in the drama of Jesus' life. He invites his disciples to share a Passover meal with him. The verses 19b–20 have been omitted by some manuscripts but most biblical scholars offer good reasons for including them as original and part of God's written Word.

PREPARATIONS (verses 7–13)

Luke tells us that it was the day when the lambs had to be slaughtered for the Passover. This was the afternoon and evening of the fourteenth day of the first month of the Jewish calendar, called Nisan (*Exod.* 12:18; *Lev.* 23:5–6). John dates Christ's death on this day (*John* 13:1; 18:28; 19:14); Luke and the other two Evangelists make it the day after. This difference in dating could be due to the use of different cultic calendars; the day and event would remain the same but the date would be reckoned differently.

What is important is the way the coming death of Jesus is tied in with the Passover feast. Deliberately he chose to be in Jerusalem for this occasion because he saw that he himself was the ideal Passover Lamb. The sentence of death was borne by the lambs which substituted for the firstborn sons of Israel. In the same way Jesus took the sentence of eternal death on himself when he was made sin for us (*2 Cor.* 5:21). Our offences were transferred to him; his righteousness was transferred to us.

Jesus is our Passover lamb through whom we can now celebrate the feast of Christian liberty from sin's control (*1 Cor.* 5:6–8). This was prefigured by the days of unleavened bread that followed the Passover sacrifice. During the period following Passover all leaven was removed from the homes of the Israelites symbolising their separation from all idolatry, to serve the Lord, the God of Israel. In the same way, Christ's death calls and empowers us for a lifetime of separated living to do his work in the world (*Heb.* 9:13–14).

As in the case of the donkey (*Luke* 19:28–34) the Master now gives detailed instructions to his disciples for finding a room for them to celebrate the feast together. A man carrying a water pot would have been an unusual sight and so a clear sign for them to follow. Not surprisingly everything came about just as Jesus had predicted.

PRELIMINARIES (verses 14–18)

A Jewish Passover meal consisted of the passing of three or four cups around the gathering (this is the reason for two different cups in Luke's account, verses 17 and 20); the recitation of a liturgy recalling the great emancipatory event of the Exodus (when Israel became a nation-state); and a meal together. Jesus adapted this practice to his own purpose because he was mediating the New Covenant between God and his people through the bread and wine of this meal. The Jewish Passover was becoming a Christian meal celebrating the exodus event of Jesus' death and resurrection (*John* 1:36). Christians mark the transition by differentiating time before Jesus as 'before Christ' (B.C.) and time after him as 'in the year of our Lord', Anno Domini (A.D.), such was the change taking place between the old order and the new (*Heb*. 8:3–13).

Jesus opens proceedings by expressing his love for his disciples, declaring his deep longing (the original is emphatic) to enjoy this meal with them. He speaks of his imminent trial, betrayal, condemnation, and death as his suffering *par excellence*. He had known suffering and rejection throughout his life but nothing to compare with this final ordeal. Rightly do Christians glory in the cross of Jesus as what is most important about their Lord (*Gal*. 6:14). He speaks of the meal being 'fulfilled' in the kingdom of God – the new order of God's rule in the hearts of men and women and throughout creation. By doing so Jesus indicates that this corporate meal (and the church meal he instituted since) is a foretaste and promise of a greater social gathering when he will sit with all his people in the glorious surroundings of heaven. At the same time Jesus puts himself under an oath of self-denial ('I will not at all eat of it', see also verse 18) as a way of showing his complete commitment to bringing it about.

Jesus takes the first or second cup in the Jewish meal and gives thanks for it before sharing it with the disciples. A second time he connects the meal with the arrival of the kingdom and again he vows to fast until it is accomplished, presumably in his resurrection. These self-imposed oaths express Jesus' single-minded devotion to go all the way to the cross (*Heb*. 12:2).

THE CENTRE-PIECE (verses 19–20)

Now comes the climax of his celebration. Jesus takes a piece of bread and breaks it in a symbolic act. He explains his action by stating that the broken bread is his body that is going to be given (a futuristic present in the original Greek). The words 'this is my body' have created all sorts of difficulties throughout the church's history. Jesus cannot mean his literal body since he was in his body when he said the words; nor can he mean to say that the mere eating of the bread conveys his flesh to those who eat (a cannibalistic and mechanical idea foreign to his whole teaching). He must mean the words metaphorically and spiritually, in the sense that his body sacrificed on the cross will be the source of believers' spiritual life and nourishment when they eat the bread in a believing way. By receiving the bread in faith believers feed on Christ himself in a sacramental way that the Holy Spirit blesses to them. When that happens the spiritual truth signified is conveyed by the sign of the bread (*1 Cor.* 10:16).

By saying 'for you' Jesus wants to remind his followers, whenever they celebrate this meal, that it is all a revelation of love. When he says, 'Do this in remembrance of me!' Jesus wants his people to remember him in person for what he has done for them. He wants them to have this constant reminder of what they owe to Christ. He also knows that by doing this they will grow in him because faith only grows as it focuses on Christ.

This command for repetition ('go on doing this in my remembrance' is what the Greek text really says) sets no limits about how often the rite should be held. The first Christians commemorated Jesus' death and love weekly (*Acts* 2:42). Paul adds that Christians should celebrate Christ's death in this way 'until he comes' (*1 Cor.* 11:26), thus making the Lord's Supper a permanent activity of the churches until the end of the age (a mark of the true church the Reformers called it). In the same verse Paul tells us that by re-enacting the actions of Jesus at the first meal Christians are proclaiming the message of Jesus' death dramatically for all to see and learn from. This is the one drama in the church's life legitimised by the word of God.

Following the bread Jesus took probably the third cup of the Jewish meal and spoke over it new words of institution. Jesus' words echo those of Moses when he mediated the covenant of the Lord with Israel at Sinai mountain (*Exod.* 24:8). But Jesus updates the words when he says 'in *my blood*' instead of 'the blood of the covenant'. Jesus was at once the priest and sacrifice of the New Covenant, whose blood ratified its promises and has made secure its blessings for all times. For this reason it is the everlasting covenant sealed in Jesus' blood (*Heb.* 13:20).

Jesus' words also echo those of Jeremiah as he foretold the coming of a new covenant between the Lord and his people (*Jer.* 31:31–34). Jesus equates his covenant with that New Covenant when he says 'this is my blood of the new covenant'. Its newness is found in its triple blessing of personal knowledge of God, full amnesty for sins, and an inner principle of obedience. The author of Hebrews is so impressed by the transition in covenantal history and administration that took place when Jesus died that he repeats the whole passage from Jeremiah (*Heb.* 8). In doing so he gives the historical and theological framework for understanding the whole life and work of Jesus Christ.

Jesus speaks of his blood being 'poured out' for his own people. 'Pouring out' is the language and symbolism of blood sacrifice as practised by the Israelites under God's provision and at his command. It signifies the giving of something entirely to God. Appropriately Isaiah uses this metaphor of the self-giving of the Messiah as the Lord's sacrifice for human sin (*Isa.* 53:12). In speaking this way about his sacrifice on the following day Jesus wanted to indicate how total was his submission to the Father's will and how complete the obedience he was offering on our behalf.

The outpouring of Jesus' life-blood on the cross made way for and secured the later outpouring of his Spirit at Pentecost (*Acts* 2:17, 33). The two are theologically connected as cause and effect. Had Jesus held back anything of himself in his self-giving at Calvary the Spirit could not have come in his lavish measures to enliven and enrich God's people throughout the ages. The outpouring of the Spirit at Pentecost and all subsequent outpourings in the life-experience of Christians and the churches are the direct harvest of Calvary (*John* 12:24; *Rom.* 5:5). The New Covenant is nothing if it is not generous, overflowing with every spiritual blessing (*Eph.* 1:3).

90

Final Tabletalk (3)

*'But behold, the hand of him who betrays me is with me on the
table. [22] For the Son of Man goes as it has been determined, but
woe to that man by whom he is betrayed!' [23] And they began to
question one another, which of them it could be who was going to
do this.*

*[24] A dispute also arose among them, as to which of them was to
be regarded as the greatest. [25] And he said to them, 'The kings of
the Gentiles exercise lordship over them, and those in authority
over them are called benefactors. [26] But not so with you. Rather,
let the greatest among you become as the youngest, and the leader
as one who serves. [27] For who is the greater, one who reclines at
table or one who serves? Is it not the one who reclines at table?
But I am among you as the one who serves.*

*[28] You are those who have stayed with me in my trials, [29] and I
assign to you, as my Father assigned to me, a kingdom, [30] that
you may eat and drink at my table in my kingdom and sit on
thrones judging the twelve tribes of Israel.*

*[31] Simon, Simon, behold, Satan demanded to have you, that he
might sift you like wheat, [32] but I have prayed for you that your
faith may not fail. And when you have turned again, strengthen
your brothers.' [33] Peter said to him, 'Lord, I am ready to go with
you both to prison and to death.' [34] Jesus said, 'I tell you, Peter,
the rooster will not crow this day, until you deny three times that
you know me.'*

*[35] And he said to them, 'When I sent you out with no moneybag
or knapsack or sandals, did you lack anything?' They said,
'Nothing.' [36] He said to them, 'But now let the one who has a*

moneybag take it, and likewise a knapsack. And let the one who has no sword sell his cloak and buy one. [37] *For I tell you that this Scripture must be fulfilled in me: "And he was numbered with the transgressors." For what is written about me has its fulfillment.'* [38] *And they said, 'Look, Lord, here are two swords.' And he said to them, 'It is enough.'* (Luke 22:21–38).

Luke's account of the Last Supper leads into Jesus' final tabletalk to his disciples. This informal discourse for the purposes of instruction reminds us of John's discourses in the upper room (*John* 13–16). Here Jesus' words of wisdom take a shorter form in four parts – prediction (verses 21–23), correction (verses 24–30), warning (verses 31–34), questioning (verses 35–38).

PRONOUNCEMENT (verses 21–23)

Having foretold his death Jesus foretells how his death will come about. It will be engineered by a traitor. Jesus faces the fact and announces it starkly – 'Behold! the hand…' The disciples are startled because Jesus can only be referring to one of them. This is a conclusion that is not lost on the disciples who fall into mutual questioning about it. Betrayal is the worst of human crimes, because it involves former friends one of whom becomes an enemy. This is the explanation of the particular bitterness that follows the experience of betrayal. That one of Jesus' own disciples could betray him was unthinkable to eleven of the disciples, a suggestion made worse by the anonymity of the traitor. That one of his own disciples was willing to betray Jesus, the heavenly Son of Man, and at the Lord's own table, gives an insight into the depth of inner darkness of the disciple in question.

Having announced the betrayal Jesus deepens the mystery by announcing that what is going to happen will be with God's approval. The betrayer will imagine that he is acting alone, but he fails to understand that by his shameful deed he is doing God's will. But God's sovereignty at work through the disciple's treachery does not exonerate the latter for a moment. God is free and man is responsible is the consistent pattern of Scripture teaching everywhere. Here is a mystery that faith can accept but reason can never unfold. Accepting both truths is the Christian way for mature thinking disciples. God's will is done through man's will being done; man's will is done because it is God's will he is doing.

Jesus pronounces a woe on the man who will carry out this dastardly deed against the Son of Man. By so saying Jesus commits that individual to a hopeless future in which he will suffer unspeakable anguish outside the reach of God's comforting mercy. For him is reserved the blackness of eternal night (*Mark* 14:21; *Acts* 1:24–25). No words could highlight more sharply the enormity of the sin of the betrayer of the Son of God. Mark intensifies the effect by adding the words of Jesus that it would have been better for his betrayer not to have been born (*Mark* 14:21). The sin of Judas stands out as the most shocking sin of human history, given the identity of Jesus and the consequence of Judas' act. Incidentally, Jesus' pronouncement rules out the theory that everybody will be saved (universalism).

CORRECTION (verses 24–30)

Like little children the disciples are easily distracted. From attending one minute to the solemn pronouncement about a traitor in their midst they fall the next into an embarrassing dispute about their own respective glories. In the very presence of the One who emptied himself to be the servant of all they exalt themselves to be the one who is over all. But Jesus, as always, has the measure of his men. He corrects them by means of an antithesis between two kinds of leadership – that practiced in the world and that exemplified by Jesus and his followers. Greatness in Jesus' vocabulary means serving others in love. How paradoxical this is for worldly-minded people – the Lord of all who waits at table on those who serve him!

Jesus has effectively burst the bubble of the disciples' pretensions after greatness. He, above all, had the right to expect others to serve him since he is none other than the heavenly Son whom angels worship. Yet he chose freely to enter this world as a servant to give his life as a ransom to set his people free (*Mark* 10:45; *Phil.* 2:5–8):

> 'This is the way the Master went,
> Should not the servant tread it still?'

The secret of Christlike service comes through a change of perspective that chooses to see greatness as generous service of others and self-giving love. How attractive Jesus' example of self-giving service is in a world that thinks in terms of power and self-interest. The disciples had still to learn the meaning of this level of self-giving but when they did, following Pentecost, their lives became fruitful and effective for Jesus. Nothing makes a Christian more like his Lord or so useful to him.

ENCOURAGEMENT (verses 28–30)

Jesus the expert Counsellor knew how to mix encouragement with reproof. Having openly exposed the pride of the disciples he now assures them of his own great goodwill towards them. They have stuck with him through the ups and downs of his three years of ministry, so he wants to reward them for loyalty and love. Just as the Father has 'covenanted' (this is the term Jesus uses twice in verse 29) with them for a kingdom, so he has covenanted the same with all who follow him. Salvation is a covenant of relationship in which disciples of Jesus stand to receive from his largesse, partially now by way of foretaste in this life and fully in the life to come (*Eph.* 1:13–14).

The final goal of salvation is therefore a shared meal – with Christ in glory! If humanity's final end or goal is to know and enjoy God then this is the way to do it, through Christ's redeeming love, the reconciling deed of his death and the indwelling of his Spirit in the heart in resurrected bodies. Nothing creaturely or material can satisfy the spiritual nature of humanity, only personal union with the one who is the infinitely good God, in Christ, through the Spirit.

But membership in Christ's kingdom will mean a share in his rule over the new creation. The promise about 'sitting on thrones judging the twelve tribes of Israel' could apply to the eleven disciples in a primary way without excluding other believers who will attain to the resurrection of life. After all, the same promise is made to them elsewhere in Scripture (*Rev.* 1:6; 22:5). Believers are united to Christ in his three-fold office as the Mediator-Priest and Prophet and King. This is why they are said to reign with Christ both now (*Eph.* 2:6) and when he comes. Ruling under God is humanity's highest calling that Christ has restored (*Heb.* 2:5–9).

PREDICTION (verses 31–34)

Always attentive to the needs of individuals and the opportunity to serve them, Jesus turns to Peter whom he calls by his natural name 'Simon'. He repeats his name as a mark of endearment and concern. Jesus gave Simon his new name 'Peter' which means a rock (*John* 1:42), that is, a strong character on whom others can rely. Sadly, Peter is about to deny his new name by denying Jesus the source of his strength (*Matt.* 16:16–18). This is because there is a spiritual realm in which the higher powers are affecting human events. Satan, as in Job's case (*Job* 1:6–12; 2:1–7), has asked God for the disciples ('you' in verse 31 is plural). This experience will be like sifting wheat to separate the chaff that is blown away. Satan's intention is the malign one of destroying the disciples' faith in Jesus but, as in Job's case again, God has set limits to how far Satan can go. The test will be real but limited.

What will balance this fiery test in the disciples' favour will be Jesus' prayers for Peter (the 'you' in verse 32 is singular). Why does Jesus now turn to Peter and single him out as an individual? Peter was about to make a boast of loyalty to Jesus whatever happened (verse 33), Peter would be shattered by his failure and would need a personal word to hang on to (60–62) and Peter was the leader of the group so that Peter's state affected the other disciples. Jesus' prayer for the disciples, starting with Peter, is found in John 17:11–12, 15.

In spite of that prayer Peter, the believer in Jesus, will fall badly, but just because of that prayer he will not fall completely. He will pick himself up (always a proof of true faith) and when he does, Christ has work for him to do – to strengthen his fellow believers exposed to the same fiery ordeals from the same source (*1 Pet.* 4:12–13; 5:8–10). This he did most effectively through being the leader of the Jerusalem church (see *Acts* 1–12) and through his apostolic letters (*1 and 2 Peter*) that still address and build up the churches.

Jesus' words informing Peter of his imminent denial of Jesus – before the night is out Peter will deny any connection with Jesus, not once but three times – must have wounded Peter's pride. These same words were going to be medicine to his wounded faith later when he remembered them (verse 61). He still relied on his own resources of strength to carry him forward. This was the door that Satan was going to enter through. Because the disciples had failed to take the advice of Jesus to pray watchfully they failed the Saviour in his hour of greatest need (*Luke* 22:39–40, 45–46). But who would have done better?

Every Christian will pass through Peter's experience of foolish self-confidence, Satan's fiery power, and the sorrows of repentance. There would be other times when he failed (*Gal.* 2:11–14). Only thus are Christ's future leaders trained for greater things. Peter learned a lot about himself, about the enemy, and about Jesus that night. The discerning reader can see this experience informing much that Peter writes and the tone in which he writes, in his first letter.

FULFILMENT (verses 35 – 38)

In the light of the impending doom the times have changed. When Jesus sent his disciples out before, he forbade them any material supports, but simply travelling in faith and the power of his name (*Luke* 9:1–6; 10:1–9). That was a time when the powers of darkness were being pressed back but now is a time of peril when the lawless powers have gained the ascendancy in human affairs. It is a time for the disciples to guard their possessions and to prepare for self-defence by buying a sword.

Does this make Jesus a terrorist or freedom-fighter? His counsel here is consistent with his predictions elsewhere (*Luke* 12:49–53) and should be read in context. The disciples took Jesus literally and made the mistake of producing two swords. In another few moments Jesus was going to rebuke the disciples for their use of violence to defend him (*Luke* 22:49–51; see *Matt.* 26:51–54). They did not yet understand that the real conflict in the world is spiritual in nature not physical, fought out in the arena of human hearts and actions. The sign of Jesus' kingdom is not a sword but a cross.

In the middle of Jesus' words to the disciples (verse 37) lies a gem of self-reflection in which he applies Isaiah's suffering servant song to himself (*Isa.* 53:12). Jesus was going to be crucified like a criminal, among criminals (*Luke* 23:32–33), because he chose to die on behalf of criminals (*John* 11:49–52; *1 John* 3:4). The Scriptures enlightened Jesus about the course of his life and its ending in darkness and solitude under judgement, for the sake of God's people. Christians are not wrong therefore when they read Isaiah 53 Christologically. Jesus reaffirmed this approach and method after his resurrection when he made the Christological reading of the Old Testament essential for understanding his own and his church's mission (*Luke* 24:44–47).

91

The Final Crisis

And he came out and went, as was his custom, to the Mount of Olives, and the disciples followed him. [40] And when he came to the place, he said to them, 'Pray that you may not enter into temptation.' [41] And he withdrew from them about a stone's throw, and knelt down and prayed, [42] saying, 'Father, if you are willing, remove this cup from me. Nevertheless, not my will, but yours, be done.' [43] And there appeared to him an angel from heaven, strengthening him. [44] And being in an agony he prayed more earnestly; and his sweat became like great drops of blood falling down to the ground. [45] And when he rose from prayer, he came to the disciples and found them sleeping for sorrow, [46] and he said to them, 'Why are you sleeping? Rise and pray that you may not enter into temptation' (Luke 22:39–46).

As the final crisis draws near Jesus goes to private prayer and draws the readers of the Gospel into the inner sanctuary of the final ordeal of the cross. Everything here is deeply sacred and fitted to make the reader spiritually-minded.

Jesus does not pray alone but takes his disciples with him for human company and support. Like Jacob in ancient times Jesus wrestles with God in his prayers and prevails for us, but at infinite cost to himself. Jesus' public ministry began with testing (*Luke* 4:1–3) it ends with testing. The Gethsemane struggle is an integral part of salvation worked out in the personal life of Jesus, the Son of God.

The fact that Jesus frequently retired to this spot (a wooded area just outside Jerusalem on the east side) explains how Judas was able to find Jesus that night and lead the gang of soldiers to him.

There are three sections to the narrative: Jesus' first words to the disciples, Jesus' private prayer words to God, Jesus' last words to his disciples. Throughout the narrative Jesus is the dominant speaker.

THE SCENE SET (verses 39–40)

The Mount of Olives was a favourite place of retirement for Jesus and his disciples. It gave him privacy and peace among the olive plantations. This night Jesus turned to his disciples and repeated to them the final petition of the prayer he had taught them, 'Pray that you will not fall into temptation' (*Luke* 11:4). This was both a warning and a prediction; a warning that they needed to pray, a prediction of how the night was going to turn out. Only earnest and believing prayer could avert the storm that was brewing and about to burst around the disciples. The tempter was abroad that night and only the spiritually empowered would stand.

JESUS' PRAYER (verses 41–44)

Jesus took his own counsel and prayed earnestly that he would not fall under the temptation that was already pressing him down. Withdrawing alone a short distance he knelt down and prayed. His very posture revealed the inner struggle. In his distress he sought the comfort of the Father's presence. The cross was going to rob him of that certainty and comfort but for now he is sure in whom he believes and that he will support him (see also *Luke* 23:34, 46). Jesus endured the test of Gethsemane by faith, as its author and finisher (*Heb*. 12:2).

His prayer was intensely personal. In it he pictures a cup being handed to him to drink from. In his anguish Jesus instinctively found meaning in the situation through this imagery of the Scriptures, so long familiar to him. The cup or goblet symbolizes God's holy anger against human sin, of individuals or of nations. The wine within it symbolizes his anger and normally overwhelms those who drink it (*Psa*. 75:8; *Isa*. 51:17; *Jer*. 25:15, 17; *Ezek*. 23:31–33).

Jesus could see that he was chosen by God to drink this cup of God's wrath against human sin in general and the sins of his people in particular. The cup that Jesus drank was foaming with the undiluted wine of God's anger (*Rev.* 14:10–11). With this deep insight into his circumstances Jesus' human frame threatened to collapse.

This moment has been deeply etched on the earliest Christian mind (*John* 12:27; *Heb.* 5:7–8). Luke tells us Jesus' experience was an 'agony' (verse 44), a word in ancient times used to refer to a death-struggle, as in gladiatorial combat. It will not do to pass over the anguish of Gethsemane by saying that Jesus was the Son of God and so assured of victory. This forgets the sensitive nature of his humanity in which he experienced the spiritual struggle much more intensely because he was personally sinless. It was more than the prospect of suffering that appalled him; it was the intimate association with the sin of the world. He who knew no sin was made sin for us (*2 Cor.* 5:21). We can only begin to imagine what that contact meant to his holy person.

The garden of Gethsemane recalls the garden of Eden (*Gen.* 3:1–6), when the first man Adam faced a similar choice but under the favourable surroundings of paradise. Jesus takes on the empire of evil, on evil's territory. He penetrates the very heart of darkness and undermines its power. Jesus reverses the results of Adam's fateful choice. As the last Adam Jesus was obedient to the point of death, even when death meant a cross (*Phil.* 2:8).

As a mere human Jesus requests for the pain to pass; as an obedient human he asks for the Father's will to be done by him. Jesus' prayer is another model one of what submission and servanthood mean in the web of circumstances that determine our lives. It is no shame to struggle to do God's will when it entails the very real death of our own self-will and a course of suffering instead. The way of the cross is the disciple's way as well. With this prayer Luke adds to the rich store of instructive data on prayer in his Gospel.

True to experience the strain of Jesus' spiritual struggle showed itself in a physical struggle in which two remarkable events were observed. First, an angel from heaven came to support Jesus. This recalls the similar event in the desert temptations (*Mark* 1:12–13). Secondly, Jesus' physique was so crushed that his perspiration began to fall to the ground, mixed with his blood. Nothing shows more clearly how human he was in the union of body and spirit and how costly in personal terms our salvation was for him.

For me it was in the garden
He prayed – 'Not my will, but Thine';
He had no tears for his own griefs,
But sweat drops of blood for mine.

In pity angels beheld him,
And came from the world of light
To comfort him in the sorrows
He bore for my soul that night.

He took my sins and my sorrows,
He made them his very own;
He bore the burden to Calvary,
And suffered and died alone.
Charles H. Gabriel

BACK TO THE DISCIPLES (verses 45–46)

What a study in contrasts between Jesus and his disciples that night! Jesus awake through faith to the point of shedding his sweat like blood; the disciples weighed down with exhaustion and grief to the point of sleeping. Because of this folly they neglected praying and so were caught out unprepared by the ferocious attack of their enemies, human and demonic.

Having won out through prayer Jesus was astonished and disappointed to find his disciples asleep and unable to help him. He confronts their failure; even yet it was not too late to pray. In opposite ways, Jesus and the disciples that night instruct Christ's followers in every age in the priority of prayer and faith, because our conflict is not in the first place with humanity but with devilry (*Eph*. 6:10–18). Divine power alone will support Christ's witnesses in days of evil (*2 Cor*. 10:3–5; *Eph*. 5:15–18).

Gethsemane was the secret of Calvary, in the sense that Jesus helped secure the victory of Calvary in Gethsemane. He went forward calmly to the cross after the settlement of his mind and heart in the garden. From there he goes to meet and greet his enemies, showing himself the lead player in the unfolding drama of his trials and crucifixion. No one took his life from him, he laid it down of himself (*John* 10:18).

92

The Arrest

While he was still speaking, there came a crowd, and the man called Judas, one of the twelve, was leading them. He drew near to Jesus to kiss him, [48] *but Jesus said to him, 'Judas, would you betray the Son of Man with a kiss?'* [49] *And when those who were around him saw what would follow, they said, 'Lord, shall we strike with the sword?'* [50] *And one of them struck the servant of the high priest and cut off his right ear.* [51] *But Jesus said, 'No more of this!' And he touched his ear and healed him.* [52] *Then Jesus said to the chief priests and officers of the temple and elders, who had come out against him, 'Have you come out as against a robber, with swords and clubs?* [53] *When I was with you day after day in the temple, you did not lay hands on me. But this is your hour, and the power of darkness'* (Luke 22:47–53).

This night incident explains how Jesus came to be in the hands of his enemies. It prepares the way for his two trials and eventual crucifixion. In the course of it Jesus converses with three different parties.

JESUS AND JUDAS (verses 47–48)

A crowd arrived led by one of Jesus' own disciples, Judas. Now it must have dawned on the other disciples why he had left the upper room early and slipped away into the night. He had acted as a spy, now as a traitor, in leading Jesus' enemies right to him, under cover of darkness. Judas had arranged with his backers that he would single Jesus out by planting a kiss of friendship on his cheek. But Jesus was never fooled by people, least of all his disciple's cunning in this play-acting. Seeing deeply into the heart of Judas Jesus calmly confronted him with his shameless deed by calling his act for what it was and addressing his tragic disciple with pity (verse 48). The words of Jesus unmasked Judas completely and would have stayed with Judas afterwards, to haunt him in a suicide's death. By betraying Jesus, the holiest and most loveable person who has ever lived, Judas showed how far he had given himself up to the devil's power (*John* 13:2, 27).

JESUS AND HIS DISCIPLES (verses 49–51)

During this exchange the rest of the disciples were beginning to waken from their torpor, to what was going on around them – the sudden arrival of Judas, a band of soldiers fully armed along with the religious leaders. They could sense immediately their malice and intentions. Their reaction was fleshly in resorting to violence, asking a question of Jesus but acting before he could give an answer. One of the disciples (John tells us it was Peter, *John* 18:10, who had acted literally on Jesus' word, verse 36) drew a sword and struck one of the attackers (a servant of the high priest), severing his ear. But Jesus' kingdom is founded on truth and so he refused to rely on armies to save him (*John* 18:33–38; *Matt.* 26:53–54). Jesus rebukes Peter and heals the damaged ear (Jesus' last healing). Even under attack Jesus' thoughts were for others, and how he could turn every situation to the glory of God.

JESUS AND HIS ENEMIES (verses 52–53)

But Jesus was not done. Having rebuked his disciples and healed his attacker's ear he turns to his opponents and challenges their actions. How easily they could have arrested him while he was teaching openly in the temple courts! But they chose to come by night under cover of darkness because they were secretly cowards who acted from pure self-interest. But by acting in these circumstances they put on display the real source of their actions, the powers of darkness that lie behind the network of evil throughout this age (*Eph.* 6:12). If they were men of the daylight they would have acted openly without shame; but they were men of the night and so had to act in a covert way.

From this point onwards Jesus appeared hopelessly in the hands of his enemies, alone and defenceless. In fact, he was entering upon his greatest triumph over the principalities and powers that were working for his destruction (*Col.* 2:15). By going forward to crucifixion Jesus was penetrating to the heart of Satan's kingdom – his power over death – and would destroy it (*1 Cor.* 15:56–57). The weakness of God in his defenceless Christ was going to prove stronger than men and Satan in their might (*1 Cor.* 1:24–25).

93

Peter's Dark Night of the Soul

> *Then they seized him and led him away, bringing him into the high priest's house, and Peter was following at a distance.* 55 *And when they had kindled a fire in the middle of the courtyard and sat down together, Peter sat down among them.* 56 *Then a servant girl, seeing him as he sat in the light and looking closely at him, said, 'This man also was with him.'* 57 *But he denied it, saying, 'Woman, I do not know him.'* 58 *And a little later someone else saw him and said, 'You also are one of them.' But Peter said, 'Man, I am not.'* 59 *And after an interval of about an hour still another insisted, saying, 'Certainly this man also was with him, for he too is a Galilean.'* 60 *But Peter said, 'Man, I do not know what you are talking about.' And immediately, while he was still speaking, the rooster crowed.* 61 *And the Lord turned and looked at Peter. And Peter remembered the saying of the Lord, how he had said to him, 'Before the rooster crows today, you will deny me three times.'* 62 *And he went out and wept bitterly* (Luke 22:54–62).

Jesus was roughly seized and taken away under cover of darkness to the private lodgings of the high priest to be interrogated by the Jewish supreme court (*Mark* 14:53, 55). Night meetings of the Sanhedrin in formal session were forbidden so this gathering may have been kept informal but its decision made official. For all their religion these men had already shown that they were capable of breaking the law with impunity. But the spotlight falls on Peter who followed Jesus at a distance, his body-language (keeping at a distance) revealing the struggle going on inside him. He had already failed his

Master twice – by relying on violence, then fleeing the scene of betrayal with the other disciples, leaving Jesus alone.

WHAT HAPPENED NEXT

No one knew how long the proceedings would take so a fire was lit to counter the cold night air. Peter slipped into the circle around the fire. He was there to watch, listen, and learn, not to be seen or questioned. But when we are away from the Lord our worst fears are sometimes realized, as Peter's were that night. A simple servant girl challenged Peter about his involvement with Jesus. How she guessed this connection we are not told but spoke more than she knew, because the Lord was calling Peter through this challenge. Already compromised, Peter roundly denied all knowledge of Jesus.

(The four Gospels' accounts of Peter's denials differ in their details yet are capable of harmonization when the reader makes use of a sympathetic imagination. For example, where an individual is singled out by one Evangelist he or she may have spoken for the group that is mentioned by another Evangelist, or perhaps more than one person at a time made the challenges to Peter, each Evangelist making his own selection from the crowd around Peter.)

If Peter thought that the danger was over he was in for a further awakening. A little later another person confronted him in the same way, accusing him of belonging to Jesus' party. His sin now became habitual for he again retorted that he had no connections with that man.

But Peter had still not escaped for shortly afterwards yet another person claimed, in the hearing of everyone present, that Peter was with Jesus, supporting this charge with the fact that Peter spoke like a Galilean (Jesus' part of the country). For the third time Peter washed his hands of Jesus and feigned ignorance. He may even have cursed Jesus (*Mark* 14:71).

In the perfect timing of God two things now happened simultaneously. First, a rooster crowed in the morning light of dawn. Secondly, Jesus was passing at that very moment and looked directly into Peter's eyes. Between the two events Peter remembered Jesus' prophecy of personal denial while the look of Jesus must have pierced Peter's conscience as a look made up of wounded but forgiving love.

The effect was crushing. Peter escaped the scene of his own betrayal of his Lord and wept alone in the bitterness of his soul. The darkness of night reflected the dark night of his soul.

SOME LESSONS

The tragic failure of Peter is one of the best known and most appreciated stories in the Gospel history. It is not difficult to understand why. All of us can identify with Peter in his personal failure and shame. We have all betrayed our Master and grieved his loving heart at some time or another. We know what Peter went through because we have been there too, so he does not weep alone. Surely it is for this reason that such an intimate story is included in the four Gospels! What is written is there for our encouragement and instruction (*Rom.* 15:4).

Secondly, it is the loving attitude of Jesus that made the difference between Peter and Judas that night. Both men failed Jesus by selfishly betraying him and both men grieved over what they had done. But Judas' sorrow had nothing of mercy in it while Peter's sorrow was mingled with love for Jesus. Theologically, Judas' repentance was legal, produced by knowing that he had done wrong; Peter's sorrow was evangelical, produced by knowing he had done wrong and that Jesus could forgive. The person of Jesus transforms our wrongs and turns them to good. There is mercy with him that he may be feared (*Psa.* 130:4); who is a pardoning Lord like him (*Mic.* 7:18) Hallelujah! What a Saviour!

Finally, Peter's failure was turned to his advantage. From now on Peter was better placed to pastor others as a tender-hearted and loving shepherd (1 *Pet.* 5:1–3). We learn from this that the Lord's oversight of all our lives is sure and wise. He turns our mourning into dancing and the night of the soul into a joyful dawn (*Psa.* 30:4–5, 11–12). We learn from our own failures to be more sympathetic and patient with others. He works everything together for good, including our shameful failures (*Rom.* 8:28).

94

The Trials of Jesus (1)

Now the men who were holding Jesus in custody were mocking him as they beat him. [64] *They also blindfolded him and kept asking him, 'Prophesy! Who is it that struck you?'* [65] *And they said many other things against him, blaspheming him.*
[66] *When day came, the assembly of the elders of the people gathered together, both chief priests and scribes. And they led him away to their council, and they said,* [67] *'If you are the Christ, tell us.' But he said to them, 'If I tell you, you will not believe,*
[68] *and if I ask you, you will not answer.* [69] *But from now on the Son of Man shall be seated at the right hand of the power of God.'*
[70] *So they all said, 'Are you the Son of God, then?' And he said to them, 'You say that I am.'* [71] *Then they said, 'What further testimony do we need? We have heard it ourselves from his own lips'* (Luke 22:63–71).

After the irregular trial of Jesus during the night the Jewish leaders convened officially as a council in the morning. Their various groups came together for the sole purpose of putting Jesus on trial and finding incriminating evidence against him. For Jesus this is the beginning of the long, final ordeal of making himself the offering for the sins of his people in fulfilment of Isaiah's servant (*Isa*. 52:11–53:12).

THE PHYSICAL TRIAL (verses 63–65)

The midnight trial involved physical and mental abuse. A blind eye was turned to their dehumanising and insensitive treatment of the prisoner. They mocked his reputation as a prophet and took full advantage of their power over him. From now until his death Jesus was to undergo this type of treatment from various groups. It is impossible to tell whether the blows or the words were more wounding to Jesus. As a sinless person Jesus' reactions would have been accentuated so that he felt the punches and the barbs more painfully than anyone else under similar circumstances. In all this ill-treatment Jesus was already paying the cost of salvation.

Peter tells us that when Jesus was insulted and physically abused he did not retaliate. Instead he committed himself to his faithful God and Father (*1 Pet.* 2:21–23). Jesus under trial is an example and inspiration for all Christians who are being subjected to unjust treatment and physical abuse. Many Christians around the world belong to the suffering, persecuted church. How reassuring and strengthening to remember that our Lord underwent similar treatment at the hands of evil and misguided people and to know that he will be with us through ordeals of the same kind. In suffering in this way Christians have the honour of making up what remains of Jesus' sufferings (non-redemptive) in this world for the sake of his church, until he comes (*Col.*1:24).

THE JEWISH TRIAL (verses 66–71)

When morning came the religious authorities convened in open court. Jesus by this time must have been in a weakened physical condition yet his captors showed him no mercy. They gather like wolves circling for the kill. They have little time so they come to the point at issue: 'Are you the Messiah?' In his response Jesus pinpoints their unwillingness to accept the substantial evidence that spoke for him, that exonerated him of all wrong. Jesus knew that he was in the hands and at the mercy of dishonest men who would not respond honestly to his honest answers. How well Jesus, the righteous Judge, knew his earthly judges (*John* 2:24–25)!

Yet Jesus had chosen the Father's way even when it meant dying at the hands of his enemies. So Jesus implicates himself in a defining moment at his own trial, not to placate his human judges but to bring about his Father's will. Joining two Old Testament passages he identified himself as the heavenly Son of Man (*Dan.* 7:12–13) and the historical Messiah (*Psa*. 110:1) whom the Lord exalts to equality with himself. Jesus had previously explained this prophecy (*Luke* 20:41–44) and the martyr Stephen would find it true (*Acts* 7:54–56).

Here was the opening his judges were craving. 'Are you the Son of God then?' they asked. Jesus is open in his reply. 'You are correct in stating this,' he said and in so saying signed his own death warrant. His judges can hardly believe their ears. Here is all the evidence they can possibly want. Jesus is self-condemned and chargeable with blasphemy. He has condemned himself in the presence of many witnesses.

But little do they know what they have done. By pushing Jesus into a free confession of his Godhead they have won grounds for indicting him; but in so doing they have made themselves chargeable with utmost wrong (*Acts* 2:22–23). In all this they have hastened the cause of world salvation.

95

The Trials of Jesus (2)

Then the whole company of them arose and brought him before
Pilate. 2 And they began to accuse him, saying, 'We found this
man misleading our nation and forbidding us to give tribute to
Caesar, and saying that he himself is Christ, a king.' 3 And Pilate
asked him, 'Are you the King of the Jews?' And he answered him,
'You have said so.' 4 Then Pilate said to the chief priests and the
crowds, 'I find no guilt in this man.' 5 But they were urgent,
saying, 'He stirs up the people, teaching throughout all Judea,
from Galilee even to this place.'
6 When Pilate heard this, he asked whether the man was a
Galilean. 7 And when he learned that he belonged to Herod's
jurisdiction, he sent him over to Herod, who was himself in
Jerusalem at that time. 8 When Herod saw Jesus, he was very
glad, for he had long desired to see him, because he had heard
about him, and he was hoping to see some sign done by him. 9 So
he questioned him at some length, but he made no answer. 10 The
chief priests and the scribes stood by, vehemently accusing him.
11 And Herod with his soldiers treated him with contempt and
mocked him. Then, arraying him in splendid clothing, he sent
him back to Pilate. 12 And Herod and Pilate became friends with
each other that very day, for before this they had been at enmity
with each other.
13 Pilate then called together the chief priests and the rulers and
the people, 14 and said to them, 'You brought me this man as one
who was misleading the people. And after examining him before
you, behold, I did not find this man guilty of any of your charges
against him. 15 Neither did Herod, for he sent him back to us.

Look, nothing deserving death has been done by him. [16] *I will therefore punish and release him.'* [17] *Now he was obliged to release one man to them at the festival [verse 17 added from footnote.]* [18] *But they all cried out together, 'Away with this man, and release to us Barabbas'* – [19] *a man who had been thrown into prison for an insurrection started in the city and for murder.* [20] *Pilate addressed them once more, desiring to release Jesus,* [21] *but they kept shouting, 'Crucify, crucify him!'* [22] *A third time he said to them, 'Why, what evil has he done? I have found in him no guilt deserving death. I will therefore punish and release him.'* [23] *But they were urgent, demanding with loud cries that he should be crucified. And their voices prevailed.* [24] *So Pilate decided that their demand should be granted.* [25] *He released the man who had been thrown into prison for insurrection and murder, for whom they asked, but he delivered Jesus over to their will* (Luke 23: 1–25).

Having secured the result they wanted from their interrogation of Jesus the Jewish leaders rush him off to Pilate the Roman governor who alone has the power to carry out a death sentence (*John* 18:28–32). By Jewish law Jesus is a blasphemer and deserves to die but other arguments and evidence will need to be presented to Pilate to secure a capital verdict under Roman law. This is the dilemma the Jewish authorities face as they hasten to Pilate's hall.

In retelling the story of Jesus' trial Luke includes the brief visit of Jesus as a prisoner to Herod in the middle of his account of the appearance before Pilate.

THE ROMAN TRIAL (Part 1) (verses 1–7)

As soon as they gain an audience with Pilate the Jews begin their attack on Jesus. It is instructive to observe their tactics. Instead of bringing religious charges against Jesus they revert to political ones that will make an impression on Pilate as Roman governor. Their charges are a biased reporting of some of Jesus' sayings, such as giving to Caesar the things that belong to Caesar (*Luke* 20:20–26) and being the messianic King (*Luke* 19:37–40). Both of these sayings of Jesus are twisted so as to put him at odds with Caesar whose authority Pilate represents. There is some historical evidence to suggest that Pilate had not enjoyed the best of relations with Caesar in Rome so that any hint of opposition to Caesar would immediately have disturbed Pilate. No doubt the Jewish authorities knew of this point of weakness in Pilate's position and exploited it.

The charge of kingship certainly got Pilate's attention because he immediately quizzes Jesus about this. Here John's account of the interview with Pilate should be read to give some more detail (*John* 19:33–38). Jesus agrees with the charge of claiming to be king but in the course of the interview Pilate becomes convinced that King Jesus is no threat to Caesar's rule.. The upshot is that Pilate comes out to the Jews to announce Jesus' innocence. Pilate will repeat this declaration of innocence another two times before he finally pronounces the death sentence. The Gospel writers want readers to be perfectly clear about the legal, personal, and political innocence of Jesus. Why then was he condemned to die and actually put to death under a legal system that was relatively enlightened and fair?

The Jews refuse to accept this finding so they expand on the charge of Jesus sowing political unrest. They explain that this is no local unrest but an unsettling of the whole country beginning from Galilee in the north and reaching all the way south to the capital city in Judea. At the mention of Galilee Pilate pricks up his ears, asking whether Jesus is from Galilee. Learning that this was so Pilate sees a way out of having to rule on this case. Herod was a puppet king of Rome, who ruled over the constituency of Galilee. It also so happened that Herod was in Jerusalem at that time for the religious festival of Passover. So Jesus became a political pawn in the game of power politics and self-interest between the leaders of Rome and Israel.

THE TRIAL BEFORE HEROD (verses 8–12)

Not unexpectedly Herod was overjoyed to receive Jesus in person. For some time he had heard reports of Jesus' miraculous powers (*Luke* 9:7–9) and now he hoped that Jesus would oblige with a private show. In addition Herod was full of curiosity and plied Jesus with endless questions. But Jesus had consistently refused to perform miracles at the whim of people, nor did he answer frivolous questions.

So in face of it all Jesus remained totally silent and maintained his dignity.

The Jewish leaders were relentless in their pursuit of Jesus and throughout his audience with Herod vehemently hurled their charges against him. Perhaps piqued that Jesus had spoiled his fun by refusing to cooperate, Herod turned Jesus over to his soldiers to enjoy themselves at Jesus' expense. The soldiers obliged by dressing Jesus up in royal robes and mocking his claims to kingly power. This was a cruel joke but typical of the ways that occupying powers torment the local people. Dressed up in this way Jesus was returned to Pilate for the final verdict. In all these encounters Jesus had the lower ground physically yet maintained the higher ground morally by his triumphant trust in God and unflinching submission to his sovereign will. Real strength comes from within, is a case of spiritual character and not of brute strength or bullying tactics.

Luke adds the sardonic remark that because of Jesus Pilate and Herod became friends that day, having previously been at odds with one another. In this unforeseen way Jesus fulfilled the terms of the great messianic Psalm 2 which describes how the rulers of the world and their peoples were united in defying the Almighty and his messianic King set on Zion's hill (*Psa*. 2:1–6). At least this is how the early Christians understood events as they unfolded on that day of Jesus' unjust trial and crucifixion (*Acts* 4:24–28; notice the careful mention of 'Herod and Pontius Pilate'). How reassuring to learn that the most traumatic experiences of Jesus' life were bringing about the world's salvation according to the predestined plan of God. Everything was on course for victory. Jesus himself was being made complete as the pioneer of his people through suffering injustice and a death-sentence (*Heb*. 2:9–10).

THE ROMAN TRIAL (Part 2) (verses 13–25)

Pilate picks up with the Jewish leaders where he had left off by announcing yet again, (now reinforced by the non-verdict of Herod), that he found Jesus innocent of the charges of political sedition. Certainly Jesus had done nothing deserving death. Pilate settled for a compromise: he would subject Jesus to a cautionary lashing then release him. By now the religious leaders were becoming desperate in their scheme to get rid of Jesus so they incited the crowds that had gathered, to cry out against Jesus and to ask for Barabbas. Each year the governor released a political prisoner out of favour to the Jews and as a way of ingratiating himself with them. The irony of the situation, that bears the hallmarks of a higher wisdom, lies in the fact that Barabbas *was* guilty of the charge of sedition, whereas Jesus was not. The exchange of Barabbas for Jesus illustrates as nothing else can, the deeper principle of substitution that underlies the death of Jesus (*2 Cor.* 5:21).

Pilate was convinced of two things: Jesus was innocent and the Jews were jealous (*Matt.* 27:18). So he tried a third time to palliate the Jews and divert them from their course of action.

But, in the plan of God, the Jews could not retract their purpose of destroying Jesus. The time for negotiation was past; they had only one word in their vocabulary now, 'Crucify, crucify!' Mob rule and mass hysteria prevailed and Pilate pathetically surrendered to the badgering of the Jewish leaders in their spite against Jesus. Against his better judgement Pilate handed Jesus over to death by crucifixion, the typical Roman way of executing criminals. In doing so he also surrendered justice and truth to be crucified with Jesus but the resurrection would shortly restore law and order to the universe and secure God's glory in man's salvation.

96

On the Way to the Cross

And as they led him away, they seized one Simon of Cyrene,
who was coming in from the country, and laid on him the cross,
to carry it behind Jesus. [27] *And there followed him a great*
multitude of the people and of women who were mourning and
lamenting for him. [28] *But turning to them Jesus said, 'Daughters*
of Jerusalem, do not weep for me, but weep for yourselves and
for your children. [29] *For behold, the days are coming when they*
will say, "Blessed are the barren and the wombs that never bore
and the breasts that never nursed!" [30] *Then they will begin to*
say to the mountains, "Fall on us," and to the hills, "Cover us."
[31] *For if they do these things when the wood is green, what will*
happen when it is dry?' (Luke 23:26–31).

The time has come for Jesus to be executed. Like other scenes from the Gospel Jesus draws a stranger into his path as a potential disciple, at the same time carrying on a conversation with the crowds who followed him everywhere, even at his death.

SIMON OF CYRENE (verse 26)

Roman soldiers had power to coerce Jews to do their bidding. Normally the victim of crucifixion was compelled to carry the wood of his own gallows, perhaps the cross-beam on which his arms would be impaled. This was part of the mental punishment (like getting prisoners of war to dig their own graves). Apparently Jesus was so weakened by the flogging (the whips used for these floggings were sharpened with bones so that they could shred a person's back and even bring on death) from the soldiers that he was unable to carry the cross by himself.

Simon (from Cyrene, a North African coastal province) was an innocent pilgrim coming up from the country that day, who ran into the grim procession snaking its way outside the walls of Jerusalem. Simon is named because he and his family were known to Luke's readers around the churches (*Mark* 15:21). Forced to manhandle Jesus' cross Simon was later going to take up his cross and follow Jesus in another way (*Luke* 14:27). Jesus was always in the right place at the right time to do his Father's will (see *Luke* 19:1–10 for another chance meeting like this). In every case salvation results.

THE WOMEN OF JERUSALEM (verses 27–31)

Throughout the whole of his trial Jesus' love for others shines out. It appeared in the garden when he healed the servant's ear; he loved Peter in his moment of greatest shame; he is about to pray for his executioners; it will surface again in his welcome to the criminal crucified beside him. Always, everywhere, Jesus is the man for others. In all of this he is a glowing example of servant love to those who follow him (*Phil.* 2:5–8).

On the way to crucifixion Jesus responds thoughtfully to the plight of the women of Jerusalem who have come out in sympathy, to bewail him. Other people would be preoccupied with their last moments on earth but Jesus, in spite of his broken body, is free from all self-pity. Instead he speaks for their forewarning and salvation.

He utters a beatitude (an exclamation of blessedness translated as 'How fortunate are those who...') that would be recited in the Jewish War (66–70 A.D.) when Jews were massacred, betrayed and killed by one another (*Luke* 21:21–24). How blessed those women would appear who had never married nor borne children – turning upside down the traditional way of looking at marriage and family joys.

Jesus quotes from the prophet Hosea who spoke on another occasion when Jews were taken prisoner and slaughtered (*Hos.* 10:8). Last of all, the book of Revelation quotes these words about the future time when Jesus returns to judge the world in righteousness (*Rev.* 6:15–17).

Finally, Jesus closes his account to the women with a proverb that speaks about green trees and dry ones (verse 31). His point is, if crucifixion can take place at a time of national peace, think what may happen when the nation is at war. He is thinking ahead to the Jewish War again. God will require from the Jews all the righteous blood they have spilt throughout their history leading up to the blood of the Son of God their rightful King (*Matt.* 23:34–35). His blood would be upon them and their children (*Matt.* 27:25) because they had failed to read the signs of the times by accepting him (*Luke* 12:54–56). For this there is no forgiveness since people crucify Jesus in their own name (*Heb.* 6:4–6; 10:26–31). God is most jealous for the glory of his Son.

97

Jesus among the Criminals

Two others, who were criminals, were led away to be put to death with him. [33] *And when they came to the place that is called The Skull, there they crucified him, and the criminals, one on his right and one on his left.* [34] *And Jesus said, 'Father, forgive them, for they know not what they do.' And they cast lots to divide his garments.* [35] *And the people stood by, watching, but the rulers scoffed at him, saying, 'He saved others; let him save himself, if he is the Christ of God, his Chosen One!'* [36] *The soldiers also mocked him, coming up and offering him sour wine* [37] *and saying, 'If you are the King of the Jews, save yourself!'* [38] *There was also an inscription over him, 'This is the King of the Jews.'* [39] *One of the criminals who were hanged railed at him, saying, 'Are you not the Christ? Save yourself and us!'* [40] *But the other rebuked him, saying, 'Do you not fear God, since you are under the same sentence of condemnation?* [41] *And we indeed justly, for we are receiving the due reward of our deeds; but this man has done nothing wrong.'* [42] *And he said, 'Jesus, remember me when you come into your kingdom.'* [43] *And he said to him, 'Truly, I say to you, today you will be with me in Paradise'* (Luke 23:32–43).

The place of execution is now arrived at. Luke tells his readers that it was known as 'the skull', because of the shape of the hillside. The name fitted the grim business of the spot which was a kind of killing field. Luke informs his readers that Jesus was not alone when he died, nor was he left alone while he died.

JESUS' PRAYER (verses 32–34)

Pilate had passed sentence on two other felons so Jesus was one of three sentenced to die that day. The other two were genuine law-breakers, terrorists on their own admission (verse 41). That Jesus did not die alone but in the company of criminals made his identification with humankind complete, just as Isaiah had predicted (*Isa.* 53:12) and as Jesus himself had wanted (*Luke* 22:37). So that this point could not be missed Jesus was crucified in between the other two criminals. His chosen company in dying was sinful men and women

Luke, like the other Gospel writers, is sparing in his information when it comes to the crucifixion itself. With an amazing economy of words he simply records, 'They crucified him.' Should we read more into this? Religious art, a recent movie and some church rituals make a strong appeal to the sense of sight by representing the dying Jesus very graphically and focusing on the physical nature of the ordeal of the cross. But the main thrust of the Gospels' accounts lies elsewhere, while not underplaying the physical pain. Jesus died in order to offer himself to God for human sin, not to satisfy the human fascination with violence (*Heb.* 2:17; 9:11–12). Other great men in history, like Socrates, have died painful and shameful deaths but only the death of Jesus can reconcile the world to God (*2 Cor.* 5:19).

There are famously seven sayings uttered by Jesus from the cross. They are windows into his self-understanding as he hung and suffered there. The first of these is recorded now (verse 34). Jesus prays to his Father for the pardon of his tormentors, a truly remarkable request from a dying man. In the face of the world's injustice and brutality Jesus thought not of himself, nor of revenge against others, but of their eternal welfare. This is where the world can see love, in God giving up his own Son for us while we were still enemies and rebels (*Rom.* 5:8). Jesus' prayer was a remarkable example of the fulfilment of his own instruction to those who follow him (*Luke* 6:27).

But was the prayer answered? Not immediately, because the soldiers for whom he prayed went on with their gruesome business of crucifying the Son of God. But later on the day of Pentecost there were those present whom Peter could accuse of the shameful deed of the crucifixion (*Acts* 2:23). Some of them were surely among the three thousand persons who were changed in heart that day (*Acts* 2:37–42).

He dies to atone
  For sins not his own;
Your debt he has paid,
  And your work he has done.
You all may receive
  The peace he did leave,
Who made intercession,
  'My Father, forgive!'

For you and for me
  He prayed on the tree:
The prayer is accepted, the sinner is free.
  That sinner am I
Who on Jesus rely,
  And come for the pardon
God cannot deny.

Charles Wesley

Finally, Luke tells his readers that the soldiers bartered for the clothes Jesus had worn before he was crucified. This was common practice and a perk connected with the heartless work of crucifying human beings. Jesus therefore was naked while he hung on the cross. There is more here than the public spectacle of nudity. Ever since Adam and Eve fell into sin physical nakedness has been associated with and become a symbol for moral guilt and shame before God (*Gen.* 3:6–11). By assuming our nakedness in this way Jesus has entered fully into the depth of our sin and provided a covering for our spiritual nakedness in God's presence. Only as we learn to trust in who Jesus is and what he has done for us, can we escape the public shame of personal exposure on the day he comes. He therefore counsels us in love to come to him for this covering of the shame of our life's story and the possibility of its being publicly shown (*Rev.* 3:18).

FINAL INSULTS (verses 35–38)

In the final hours of his life on earth four groups of people added to the psychological and emotional pain of Jesus.

First, the people stood around passively watching but doing nothing. Such indifference is typical of fallen human beings in the face of human wrong. In the presence of the dying Son of Man people remained aloof and apathetic. Their absence of sympathy and love must have added greatly to Jesus' sense of final rejection and isolation. Like people who stop to gawk and gaze at a gory scene the people that day lingered around the cross as though Jesus' dying was a kind of blood sport that transfixed them.

Secondly and predictably, the religious leaders showed no such indifference. They were actively outspoken in their hatred of Jesus to the end. Like wolves baying for the blood of their victim, even when impaled on the cross, they cannot satisfy their blood-lust for more of the same. Their reasoning was perverted – 'He saved others, let him now save himself.' That would prove him to the Messiah he claims to be. To the end they were obsessed with the evidence for Jesus' claims, like troubled men. Their logic was flawed on two counts: first, they ignored the scripture that spoke of the terminal sufferings of the Lord's Christ; secondly, they failed to understand the spiritual nature of God's salvation, seeing his physical death as his defeat.

Thirdly, as though they had not inflicted enough pain on their victim, the soldiers continued to mock Jesus hanging on the cross. They ridicule his royal claims verbally and by offering him royal wine to drink. They played the devil's advocate by appealing to the last vestiges of his natural desire for self-preservation by calling on him to save himself. The inspiration for their taunts came from the inscription above Jesus' head (it was customary to attach the main charge against criminals to the wooden beam above the prisoner's head). In Jesus' case it read, 'This is the King of the Jews'. Pilate had written this against the offended protests of the Jews (*John* 19:19–22). In God's overriding providence Pilate's inscription told the truth about Jesus to the whole inhabited world because it was written in the major languages of the empire (Latin, Greek and Aramaic). From this we learn that the cross is an event that God wants everyone everywhere to know about.

The fourth group to participate in Jesus' final hours was the criminals on either side of him, but they deserve a separate treatment.

THE TWO CRIMINALS (verses 39–43)

More drama follows when the two criminals on either side of Jesus begin to interact with him. This is some indication of how close the crosses must have stood to each other. The two criminals sound and look the same in their dying state but their final end is different because of Jesus. Right up to the point of death Jesus was dividing and saving lost men and women, reconciling them to God through his own intervention.

Spurred on by the chorus of voices around the cross and the superscription above it, one of the criminals appeals to Jesus to save himself and them. The request is wholly selfish, the desperate cry of a man who will clutch at any last straw of hope. It is also naturalistic, his plea looking to the prolongation of life rather than any higher hope. Having made his play the first criminal is not heard from again though the second criminal addresses him without reply.

The reader is allowed to eavesdrop on this personal conversation between dying men. The second criminal's response is diametrically different from his fellow's. His utterances are remarkable for several reasons. First, he rebukes wrong-doing in himself and in his fellow. He has developed a sense of sin and recognises what their wrongdoing deserves. Secondly, he declares the innocence of Jesus, just like Pilate had done. The death of Jesus must be a gross miscarriage of justice or the working out of a divine plan. In all this he shows the evidence of saving faith in Jesus (*Heb*. 6:1). Next, he appeals directly to Jesus as his Saviour, calling him by name ('Jesus', that is, *the Lord saves*). Only a one to one relationship will bring about the desired result. Lastly, he expresses his faith in Jesus by looking to the arrival of his kingdom. In this he shows that he has grasped something of the spiritual nature of Christ's authority. In these few words the second criminal shows himself a new man who is ready for the great changeover that death will bring. He has been snatched by Jesus from the valley of death and the jaws of hell.

The last word is with Jesus who assures his new friend that he will go with him into the heavenly paradise. This is another of Jesus' special sayings from the cross, most of them directed to God or to others. Here is Jesus the man of love, the crucified, at work. That this change will come 'today' supports belief in an intermediate state in which the believer in Jesus goes immediately into his presence (*Phil.* 1:23) and awaits the bodily resurrection when Jesus comes again (*2 Cor.* 12:2–4; *Rev.* 2:7). 'Paradise' is literally a pleasure park, symbolising not the indulgence of the senses so much as the satisfaction of the mind and affections in the enjoyment of God through the Son and Spirit.

The dying criminal, in effect, has borne witness to the effectiveness of Jesus' dying sacrifice.

There is a fountain filled with blood
  Drawn from Immanuel's veins;
And sinners plunged beneath that flood,
  Lose all their guilty stains.

The dying thief rejoiced to see
  That fountain in his day;
And there have I, though vile as he,
  Washed all my sins away.

Dear dying Lamb, Thy precious blood
  Shall never lose its power,
Till all the ransomed church of God
  Be saved, to sin no more.

William Cowper

98

The End

It was now about the sixth hour, and there was darkness over the whole land until the ninth hour, [45] *while the sun's light failed. And the curtain of the temple was torn in two.* [46] *Then Jesus, calling out with a loud voice, said, 'Father, into your hands I commit my spirit!' And having said this he breathed his last.* [47] *Now when the centurion saw what had taken place, he praised God, saying, 'Certainly this man was innocent!'* [48] *And all the crowds that had assembled for this spectacle, when they saw what had taken place, returned home beating their breasts.* [49] *And all his acquaintances and the women who had followed him from Galilee stood at a distance watching these things* (Luke 23:44–49).

Luke reports Jesus' end simply and briefly. Yet in spite of this Luke manages to convey something of the wonder and achievement of the most momentous event in the history of our planet. Four incidents make up the mystery of those hours during which Jesus died.

DARKNESS COVERS THE LAND (verses 44–45)

It was now noon or the sixth hour by Roman reckoning. Just when the sun would have reached its zenith an unearthly darkness fell over the whole land. How far this darkness extended or what caused it, Luke chooses not to tell. The time of full moon, when the Passover was held, would rule out the possibility of an eclipse. Others have suggested a freak sirocco blowing in from the desert. Whatever the physical explanation the event itself was clearly timed to coincide with the period of Jesus' dying and to pass when he died three hours later.

Various explanations of the darkness have been offered of a religious kind. The external darkness was symbolical of the inner darkness through which Jesus was passing in bearing the sin of the world; the darkness was physical and was a display of creation's grief and shame over the banishment and death of her Creator king. That the sun, the centre of the earth's solar system, was drawn into the events surrounding the death of Christ reminds us that when Jesus died he included the whole material creation in his redemptive work (*Col.* 1:19–20).

THE TEMPLE'S CURTAIN IS TORN (verse 45)

At the close of the three hours the curtain inside the Jerusalem temple was torn in two from top to bottom (*Matt.* 27:50–51). Like the noontime darkness this was a supernatural incident that throws great light on the meaning of Jesus' death by witnessing to something momentous taking place in the spiritual world beyond human sight. The temple was the symbol of God's presence among his redeemed people but the curtain across the middle of the temple signified that direct access to God was not yet available (*Heb.* 9:6–9a). The death of Jesus changed all that by being a prefect sacrifice for sin, offered once for all (*Heb.* 9:11–14). In token of this change in divine-human relations the curtain not only could now come down but effectively *must* come down. Significantly, it was torn from top to bottom thus throwing open the way into the most holy part of the temple where God's presence was believed to be, above the ark of the covenant and the mercy seat. The Lord could now deal with sinful and erring men and women on the basis of justified mercy or free grace; he could be just and the justifier of those with faith in Jesus (*Rom.* 3:26).

Jesus' self-offering on the cross to God was and is, a new and living way into the heavenly temple where God resides, for fallen men and women in this life and the next (*Heb.*10:19–22).

> For in his death our death
>   Died with him on the tree,

And a great number by his blood
Will go to heaven made free.

When Jesus bowed his head
And, dying, took our place,
The veil was rent, a way was found
To that pure home of grace.
John Elias

JESUS PRAYS AND DIES (verse 46)

Six times already Jesus has spoken from the cross (*Mark* 15:34; *Luke* 23:34, 43; *John* 19:26–28, 30). For the seventh and last time he utters words that have been recorded for human reflection and encouragement to the end of time. Once more he addresses his Father by name, with a clear mind and trustful heart (*Luke* 23:34); once again he uses the words of Scripture to express his deepest emotions (*Psa*. 31:5). He entrusts himself into the safe hands of his God and Father as he reaches the doorway of death. These are the final recorded words of the pre-Easter Jesus and act as a pointer to his perfect faith in God and acceptance of the Father's will. They are the words of a man who is at perfect peace with God and who fears nothing from the judgement that follows death (*Heb*. 9:27). Jesus' faith in the Father's care and justice was vindicated because his body was kept from the normal process of decomposition throughout his entombment that follows. Every true believer in Jesus can pray this peaceful and radiant prayer because they are one with him in his victory over death and the grave.

THE CENTURION PRAISES GOD (verse 47)

The final incident that Luke weaves into the crucifixion scene is the spoken witness of the Roman centurion, delegated to supervise the execution of Jesus. That such a man could openly confess the innocence of Jesus is surely evidence of the power of Jesus' words and the purity of his spirit in dying. In all his years of public service this centurion had never encountered a criminal like Jesus whose personal innocence was overwhelmingly obvious.

In declaring Jesus a just man who did not deserve to die this centurion is siding with Pilate in his better moments and the body of evidence from the whole lifetime of Jesus. The sincere reader who has followed the narrative to this point will want to echo the centurion's opinion as his own: Jesus is innocent of the charges against him and did not deserve to die. His death was unjust yet willed by God for the salvation of humankind for whom he died.

Again Luke works the note of praise into the narrative of his Gospel. Wherever Jesus went, praise to God was the response of men and women to the wonders of his love and the works of his power. Jesus was the sacrament of God's gracious presence in the world for those who believed. This happened at Jesus' birth (*Luke* 2:13), it happened when Jesus healed (*Luke* 5:25–26; 7:16; 18:43), it happened when he entered the holy city (*Luke* 19:37) and it will happen again when he returns to heaven (*Luke* 24:53). Jesus brought joy into the world and bequeaths it to all those who take him at his word and commit to him as Lord.

THE SPECTATORS DISPERSE (verses 48–49)

Luke winds down his narrative of Jesus' passion by commenting on those who were there to observe his final moments. As is often the case with crowds on public occasions the people were divided into two groups. Those who were present out of curiosity showed deep emotion at what they had seen and heard, and returned home in a mood of sombre reflection, even foreboding. But those who were there from personal loyalty to Jesus lingered at the cross because they knew him and were known to him. Some, like the Galilean women, had travelled far to be there that day, to show solidarity with him, even though they felt helpless in the face of events.

Everyone ought to spend time at the cross of Jesus, for the deepening of faith and spiritual life. 'To live *for Christ* is to live always within sight of the cross' (John Stott). The largest section in hymn-books is often the one on the sufferings and death of Jesus. This is a clue to their importance in the individual experience and collective witness of God's people. In heaven as on earth the subject of greatest interest is the majesty and the mystery of the dying Lamb of God (*Luke* 9:30–31; *Eph.* 3:17–19; *Rev.* 5:6–14). As a guide and example the words of one of these great songs of the blood-bought church of God may conclude this section.

There is a green hill far away,
  Outside a city wall,
Where the dear Lord was crucified
  Who died to save us all.

We may not know, we cannot tell
  What pains He had to bear;
But we believe it was for us
  He hung and suffered there.

He died that we might be forgiven,
  He died to make us good,
That we might go at last to heaven,
  Saved by his precious blood.

There was no other good enough
To pay the price of sin;
He only could unlock the gate
Of heaven and let us in.

Oh, dearly, dearly has He loved,
  And we must love him too,
And trust in his redeeming blood,
  And try his works to do.

Cecil Frances Alexander

99

Jesus' Burial

Now there was a man named Joseph, from the Jewish town of Arimathea. He was a member of the council, a good and righteous man, [51] *who had not consented to their decision and action; and he was looking for the kingdom of God.* [52] *This man went to Pilate and asked for the body of Jesus.* [53] *Then he took it down and wrapped it in a linen shroud and laid him in a tomb cut in stone, where no one had ever yet been laid.* [54] *It was the day of Preparation, and the Sabbath was beginning.* [55] *The women who had come with him from Galilee followed and saw the tomb and how his body was laid.* [56] *Then they returned and prepared spices and ointments. On the Sabbath they rested according to the commandment* (Luke 23:50–56).

Jesus had died around three o'clock on Friday afternoon. The Jewish Sabbath followed and began at six o'clock the same evening. He had also died as a criminal by being hung on a tree. Jewish law required that the body of the deceased should be brought down before sunset on the same day and buried, otherwise the whole land would be polluted by the corpse (*Deut*. 21:22–23; *Jos*. 8:29; 10:26–27). This meant that Jesus' followers had only three hours in which to gain permission to remove the body, actually take it down and find a place to bury it. The burial of Jesus was therefore a matter of some urgency.

JOSEPH (verses 50–54)

In this moment of need Joseph stepped forward to do the honours for Jesus. Joseph came from a town in southern Judea called Arimathea and was a member of the national council called the

Sanhedrin. Joseph represents that rare breed of politician or public servant who is willing to stand up for Jesus openly, even when he stood virtually alone (*John* 19:38–39). Like Nicodemus he had objected within the council to the crookedness of the decision to be rid of Jesus (*John* 7:50–52). As a true believer in the coming of God's final kingdom he had become a disciple of Jesus (*Matt.* 27:57). Joseph fronted up to Pilate in person and requested the body of Jesus for burial.

The next problem was where to bury Jesus since the Sabbath was coming on when no burial work was permitted. If only Joseph had realised that he belonged to the script written long ago by the prophet Isaiah when predicting the death, burial, and resurrection of the Messiah. There it was stated that the Messiah would be buried with a rich man in his death (*Isa.* 53:9). Joseph owned a private tomb next to the place of Jesus' execution. Appropriately this tomb had never been used, being newly cut from the rock (*Matt.* 27:60). Only pristine things were suited to the usage of the Son of God (*Luke* 1:26–31; 19:29–31). This is where they laid the lifeless body of Jesus.

THE WOMEN (verses 55–56)

Joseph was not the only one active in Jesus' service that day. Some of the same women who had provided for Jesus and the disciples (*Luke* 8:1–3), had accompanied him all the way to Jerusalem and were round the cross (*Luke* 23:49), they took note of what Joseph had done and where. Only a short part of the day was left so the women only had time to note where Jesus was buried, before going home to prepare the spices for Jesus' body. Being women of faith they kept the fourth commandment by resting all that day until early on our Sunday / Lord's Day morning (*Luke* 24:1).

Women can be strong in their attachments. Without aspiring to membership in the leadership band of Jesus' disciples these women displayed a faith of friendship that equalled that of the men. They passed every test of faith and loyalty to Jesus. By being there at the end they were rewarded with being there at the beginning of his resurrection.

Someone might ask, 'Why did Jesus have to be buried?' and, 'Why could he not have immediately come back in resurrection power?' The burial of Jesus should not be passed over too easily because it lines up with his death and his resurrection as an integral part of the history of salvation (*1 Cor*. 15:3–5). The burial of the Son of God injects a real break between Jesus' death and his resurrection; it tells us that Jesus really died and that his resurrection was physical as well as spiritual. The burial affects the way people read and interpret the narrative. It means the closure of Jesus' earthly life and work; it preludes the way for his resurrection as the Son of God with power, through the Spirit of holiness (*Rom*. 1:3–4).

Theologically and pastorally the burial of Jesus is important for it assures the believer that his burial is covered by Jesus as his representative. Jesus acts for the believer at every stage of the earthly journey, including the period after death when the body decomposes and is disposed of. That period too is sanctified by the burial of the sinless Saviour on our behalf, in expectation of the resurrection of the body on the day he comes again.

Incidentally, the story of Joseph and the women shows us how godly men and women can and should work together creatively for the greater good of the community and the advancement of the gospel. Theirs is a working relationship of complementarity and mutual support in which each play their part and together praise and serve God with a single voice and design (*Rom*. 15:5–6).

The scene is now set for the greatest of all the reversals that Luke records in his Gospel – the resurrection of Jesus from death to life, from shame and rejection to freedom and victory, from earthly weakness to heavenly power.

100

Jesus Is Risen!

But on the first day of the week, at early dawn, they went to the tomb, taking the spices they had prepared. [2] *And they found the stone rolled away from the tomb,* [3] *but when they went in they did not find the body of the Lord Jesus.* [4] *While they were perplexed about this, behold, two men stood by them in dazzling apparel.* [5] *And as they were frightened and bowed their faces to the ground, the men said to them, 'Why do you seek the living among the dead?* [6] *He is not here, but has risen. Remember how he told you, while he was still in Galilee,* [7] *that the Son of Man must be delivered into the hands of sinful men and be crucified and on the third day rise.'* [8] *And they remembered his words,* [9] *and returning from the tomb they told all these things to the eleven and to all the rest.* [10] *Now it was Mary Magdalene and Joanna and Mary the mother of James and the other women with them who told these things to the apostles,* [11] *but these words seemed to them an idle tale, and they did not believe them.* [12] *But Peter rose and ran to the tomb; stooping and looking in, he saw the linen cloths by themselves; and he went home marvelling at what had happened* (Luke 24:1–12).

This is Luke's account of the resurrection of Jesus, an event that is presented with different details by all four Evangelists. The fact that it is repeated four times points to its importance for early Christianity and all later faith and preaching (*1 Cor.* 15:1–34). Authentic faith and life in Christ cannot survive where the bodily resurrection of Jesus is reduced to a religious symbol or denied as a factual happening. Jesus in his resurrection is the first-fruits of that human harvest that will rise to greet him at his second advent. His re-embodied self is the model of the new humanity fitted for the new environment of God's kingdom that all his people will inherit and inhabit.

THE EMPTY TOMB (verses 1–3)

The account begins with the women since Luke has just told of their visit to the tomb. Their names are given later (verse 10). Luke tells the resurrection story through the eyes of these women. Their eagerness was shown by their coming to the tomb at first light. To their utter surprise they found the stone rolled away from the tomb and the tomb emptied of Jesus' body. By itself the empty tomb did not convey to them the fact of Jesus' resurrection since someone could have preceded them and removed the body. This was the first possibility that Mary thought of (*John* 20:1–2, 11–15).

Faith in Jesus' bodily resurrection depends on a complex set of circumstances that provide substantial evidence (for example, the sudden change in the disciples, the vigorous rise of Christianity and its inexplicable survival through two millennia of persecutions) but the empty tomb is a crucial piece of the evidence. Two angels at the tomb give the women the only meaningful interpretation of the empty tomb – Jesus has risen from the dead. All other explanations are less credible than this one.

THE FIRST WITNESSES (verses 4–7)

Naturally the women were perplexed about their discovery, though at a loss for answers, until two angels appeared beside them. Already unsettled by the empty tomb the sudden appearance of angels quite terrified the women who bowed their faces to the ground at the presence of heavenly beings.

The angels address the women with inside information on what has really happened and with insight into the thinking and fears of the women. Their tone is firm but reassuring. They come straight to the point with a question that says it all: 'Why are you women looking for a dead person when he has actually risen and is out and about in the community of the living?' Their question, which is virtually a statement of fact, is followed by the first affirmation of the resurrection faith: 'He is not here, he has risen!'

Placing their message beyond all doubt the angels recall what Jesus said while he was among them. Due to a strange lapse of memory the women had failed to match these words to the experience they had just come through. Now they do remember and are convinced that Jesus is alive again (*Luke* 9:43–45; 18:31–33).

Christians take a realist view of the resurrection of Jesus. This means that they believe in real women and real angels speaking to them at a real tomb that was really empty because its occupant had been raised in bodily form. The resurrection of Jesus is a fact that is true and reliable, no matter how few or many people believe it is so.

BELIEVING WOMEN (verses 8–10)

Convinced by the angels and incited by their own discovery of the empty tomb the women rush off to share first-hand with the disciples the good news of Jesus' personal resurrection. So notable is their witness at this strategic point in the story of Jesus that Luke records the names of three of the women. He may have done this not only as a historian interested in the details, but because these women were known in the early churches.

Just as with the news of Jesus' conception and birth Luke brings different witnesses together to share their experiences of God's grace (*Luke* 1:39–56). Again women are involved and appear in a good light. Like Mary at the annunciation they believed what the angels told them without requesting a full explanation before they believed. Then they reported their news to the apostles as leaders of the disciple band. In contrast to the women's readiness to believe, the disciples are slow, even unwilling, to believe what is reported.

Though the example of the women here gives no support to women's ordination (which is another issue), readers are left in no doubt about the capabilities and valuable contribution of women in the public witness and life of the churches.

DISBELIEVING APOSTLES (verses 10–12)

Not for the first the apostles were in the grip of unbelief rather than faith. Perhaps from male pride and cultural convention they refused the forthright evidence of the women. Their faith in Jesus had suffered a crushing blow from his death and the silence that had followed. Even when Jesus appeared to them in person they had difficulty accepting the evidence (*Luke* 24:36–43)!

Some spark of hope still lived in Peter's heart though; he tests the story of the women by going out to the tomb to see for himself. Typically he reacted instinctively, running all the way to the tomb, a sign perhaps of his longing to be restored with Jesus. He found the burial vestments but Jesus was nowhere to be seen. No angels! No body! Yet Peter returned home amazed, unable to make sense of all that was happening to him in these days.

It is easy for us in hindsight to fault the disciples for their unbelief in the face of the emergent evidence for Jesus' resurrection. But millions have read or heard the accounts and give no credence to the event of Jesus' rising. They are worse than the disciples who in time came to complete faith in the resurrection of Jesus and proclaimed it as a first-order belief for personal salvation. Where do you stand on the resurrection of Christ? – with the angels, the women and (eventually) the apostles? Or do you side with the many who throughout Christian history have chosen to escape the searing light of the resurrection by adhering to one of the alternative explanations put forward by rationalistic scholars or naturalistic scientists?

101

A Journey with a Difference

*That very day two of them were going to a village named
Emmaus, about seven miles from Jerusalem, [14] and they were
talking with each other about all these things that had happened.
[15] While they were talking and discussing together, Jesus himself
drew near and went with them. [16] But their eyes were kept from
recognizing him. [17] And he said to them, 'What is this conversation that you are holding with each other as you walk?' And
they stood still, looking sad. [18] Then one of them, named Cleopas,
answered him, 'Are you the only visitor to Jerusalem who does
not know the things that have happened there in these days?'
[19] And he said to them, 'What things?' And they said to him,
'Concerning Jesus of Nazareth, a man who was a prophet mighty
in deed and word before God and all the people, [20] and how our
chief priests and rulers delivered him up to be condemned to death,
and crucified him. [21] But we had hoped that he was the one to
redeem Israel. Yes, and besides all this, it is now the third day
since these things happened. [22] Moreover, some women of our
company amazed us. They were at the tomb early in the morning,
[23] and when they did not find his body, they came back saying
that they had even seen a vision of angels, who said that he was
alive. [24] Some of those who were with us went to the tomb and
found it just as the women had said, but him they did not see.'
[25] And he said to them, 'O foolish ones, and slow of heart to believe
all that the prophets have spoken! [26] Was it not necessary that
the Christ should suffer these things and enter into his glory?'
[27] And beginning with Moses and all the Prophets, he interpreted
to them in all the Scriptures the things concerning himself.*

> [28] *So they drew near to the village to which they were going. He*
> *acted as if he were going farther,* [29] *but they urged him strongly,*
> *saying, 'Stay with us, for it is toward evening and the day is now*
> *far spent.' So he went in to stay with them.* [30] *When he was at*
> *table with them, he took the bread and blessed and broke it and*
> *gave it to them.* [31] *And their eyes were opened, and they*
> *recognized him. And he vanished from their sight.* [32] *They said*
> *to each other, 'Did not our hearts burn within us while he talked*
> *to us on the road, while he opened to us the Scriptures?'* [33] *And*
> *they rose that same hour and returned to Jerusalem. And they*
> *found the eleven and those who were with them gathered together,*
> [34] *saying, 'The Lord has risen indeed, and has appeared to*
> *Simon!'* [35] *Then they told what had happened on the road, and*
> *how he was known to them in the breaking of the bread* (Luke
> 24:13–35).

After the appearance of Jesus to the women Luke alone records the following story about two disciples and their encounter with the risen Lord. It is a masterful account, full of humanity and spiritual lessons. As well as being further evidence for the actual existence of the risen Jesus it can function as a parable of the Christian life. Like the two disciples, believers today journey together with Jesus as he refreshes and strengthens them through the Scriptures and by making himself known in the ordinary events of life.

THE SCENE SET (verses 13–16)

The story is about two disciples travelling home to Emmaus about twelve miles out of Jerusalem. One is named Cleopas (see also *John* 19:25). This has led to the idea that his travelling companion was his wife Mary, but the remark about 'our women' (verse 22) could mean that the two travellers were men. What is more important is their topic of conversation – the events of Jesus' execution three days before, which all Jerusalem was talking about. When Jesus joins them on the road he remains incognito. Their failure to begin with in recognising Jesus was ordered by God (as in *Luke* 8:10; 18:34) so that they might come to a clearer belief in the resurrection of Jesus and his abiding presence (verse 31).

THE CONVERSATION (verses 17–27)

When Jesus opens the conversation with a leading question, 'What are you talking about?' he knows exactly where he is taking the conversation and what he is going to do. The two stop in their tracks, their faces conveying their grey mood of despair. Jesus' question moves Cleopas to suggest their new friend must be a visitor in Jerusalem since there was only one topic of conversation in the city these days – the crucifixion of Jesus of Nazareth.

Jesus then pretends ignorance a second time, 'What things are being talked about?' 'About Jesus of Nazareth, whom we supposed a prophet because of his powerful words and acts. Unfortunately the religious leaders did not like him and handed him over to the Roman authorities who duly crucified him.'

Tragically, Cleopas and his friend had nurtured the hope that Jesus might have been the long-awaited Deliverer of Israel. Cleopas had not yet grasped the need for a Messiah who would suffer and die for God's people, a point that Jesus was going to explain (verses 26–27, 32). Cleopas was grappling with the contradictory evidence about Jesus. In verses 20–21 he weighs the negative evidence suggesting that Jesus was mistaken; in verses 22–24 he weighs the positive evidence suggesting that Jesus may be the Messiah.

This teaches us the need to master the evidence about Jesus in his life, death and resurrection if we are to believe properly in his name. The death of Christ and his resurrection lie at the heart of Christian faith and discipleship. Without them Christianity loses its distinctiveness. These are also the very points that other religions or secular opponents object to or pass over in their assessment of the case for Christianity. Paul clearly argues that without the actual resurrection of Jesus evangelism and faith are meaningless and Christian suffering is pointless (*1 Cor*. 15:12–19).

Cleopas clinches his doubts by adding that it is now 'the third day' since these things happened. Yet Cleopas also shares that some of their women had visited the tomb of Jesus that very day without finding his body. Angels had appeared instead who witnessed that Jesus was alive. This was confirmed by other friends who could not find any trace of Jesus.

In the light of what immediately follows it is clear that presenting the evidence alone is not sufficient to make people believers in Jesus' death and resurrection. There is needed a further factor – the explanation of the Scriptures that record the history of these events in the life of Jesus. Along with this there is needed the inner, secret but effective illumination of the mind and heart to the spiritual light and truth of God's word. All this belongs to the epistemology[1] of faith.

Only the Lord himself can do this by opening the inner eyes of understanding to grasp spiritual meaning (verse 31), but once this happens all the evidence makes sense so that truth comes alive and controls the mind and heart (verses 31–35).

Jesus has led the disciples to the point where he can conclude the conversation by revealing the truth about himself. He scolds them for their foolishness in not believing the Scriptures that speak so plainly about him (*Acts* 2:22–35; 3:17–26; 13:26–37). So Jesus takes them on an expository tour of the Old Testament. In doing so he emphasises two things: first, the messiah had to suffer the way he did if he was going to take away the world's sin and reconcile the world to God. The atonement of his death was necessary as a prelude to his glorification afterwards through resurrection and ascension. Secondly, he explained that he was the key to Old Testament revelation in the law and the prophets. His understanding of the Old Testament was Christological and so should ours be. The Old Testament is a Christian book for using by all believers today.

AN ACT OF HOSPITALITY (verses 28–31)

The road and the miles had been gobbled up in the riveting words of Jesus. Emmaus was in sight and their friend would be leaving them. Since it was almost the end of a long day Cleopas and his companion urged Jesus to stay with them that night. By practising hospitality the two friends entertained more than angels; in their generosity they were rewarded with a sighting of Jesus the risen Lord (*Heb*. 13:2). Jesus accepted their invitation and joined them at a meal. It was when he handled the bread by breaking it that their memories were jolted and they realized that their guest was Jesus.

[1] Epistemology: the theory of knowledge, how we know what we know.

Since Cleopas and his friend were not present at the last supper Jesus' action in breaking the bread must have been a well-known trait to them from somewhere else. Apparently Jesus had his own distinctive way of doing things (*Luke* 9:16). Before they could ask Jesus anything he vanished from their sight.

Our Lord comes to us in the ordinary meetings, events and actions of daily life. What is more common than sitting at a table to eat together? The whole of life is sanctified for the believer in Jesus. This means that he is actively engaged for the believer's up-building in everyday occurrences such as through another person, a piece of music, a book, an accident, a memory, a picture and so on. All things are ours in Christ (*1 Cor*. 3:21–23). The spiritually-minded Christian should be alert to these visits of the Lord in daily life that assure us of his attentiveness and company though we cannot see him.

THE RETURN JOURNEY (verses 32–35)

There was only one thing to do – go back to Jerusalem and report to the Eleven. So off they went without delay (we can picture the unfinished meal on the table), in their eagerness to tell what they had just experienced. Their mood on the return journey is quite the reverse of their earlier one. Then they were down-cast, now they are upbeat. It was Jesus' exposition of the Scriptures that did it. Their hearts burned inside them as he spoke so candidly about heavenly things. In this we are reminded that it is primarily through the Scriptures that Jesus meets with his disciples and nurtures them. The most pure joys and the greatest gains for faith come through knowing him in his word, read privately or in groups, especially through the preaching of it publicly by gifted and experienced teachers.

In the city the two found the Eleven who greeted them with their own news about Jesus – that he had appeared in person to Peter. To this the two disciples were able to add their own story of Jesus' resurrection appearance. By now the mood of the disciples was rapidly improving and about to get a whole lot better by two more appearances of Jesus. The resurrection of Jesus is still one of the pillars of Christian faith and the source of Christian joy, assurance and mission. The Easter faith is everyday faith for living and sharing around. The resurrection is the beginning of the new creation in which believers now share and are the first-fruits (*2 Cor.* 5:17; *James* 1:18).

It is the same evidence that reaches us today, two millennia later. Either the resurrection is a real event or the disciples and millions like them, have been self-deceived. But it is difficult to square a falsehood of such magnitude with the –

- global expansion of Christianity
- morally uplifting effects of Christianity on human life and culture
- ability of believers to glorify God through intense suffering
- willingness of so many to die for a Person who is now long gone.

All the evidence makes much more sense when the resurrection of Jesus is taken at face value as a real event, the cause behind the above effects.

As we have tried to show, the Emmaus story is a kind of typology of the Christian life. Christians struggle with their faith and doubts in the face of negative experiences in a hostile world. But Christ himself waits on the Christian and refreshes every believer through the power of his word. He also makes himself known periodically through the providences of daily life when we may least expect him. Also through the company of like-minded believers hearts are warmed and faith revived as personal testimony is shared in the light of truth. In all three ways Christ keeps his own and leads them safely to heaven.

102

The Real Presence of Jesus

As they were talking about these things, Jesus himself stood among them, and said to them, 'Peace to you!'
[37] *But they were startled and frightened and thought they saw a spirit.* [38] *And he said to them, 'Why are you troubled, and why do doubts arise in your hearts?* [39] *See my hands and my feet, that it is I myself. Touch me, and see. For a spirit does not have flesh and bones as you see that I have.'* [40] *And when he had said this, he showed them his hands and his feet.* [41] *And while they still disbelieved for joy and were marvelling, he said to them, 'Have you anything here to eat?'* [42] *They gave him a piece of broiled fish,* [43] *and he took it and ate before them.* (Luke 24:36–43)

No sooner had the disciples heard the reports about Jesus than he stood among them in person. Here was a first-hand viewing of the risen Son of Man that they could never gainsay! But their first emotion was terror because his appearance was ghostly. But Jesus quickly set their minds at rest by challenging their fears, showing them his bodily scars and inviting their touch (*John* 20:24–28). He might have appeared like a ghost but he had a material body, just like believers in their resurrection (*1 Cor.* 15:42–50).

Jesus appeared repeatedly to groups of disciples and individuals during forty days after his resurrection to provide 'infallible proofs' (*Acts* 1:3) of his being alive. Some of that circumstantial and factual evidence reaches us today in the four Gospels for the same purpose. Luke's account helps believers base their faith in the events of this world's history as a guarantee and guide to truth.

Since the disciples were by now on the brink of complete persuasion and showing the emotions of uncontrollable joy in spite of remaining disbelief, Jesus clinches his presentation as a risen Person by asking them for food. Ghosts don't eat food (though people may leave food out for them), but real people with physical needs do! Having received their offer of food he ate it in front of them to allay their remaining doubts and fears.

The Jesus of the resurrection was the same yet different from the Jesus who was crucified and died. For example, he suddenly appeared among the disciples, entering through the door of the room where they were meeting. At the same time he could eat and process food. Continuity and discontinuity with Jesus of Nazareth mark the new Man Christ Jesus, the first-fruits of the harvest of all those who have fallen asleep in him. Scripture encourages believers to know that what was true for him will become true for them on the day he returns. They should be looking out for a Saviour from heaven who will transform their lowly and weak bodies to become like the body of his glory (*Phil.* 3:20–21). Like Jesus before and after the resurrection believers will be essentially the same, yet different and more liberated in many ways.

103

Retrospect and Prospect

Then he said to them, 'These are my words that I spoke to you while I was still with you, that everything written about me in the Law of Moses and the Prophets and the Psalms must be fulfilled.' [45] *Then he opened their minds to understand the Scriptures,* [46] *and said to them, 'Thus it is written, that the Christ should suffer and on the third day rise from the dead,* [47] *and that repentance and forgiveness of sins should be proclaimed in his name to all nations, beginning from Jerusalem.* [48] *You are witnesses of these things.* [49] *And behold, I am sending the promise of my Father upon you. But stay in the city until you are clothed with power from on high'* (Luke 24:44–49).

Reading in one sitting the closing chapter of Luke's Gospel makes it seem that Jesus rose from his grave, appeared to his followers, commissioned his apostles and ascended to heaven, all within a twenty-four hour period. In fact, Acts tells us that chapter twenty-four covers a period of virtually six weeks (*Acts* 1:3). Luke has compacted his narrative so as to move quickly to the finale of his account of Jesus' earthly journey – the ascension. But first Jesus must sum up his earthly ministry and commission the disciples who will henceforth act under his authority, in the absence of his physical presence.

LOOKING BACK (verses 44–45)

First, Jesus recalls his teachings to the disciples while he was still with them. His teaching was that he was the goal and meaning of the Old

Testament Scriptures and that everything there written about him had to be fulfilled. Jesus found himself written about in every part of the Jewish canon. The foundational part was the Law that consisted of the first five books of Moses (a reader can think here of the promised 'seed' of Abraham, the figure of Melchizedeck, the Passover sacrifice and other institutions); the second part was the Prophets which included the historical books starting with Joshua (here think of the Davidic covenant about a great descendant whose kingdom will never end, along with the many messianic promises of the great prophets); the third part began with the Psalms and included all the poetical and wisdom books ending with the Chronicles (think of the messianic Psalms or the prophetic utterances of the book of Daniel).

The Old Testament is a Christian book because it predicts Christ in a variety of ways. The Old Testament in its covenants of promise, history of salvation, worship regulations, historical and personal typologies, institutions of sacrifice, liturgy of faith and confession, offer Christ to modern readers. From these sources and aids Jesus understood himself to be the suffering servant of the Lord whose death would atone for the sins of many and set them free (*Luke* 20:41–44; 22:37). Without him the Old Testament remains unfinished business, enigmatical, literal and lifeless. But through him it becomes illumined and a source of delight and spiritual refreshment to the Christian. With this explanation Jesus was repeating the exposition of the Scriptures that burned the hearts of the two disciples on the Emmaus road (*Luke* 24:25–27).

Yet something more is needed for a spiritual understanding of the Scriptures and that is spiritual enlightenment. Christ alone can give this, which is what he did for his disciples (verse 45). The letter of the Bible without the Spirit to interpret it is deadly and ineffective (*2 Cor.* 3:4–18). Both the outward reading and teaching of the written word of God *and* the inner enlightenment and assurance of the Holy Spirit are necessary for the desired effect. The Spirit without the word leads to mysticism, the word without the Spirit leads to nominalism.

LOOKING FORWARD (verses 46–49)

What follows is Luke's account of the Great Commission, better known from Matthew (*Matt.* 28:18–21). Jesus highlights five items for attention.

- The message about Jesus as Messiah is a scriptural one. The Scriptures foretold the sufferings of the Messiah and his resurrection (*Psa.* 22; *Isa.* 52:13–53:12; *1 Cor.* 5:7).
- Repentance and forgiveness are the first requirements of Christ's rule. Without these none can relate rightly to God who is equally holy and gracious (*Acts* 2:37–38).
- The message of the messiah is for the whole of humankind. It should be proclaimed to the whole world in a non-sectarian way (*Isa.* 2:1–4; *Luke* 2:27–32). Acts records this global mission of Christ's followers.
- The apostles are the official witnesses of the truth about the Messiah. Their oral and written witness, distilled in the New Testament, becomes the pattern of Christian witness to Christ forever.
- The power of the Holy Spirit is needed to accomplish this global task. Just as Jesus had received the Spirit of mission and power (*Luke* 3:21–22) so would his followers while waiting in Jerusalem at Pentecost (*Acts* 1:4–8; 2:1–4).

The commission then and now consists of four parts: the message of the historical events of Jesus' death and resurrection; the appropriation of the message through personal repentance and faith in Jesus Christ; the world outreach of the gospel message; the empowerment for mission through the Holy Spirit. No theology of mission or evangelism can afford to omit any one of these four elements.

104

Leave-taking

Then he led them out as far as Bethany, and lifting up his hands he blessed them. [51] *While he blessed them, he parted from them and was carried up into heaven.* [52] *And they worshipped him and returned to Jerusalem with great joy,* [53] *and were continually in the temple blessing God* (Luke 24:50–53)

Luke comes now to the last moments in Jesus' earthly life. We call this parting the Ascension because Jesus rose or ascended physically from the earth. For this final episode Jesus led his disciples out to Bethany at the Mount of Olives (*Acts* 1:12), a short distance from Jerusalem. He wanted to be alone with his disciples in these final moments of earthly contact. Historically the ascension of Jesus was the moment of his transition from an earthly existence to a heavenly one. Scientifically it presents no greater difficulties than the resurrection. Both testify to the innovative power of God in working out his salvation plan in and for the world.

Only Luke records the ascension because he wanted to make it the end-point of Jesus' pilgrimage of faith. But just as it is the goal of the Gospel so it is the starting-point of Acts (*Acts* 1:9–11). By overlapping his accounts of the ascension in this way Luke creates a strong sense of continuity between the earthly life of Jesus and the Christian history of mission that follows. The same Jesus is Lord of both (*Acts* 1:1–2).

The ascension puts the finishing touches to Luke's picture of Jesus as the last and greatest prophet of the Lord. Jesus himself linked his life-work to that of Elijah (*Luke* 4:24–27). He had talked with him on the mountain (*Luke* 9:30–31); now, like Elijah, Jesus is carried up into heaven (*2 Kings* 2:1–12), having also made pronouncements about a future giving of the Lord's Spirit to his followers (*2 Kings* 2:9–18).

So Jesus' earthly life comes to a close on a high note of triumph and blessing, with one important difference. By finishing with an act of blessing Jesus was playing the part of a departing priest who had offered his sacrifice and made propitiation for the sins of his people. This is something Elijah could never do, nor any of the prophets. Further, Elijah departed as an individual, Jesus was taken up into heaven as a representative of many others, whose presence there gives God the right to make everything new (*Rev.* 21:5).

Luke explains (accepting the longer reading of verse 51) what happened next and what it means. Jesus was parted physically from the disciples by being lifted up from the ground, rising into the air until he was out of the disciples' sight (*Acts* 1:9). This was a physical event described in spatial terms but has nothing to do with a primitive view of the universe. There is no other language with which to describe an exceptional event like the ascension. What it meant is more important than its physical explanation. Jesus was now transferring from the present age to the one to come, from this space-time creation to the new creation inaugurated in his resurrection, with its greater properties of power, glory, and spirituality (*1 Cor.* 15:42–44). When Jesus returns he will reverse his ascension with a descension (*Acts* 1:11).

Luke closes his Gospel where he opened it – inside the temple with people praising God. How much has happened since the angel appeared to Zechariah in the temple with the breaking news of Elizabeth's conception of John! The eleven disciples have so much more to praise God for than Zechariah had. This is because Jesus the Messiah has come into the world, lived, died, risen again, and ascended into heaven. Now the disciples were waiting expectantly for another moment in the unfolding of God's saving design – the coming of the Holy Spirit to empower and motivate them for the endless task of discipling the nations of the world. Together, the coming of Jesus and the coming of the Spirit are the true temple theology of the Bible – God's personal dwelling with humankind and in the church as Christ's body.

In Acts Luke shares the next instalment of the greatest story ever told – God's saving love for the world. In the meantime the first disciples worshipped Jesus. They had come at last to see him as the eternal Son of God – not by adoption but intrinsically and in his very Being. They agreed now with the angel of the annunciation (*Luke* 1:31–37). Modern readers of Luke's Gospel are meant to do so too, having followed everything from the beginning along with Theophilus (*Luke* 1:1–4).

Group Study Guide

SCHEME FOR GROUP BIBLE STUDY

(Covers 26 Weeks; before each study read the passage indicated and the chapters from this book shown below.)

Study Passage	Chapters
1. Luke 1	1–5
2. Luke 2	6–8
3. Luke 3	9–11
4. Luke 4	12–15
5. Luke 5	16–20
6. Luke 6	21–23
7. Luke 7	24–27
8. Luke 8	28–33
9. Luke 9	34–42
10. Luke 10	43–46
11. Luke 11	47–50
12. Luke 12	51–54
13. Luke 13	55–60
14. Luke 14	61–62
15. Luke 15	63–64
16. Luke 16	65–67
17. Luke 17	68–70
18. Luke 18	71–76
19. Luke 19	77–79
20. Luke 20	80–85
21. Luke 21	86–87

	Study Passage	Chapters
22.	Luke 22	88–94
23.	Luke 23:1–31	95–96
24.	Luke 23:32–56	97–99
25.	Luke 24:1–35	100–101
26.	Luke 24:36–53	102–104

This Study Guide has been prepared for group Bible study, but it can also be used individually. Those who use it on their own may find it helpful to keep a note of their responses in a notebook.

The way in which group Bible studies are led can greatly enhance their value. A well-conducted study will appear as though it has been easy to lead, but that is usually because the leader has worked hard and planned well. Clear aims are essential.

In all Bible study, individual or corporate, we have several aims:

1. To gain an understanding of the original meaning of the particular passage of Scripture;

2. To apply this to ourselves and our own situation;

3. To develop some specific ways of putting the biblical teaching into practice.

2 Timothy 3:16–17 provides a helpful structure. Paul says that Scripture is useful for:

(i) teaching us;
(ii) rebuking us;
(iii) correcting, or changing us;
(iv) training us in righteousness.

Consequently, in studying any passage of Scripture, we should always have in mind these questions:

What does this passage teach us (about God, ourselves, etc.)?

Does it rebuke us in some way?

How can its teaching transform us?

What equipment does it give us for serving Christ?

In fact, these four questions alone would provide a safe guide in any Bible study.

PRINCIPLES

In group Bible study we meet in order to learn about God's Word and ways 'with all the saints' (*Eph.* 3:18). But our own experience, as well as Scripture, tells us that the saints are not always what they *are* called to be in every situation – including group Bible study! Leaders ordinarily have to work hard and prepare well if the work of the group is to be spiritually profitable. The following guidelines for leaders may help to make this a reality.

Preparation:

1. Study and understand the passage yourself. The better prepared and more sure of the direction of the study you are, the more likely it is that the group will have a beneficial and enjoyable study.
Ask: What are the main things this passage is saying? How can this be made clear? This is not the same question as the more common 'What does this passage "say to you"?', which expects a reaction rather than an exposition of the passage. Be clear about that distinction yourself, and work at making it clear in the group study.

2. On the basis of your own study form a clear idea *before* the group meets of (i) the main theme(s) of the passage which should be opened out for discussion, and (ii) some general conclusions the group ought to reach as a result of the study. Here the questions which arise from 2 Timothy 3:16–17 should act as our guide.

3. The guidelines and questions which follow may help to provide a general framework for each discussion; leaders should use them as starting places which can be further developed. It is usually helpful to have a specific goal or theme in mind for group discussion, and one is suggested for each study. But even more important than tracing a single theme is understanding the teaching and the implications of the passage.

Leading the Group:

1. Announce the passage and theme for the study, and begin with prayer. In group studies it may be helpful to invite a different person to lead in prayer each time you meet.

2. Introduce the passage and theme, briefly reminding people of its outline and highlighting the content of each subsidiary section.

3. Lead the group through the discussion questions. Use your own if you are comfortable in doing so; those provided may be used, developing them with your own points. As discussion proceeds, continue to encourage the group first of all to discuss the significance of the passage (teaching) and only then its application (meaning for us). It may be helpful to write important points and applications on a board by way of summary as well as visual aid.

4. At the end of each meeting, remind members of the group of their assignments for the next meeting, and encourage them to come prepared. Be sufficiently prepared as the leader to give specific assignments to individuals, or even couples or groups, to come with specific contributions.

5. Remember that you are the leader of the group! Encourage clear contributions, and do not be embarrassed to ask someone to explain what they have said more fully or to help them to do so ('Do you mean . . . ?').

Most groups include the 'over-talkative', the 'over-silent' and the 'red-herring raisers'! Leaders must control the first, encourage the second and redirect the third! Each leader will develop his or her own most natural way of doing that; but it will be helpful to think out what that is before the occasion arises! The first two groups can be helped by some judicious direction of questions to specific individuals or even groups (for example, 'Jane, you know something about this from personal experience . . .'); the third by redirecting the discussion to the passage itself ('That is an interesting point, but isn't it true that this passage really concentrates on . . . ?'). It may be helpful to break the group up into smaller groups sometimes, giving each subgroup specific points to discuss and to report back on. A wise arranging of these smaller groups may also help each member to participate.

More important than any techniques we may develop is the help of the Spirit enabling us to understand and to apply the Scriptures. Have and encourage a humble, prayerful spirit.

6. Keep faith with the schedule; it is better that some of the group wished the study could have been longer than that others are inconvenienced by it stretching beyond the time limits set.

7. Close in prayer. As time permits, spend the closing minutes in corporate prayer, encouraging the group to apply what they have learned in praise and thanks, intercession and petition.

STUDY 1: Luke 1

1. What was Luke's standpoint in writing his Gospel?
2. Why should the Gospels have a special place in the reading of Christians?
3. Does the story of Elizabeth and Zechariah contain any wisdom for childless or infertile couples?
4. What does this story teach us about failure and backsliding in Christian life and service? Discuss 1 Corinthians 9:24–27 in relation to the story of Zechariah.
5. Why was Zechariah wrong to doubt the angel's announcement? Can we learn from Zechariah's mistake?
6. Does the incarnation teach us anything about when human life begins (verses 31, 35)?
7. What spiritual lessons can we learn from Mary's personal example (verses 38, 45)?
8. Can we learn anything about the status of the human embryo from the story of Mary's visit to Elizabeth (verses 39–44)?
9. Discuss the importance of personal experience in religious profession (verses 47-49).
10. What attributes of God does Mary celebrate in her song?
11. What can we learn about personal recovery in the Lord's service from the experience of Zechariah (verse 64)?
12. What is the heart of the gospel message according to Zechariah?

STUDY 2: Luke 2

1. What historical difficulties are raised by Luke's chronology of Jesus' birth (verses 1–2)?
2. Why does Luke draw attention to the fact that Joseph belonged to the family of David (verse 4)?
3. How foundational is the incarnation for the history of salvation?

4. Discuss the meaning and relevance of the angels' message about Jesus (verse 11).

5. What does God's peace mean in a world that is often in conflict?

6. How do Isaiah chapters 40–55 help us to understand Simeon's prophecy about Jesus (verses 30–32)?

7. How does Luke bring out the global reach of Jesus' mission?

8. Give examples from Luke's Gospel of Jesus causing the rise and fall of many in Israel, and of Jesus being spoken against.

9. What does reference to his Father's things or house tell us about the consciousness of Jesus?

10. Did Jesus disobey his parents in obeying God? Would it matter if he had?

11. Were Joseph and Mary right to be anxious and to scold Jesus?

12. Would you expect this kind of behaviour from your twelve-year old? If not, why not?

13. What should Christian young people and Christian parents take from this story of Jesus?

STUDY 3: Luke 3

1. Why is Luke so careful to inform us of the world and regional rulers of that time (verses 1–2)?

2. Give some modern equivalents of people saying, 'We have Abraham for our father', as a reason for declining the call to personal repentance (verse 8).

3. What do John's counsels teach us about Christian social ethics (verses 10-14)?

4. What does baptizing with the Holy Spirit and with fire mean?

5. Why was Jesus baptized?

6. What were the roles of the Father and the Spirit in the ministry of Jesus?

7. Who are the most important human links in Jesus' family tree? What do these individuals tell us about Jesus?

8. Can *we* be related to Jesus? How?

STUDY 4: Luke 4

1. In what ways do the original temptation of Adam and Eve and the later temptation of Israel help us to understand the temptations of Jesus?

2. What lessons can we learn for own battle with temptation from the ways Jesus handled his own?

3. Discuss the place of the Bible in facing temptation?

4. What were the main points of Jesus' sermon in Nazareth?

5. Read the stories of Elijah and Elisha and see what similarities you can find with the ministry of Jesus.

6. What sort of authority did Jesus have?

7. What sort of faith did the demons have?

8. What can we learn about the priorities of Jesus' human work from the ordering of events in chapter four?

STUDY 5: Luke 5

1. Why did the catch of fish give Peter a sense of his sinfulness?

2. What did Peter mean by saying, 'I am a sinful man' and why did he ask Jesus to leave him (verse 8)?

3. What can we learn about evangelism from fishing, ancient and modern (verse 10)?

4. How does the leper represent sinful human nature (verse 12)?

5. What place should the willingness of Jesus have in presenting him as a Saviour and Helper (verses 12–13)?

6. Give other examples of the power of the Lord at work in Jesus' ministry (verse 17).

7. What is the significance of faith from this story (verse 20)?

8. Why is it that only God can forgive sins (verse 21)?

9. Should fear have any place in religion (verse 26)?

10. What does Jesus' illustration tell us about the natural spiritual condition of human beings (verse 31)?

11. Did Jesus mean that there are righteous people who do not need his healing (verse 32)?

12. Why do praying and fasting so often go together and is fasting a Christian practice (verse 33)?

13. Develop the thought of Jesus as the heavenly Bridegroom .

14. What did Jesus have in mind when he spoke of new wine and new wine-skins and what applications does this have for Christians and the churches today (verses 37-38)?

15. Does verse 39 contradict what Jesus has just been saying about the new age? Give examples from modern church life of what Jesus teaches in this verse.

STUDY 6: Luke 6

1. Does Jesus do away with the Sabbath commandment?
2. Can we justify the change from the Sabbath day to the Lord's Day (*Rev.* 1:10)?
3. How should Christians keep the Lord's Day in a modern, secular city or in an Islamic or Hindu culture?
4. What are some of the ways Christians can do good and save life on the Lord's day?
5. What does it take to be a leader in Christ's service?
6. What general lessons for church life can we learn from the types of men Jesus gathered round him as apostles?
7. How should we understand being poor, sad, and hungry or rich, full, and happy in Jesus' teaching (verses 20–26)?
8. How can we learn to love our enemies and why is this important?
9. Give examples from your daily life in which you could practise Jesus' ethic of generosity better.
10. How can we ensure that our hearts are filled up with good things (verse 45)?

STUDY 7: Luke 7

1. In what ways did the faith of the centurion show itself? Find at least three evidences.
2. Consider the place of soldiers in Luke's Gospel.
3. What were the special circumstances of the woman that moved Jesus to compassion and what does this tell us about God's compassion for the sufferings of humanity?
4. What does this story teach us about the life-giving Saviour?
5. Discuss the various uses of the beatitudes of Jesus (verse 23) in the 21st century.
6. In what ways did John show himself a true prophet of God? What lessons can we learn from this for public preaching today?
7. How should Christians respond to Jesus' saying in verse 28?
8. Can you think of some modern applications of the principle of verse 35?
9. In what ways can we express our personal love for Jesus?
10. If loving much depends on being forgiven much is it better to have lived a very sinful life before coming to Jesus?
11. What was wrong with Simon's attitude?

STUDY 8: Luke 8

1. Why did Jesus not appoint any women apostles?

2. Why is God's Word like seed (verse 11)?

2. If spiritual understanding is God's gift, why evangelize (v.10)?

3. Give modern examples of each of the first three soil types (vs. 12–14).

4. What are the best ways to hold Christ's word fast and bring forth good fruit with patience (verse 15)?

5. Why is God's Word like light?

6. How does anyone become a member of the family of God?

7. What does this story in vs. 22–25 tell us about the humanness of Jesus?

8. How from the story can we answer the question, 'Who is this?'

9. Can a Christian be demon-possessed (*Col.* 1:13, *1 John* 5:18)?

10. Show from the story how Jesus restores all our human relationships – with God, ourselves, others, nature.

11. Talk about witnessing in your own family (verse 39)?

12. What can we learn from the way the woman touched Jesus?

13. What does verse 46 teach us about the way faith operates in relation to God?

14. Why did Jesus say that the girl was only sleeping when she had in fact died (verses 52–53)?

STUDY 9: Luke 9

1. Why did Jesus send out the twelve disciples without provisions?

2. Does shaking off the dust of unwelcoming villages show an intolerant attitude unbecoming of the Christian gospel (verse 5)?

3. What did Herod's perplexity amount to?

4. What can we learn from the welcoming attitude of Jesus (v.11)?

5. What was the difference between the way the disciples planned to solve the problem of hunger and the way Jesus responded to the same problem?

6. What can we learn from the way Jesus used the five loaves and the two fish?

7. What is the relation between who Jesus is and what he did for us?

8. Why did Jesus have to suffer, and be rejected and crucified?

9. What does it mean to say that Jesus is the Christ?

10. What makes discipleship so costly?

11. What resources does Christ give us for living in self-denial and obedience?

12. Is discipleship really worthwhile?

13. How was this mountain-top experience a coming of the kingdom of God (verse 27)?

14. What is the significance of Moses and Elijah appearing with Jesus in glory? Why were they talking about Jesus' death?

15. What do we learn about Jesus from the heavenly voice?

16. Why could the disciples not cast out the evil spirit?

17. Why was Jesus exasperated with the disciples?

18. Why did Jesus choose to foretell his suffering at this time?

19. Why are people so concerned about greatness?

20. What is the message of the little child?

21. What is the 'taking up' of Jesus and why does Luke make it the end-point of his life of Jesus?

22. Discuss examples of the ways modern Christians may share in the ungenerous and judgemental attitudes of the disciples.

23. Explain the point of Jesus' reply in verse 58.

24. Explain what Jesus was really saying in verse 60.

25. What may people put first today, before following Jesus?

26. What is the spiritual principle at stake in verse 62?

STUDY 10: Luke 10

1. What does verse 2 say to us in a day when there appears to be little response to gospel preaching?

2. Does this passage support 'faith missions'?

3. Discuss principles and practices of church growth from this passage.

4. Are the woes of Jesus (v. 13–15) consistent with him as compassionate and forgiving?

5. Are there stages in the 'fall' of Satan?

6. What does Jesus' prayer teach us about God's saving grace?

7. Discuss the connection between keeping God's law (loving God and neighbour) and gaining eternal life in the biblical story.

8. Discuss the way love works from the story of the good Samaritan.

9. What does the story in verses 38–42 tell us about Jesus' view of family life?

10. Discuss the strengths and dangers that arise for us from our different temperaments?

11. What does this story teach us about the role of women and their relationships to one another?

STUDY 11: Luke 11

1. Why do we find praying difficult and need to be taught (v. 1)?

2. Why is it normal practice to pray to the Father, through the Son, with the help of the Holy Spirit (*Eph*. 2:18)? May we not pray to Jesus or the Spirit directly?

3. In what ways does Jesus help us to pray?

4. Why should we believe in a personal devil (verses 16, 18)?

5. Discuss signs of the kingdom of evil in the world today.

6. Explain the meaning of verse 23 and reconcile it with what Jesus says in Luke 9:50.

7. Discuss the death of Christ in relation to the kingdom of Satan (verses 21–22).

8. Discuss the value of moral education in reforming people's lives (verses 24-26).

9. Why does the Word of God take priority over every other interest or relationship of life (verses 27-28)?

10. What was wrong with asking for a sign to help people believe in Jesus (verse 29)?

11. In what way was Jonah a sign to the Ninevites (verse 30)?

12. Why was the guilt of Jesus' peers greater than that of the Ninevites (verse 32)?

13. What was the main fault of the Pharisees and what relevance does this have for religious practice today (verses 39–41)?

14. What does verse 42 teach us about tithing as a practice?

15. Why does religious office appeal to human vanity (verse 43)?

16. Why is religion so often legalistic and burdensome (verse 46)?

17. What do we learn from verses 50–51 about Jesus' attitude to the Old Testament as a source of historical knowledge?

18. What is 'the key of knowledge' and how may religious experts misuse it (verse 52)?

STUDY 12: Luke 12

1. How does the teaching of verse 56 affect the reading of the contents of this chapter?
2. What is particularly dangerous and damaging about double standards?
3. What does the Bible mean by fearing God? Is it a Christian virtue?
4. Discuss, in a pastorally helpful way, the sin against the Holy Spirit.
5. Discuss modern examples of the thinking of the rich farmer.
6. What remedies does Jesus give for the problem of anxiety?
7. How can we secure true wealth (verses 32–34)?
8. In what practical ways should the return of Jesus affect us?
9. Discuss the interplay of imminence and delay in the teaching of Jesus about his return.
10. In verse 48, people do not know yet deserve to be beaten, even lightly. How can these both be true?
11. Can we reconcile Jesus the peace-maker with his dividing families?
12. How does the time of Jesus help us to understand and evaluate our own times?
13. Why is being reconciled with God the greatest priority?

STUDY 13: Luke 13

1. Is there a connection between human suffering and human sinfulness (verses 2, 4)?
2. Why is repentance essential for salvation (verses 3, 5)?
3. What was the 'perishing' that Jesus refers to (verses 3, 5)?
4. How does Jesus' preaching square with the postmodern virtue of universal tolerance?
5. What was the fruit that God wanted from national Israel (6)?
6. What does the parable teach about the patience of God?
7. What was wrong with calling healing 'work' (verse 14)?
8. What healing was appropriate on the Sabbath day according to Jesus (verses 15-16)?
9. Why does Jesus refer to the woman as 'a daughter of Abraham' (verse 16)?

10. What is the main point of the parable in verse 19?

11. How does the second parable (verse 21) differ from the first?

12. Why does entering the kingdom require such effort (v. 24)?

13. What do Jesus' words about the closed door tell us about belief in universalism (verses 24–27)?

14. Why will hell be a sad existence (verse 28)?

15. What does verse 29 tell us about the success of the gospel?

16. What do we learn from verses 32 and 33 about Jesus' understanding of his own mission?

17. Read Luke 13:35 with 21:24. Then read Romans 11:11–15, 23, 25–27. Do these verses make a case for a future conversion of the Jewish people to evangelical faith?

STUDY 14: Luke 14

1. What general moral principle was Jesus establishing in his two questions (verses 3, 5)? What situations could this illumine today?

2. As well as a wedding, what other social settings could Jesus' teaching about humility (verse 11) have relevance for?

3. What principle is Jesus promoting in verses 12–14? How might you practise that in your world of friendships and contacts?

4. Is the prospect of a heavenly reward a worthy reason for doing good (verse 14)?

5. What lessons does the parable of the guests and the banquet teach us about Christian missions? Be specific in your answers.

6. Is there any place for hate in following Christ today (verse 26)?

7. What does the cross mean for Christians living, working and witnessing in a western society?

8. What difference should the need for counting the cost (verses 28, 31) make to the way we approach gospel preaching and evangelism today?

9. What causes us to lose our spiritual and moral saltiness and how can we preserve this in a secular and relativistic culture?

STUDY 15: Luke 15

1. What do Jesus' parables teach us about God's seeking love?

2. The parables contain a lot of joy. What does this tell us about the kind of God he is and the kind of place heaven is?

3. Were both of the sons *prodigal* sons, but in different ways?

4. What was the basic problem with each of the sons?
5. Identify some counterparts of the two sons in society today.
6. What does this parable teach us about the character of God?
7. Why is this parable such a popular one throughout the world?

STUDY 16: Luke 16

1. Does Jesus commend dishonesty in this parable (vs. 1–12)?
2. In what ways can unbelievers be more shrewd than believers?
3. Discuss good ways of stewarding our wealth and possessions.
4. Discuss the place in the religious life of the honest and open heart that pleases God (verses 14-15).
5. Discuss ways in which the law and the prophets differ from the gospel of the kingdom of God and where they overlap and agree.
6. Is verse 18 a blanket ban on divorce by Jesus? Consider the other gospel references in giving your answer.
7. Does Lazarus teach us that God receives into heaven the poor because they are poor, vulnerable and have experienced injustice in this world?
8. What are the main truths of the after-life that Jesus teaches us in this parable (verses 22-27)?
9. Compare the power of the Scriptures with the power of miracles to persuade people to repent and turn to God.

STUDY 17: Luke 17

1. Discuss the dynamic between repentance and forgiveness both in our relation to God and to brothers and sisters in Christ.
2. How does the greatness of faith consist in?
3. What does the parable tell us about *works of supererogation* (doing more than God requires)?
4. What is the place of faith in the story in verses 11–19 and how does that translate into our world?
5. What place should gratitude have in our relationship to and worship of God through Jesus?
6. What other biblical references can you think of that teach the inwardness and spiritual nature of the kingdom (verse 21)?
7. What are some of the characteristics of the day of Christ's return hat he highlights in this passage?
8. How should we prepare and be ready for Christ's return?

STUDY 18: Luke 18

1. Why do we lose heart in prayer?
2. How does this parable encourage us in praying?
3. What was wrong with the praying of the Pharisee?
4. What was right about the praying of the tax-collector?
5. In what sense does the kingdom of God belong to children?
6. Why does Jesus draw attention to the need for a correct view of goodness in seeking eternal life (verses 18–19)?
7. What use is the moral law in evangelism (verses 20–21)?
8. What is the one essential in becoming a disciple of Jesus?
9. Why does Jesus dwell on the various abuses he will suffer in Jerusalem at the hands of his enemies?
10. Jesus always responded to an appeal for mercy from people. What does that teach us today about Jesus?
11. How does the blind man show his faith in Jesus and how should we do so?
12. Is the fact of people glorifying and praising God the best evidence of a genuine work of God going on among us?

STUDY 19: Luke 19

1. What is most attractive about Jesus in the story of Zacchaeus?
2. Discuss other examples from Luke's Gospel of Jesus seeking and saving lost men and women.
3. Compare the parable here with the similar one in Matthew 25.
4. What does the parable teach us about individual initiative in the conduct of our lives in Jesus' service?
5. What does the parable tell us about having a right view of God if we are to be productive servants of the Kingdom?
6. Explain from verse 26 how heaven will mean having more, and hell will mean having less, than we all have now.
7. Why would the messianic king of Israel ride into the royal city on a donkey?
8. Why was the spiritual song so similar on the occasion of Jesus entering the holy city (verses 37-38) as when he was born (2:14)?
9. What do the tears of Jesus over the lost city of Jerusalem tell us about emotional engagement with the world of our day which is also lost?

10. Is the cleansing of the temple a warrant for violent revolution against injustice and moral corruption in society?

STUDY 20: Luke 20

1. Why is the question of authority so fundamental?
2. Does Jesus' refusal to tell the Pharisees everything mean that there are times when we should withhold the truth from people?
3. Give some Old Testament examples of the tenants beating and throwing out the servants ('my servants the prophets') sent by the master of the vineyard to Israel.
4. Explain how Jesus, having been rejected by the builders, has become the head stone of the corner of the whole building.
5. What was the catch in the question the spies asked Jesus?
6. What does Jesus tell us about the respective roles of God and Caesar in our lives?
7. Does the law of levirate marriage have any application to Christian behaviour or relations today?
8. What will the resurrection mean for our gender and sexuality?
9. What support do Jesus' words give for belief in an after-life?
10. What was wrong with the scribes saying that the Messiah was David's son?
11. How does Psalm 110 prove the divinity of the Messiah?
12. What is the full truth about himself that Jesus implies from this exchange with the scribes?
13. Is there a place for ceremonies in the public life of the churches?
14. Jesus teaches degrees of condemnation and punishment in the final judgement. Discuss.

STUDY 21: Luke 21

1. What does the widow teach us about Christian generosity?
2. What are some of the spiritual qualities that go towards Christian giving (see *2 Cor*. 8–9)?
3. Can we be precise about the signs of the end of the world (v. 7)?
4. Have the major signs Jesus mentions always been present in history or will they proliferate towards the end of the age?
5. What are the major signs of the end and are they especially apparent now (verses 8–19, 25–28)?

6. What dangers and temptations attach to the period before the coming of the Lord (verse 34)?

7. How may we best prepare for the end of the age?

STUDY 22: Luke 22

1. Was Judas demon-possessed?

2. Why did Jesus suffer and die at Passover time?

3. How is the Passover meal fulfilled in the Kingdom of God?

4. What is the biblical background to Jesus' words in verse 20?

5. If the Son of Man went to his death as God appointed how could Judas be guilty of his blood (verse 22)?

6. How does Jesus' style of leadership differ from other kinds?

7. What can we learn from Jesus' words to Peter (v. 31–32)?

8. Does Jesus mean that there are times when his followers can legitimately take up arms in their defence (verse 36)?

9. Does Jesus promise that if we pray we will never face testing (verse 40)?

10. Is there a relation between the cup that Jesus drank on the cross (verse 42) and the cup that we drink at the Lord's Supper?

11. What should we learn about the humanity of Jesus from his physical and mental struggle in Gethsemane (verse 44)?

12. What does it tell us about Judas that he could betray the Son of Man with a kiss?

13. What does it tell us about Jesus that he healed the servant's ear in these circumstances?

14. What steps led to Peter's denial?

15. What steps led to Peter's repentance?

16. How does Jesus make use of the passage in Daniel 7:12–13 for his own purposes (verse 69)?

17. Why did Jesus implicate himself (verse 70)?

STUDY 23: Luke 23:1–31

1. The Jews bring three related charges against Jesus (verse 2). Is there truth in any of these charges?

2. Discuss the significance of the trial of Jesus before Herod.

3. If Jesus did no crime deserving death then why did he die?

4. Put yourself in the place of Simon of Cyrene as he reflected on the events of that day at its close.

5. What do the sayings of Jesus to the women of Jerusalem teach us about our attitudes to the events of this life?

STUDY 24: Luke 23:32–56

1. On a scale of 1 to 10 grade the guilt as you see it of:
   i. the soldiers who crucified Jesus; ii. the people standing by;
   iii. the religious leaders scoffing at Jesus; iv. the first criminal.
2. What does the first word of Jesus from the cross (verse 34) teach us about the love of Christ?
3. Can you explain the different responses to Jesus of the two criminals beside him?
4. What can we learn from the attitude and utterances of the second criminal about the signs of saving faith in a human being?
5. How is our understanding and acceptance of the death of Jesus helped by the symbolism of the darkness that came over the landscape and the torn curtain in the temple?
6. Discuss the seven sayings of Jesus from the cross and explain how they help us to understand his ordeal from the point of view of God, Christ himself and us.
7. How far do you agree with the centurion's judgement about Jesus and on what grounds?
8. How do you think you would have responded if you had witnessed Jesus' death?
9. Does the burial of Jesus matter for salvation?
10. What lessons of faith can we learn from Joseph? the women?

STUDY 25: Luke 24:1–35

1. Discuss the religious significance of the empty tomb of Jesus?
2. What place should the resurrection of Jesus have in our faith?
3. Discuss the role of the women in the proclamation of the resurrection and how that may affect the way they function in the corporate witness of the churches today.
4. Can you explain the disbelief of the apostles (verse 12)?
5. Discuss the story of the walk to Emmaus as a parable of the Christian life. What lessons or principles can we glean from it?
6. Pick out and explain some of the references in verse 27 to Jesus as Messiah in the writings of Moses and the Prophets.

7. Why did the two disciples recognize Jesus from the breaking of the bread but not in the opening of the Scriptures?

STUDY 26: Luke 24:36–53

1. If the risen Jesus was not a spirit, then what was he?
2. Why was Jesus so anxious to persuade the disciples of his material presence and reality?
3. Discuss with further examples the connection between faith and joy (verse 41).
4. Pick out examples of messianic passages in some of the Psalms and discuss what they tell us about Christ.
5. Discuss the opening of the mind to spiritual truth in Christian experience.
6. Why are the death and the resurrection of Jesus so often paired together?
7. Discuss the differences between repentance and forgiveness with regard to sin. Why are both necessary?
8. What is the value of Christ's promise of the Holy Spirit (verse 49) in doing Christian mission work today?
9. Why does Luke end his Gospel with the ascension rather than the resurrection?
10. What is the theological message of the ascension?
11. Discuss the place in Luke's Gospel of joy, and praise of God.

FOR FURTHER STUDY

The following books are recommended for study of Luke's Gospel:

Michael Bentley, *Saving a Fallen World: Luke Simply Explained*, (Durham: Evangelical Press, 1992)

Norval Geldenhuys, *Commentary on the Gospel of Luke* (London: Marshall, Morgan & Scott, 1965)

William Hendriksen: *The Gospel of Luke* (Edinburgh: Banner of Truth, 1978)

J. C. Ryle, *Expository Thoughts on the Gospels – Luke* (2 vols.) (1858; repr. Edinburgh: Banner of Truth, 1986).

Thomas Schreiner, 'Luke', in Walter Elwell (ed.), *Evangelical Commentary on the Bible* (Grand Rapids: Baker Book House, 1989).